Cultivating Virtue

Cultivating Virtue

Perspectives from Philosophy, Theology, and Psychology

Edited by Nancy E. Snow

OXFORD
UNIVERSITY PRESS

OXFORD
UNIVERSITY PRESS

Oxford University Press is a department of the
University of Oxford. It furthers the University's objective
of excellence in research, scholarship, and education
by publishing worldwide.

Oxford   New York

Auckland   Cape Town   Dar es Salaam   Hong Kong   Karachi
Kuala Lumpur   Madrid   Melbourne   Mexico City   Nairobi
New Delhi   Shanghai   Taipei   Toronto

With offices in

Argentina   Austria   Brazil   Chile   Czech Republic   France   Greece
Guatemala   Hungary   Italy   Japan   Poland   Portugal   Singapore
South Korea   Switzerland   Thailand   Turkey   Ukraine   Vietnam

Oxford is a registered trade mark of Oxford University Press
in the UK and certain other countries.

Published in the United States of America by
Oxford University Press
198 Madison Avenue, New York, NY 10016

Library of Congress Cataloging-in-Publication Data
Cultivating virtue : perspectives from philosophy, theology, and
psychology / edited by Nancy E. Snow.
       pages   cm
Includes index.
ISBN 978-0-19-996742-1 (hardcover : alk. paper)—
ISBN 978-0-19-996744-5 (pbk. : alk. paper)
1. Virtue.   2. Ethics.   I. Snow, Nancy E., editor.
BJ1521.C87   2014
179'.9—dc23   2014018467

1 3 5 7 9 8 6 4 2

Printed in the United States of America
on acid-free paper

CONTENTS

Contributors   *vii*

Introduction   1

1. Aristotle on Cultivating Virtue   17
   Daniel C. Russell

2. Mill, Moral Sentimentalism, and the Cultivation of Virtue   49
   Julia Driver

3. The Roots of Empathy   65
   Michael Slote

4. Kant on Virtue and the Virtues   87
   Adam Cureton and Thomas E. Hill

5. Cultivating Virtue: Two Problems for Virtue Ethics   111
   Christine Swanton

6. The Situationist Critique and Early Confucian Virtue Ethics   135
   Edward Slingerland

7. It Takes a Metaphysics: Raising Virtuous Buddhists   171
   Owen Flanagan

8. Islam and the Cultivation of Character: Ibn Miskawayh's Synthesis
   and the Case of the Veil   197
   Elizabeth M. Bucar

9. Frailty, Fragmentation, and Social Dependency in the Cultivation
   of Christian Virtue   227
   Jennifer A. Herdt

10. The Co-Construction of Virtue: Epigenetics, Development,
    and Culture   251
    Darcia Narvaez

11. The Development of Virtue: A Perspective from Developmental
       Psychology   279
       Ross A. Thompson

12. Psychological Science and the *Nicomachean Ethics*: Virtuous Actors,
       Agents, and Authors   307
       Dan P. McAdams

Index   337

CONTRIBUTORS

Elizabeth M. Bucar is Associate Professor of Religious Studies at Northeastern University.

Adam Cureton is Assistant Professor of Philosophy at the University of Tennessee, Knoxville.

Julia Driver is Gilbert L. Stark Professor of Christian Ethics at Yale Divinity School.

Owen Flanagan is the James B. Duke Professor of Philosophy and Professor of Psychology and Neuroscience at Duke University.

Jennifer A. Herdt is Professor of Christian Ethics at Yale Divinity School.

Thomas E. Hill is Kenan Professor of Philosophy at the University of North Carolina, Chapel Hill.

Dan P. McAdams is the Henry Wade Rogers Professor and Chair of the Psychology Department at Northwestern University.

Darcia Narvaez is Professor of Psychology at the University of Notre Dame, Indiana, USA.

Daniel C. Russell is Professor of Philosophy in the University of Arizona's Center for the Philosophy of Freedom and the Percy Seymour Reader in Ancient Philosophy at Ormond College, University of Melbourne.

Edward Slingerland is Professor of Asian Studies, Canada Research Chair in Chinese Thought and Embodied Cognition, and Associate Member, Departments of Philosophy and Psychology, at the University of British Columbia.

Michael Slote is UST Professor of Ethics in the Philosophy Department at the University of Miami.

Nancy E. Snow is Professor of Philosophy at Marquette University in Milwaukee, Wisconsin.

Christine Swanton is professor in the Department of Philosophy at the University of Auckland, New Zealand.

Ross A. Thompson is Distinguished Professor of Psychology at the University of California, Davis

Introduction

The last thirty years have seen a resurgence of interest in virtue in Anglo-American philosophy. Virtue ethics, an approach to norma-tive theory that focuses on the character of the agent, has estab-lished itself as a legitimate alternative to consequentialism and deontology.[1] Work elucidating theories of virtue within these competing traditions has also moved forward.[2] Despite the rising interest in virtue, however, little attention has been paid to the question of how virtue is developed.[3] This volume aims to address that gap in the literature. It is a collection of mostly new essays solicited from philosophers, psychologists, and theologians, all in the forefront of research on virtue.[4] Each of their contributions focuses on some aspect of virtue development, either by highlighting virtue culti-vation within distinctive traditions of psychological, ethical, or religious thought, by taking a developmental perspective to yield fresh insights into criticisms of virtue ethics, or by examining the science that explains virtue development. Russell and Driver investigate virtue cultivation or problems associated with it from Aristotelian and utilitarian perspectives, the latter focusing on sentimentalist virtue development, a theme taken up by Slote. Cureton and Hill and Swanton explore self-improvement, the former from a Kantian vantage point, the latter with an eye toward offering solutions to the problems of self-centeredness and virtue ethical right action. Slinger-land examines contemporary psychology as well as virtue development in the Confucian tradition to counter situationist criticisms of virtue ethics. Flanagan, Bucar, and Herdt examine virtue cultivation in the Buddhist, Islamic, and Christian traditions, respectively. The essays by Narvaez, Thomp-son, and McAdams offer descriptive insights from psychology into virtue development. The result is a collection of extremely creative essays that not only fills the current gap but also promises to stimulate new work on a relatively neglected yet vital topic.

Stimulating new work on virtue cultivation and related topics is a second aim of the volume. The deeper idea here is to shape the trajectory of research on virtue in new and fruitful ways. Focusing the attention of the best minds in the field on virtue development is a way of rounding out current research on virtue and offering new directions forward. As research on virtue cultivation progresses, the hope is that investigations of related areas will advance as well. For example, in saying something about virtue cultivation, we must also think about the development of personality, rationality, motivation, and emotions, and consider the roles of parents and supportive communities in virtue education. We must think about habituation and bodily practices. We must seek to integrate science into our thinking, investigate non-Western conceptions of virtue, and compare and contrast them with more familiar Western accounts. Finally, we should begin to acknowledge that theological perspectives on virtue can add value to philosophical discussions. In short, this volume aims to suggest to readers further research opportunities in multiple directions.

The volume is arranged in the following order. Russell begins with an Aristotelian perspective on virtue development, followed by Driver on utilitarianism, Slote on sentimentalism, Cureton and Hill on Kantianism, and Swanton on self-improvement. Slingerland and Flanagan leave the Western tradition to take readers into the nuances of Confucianism and Buddhism, respectively. Religious ethicists Bucar and Herdt follow with explorations of Islamic and Christian virtue cultivation. Finally, psychologists Narvaez, Thompson, and McAdams are given the last word, discussing virtue development from three different psychological perspectives.

Despite their differences, several common themes emerge in these presentations. The importance of early upbringing for the development of virtue is highlighted by Russell, Slote, and Flanagan, and reinforced in the essays by psychologists. Driver, Slote, Thompson, and Narvaez stress the importance of affect for the growth of virtue. Driver mines early sentimentalist thinkers for insights into virtue development, and Slote continues that tradition with a contemporary account. Slingerland and Swanton use developmental approaches to virtue to counter criticisms of virtue ethics. In the traditions explored by Bucar and Slingerland, bodily practices contribute to virtue development. Metaphysical assumptions form the background for virtue cultivation in the Buddhist and Kantian thought examined by Flanagan and Cureton and Hill. The importance of motivation is underscored by Russell, Swanton, and McAdams. McAdams explicitly relates his psychological view of virtue development to Aristotle's perspective. Bucar and Herdt accentuate God's role in the acquisition of virtue. Finally, the importance of community is integral to the views of virtue cultivation offered by Herdt, Narvaez, and McAdams. Let us turn to an examination of each author's contribution.

In "Aristotle on Cultivating Virtue," Daniel C. Russell sketches an Aristotelian research program for virtue development. He articulates what Aristotle thinks virtue is and how it is acquired. Russell here seeks to show that Aristotle thinks virtue, its acquisition, and the competencies needed for it are mundane—that is, parts of our daily lives and of the ordinary ways in which we try to better ourselves. To develop virtue we must develop dispositions to choose and act for virtue-relevant goals. Virtue is dynamic; though virtue acquisition takes place as a person develops, it is an ongoing process, occurring even among mature agents. Russell's central contention is that light can be shed on our understanding of virtue acquisition by studying how skills are acquired. Thus, the notions of skill and of skill acquisition are at the heart of an Aristotelian perspective on cultivating virtue.

Russell argues that this emphasis on skill meshes well with contemporary psychology in two important respects. To understand the first respect, we need to note the distinction between path-dependent and path-independent ways of becoming moral. Path-independent approaches specify a moral ideal and then chart ways of reaching it. Lawrence Kohlberg's model of universal moral thinking is a case in point. By contrast, path-dependent approaches survey how people generally improve themselves, then extend this knowledge to an account of character development. As Russell notes, the psychologists Darcia Narvaez and Daniel K. Lapsley call these contrasting approaches "moralized psychology" and "psychologized morality," respectively. Russell argues that Aristotle's is a path-dependent approach, and hence, an example of psychologized morality.

A second respect in which Aristotle's view of virtue acquisition meshes well with contemporary psychology is in its emphasis on skill. Much work in psychology has been done on skill acquisition and expertise that is potentially useful for understanding character development. Since Aristotle was not concerned with specifying in fine detail the competencies needed for virtue, he can be viewed as setting out the broad contours of a research program to be filled in by later generations. In this regard, the psychology of skill acquisition is a promising area for ongoing research into virtue cultivation. Yet, Russell cautions that such a program faces hurdles. Unlike many contexts in which we acquire skills, virtue is messy. We cannot always learn it in structured environments that afford us opportunities to learn predictable regularities, nor do we always have the advantage of clear feedback. Despite these challenges, the psychology of skill acquisition remains a fertile resource for further investigation into the nuances of Aristotelian virtue cultivation.

Julia Driver's piece, "Mill, Moral Sentimentalism, and the Cultivation of Virtue," examines utilitarian virtue cultivation through the work of John Stuart Mill. Driver begins by making the point that many virtues, for Mill, involve the perfection of our higher capacities for happiness or pleasure. Improvement in the virtues, Mill thinks, can be aided by higher educational institutions, but also by engaging with good literature. Through our reading of literature, history, and documentaries, Driver argues, we develop our abilities to put ourselves in the positions of others and take their perspectives. She develops this theme by examining the influence of moral sentimentalism on Mill's thought.

Though not all utilitarians are sentimentalists, Mill is influenced by sentimentalist concerns, such as the importance of natural sentiment—in particular, sympathy—as the basis for the other-regarding conduct utilitarianism requires. In this respect, Driver contends, Mill is similar to Hume. To be sure, Mill and Hume diverge in their accounts of virtue, yet a broadly sentimentalist approach, Driver urges, helps us to interpret Mill's cryptic remarks on the "art of life."

In *A System of Logic*, Mill discusses the art of life in terms of three separate spheres: prudence, morality, and aesthetics. He associates aesthetics with virtue and morality with right. Driver offers a way to conceptualize the spheres by taking Mill to separate being virtuous from acting rightly and wrongly. Her focus, however, is on how goodness in each sphere is to be realized. Among the qualities needed to realize goodness in one's life, Driver contends, is the ability to make good judgments about what it means to be virtuous and/or do one's duty. That is, being dutiful as well as virtuous are connected with the ability to make reliable judgments about duty and virtue. Virtue and aesthetics are related through attention, as Iris Murdoch urged, as well as through perspective-taking. Many philosophers endorse the view that one's moral sensitivities are enlarged by the ability to take the perspectives of others. Important information, such as the kinds of reasons that motivate others, is thereby attained. Perspective-taking is also a way of correcting emotions and of allowing us to shed idiosyncratic concerns and enlarge our social sympathies. We cannot be a fully utilitarian agent, Driver argues, unless we are virtuous—and that requires developing the kinds of qualities and skills needed to take the "larger view" made possible by expanded social sympathies.

Sentimentalist virtue development is the theme of the next essay. Michael Slote expands upon previous work to give a sentimentalist account of moral development in "The Roots of Empathy." Noting that explanations of moral growth often begin with how children learn good behavior from loving parents, Slote urges us take a step back and examine how early parent-child interactions make these later educational processes possible or impossible. His account, though consistent with the view that genetic or brain abnormalities play a role in psychopathy, focuses on the need for parental love, and in particular, on the kinds of reactions to parental attitudes and behavior that can inhibit or facilitate moral development. Children who are denied parental love react with rage, which forecloses their capacities for basic associative or receptive empathy. This is the kind of empathy that allows us to feel what others are going through, and is the *sine qua non* of further moral development. By contrast, children who are loved by their parents respond with gratitude. Gratitude, Slote argues, is the emotional basis for further moral growth.

He begins by situating his account of gratitude within a sentimentalist framework in which empathy has a central role to play in moral development. Just as empathy and sympathy have been found to contribute to altruistic behavior, so, too, Slote contends, gratitude can facilitate altruism. Of special importance in moral development is a kind of diffuse or generalized gratitude that infants and children feel on having their need for parental love met. This generalized gratitude contrasts with the generalized rage or anger that those denied parental love can come to feel. Slote clarifies his points about diffuse or generalized gratitude by examining cases of adult gratitude. Not only are we grateful for benefits we are given, we are also grateful for the sympathetic attitudes and motives with which those boons are bestowed. In Slote's view, we "take in" those sympathetic attitudes and motives by a kind of associative or receptive empathy. Through this receptivity, we become sympathetic too, and this aroused sympathy, which Slote believes is gratitude, though focused mainly on our benefactor, can be spread to others or generalized. We feel gratitude intensely because it is aroused by benefits warmly bestowed on us, and this intensity of feeling makes it less likely than other emotions to lose its force when it is generalized.

Essentially the same processes that explain adult gratitude apply to gratitude in early childhood. Young children have basic capacities for empathy, Slote contends, which allow them to take in the love and sympathy they feel from their parents. This then generates gratitude—the diffusion to others of the love and sympathy the child has taken in. The early gratitude is necessary for further moral development. Children who do not receive parental love, but instead, are neglected or abused, respond with anger or rage—emotions which undercut their empathic capacities and preclude the possibility of moral growth. Slote concludes his piece by exploring some implications of his sentimentalist account of the early wellsprings of moral development in empathy and gratitude for understandings of psychopathy and, especially, of care ethics.

Adam Cureton and Thomas Hill examine a different approach to virtue and moral education in their piece, "Kant on Virtue and the Virtues." They offer an overview of Kant's conception of virtue and discuss his views on education and moral self-improvement. Kant's most thorough discussion of virtue, they explain, is found in the Doctrine of Virtue, which is the second part of *The Metaphysics of Morals*. To be fully virtuous, for Kant, is to have a good will that is firmly resolved and fully ready to overcome temptations, both internal and external, to immorality. The aim of the virtuous is not only to avoid acting wrongly and to pursue moral ends, but also to do so for the right reasons. The good will is that faculty that enables imperfect humans to act for the right reasons—that is, to act from respect for the Moral Law. Virtue is the strength of will always to do our duty and to act from right reasons. Though we cannot attain it in this life, perfect virtue is, nonetheless, an end to which we should aspire.

Kant's conception of virtue has several interesting features. First, unlike some ancient virtue theorists, Kant maintains that we all have the capacity to become virtuous. This is because being and becoming virtuous depend so heavily on choice. We should strive to become virtuous and can become virtuous despite impediments, such as innate personality traits and early upbringing, which might not conduce to virtue. Second, like other virtue theories, Kant's account has several roles for feelings. Third, Kant does not hold that success is a condition of being virtuous; that is, the moral goodness or virtue of the agent does not depend upon the results she achieves. Fourth, Kant takes an interesting position on the question of the unity of the virtues. *Virtue* is the strength of will to fulfill our duties, whereas *virtues* are commitments to specific moral ends. If, from a sense of duty, I set the happiness of others as a moral end and structure my choices around that commitment, I have the virtue of generosity. It is a duty of virtue to be generous in this sense. Kant maintains that there is only one virtue: the second-order commitment to do one's duty for the sake of duty, but he denies that particular virtues, such as generosity or courage, mutually entail one another. The authors go on to discuss Kant's list of virtues and vices, and explain how virtue fulfills our moral nature. Though virtue fulfills us morally and can help us to be cheerful and tranquil, Kant acknowledges that we can be virtuous but also destitute, despised, and unhappy.

Kant's views on moral education include discussions of the education of children and adolescents, as well as the duty of moral self-improvement possessed by adults. The education of children is rule-governed: children are taught to conform their behavior to rules by being subjected to family rules, school rules, and the rules of games. These rules are meant to train children to control their emotions, and to curb their "lawless freedom," while yet allowing them to develop naturally. The authors note that Kant's account of these rules, as well as his views of the nature of punishment, are similar to his ideas about the state and legal punishment. The education of the adolescent is meant to enable her to make "good use" of freedom under constraints—that is, to elicit her nascent sense of dignity—and to foster her ability to represent to herself a sense of duty. Adolescents should be given moral problems to ponder in order to develop and encourage rational habits of moral approval and disapproval, among other desiderata. Upon reaching adulthood, an individual's rational capacities should be sufficiently developed so that she is able to continue perfecting her moral powers. The authors discuss the duty of moral self-improvement in terms of Kant's scheme of perfect and imperfect duties, and conclude their piece by considering objections and replies.

In "Cultivating Virtue: Two Problems for Virtue Ethics," Christine Swanton examines two problems internal to virtue ethics that apparently arise from the commitment to be virtuous and to develop one's virtue. They are the self-centeredness objection—that is, the claim that virtue ethics requires the agent to focus on her own virtue and flourishing, thereby undervaluing the regard due to others; and the charge that virtue ethical criteria of right action, which rely on the notion that right action is what the virtuous person would characteristically do, cannot account for acts that should be taken by imperfect agents seeking to improve their virtue.

Though arising in several answerable forms, the self-centeredness objection, Swanton contends, is especially problematic for virtue ethics when it is making a particular claim about the deep structure of the virtuous agent's motivation. The claim is that having virtue is the most practically important aspect of an agent's life, and that the virtuous agent must subordinate everything else to this end. Swanton maintains that arguments against the objection in the form in which it relies on this claim fail, then argues that virtue ethics is not committed to the value structure at the heart of the self-centeredness objection. She draws on her own view of virtue ethics as pluralistic and non-eudaimonistic to make her case. What makes traits virtues, she contends, is not their contribution to the flourishing of their possessor, but their targets or aims. What motivates the agent who seeks to be virtuous is the desire to attain the targets of virtue, and developing virtue is secondary to that aim. This circumvents the self-centeredness objection, and derails the notion that the desire to cultivate virtue must always be self-centered or egoistic.

Swanton also uses her account of virtue ethics to answer the charge that virtue ethical theories of right action cannot explain the rightness of actions taken by imperfect agents in efforts to cultivate their virtue. She proposes an aspirational virtue of self-improvement, and offers a "thick" description of it in terms of extent, motive, time, people, manner, and instruments for its sustenance, such as good political structures. This account draws on a variety of philosophical and psychological views to show how the virtue is dynamic and satisfies the conditions that Aristotle puts on virtue, while not being overly burdensome or self-consuming for the agent. Swanton also describes various perils into which unwary self-improvers might fall, such as susceptibility to feelings of self-righteousness and sanctimoniousness.

Self-improvement is central to the Confucian tradition in ethics. Edward Slingerland mines the insights of early Confucians to offer responses to the situationist critique of virtue ethics in his chapter, "The Situationist Critique and Early Confucian Virtue Ethics." A reworked version of the article that originally appeared in *Ethics*, the piece offers empirical as well as conceptual critiques of the situationist challenge, then explores the views of early Confucians, such as Confucius, Mencius, and Xunzi, on virtue education. Situationism interprets classical virtue ethics as setting a "high bar" for living virtuously, but the early Confucian tradition, through a combination of rigorous education and carefully chosen situational reinforcements, offers ways for learners of virtue to meet the challenge.

The situationist critique of virtue ethics is the argument, made most prominently by Gilbert Harman and John Doris, that social psychological studies show that global traits—traits that produce behavior that is consistent across different types of situations—either do not exist or exist so rarely that they are unlikely to have significant effects on behavior. Most philosophical traditions assume that virtues are global traits—that if a person is honest, for example, he will be honest in business dealings, when under oath in court, in taking tests, and so on. The non-existence or paucity of such traits, situationists contend, should force us to abandon virtue ethics. Empirical studies show that situations have far more effect on behavior.

Slingerland criticizes situationism on a variety of grounds. First, he adduces psychological studies to show that the person–situation debate in psychology is passé. Second, he criticizes the situationists' reading of the 0.3 personality coefficient for correlations of traits with behavior across situations, contending that it is more significant than situationists typically allow. Finally, he criticizes the conceptual distinction between local and global traits, arguing that there is no analytic dichotomy between such traits, but instead, a spectrum. What counts as local and global traits is often determined pragmatically. Despite these drawbacks, situationism has a point that needs to be addressed: classical virtue traditions assume that virtuous behavior must approach 1.0. Virtuous people are not allowed to steal or cheat only once or a few times; they must strive to be virtuous at all times. Early Confucian virtue ethics, Slingerland argues, offers a program for how this might be achieved. Rigorous training in virtue, or extension, helps learners to develop their positive traits and curb their negative tendencies. This helps learners to clear the situationists' "bar." Yet the bar is lowered by the ongoing presence of situational factors, such as ritual practice, the study of ancient texts, the presence of a teacher, and other environmental stimuli that chronically prime learners to think, feel, and act virtuously. The combination of a lowered bar and intensive education helps Confucian learners to "jump" the situationist hurdle. Or so we can hope—a hope that is reinforced, Slingerland notes, by recent psychological work on roles for nonconscious processing in the acquisition of virtue.

Owen Flanagan takes readers into the complexities of Buddhism in "It Takes a Metaphysics: Raising Virtuous Buddhists." Flanagan offers a rational reconstruction of Buddhist moral education by advancing the view that Buddhism requires learners to know more than the ethical truths espoused by their tradition: it requires them to absorb key metaphysical truths that ground a calling or commitment. Buddhists must feel and embrace this calling to be able to live their lives in accordance with Buddhism's distinctive, and very demanding, set of values. Flanagan's aim is to answer a central question: How do Buddhists get from the "is" of metaphysical and natural facts to the "ought" of living a certain kind of ethical life?

Though Buddhism has many sects and invokes many concepts, the common core that Flanagan identifies consists of the Four Noble Truths the Noble Eightfold Path, and the Four Immeasurables. These doctrines contain diagnoses of the human condition, such as the notion that all sentient beings suffer, as well as ethical prescriptions and prohibitions for relieving this suffering. At one level, what seems required of the Buddhist practitioner is that some actions be taken and others avoided—a kind of continence. But at a deeper level, more challenging self-cultivation is required. At this level, the Buddhist is trying to develop difficult dispositions that should be universal in applicability, such as the Four Immeasurables—compassion, loving-kindness, sympathetic joy, and equanimity. These are the virtues possessed by the saint or sage who is on the verge of enlightenment. Why struggle to attain these, and other demanding Buddhist virtues? To answer this, a rather complex story needs to be told.

Naturalistic as well as non-naturalistic versions of Buddhism and of the motivations for Buddhist virtue cultivation are available. Flanagan opts for a naturalistic understanding. His story recognizes the deeply integrated Buddhist worldview, according to which metaphysical doctrines, such as impermanence, dependent origination, and "no-self" are the background conditions within which Buddhist ethical strictures are to be understood and taught. We suffer because we seek permanence in an impermanent world and because our egos separate ourselves from others with whom we are dependently related. There are no unique essences, including persons. Though we perceive individuated entities, they are in reality aspects of being that is in a continual state of unfolding. We must come to understand these and other truths through instruction in philosophy, and to grasp some of them in non-conceptual ways through mindfulness practices, such as forms of meditation. Yet none of these ideas, Flanagan argues, is sufficient to ground the "ought" of Buddhist ethics. We could accept Buddhism's metaphysical doctrines and become nihilists. The crucial moment in the psychology of moral development is when the Buddhist learner experiences an overpowering desire or "calling" which, due to prior philosophical reflection, she has no reason to refuse. To embrace this calling is to enter fully the stream of Buddhist life.

In "Islam and the Cultivation of Character: Ibn Miskawayh's Synthesis and the Case of the Veil," Elizabeth Bucar uses the writings of the tenth-century Islamic thinker Ibn Miskawayh to elucidate an Islamic view of virtue and apply it to the practice of veiling. In the first part of her chapter, she introduces the thought of Ibn Miskawayh, and in the second, she analyzes the practice of veiling and the virtue of modesty in terms of the framework his work provides. She concludes with some observations about the virtue of modesty in contemporary contexts.

Sacred texts, Bucar explains, are not the only sources of Islamic ethics. Ethics in the Islamic tradition has been articulated through various "special sciences." Among these, Islamic jurisprudence, or *fiqh*, has been perceived to hold pride of place in matters of morals rules and codes. The cultivation of virtue and character is the province of another special science, namely *adab*, or Islamic etiquette. *Adab* tells practitioners of Islam how to acquire manners, morals, and character. Ibn Miskawayh's writings contribute to this area; indeed, he is regarded as the father of Islamic virtue ethics, as his writings attempt to synthesize revealed truths of Islam and the insights of ancient Greek philosophy. Ibn Miskawayh adopts Plato's view of the soul as a self-subsisting entity, and Aristotle's conception of virtue as an entrenched, habituated disposition that goes "all the way down"—that is, as deeply embedded in the personality of the agent. Yet he views human nature as religious; we are creatures of God and follow a divine plan. Character formation is a process of perfecting the soul for God. Three aspects of Ibn Miskawayh's view are crucial: the centrality of bodily practices, the habituation of sexual appetites, and the social dimensions of virtue. Through bodily practices we are able to grow in virtue. Frequently, the action precedes the virtuous intention or disposition. We act as if we are virtuous first, then eventually come to be virtuous. Sexual appetites, though not intrinsically evil, need to be regulated and properly ordered in a virtuous life. Finally, virtue is a public or social matter. We become virtuous with and through the influence of others, and we strive to achieve societies that exemplify forms of corporate virtue.

With this framework in hand, Bucar explains the practice of veiling and its centrality to the virtue of modesty by addressing the questions: What does veiling ethically do? and, What role does veiling play in character formation? Her aim is to reveal veiling as something more than a symbol of religious fundamentalism: it is a practice that helps Muslims to acquire virtue. Though Qur'anic texts on veiling raise interpretative difficulties, they have implications for the modesty of both men and women. Men are instructed to avert their gazes; women, to cover various body parts. The idea is that women must cover themselves in certain ways in order to affect how men look at them. Women are admonished to dress and act, and men, to act in ways designed to avoid inflaming illicit sexual desires. Veiling takes place in public. It is an ethical practice that creates a "public virtue zone," in which Muslim men and women are reminded of the need for, and encouraged to strive toward, sexual modesty.

In her concluding observations, Bucar points out two interesting dimensions of veiling. First, veiling is a gendered practice. Might it be true that the Islamic virtue of modesty is also gendered? Second, what counts as modesty in dress and comportment varies in different Muslim countries in the twenty-first century. Does this entail relativism—that modesty itself, and perhaps other Islamic virtues, vary according to time and place? Perhaps not, as Bucar identifies three common features of Islamic modesty: its focus on women; its insistence on personal dispositions, and not merely outward dress and behavior; and its contribution to a visual culture of Islam: shared images and perceptions co-construct personal religious identity and virtue.

Jennifer A. Herdt explores the history of character cultivation in the Christian tradition in "Frailty, Fragmentation, and Social Dependency in the Cultivation of Christian Virtue." Herdt stresses that Christianity is a living tradition of character formation; Christians have been interested not only in a correct understanding of reality but also in moral ways of living— ways that bring believers closer to God through the emulation of Christ. Christ is the exemplar for those who want freedom from sin and death, and he provides the power to emulate him for those seeking to do so. How Christ is best emulated is a complex story with many levels of interpretation, but at the heart of it, Herdt contends, is the need for character formation.

Though some early Christians emulated Christ through the idealization of martyrdom and ascetic practice, others believed that another path was open to people in all walks of life. They found sustenance in the writings of the *Didache*, an early list of precepts whose central commandment was to love—love God, one's neighbors, one's enemies, and oneself. The commandment to love, Herdt maintains, was at bottom an injunction to character formation. Christians should become people with certain kinds of characters, intentions, and motives. Practices relating to self-control and meditation, which can be conceptualized as forms of spiritual exercises, were stressed. By the fourth century, two common factors had emerged: the centrality of love and humility. Humility is crucial to the story of Christian character, for it highlights human dependency on God's grace, frailty in the face of temptation and sin, and egalitarianism—we are all weak and sinful before God. Practices of self-examination and of repentance and individual and communal healing went along with the stress on humility.

Christian theologians and philosophers transformed many debates about the virtues from ancient Greek and Roman thinkers. The medieval scholastics, especially Aquinas, brought thinking about virtue to new levels of systematicity. Aquinas saw that the final end of humankind, fellowship with God, could not be attained without divine grace. Faith, hope, and charity were three theological virtues that are infused in us through the sacraments to help us achieve that end, but so, too, were many other moral virtues supplemented by divine power in order properly to orient us beyond the end of human happiness. The Reformation theologian Martin Luther repudiated virtue, with its resonances in pagan philosophy. He emphasized grace and not works. Communities that embraced Luther's thought formed Christian character through practices such as prayer, corporate worship, preaching, fasting, and meditation. In the twentieth century, philosophers as well as Catholic and Protestant theologians have again become interested in virtue. Many of the characteristics of virtue in the Christian tradition, Herdt argues, could indemnify it against recent situationist attacks on Aristotelian virtue. For example, recognizing the fragility of virtue and the need for God's grace to sustain it, as well as the injunction to see others as neighbors, are aspects of Christian virtue that offer a more realistic picture of humanity's prospects than Aristotelianism.

Darcia Narvaez takes an evolutionary view of the conditions needed for the development of virtue in "The Co-Construction of Virtue: Epigenetics, Development, and Culture." She identifies the care conditions necessary for the healthy growth of the physiological and brain capacities required for virtue, and calls this environment, the "evolved developmental niche" (EDN). Depending on the early care a child receives, he or she can come to have different ethical orientations, each with multiple subtypes: the Safety ethic, the Engagement ethic, or the Imagination ethic. Narvaez contends that the conditions for developing the optimal ethical orientation, the Imagination ethic, are found in hunter-gatherer societies, and offers suggestions for how the wisdom of hunter-gatherers can be reclaimed for virtue cultivation in our own day and age.

Proper brain and body functioning, Narvaez contends, are required for the development of capacities, such as perception, attention, emotional self-regulation, empathy, and social skills, all of which are needed for virtue. Scientific studies support the view that forms of early caregiving, such as frequent touch, breastfeeding, play, nurturing social support, and even natural childbirth, are vital for the development of these capacities. These forms of care mark the optimal environment of early nurturance, the EDN. Though care received under these conditions can set children on the path to virtue, there are ways in which care can go awry. Narvaez explores these by reference to the triune ethics theory. According to this theory, the Safety ethic is the most primitive moral response, focusing on "me and mine." It develops through undercare in early childhood. More promising is the Engagement ethic, which gives rise to prosocial, compassionate response, is fostered in the EDN, and is primed by caring, supportive relationships. The most highly evolved ethic is the Imagination ethic, which uses abstraction, deliberation, and imagination to expand capacities for empathic engagement beyond face-to-face interaction.

Hunter-gatherer societies, Narvaez argues, support the EDN for children and others throughout life. Allowing for autonomy yet emphasizing community, such societies stress social interconnections as well as unity with nature. Contemporary Western societies do not emphasize these interconnections, and, indeed, create conditions that undermine them. In Narvaez's view, these conditions constitute cultures of competitive detachment within which the EDN is not supported. The recovery of hunter-gatherer values and mindsets, she contends, can be achieved by emphasizing cultures of cooperative companionship, which rekindle the need for and value of "being with" others and the world in interdependent relationships, as well as autopoeisis, or the active participation of the self in its own development and organization. Companionship virtue and autopoesis in virtue development are ways in which mindful morality and communal imagination can take hold.

Moral development in early childhood is Ross A. Thompson's topic in "The Development of Virtue: A Perspective from Developmental Psychology." Thompson reviews a number of psychological studies of children under the age of five years that counter common misconceptions of toddlers as either egoists or as budding altruists. Studies of early childhood provide evidence of the emergence of a premoral sensibility that could serve as the foundation for further character development.

Studies show that twelve- to eighteen-month-old toddlers interpret the actions of people they watch in terms of inferred goals and intentions. This seems to be evidence of early social understanding, which, researchers believe, is nonegocentric in the sense that young children do not confuse their own intentions and goals with those of the adults they observe. These achievements provide the basis for a range of skills and capacities which, taken together, shape the contours of a premoral sensibility. For example, studies indicate that toddlers are capable of shared intentionality—that is, the ability to have psychological states similar to those of others, including shared goals and intentions. Shared intentionality is essential for cooperative, prosocial behavior. Studies suggest that young children engage in such behavior as result of spontaneously understanding, sharing, and knowing how to assist in the achievement of others' goals, and not from the desire to obtain extrinsic rewards. Experiments also reveal that toddlers are able to appraise others' behavior in terms of its effects on goal attainment, punish those who obstruct the efforts of others to reach goals, reward those who help, and provide benefits to those who are victimized. Emotion understanding is another aspect of a premoral sensibility that young children display. Young children show skills in interpreting others' emotions, including capacities for empathy. In agreement with Slote's general line of argument, Thompson contends that these abilities are important for moral development, as parents often enlist emotional responses in attempts to teach children about values and how to behave morally.

Young children's' premoral sensibility is an important precursor for further moral development. The foundations of conscience, for example, seem to be established in early childhood—evidence for this is found in studies of children as young as age two and a half. "Conscience" is understood by developmental psychologists to refer to the processes by which children construct and act consistently with internal generalizable standards of conduct. Echoing themes from Narvaez, studies show that the quality of parent-child relationships is crucial to the growth of conscience and individual differences in moral conduct. Finally, Thompson discusses research on moral identity, or the construction of a sense of self around moral values. Significantly, a longitudinal study found correlations of conscience development in children from ages two to four and a half with the emergence of a "moral self" at age five and a half, and socially and emotionally competent behavior at age six and a half. Despite evidence for a developmental trajectory from a premoral sensibility through the growth of conscience and the formation of moral identity, Thompson notes that many questions remain unanswered.

In "Psychological Science and the *Nicomachean Ethics*: Virtuous Actors, Agents, and Authors," Dan P. McAdams draws on empirical work from a variety of fields to advance a three-stage perspective of the development of virtue, ranging from infancy through adulthood. He argues that this tripartite developmental scheme is broadly consistent with the account of virtue given by Aristotle in the *Nicomachean Ethics*. According to this scheme, different layers of the self contribute to full virtue: the self as a social actor, as a motivated agent, and as an autobiographical author. Each layer represents a form of growth or maturation into virtue.

After briefly remarking on the death of situationism in psychology and recent trends in the empirical study of virtue, McAdams turns to an account of the earliest stage of virtue development, that of the social actor. This stage, he believes, resonates with Aristotle's views of how families and the state must provide the social supports and guidance needed to habituate and educate children into virtuous behavior. Temperament and sociality are key influences here. As social beings, we are taught to be virtuous. Social action that ostensibly accords with virtue precedes action produced by the motivation or desire to act virtuously. A child might share her toys, for example, only because her parents tell her to and not because she genuinely desires to be fair or generous. Moreover, temperament makes a difference to the personality traits children come to have as well as to how they develop in virtue. Positive emotionality can give rise to extraversion, prosocial behavior, and hope, whereas negative emotionality can lead to neuroticism. Being low in neuroticism correlates with virtues such as humility and serenity. Effortful control can lead through experiences of empathy and guilt to agreeableness and conscientiousness. These traits provide resources for the development of several virtues, including prudence, order, and resolution.

Consistently with studies mentioned by Thompson, ages five through seven mark notable advances in the child's development. Several developmental psychologists note that during this period, the child becomes capable of rational choice and deliberation. She acquires personal goals and begins to exercise her own agency in pursuit of them. She comes to see herself as a motivated agent. Her agency does not supplant her traits, but is layered in with them. At this second stage, the child displays genuine virtue. The third stage McAdams discusses is that of the autobiographical author. Here he invokes Aristotle's views on wisdom and contemplation. This is the pinnacle of virtue, available only to the mature, perhaps older, adult. The autobiographical author takes a retrospective view of her life; she is able to look back over the years and form a narrative that gives her life meaning. McAdams and others have found evidence that the lives of moral exemplars who excel in specific virtues, such as caring or courage, are sometimes characterized by redemption sequences—accounts of emerging from hardship or other negative experiences strengthened, or with insight, or transformed. Such individuals, whose narratives are often influenced by their cultures, display high levels of generativity through activities, such as teaching, mentoring, and other forms of prosocial involvement, aimed at leaving a positive legacy.

I have given the psychologists the last word in this volume for two reasons. One is that their work reinforces, from a scientific perspective, views articulated earlier in the collection by philosophers and theologians. The other is that their contributions necessarily remain open-ended. As Thompson points out, there is much about virtue development that we do not know. So we end, then, not only by presenting new perspectives on virtue cultivation but also with an invitation to readers to press ahead with their own ideas on this subject. The positive legacy of this volume, I hope, will be to move research on virtue cultivation forward.

NOTES

1. See Rosalind Hursthouse, *On Virtue Ethics* (Oxford: Oxford University Press, 1999); Michael Slote, *Moral Sentimentalism* (New York: Oxford University Press, 2010), and *Morals From Motives* (Oxford: Oxford University Press, 2001); Christine Swanton, *Virtue Ethics: A Pluralistic View* (New York: Oxford University Press, 2003); and Daniel C. Russell, *Practical Intelligence and the Virtues* (New York: Oxford University Press, 2009).
2. For Kantianism, see, for example, Anne Margaret Baxley, *Kant's Theory of Virtue: The Value of Autocracy* (New York: Cambridge University Press, 2010). For utilitarianism, see Julia Driver, *Uneasy Virtue* (Cambridge: Cambridge University Press, 2001).
3. Notable exceptions include Julia Annas, *Intelligent Virtue* (New York: Oxford University Press, 2011); David Carr and Jan Steutel, eds., *Virtue Ethics and Moral Education* (New York: Routledge, 1999); and Brad K. Wilburn, ed., *Moral Cultivation: Essays on the Development of Character and Virtue* (Lanham, MD: Rowman & Littlefield, 2007).
4. Slingerland's essay is a reworked version of the article that originally appeared in *Ethics*.

BIBLIOGRAPHY

Annas, Julia. *Intelligent Virtue*. New York: Oxford University Press, 2011.
Baxley, Anne Margaret. *Kant's Theory of Virtue: The Value of Autocracy*. New York: Cambridge University Press, 2010.
Carr, David, and Jan Steutel, eds. *Virtue Ethics and Moral Education*. New York: Routledge, 1999.
Driver, Julia. *Uneasy Virtue*. Cambridge: Cambridge University Press, 2001.
Hursthouse, Rosalind. *On Virtue Ethics*. Oxford: Oxford University Press, 1999.
Russell, Daniel C. *Practical Intelligence and the Virtues*. Oxford: Clarendon, 2009.
Slote, Michael. *Morals From Motives*. New York: Oxford University Press, 2001.
Slote, Michael. *Moral Sentimentalism*. New York: Oxford University Press, 2010.
Swanton, Christine. *Virtue Ethics: A Pluralistic View*. New York: Oxford University Press, 2003.
Wilburn, Brad K., ed. *Moral Cultivation: Essays on the Development of Character and Virtue*. Lanham, MD: Rowman & Littlefield, 2007.

CHAPTER 1

⌁

Aristotle on Cultivating Virtue

DANIEL C. RUSSELL

INTRODUCTION

It is curious that many of us philosophers who talk about what the virtues are so rarely stop to consider how the virtues come to be. That is particularly curious, considering that <u>to have a virtue is an achievement. </u>We say things like "Louise is generous," and maybe she is and maybe she isn't; but to say "By accident, Louise is generous" would be bizarre, like saying "By accident, Louise is an extremely good plumber." What is more, being a generous person, like being a good plumber, is not "once and done." <u>It is not the sort of achievement that reaching the peak of a mountain is—once it is done, it is done forever—but the sort that involves keeping sharp, learning, and improving. </u>It seems, then, that built into the very idea of what a virtue is are certain ideas about how such a thing develops.

It is with exactly those ideas—in a word, the idea that the virtues are dynamic—that Aristotle begins his discussion of what the virtues are. When Aristotle considers the nature of a virtue, he begins with the fact that a virtue is something we do not start life with, and that does not simply emerge no matter what we do. It is something that we have to acquire, first through favorable upbringing and then with more focused effort as one matures.[1] Aristotle's point is not to analyze "virtue" as a concept, as if it were something that had fallen from the sky. His point is that character and intellect do develop, either well or badly, and that the difference is not entirely out of our hands; to talk about "virtue" is to talk about what it looks like when that development goes well, so that we can have a clearer picture of what it takes for us to get better at living our lives.[2] To have a virtue is to have developed in a certain way, so for Aristotle the nature of the virtues is not a separate issue from how we cultivate the virtues.

Put simply, Aristotle's theory of the virtues is a theory of getting better, in one's character and in one's intellect. Yet for all that, Aristotle does not offer any special theory of how we get better with respect to the virtues— and that, I think, is one of the most telling features of Aristotle's approach: he offers no special theory of acquiring the virtues because he thinks that there is no special problem involved in understanding how virtues are acquired. On the contrary, Aristotle thinks of that process as a particular instance of something people do all the time: getting better at something through practice and training. That is why Aristotle says that cultivating a virtue is like acquiring a skill, such as learning to play a musical instrument or to build a house. In each case, we develop a certain capacity through the things we do. In this way such capacities are unlike, say, the capacity for vision, since we do not become able to see by repeatedly seeing—that is just the way we naturally are. The way we turn out with respect to (say) courage, though, or building, will depend on the actions we make customary. We become courageous through one course of actions, and cowardly or reckless through other courses, just as apprentice builders become either good or bad builders depending on how they train.[3]

So, when Aristotle thinks about how we become virtuous, he thinks immediately of how we become skilled. Becoming virtuous is a special case of the general phenomenon of getting better—better at succeeding in the sorts of things where succeeding is not the default. The central contention of Aristotle's approach, then, is that the study of the nature of virtue is best begun with a study of how skills are acquired. The question I want to consider in this chapter is whether that contention points to a promising line of investigation in the psychology of moral development.

Believe it or not, just that brief description of Aristotle's central contention is enough to align it with one side of a major division between modern approaches to the psychology of moral development. Understanding that division will point to features of Aristotle's account that are particularly salient for thinking about it as a line of psychological research, so I want to begin by briefly laying out some broad structural features of that division between the main alternative approaches (section 1). I then want to lay out Aristotle's central contention in fairly close detail, looking at the kind of thing he thinks a virtue is (section 2), how he thinks a virtue is acquired (section 3), and what he thinks one learns to do in acquiring a virtue (section 4). After a brief summary of Aristotle's approach to cultivating virtues (section 5), I turn in the last two sections to assessing Aristotle's approach as a research project in the psychology of moral development, looking at some current research on the psychology of skill as a model for moral development (section 6) before discussing what I think are some major hurdles for any such project, including Aristotle's (section 7).

1. TWO WAYS OF THINKING ABOUT MORAL DEVELOPMENT

I said above that Aristotle thinks that a key to understanding the nature of the virtues is the fact that we have to acquire them, and in particular that we acquire them by the same sorts of processes by which we acquire skills like building or playing an instrument. Aristotle's approach is therefore an example of what I shall call a path-dependent approach: we study the psychology of moral development starting from what we know about how people develop and improve generally, and extend this knowledge to an account of improving in character in particular. On this approach, the job for psychology is to tell us what we are actually able to do to develop practical competencies, and the job for philosophy is to tell us which of those real alternatives would count as improvement. In other words, the path-dependent approach merges a psychological picture of the available paths for improvement with a philosophical picture of what creatures to whom those paths are available might aspire to become. The alternative approach is path-independent, since the order of investigation is reversed: we begin with a philosophical account of the virtuous person, understanding moral development as the process of becoming that sort of person. Put another way, it is philosophy's job to give us an ideal to aspire to and psychology's job to tell us how to get there from here.

In the case of virtues, the distinction between these two approaches comes down to whether or not we can properly understand the nature of the virtues in advance of knowing how people develop and acquire the virtues. Psychologists Darcia Narvaez and Daniel Lapsley call the path-dependent and path-independent approaches "psychologized morality" and "moralized psychology," respectively, and they note that moralized psychology was the dominant approach in the latter decades of the twentieth century, best known from the work of Lawrence Kohlberg and his colleagues.[4] As Kohlberg himself described his approach, it was an explicit and self-conscious embracing of a prior philosophical view of morality as a matter of conscious reasoning about moral principles.[5] Kohlberg began with a purely philosophical picture of moral maturity—in particular, an explicitly neo-Kantian picture drawn from the work of philosophers like Hare, Frankena, and Rawls—and developed a theory of moral development as a progression through a series of developmental stages by which moral reasoning becomes increasingly explicit, and explicitly focused on purely formal and universal moral principles.[6]

By contrast, Narvaez and Lapsley themselves are at the frontier of a psychologized morality approach, and in particular they approach moral development by way of discoveries already made in the psychology of skill acquisition.[7] This new, path-dependent approach is what the field needs, they argue, because the once-dominant path-independent approach, it turns out, has doomed the field to stagnation. For one thing, everywhere else in psychology the evidence suggests that human action in general is not based on conscious reasoning, much less on deliberation that focuses on universal principles. A path-independent methodology in the field of moral development has therefore isolated it from the study of human psychology more generally. So, for example, if the study of expert behavior finds that as performance becomes more intelligent it also becomes less explicit or self-conscious, then the study of moral development will be kept from integrating these findings due to its stipulating at the outset what sort of thing moral maturity would have to be.[8] For another, such isolation also forces us to see morality as foreign and isolated from the rest of human life, like an island in a vast sea of non-moral behavior.[9]

Now, as I have put it, Aristotle's central contention about acquiring the virtues is that the process of acquiring the virtues should be modeled on acquiring skills. If I am correct to put Aristotle's view that way, then we are at a particularly interesting point in time to ask how promising a line of research Aristotle's approach might point to. It is a good time, then, to look at Aristotle's approach in detail, and I want to structure my examination here in terms of three chief differences between the path-dependent and the path-independent approach to moral development. First, Aristotle's approach is path-dependent insofar as he takes virtue itself to be something mundane: psychologically speaking, it is like other, thoroughly ordinary and familiar types of being good at doing things (section 2). Second, Aristotle also thinks that the acquisition of a virtue is mundane, like other processes by which people become good at doing things (section 3). And third, Aristotle takes what one learns in acquiring a virtue to be mundane as well: the competencies that a virtuous person has are of the same sort as those of people with practical skills (section 4).

2. VIRTUE IS SOMETHING MUNDANE

For Aristotle, a virtue (*aretê*) in the broadest sense is simply an "excellence," the goodness peculiar to a living thing as the kind of thing it is. Of course, Aristotle recognizes that *aretê* is used primarily to talk about those living things that exercise choice (*prohairesis*)—that is, people—but the concept is one that also gets used more broadly to identify the good cases as apart from the bad cases.[10] This is not because things in nature have some higher purpose; for Aristotle, the "purpose" or "final cause" of a living thing is simply to have the mode of life characteristic of the kind of thing it is.[11] Rather, notions like "excellence" and "badness" have a place in the study of the world for the simple reason that a thing can be either complete or deficient as the kind of thing that it is,[12] and so anyone who proposes to study plants or animals will have to distinguish good specimens from bad ones.[13]

Excellence, then, is a kind of "quality" (*poiotês*), since it answers questions of the form "what is it like?" (*poion*)[14] and thus sorts things by what they are like.[15] Excellence does not sort things into different kinds, like "two-footed"; rather, it is a quality of being "in a good way," so to speak.[16] As such, excellence is a specific kind of quality that Aristotle calls a thing's "condition" or "comportment" (*diathesis*).[17] Some conditions say only what something is like right now (as when we say, "This tea is hot"), but other conditions are long-lasting and entrenched, as when we say that someone has knowledge; excellence is a condition of this second, long-lasting kind.[18]

A condition of the long-lasting sort Aristotle calls a *hexis*, which comes from the Greek word "to have" (*echein*), and specifically from that word's usage in a peculiar Greek idiom for "how things are" (*pôs echein*) with someone or something. *Hexis* is notoriously difficult to translate into English, which has no equivalent idiom; I shall simply call a *hexis* an "attribute." More specifically, Aristotle says that excellence is a *hexis* or attribute in virtue of which things can be said to be well with someone or something.[19] And this is what Aristotle says in *NE* II.5 as well, where he classifies virtue in a generic way as an attribute as opposed to other kinds of qualities.

In sum, Aristotle thinks that excellence or virtue belongs to a class of attributes in virtue of which things go well for a living thing not just at the moment but in a long-lasting way. In this most generic sense, an excellence is a kind of completeness or fulfillment a thing has when it is not deficient as the kind of thing it is.[20] So, for example, health is an excellence,[21] specifically an excellence of the body's narrowly biological capacities.[22] However, health is an excellence that all living things can have; to talk about distinctly human excellence (*aretê anthrôpinê*)[23]—that is, excellence strictly speaking, of the sort limited to creatures with choice[24]—Aristotle looks at the distinctly human capacity for excellence in both our reasoning (*aretê dianoêtikê*) and our affective nature (*aretê êthikê*).[25] These excellences are attributes for which we praise people[26]—that is, for which we say that things are well with someone in a way that makes sense only when speaking of a human being, whose choices are part of the process of development. "Human excellence" includes scientific knowledge or *epistêmê* (a "demonstrative-knowledge attribute," *hexis apodeiktikê*),[27] skill or *technê* (a "making attribute," *hexis poiêtikê*),[28] practical intelligence or *phronêsis* (a "doing attribute," *hexis praktikê*),[29] and virtue of character (*aretê tou êthous*, which is a "choosing attribute," *hexis prohairetikê*).[30]

What all human excellences have in common, we might say, is that they are all ways of being good at something within the distinctly human sphere of life. But since Aristotle's focus in the *Ethics* is on being good at things to do with how we act and lead our lives,[31] he sets aside knowledge right away: knowledge—by which he means knowledge of some particular discipline of learning or other[32]—is something we acquire through study, not practice.[33] And no wonder, since that study is of things that we cannot do anything about;[34] as Aristotle says, we can investigate geometry, or the weather, but we cannot deliberate about it.[35]

Now, Aristotle says that skill, practical intelligence, and character virtue are alike in being about things we can do something about,[36] and in being acquired through practice.[37] However, while this similarity with skill is, for Aristotle, the key to understanding how we acquire practical intelligence and character virtue, he is adamant that the latter sorts of virtues are not kinds of skills themselves. Unlike virtuous actions, acts of skill have separate products that can be evaluated strictly on their observable or structural properties;[38] and unlike practical intelligence, skill is concerned with some specific kind of making, whereas practical intelligence is concerned with acting, and not just in some specific domain but all the way across one's life.[39] So although skill is a human excellence, it is not the sort of excellence that is the topic of the *Ethics*, a collection of treatises on action and emotion.

For Aristotle, the idea behind excellence in the strictest sense—the sense of virtue—is the idea of being good at living one's life. More precisely, it is the pairing of character virtues and practical intelligence,[40] a pairing of the following sort. Aristotle says that people with character virtues—or more commonly, just "virtues," such as courage and generosity—have the right sorts of goals (such as standing for good in the face of danger or helping others with one's resources), and that it is practical intelligence that enables those people to determine what it would mean to realize those goals.[41] Put another way, virtue is a long-term attribute (*hexis*) of aiming at appropriate things (recall: it is a "choosing attribute"), and practical intelligence is a long-term attribute of deliberating well about acting for the sake of those things (a "doing attribute").

There are a couple of things we should notice about Aristotle's account of virtue at this generic level. One is that the topic of virtue is part of a broader outlook on the world, and therefore is literally mundane. In the end, a virtue is just an attribute of being in a good way, and attributes like that are among the things there are in the world. People become good at playing a musical instrument or practicing medicine or understanding geometry; getting better is a familiar phenomenon in our world. And people also seem to get better at helping others, better at facing challenges, better at being a friend. Aristotle finds the occurrence of all forms of excellence to be something to discover and try to understand as part of the world as we find it.

The other thing to notice is that even though Aristotle sets apart the virtues in the strictest sense—practical intelligence and the various character virtues—his approach is still mundane here, too. The virtues are different from knowledge because of how we acquire them: it takes repeated, focused practice, just as in the case of skill. The virtues are different from skill also because of our aim in acquiring them, namely to be good at certain sorts of choosing and doing rather than at certain sorts of making. What is conspicuous by its absence here is any prior moral ideal or principle that marks the virtues as different from everything else in the world. Virtue is a kind of getting better and becoming good at something; in that respect, it is no different from mastery of a skill or a science. What is distinctive about it is what we hope to become good at by acquiring the virtues, namely to become good at setting our aims, making choices, and pursuing ends—good, in other words, at being creatures who have lives they put together in that way.

3. THE ACQUISITION OF VIRTUE IS MUNDANE

Aristotle's main treatise on the virtues—the second book of the *Nicomachean Ethics*—begins with where the virtues come from, namely from what he calls *ethos*.[42] In fact, he says that this is why excellence of character (i.e., of *êthos*) is so called, since the word *êthos* is only a slight variation on *ethos*.[43] Etymology aside, Aristotle's linking of them illustrates how tightly he wants to connect the nature of virtue and the route by which virtue is acquired. So what is that route exactly?[44]

Ethos is a noun that derives from the verb *ethein*, "to be accustomed" or "wont" to do this or that, and to say that something comes about from *ethos* is to say that it comes about by a process that makes some kind of action customary and familiar—we might even say "characteristic." And that makes it easier to see why Aristotle would make such a close link between character and *ethos*: <u>character is what one has as a result of building up of customary and familiar ways of acting.</u> Now, if we say only that much, then we might imagine that *ethos* is a kind of passive absorption of routine, and in fact the standard English rendering of *ethos*, "habit" or "habituation,"[45] can suggest exactly that in everyday usage. We might worry, then, that Aristotle's account of how we acquire virtues is all too mundane—in particular, too mundane to result in what we would really think of as virtue.

However, that conclusion would seriously misconstrue Aristotle's point in at least a couple of ways. For one thing, for Aristotle *ethos* contrasts not with, say, focused and mindful effort, but with developmental paths that are merely natural, such as the development of our perceptual capacities.[46] Making the point that character comes from *ethos*, then, is supposed to draw attention to the fact that it comes about in ways that people can do something about.

<u>For another, Aristotle notes that *ethos* is the same process by which skills are acquired, such as building or playing a musical instrument: character, like skill, comes from repeated action.</u>[47] More than that, good character, like being good at building or playing an instrument, <u>comes from repeated action that is focused in the appropriate way</u>: you do not become a courageous person just by coming through a lot of frightening situations, any more than you become a good builder just by doing a lot of building.[48] In both cases, the process has to be directed so that it is not merely repetition but focused on the specific kind of actions that will train you to do well. That is why aspiring builders and musicians seek out qualified instructors,[49] and it is why we try to surround young people with the right kinds of social institutions,[50] examples, and guidance, right from childhood.[51]

So I suggest that, in this context anyway, we would do best to think of *ethos* as "practice" or "training," preserving the analogy with the process by which we acquire skills. This also confirms that *attribute* is (though not ideal) a better rendering of *hexis* than the more traditional *habit*. A good builder's skill, for instance, is an entrenched attribute (*hexis*) of that person in virtue of which he or she builds well, on account of having trained to do so (*ethos*); but we certainly would not describe a builder's skill as a "habit" built up through rote "habituation."[52] <u>An excellence, whether it is a virtue or a skill, is an entrenched attribute of a person that results from practice and training.</u>

But perhaps that is too quick; after all, a lot of what goes on in practice or training is what we might call "conditioning," as when we build up physical strength through repeated exercise.[53] In the case of self-control, the analog of exercise is getting used to walking away from pleasant temptations; in the case of courage, it is getting used to the things that frighten us and resisting the tendency to exaggerate them.[54] It is no accident that these examples involve pleasure and pain, which Aristotle acknowledges both as powerful motivating forces and as among the chief components of the character virtues.[55] At this point Aristotle explicitly refers to Plato's view that it is through our experience of pleasure and pain that we begin, while still children, to develop better or worse character.[56] Aristotle seems to think that Plato was on the right line here; but does this talk of shaping or conditioning children to find some things nice and other things nasty suggest that Aristotle thinks of *ethos*, when it comes to character, more along the lines of simple "habituation," after all?

I think such a conclusion would get both Plato and Aristotle wrong. It would get Plato wrong because he thinks of this early conditioning as a kind of preparatory education. As Aristotle notes, Plato says that to be "educated" (to have *paideia*) is to be pleased and to be pained at—more generally, to like and to detest—the appropriate things. To be sure, Plato says that this is not a kind of intellectual learning: someone might be extremely well educated in liking and detesting the right things, he says, despite lacking all sophistication in articulating just what he or she has learned. But he does think of it as learning just the same, insisting that such a person is actually better educated—"there is a great difference in education" between them, Plato writes—than someone who is more sophisticated about the difference between good and bad but whose emotions do not track that difference.[57] This education is preparation for agreement between reason and emotion as one becomes mature enough to grasp the reasons why good things should be liked and bad things detested.[58]

More important at present, we would misunderstand Aristotle if we assumed that the early shaping of pleasure and pain is a kind of rote habituation. To be sure, Aristotle does divide the mind into a rational and a non-rational part,[59] and he then proceeds to discuss the virtues of these parts—practical intelligence and the virtues of character, respectively—in separate treatises.[60] But although Aristotle thinks that character has both rational and non-rational dimensions, this does not mean that character is literally complex, an aggregate of distinct parts.[61] On the contrary, when Aristotle distinguishes the rational and non-rational parts of the mind, he goes out of his way to say that he does not care whether these are distinct parts, as arms and legs are, or whether they are different in "definition" only but not actually distinct, as concavity and convexity are merely two aspects of the same arc.[62] What is more, Aristotle clearly believes that *ethos* is a single process that results in both character virtue and practical intelligence. That process is the one by which, in ethics, we learn that such and such is good,[63] and in character training that process involves simultaneously learning why such and such is good.[64] And of course, virtue of character is a *hexis* in virtue of which one acts and chooses in accordance with a "mean," and with "right reason"—which is to say, with practical intelligence.[65] So the developmental process that results in the virtues of character is the same process that results in practical intelligence.[66]

For Aristotle, training in virtue is simultaneously a blend of rational and non-rational training; and in fact, that simultaneous blend seems to be what we actually observe. Rosalind Hursthouse gives the example of saying to a small child who has just taken something from the cat's dish, "You don't want that dirty nasty thing!" Obviously, the child does want the thing, but of course the statement is a prescriptive one: we say things like that to children both to teach them "not to want that sort of thing, and also . . . that the nasty and dirty is such as to be undesirable and bad."[67] The example illustrates that, in general, we do not teach children what to like or detest and then introduce normative concepts at some other time. And similarly in the teaching of virtue there are rational and non-rational dimensions, but that does not mean that there are literally distinct parts, much less stages, of such training.

For Aristotle, the clearest picture we have of the kind of "training" that goes on in acquiring a virtue is the kind of training by which we acquire a skill. Twice in a short span Aristotle makes the point that with virtue, it is action that precedes the capacity, and not vice versa. The first time, Aristotle observes that in this respect virtue is unlike seeing or hearing, since we obviously do not acquire the capacity to see or to hear by repeatedly looking or listening.[68] And Aristotle immediately compares virtue to skill in this respect,[69] as if sensing that this phenomenon—doing something so as to acquire a capacity for doing it—requires explanation. The explanation, quite simply, comes by pointing to a context in which it is obvious how this happens, as one acquires the capacities a builder or musician has by practicing building or music.

The second time, though, Aristotle raises a paradox about this kind of learning: how can it be that doing certain sorts of actions has to precede the capacity for doing those sorts of actions?

> But one might find it puzzling how we say that people have to become fair by doing fair things, and temperate by doing temperate things; after all, if they are doing fair things and temperate things, then they are fair and temperate, just as they are literate and musical if they are doing literate things and musical things.[70]

Aristotle finds this a very easy paradox to solve, since the comparison with literacy and musical skills is actually the solution itself:

Or isn't that how things are in the case of the skills? For it is possible to do something grammatical both by chance and at someone else's direction; so one will be grammatical if he should both do something grammatical and do it grammatically, that is, according to the grammatical skill within himself.[71]

Aristotle's response to the puzzle, then, is to make a distinction between doing something in a beginner's way and doing it in an accomplished way; so, in the case of virtues like fairness and temperance, one acquires the capacity to do fair or temperate things in an accomplished way through doing the same kind of things in a beginner's way.[72] The comparison of virtue to skill is significant, not only or even chiefly because it offers a way out of the puzzle, but because it shows Aristotle explicitly considering a question about cultivating virtue and arriving at an answer by considering how mundane that process is—it is just like other everyday ways in which we get better at something. What is more, cultivating virtue is like those other kinds of getting better in that, in those cases too, it takes focused effort and practice on the part of the learner to acquire the capacity. That, he says, is where most people go wrong: they "know" what they ought to do in the sense in which people sometimes know what the doctor has ordered but still do not do it.[73] Elsewhere, he notes that we speak even of small children as having "virtues," as when we say that a child has a kind or courageous nature; but children—and immature adults, for that matter—do not have their own practical intelligence to guide them, and in that respect they still need to grow up.[74] Our early development is, for the most part, something that happens to us; but eventually cultivating virtue is something that we have to do, and that takes focus, effort, and the right kind of practice.

4. WHAT ONE LEARNS TO DO IN ACQUIRING A VIRTUE IS MUNDANE

Aristotle thinks that the process of acquiring a virtue is a lot like the process of acquiring a skill. But what about the attributes themselves—the *hexeis*—that result from those two processes: how alike are they? We have already seen several respects in which Aristotle insists that they are not alike at all.[75] The chief difference is that skills like building have a product that is distinct from the act of building, and can be assessed independently of that act, whereas the same is not true in the case of virtuous actions.[76] But for all that, Aristotle is also deeply impressed by a couple of crucial similarities between virtue and skill. One similarity is this: in each case, to say that someone has such an attribute is to say that that person both (a) has certain standing goals and (b) is intelligently oriented toward those goals.[77]

Now, what Aristotle says here is extremely compressed, but the idea behind (a) seems to be this: to say that a person is a physician, or a generous person, is to build a standing goal right into that description—to heal by use of medicine, or to help by use of resources. And the idea behind (b), I think, is that in both cases the goal is determinable but not yet determinate: the physician knows what to do for a given patient only after specifying what healing would amount to in that patient's case. Likewise, a generous person must also determine what would actually count as helping, given the particulars of the case at hand.

It is that "specificatory" ability, I think, that goes into being intelligently oriented toward one's goals, in the case of skill as well as virtue. The issue here is not (or not merely) finding the means to one's end: another attribute, "cleverness" (*deinotês*), is concerned with that.[78] Rather, Aristotle says that there is an excellence that arrives at a decision, and that that excellence is practical intelligence, or *phronêsis*;[79] the idea seems to be that before one can decide just how to achieve what one has decided to do, one must first decide what to do, here and now, in a concrete way, given all the particulars. This way of reconstructing the analogy with skill jibes with what Aristotle says elsewhere about that analogy: insofar as a physician, or an orator, or a statesman is deliberating about what to do, that person does not deliberate about whether to heal or to persuade or to govern well, but about what to do given such a goal.[80] Here, too, what is so striking about saying that the physician's goal is "to heal," that the orator's goal is "to persuade," and that the statesman's goal is "to govern well" is how uninformative those goals are in any concrete, here-and-now setting. It is impossible to jump from that sort of goal directly to thinking about the means to it. First, we must decide exactly what realizing that goal would look like, here and now.[81]

The other main way in which skill and practical intelligence are similar attributes is that each of them is prescriptive with respect to what to do, where "doing" is a matter of making or producing in the case of skill[82] and of acting, more generally, in the case of practical intelligence.[83] Each of them, Aristotle says, aims at a "mean" and avoids what is either "too much" or "too little,"[84] although each skill is concerned only with its particular sphere whereas practical intelligence is concerned with every area of human life.[85] For these reasons too, then, Aristotle takes skill and virtue to be different attributes, but he is nonetheless impressed by the fact that virtue, just like skill, is about success at determining what to do.

Aristotle elaborates both of these similarities between skill and virtue by focusing on several ways in which practical intelligence involves extracting crucial information from one's surroundings. Here Aristotle makes it clear that practical intelligence is not some monolithic attribute but actually is an array of more specific functions.[86] One of these functions is a certain ability to judge what situation one is actually in; Aristotle calls this ability "comprehension" (*sunesis*),[87] which he describes as a "critical" or "discriminatory" ability (*kritikê*).[88] Although his discussion is highly compressed, it is suggestive of an ability to do well on the "front end" of deliberation, so to speak, taking a careful and critical look at the available information in order to formulate an accurate view of just what the case at hand is, about which one must make a decision.

Another ability Aristotle calls "sense" (*gnômê*),[89] which is another discriminatory ability (*kritikê*) that involves looking at one's situation from multiple perspectives so as to determine what would be "sensible" or reasonable in that situation, all the way around. Lastly, Aristotle focuses on practical intelligence as a problem-solving ability, and identifies what he calls *nous* or "intelligence," the ability to bring deliberation to a successful conclusion with respect to what, concretely, is to be done in particular circumstances for the sake of one's goal.[90]

All of these attributes (*hexeis*), he says, converge toward the same point, since it takes all of them together to arrive at the right decision, some of them by formulating the relevant information and some by arriving at a decision on the basis of that information.[91] The idea, then, seems to be that practical intelligence, like skill, involves a host of more fine-grained abilities to "read" situations so as to extract goal-relevant information from them and then identify what it would be best to do toward that goal, given one's actual situation. This, I take it, is why Aristotle so frequently compares practical intelligence to a kind of perception,[92] since practical intelligence, like skill, enables one to extract relevant information from one's surroundings that might well be lost on others.[93]

For Aristotle, then, virtue and skill are importantly alike both in how they are acquired and in the kinds of attributes they are. What explains both of these similarities is the fact that virtue and skill are both goal-oriented. Because of their orientation toward certain kinds of goals, each must be acquired by constant practice focused on realizing those goals in an intelligent way. And again because of their goal orientation, each of them is a *hexis* in virtue of which one is able to gather goal-relevant information from one's current circumstances, determine what achieving that goal would look like within those circumstances, and orient one's actions with respect to that goal. That is why, as Aristotle puts it, both skill and virtue are concerned with "things that can be otherwise"[94]—that is, circumstances that vary from case to case and from time to time, and which therefore require us to carefully adjust our actions to the particular demands of a given situation, as if aiming at a target.[95]

5. ARISTOTLE ON CULTIVATING VIRTUE: A RESEARCH PROGRAM

We can summarize the main points of Aristotle's account of moral development as follows:

- Moral development consists of acquiring certain long-term attributes (*hexeis*), called virtues.
- The virtues are acquired through practice and training that must ultimately be focused and directed. In other words, the virtues are like skills in how we go about acquiring them.
- The virtues combine the pursuit of certain kinds of goals with practical reasoning that is effective in making and executing plans for realizing those goals. In other words, the virtues are also like skills in their cognitive structure.

Taken together, these features of Aristotle's approach add up to what I have called Aristotle's central contention about moral development, namely that we can understand the nature of virtue only by understanding how virtue is acquired, and in particular how acquiring a virtue is like acquiring a skill. This approach to virtue cultivation is of the path-dependent, "psychologized morality" variety; that is, it begins with what we might know about development and "getting better" in general, and extends that knowledge to getting better at living our lives in particular.

This way of understanding Aristotle's approach to virtue cultivation leaves us with an observation to make and a question to ask. First, the observation: as I have presented him here, Aristotle offers a thoroughly mundane, path-dependent approach to moral development. As such, the mundane Aristotle I have presented here is in stark contrast with a more heroic Aristotle that we find in descriptions like the following:

According to Aristotle ([*NE* II.4] 1105a27–b1), genuinely virtuous action proceeds from "firm and unchangeable character" rather than from transient motives. The virtues are *hexeis* ([II.5] 1106a11–12), and a *hexis* is a state that is "permanent and hard change" ([*Cat.* 8] 8b25–9a9). Accordingly, while the good person may suffer misfortune that impairs his activities and diminishes happiness, he "will never [...] do the acts that are hateful and mean" ([*NE* I.10] 1100b32–4...). The presence of virtue is supposed to provide assurance as to what will get done as well as what won't; for Aristotle ([I.10] 1101a1–8; [VI.5] 1140a26–b30), the paradigmatically virtuous *phronimos*, or practical wise man, is characterized by his ability to choose the course of action appropriate to whatever circumstance he is in, whether it be easy or excruciating.[96]

This is not at all an unusual reading of Aristotle; if anything, it will probably seem utterly familiar. Here, we depict Aristotle as starting with a robust ethical ideal: the paradigmatic virtuous and wise person who always and unfailingly does the right thing. The idea that there could be such a person calls for explanation, of course—what could possibly ensure such perfect steadfastness? The answer comes in the form of a bold, even shocking psychological posit: there must be—somehow, and strange as it seems—such things as permanent, unchangeable states that just do generate that sort of constancy; and let's call those states "virtues."

Notice that on this picture, the question of virtue cultivation is the question of looking up at such an ideal and asking how to get there from here. Now, it is of course true that Aristotle does rely on ideals and paradigms, but then so too does every study, whether explicitly or not: after all, much of the reason for talking about "excellence" in the case of plants or animals is to distinguish between good specimens and defective ones, so that defects are not included as part of the anatomy of the species (as opposed to one of its pathologies). The same will be true of skills like playing a musical instrument, since we do not understand the skill in question unless we understand how it helps people avoid musical mistakes; and yet recognizing that fact never leads us to suppose that learning an instrument is the task of figuring out how to get from here to musical perfection. So too for virtues: if the aim is to get better, then it is no good building up a picture of "better" that features our failings and defects, even though failings and defects are inevitable for us.[97] There is a role for "paradigms" in understanding the virtues, but for Aristotle "virtue" is not brought in as a posit, a name for the kind of psychology we would have to have to live up to some pre-established ethical ideal.

Now for the question: when it comes to understanding the cultivation of virtue, what has Aristotle left us—a codified theory or a research program? Put another way, when we assess Aristotle's relevance to our thought in this area, are we assessing a set of things to believe—doctrines about what character and skill are, and how they are related? Or are we assessing a way of figuring out what to believe—the decision to study character by starting with the nature of skill and seeing what the evidence suggests? We might see this as a question about what Aristotle intended; if so, I think Aristotle would have preferred to leave a program, rather than a pronouncement, as his philosophical legacy. Despite later being branded as "The Philosopher," Aristotle himself saw the history of philosophy as the evolution of research programs: our knowledge grows, he said, when philosophers both learn all they can from others who went before and leave something new for others who come after.[98] In other words, if Aristotle was right about philosophy, then his intentions are not really the point. The question is really a question for us, because it is a question about what we would do best to take away from Aristotle, if anything.

I do think Aristotle was right about how philosophy grows, and my own choice is to take Aristotle's chief contribution in the area of virtue cultivation to be a certain direction for research. This means, for one thing, that we can draw inspiration from Aristotle for future research in moral development that focuses on skill, even though there will be numerous points at which we would do better to revise or even scrap things that Aristotle himself believed about either moral development or skill. For example, many scholars read Aristotle as maintaining that a person who has a skill must also be able to teach that skill to others, and yet it is at best odd to suppose that implicit in the skill of building is the skill of teaching that skill.[99] I am not convinced that that is Aristotle's view, but the more important point at present is that even if it were, there would still be no reason to think that his research project on the virtues modeled on the skills comes with that string attached.

Even more unsettling is Aristotle's unambiguous belief that cultivating virtue takes not just a community but also the full force of political power, centralizing control of every aspect of social and family life in order to engineer, as far as possible, the production of virtuous citizens in accordance with a state-approved vision of the virtues and human well-being.[100] I do not see Aristotle's research program as having that string attached, either. On the contrary, the skill analogy itself provides a reason for skepticism about Aristotle's politics: everyone knows it takes a community to make a builder, but no one moves from that to the idea that it takes as much intervention as the state can muster to turn out builders properly.

When we assess Aristotle's account of moral development, then, the question is not whether we would do well to take our cue from what Aristotle believed, but whether there is any reason to follow in the direction of thinking about skill as a way of shedding light on the nature of the virtues.

6. MORAL DEVELOPMENT AND THE PSYCHOLOGY OF SKILL

Logically, the study of skill begins by identifying the main features of skilled performance as opposed to novice performance, before moving on to the psychological mechanisms that underwrite that performance;[101] my discussion here will focus mostly on the former. At a very general level, Narvaez and Lapsley identify three main things that separate experts from novices:[102]

- Experts bring to bear on problems a much greater wealth of background information and experience than novices do, and that information is better organized into a coherent whole.
- Experts have richer perceptions of the situations in which they act than novices do, and are able to survey a wide array of information and discover the most salient opportunities for action.
- Experts are both much more prone and much better able to define their situation and their problem than novices are.

Furthermore, experts develop these superior abilities by learning in contexts that provide reliable feedback, that combine learning of what to do and why to do it (instead of separating theory from application), and by spending a lot of time on focused practice.[103] To borrow Aristotle's language, what separates experts from novices is their *hexeis*: through practice, experts have developed entrenched abilities to extract relevant information from their surroundings so as to adjust their actions intelligently with respect to their goals. But what more precisely can experts do?

Arguably the most groundbreaking work in the modern study of skill was done by William Chase and Herbert Simon in their research on chess skill.[104] Chase and Simon wanted to explain why, as they discovered, expert players could reconstruct a particular arrangement of pieces on a chessboard from memory with more speed and accuracy than less expert or novice players could. They noticed that all of the players they observed reconstructed the boards in "chunks"—that is, groups of related pieces—as opposed to, say, row by row. Somehow, expert players were able to extract more information from their views of the boards they were then supposed to reconstruct.[105] But how?

One hypothesis would be that the better players had better general powers of memory. However, Chase and Simon ruled out this hypothesis because all the players performed similarly when the boards they reconstructed had randomly assembled pieces. Evidently, then, superior performance at reconstructing chess boards is a function of breaking the board down into chunks of pieces related in ways that are meaningful in chess play. What makes those chunks meaningful, of course, is that the pieces in them are arranged in strategic patterns that are familiar from chess play—in a word, the chunks are goal-salient. The better a chess player you are, the better you are at extracting information from a chessboard, representing it as a concatenation of goal-salient chunks.

However, strategically salient patterns will also tend to be visual patterns that are very familiar to experienced chess players, so one further hypothesis would be that the experts were "chunking" according to the visual familiarity of the patterns, and another hypothesis would be that they were chunking according to the strategic salience of the patterns as such. To find out which, Chase and Simon turned from static chessboards to reconstructions of a particular stage of a board within a game that the players had already memorized.[106] Players still used chunks just as they did when reconstructing static boards, but when players gave a verbal narrative of the process of reconstruction, Chase and Simon found that more skilled players tended to focus on a strategic move being made at that stage of play, labeling chunks in terms of strategic moves and placing the pieces relevant to that strategy first before filling in the other patterns. "Memory for moves," Chase and Simon concluded, "is probably segmented into little episodes, each organized around some goal."[107] In that case, better players are better because they have developed a better ability to focus on strategically relevant patterns.[108]

Similar results have been found elsewhere as well. For example, Marina Myles-Worsley and her colleagues found that among the radiologists they studied, the more experienced ones were more accurate in their recognition of abnormal chest X-rays than the less experienced radiologists.[109] This was, again, not because the experts had better general memory—all subjects performed about the same on face-recognition tasks, for instance. Interestingly, it was also not because they were better at X-ray recognition over all: on the contrary, the more experienced radiologists were actually less accurate in their recognition of normal chest X-rays. Evidently, then, the expert radiologists were quicker both to recognize disease-relevant identifying features and to disregard other identifying features when these were not disease relevant.[110]

Further research on such "expertise effects" has placed increased emphasis on the goal-oriented nature of skillful reasoning.[111] Kim Vicente and JoAnne Wang have developed a theory of skill that they describe as "ecological," insofar as it understands skill as a matter of successfully "adapting" to the environment of action: expertise effects can be expected, on their view, when both (a) stimuli can be structured according to goal-relevant constraints and (b) experts attend to those constraints.[112] For example, on their view a random chessboard can be defined as one lacking goal-relevant structure: the pieces are so haphazardly arranged that the strategic opportunities they afford—or the "affordances"—are very unclear. Put another way, with a regular board experts see not merely where a piece is but why it is there; on a random board there is no "why" to a piece's position, and that is why there are no experts with respect to random boards.[113] In such unstructured environments, Vicente and Wang predict that experts will show little or no advantage over novices. In a more structured environment, such as in a regular game of chess, strategies can be formulated with respect to goals like defending, capturing, and ultimately winning, and it is here that expertise makes an important difference. The level of structure in the environment is crucial, on this view, since the advantage of experts over novices is that they "are able to evaluate effectively what is relevant in specific contexts and are thereby able to focus primarily, or exclusively, on the information that is of value for the task at hand.... [O]ne of the hallmarks of expertise is attunement to goal-relevant constraints."[114]

Clearly, the psychological study of skill has led to a focus on the sort of goal-oriented competence that is central in Aristotle's thinking about skill as well. The extent to which understanding the psychology of skill will illuminate moral psychology, though, is a question for ongoing research—it is simply too early to say. The impetus for that research is (a) the striking isomorphism between skill and personality attributes in general and (b) the hope that this isomorphism should still hold when we think about character in particular. Personality psychologists have noticed a remarkable convergence between the developing "social-cognitive" models of personality and research on the nature of skill: in both fields, the basic psychological unit that has emerged is an entrenched attribute in virtue of which one is specially attuned to regions of experience that are salient to the person's goals and interests.[115] In particular, in both cases the attribute is acquired in similar ways, being built up from repetition and practice, and highly reinforced by environmental feedback. And in these two cases the structure of the attribute is similar as well. On the one hand, part of the attribute is an entrenched pattern of focusing attention on items of personal salience so as to extract information from one's surroundings that tends to be missed by people who do not share that attribute. And on the other, it is part of that attribute that one has become particularly adept at drawing on one's own relevant background information to process the extracted information in goal-relevant ways.

Such an isomorphism between personality and skill would cast light on the cultivation of virtue: becoming virtuous, like becoming skilled, is a matter of having certain goals and values in terms of which to focus one's attention on one's environment; it is a matter of learning how to focus that attention effectively so as to extract information salient to those goals and values; and it is also a matter of learning enough about how the world works to process that information so as to formulate intelligent plans and adjust one's behavior accordingly.[116] In other words, having a virtue, just like having a skill, means both getting the goal right and getting things right with respect to that goal,[117] not by chance but in accordance with an entrenched personal attribute.[118]

Unsurprisingly, though, the overlap between this approach to moral development and Aristotle's is not exact. Perhaps the chief divergence is that whereas modern research on the psychology of skill focuses on automaticity, Aristotle himself was ambivalent about it. To make some process "automatic" in the psychologist's sense is not to make it mindless, but to decrease its draw on the scarce resource of attention so that more of one's attention can be given elsewhere. For example, expert chess players excel not by seeing more possible strategies than novices do but by eliminating more strategies from their attention right away, allowing them to divert their attention away from a host of dead ends and toward a much smaller set of hopeful possibilities. By doing automatically what novices must do deliberately, experts are able to be more mindful players, players who put their attention where it really counts.[119] If that is right, then it is worth considering that certain forms of increased automaticity may be involved in acquiring the virtues, since attention is obviously a scarce resource for character as well.[120]

Unfortunately, Aristotle himself does not have a clear view about automaticity.[121] On the one hand, he says that things we do "immediately" (*exaiphnês*) are not done from choice (*prohairesis*)[122] since choice involves deliberation,[123] and deliberation takes time.[124] But on the other, he also says that a courageous person can decide "immediately" in virtue of his or her *hexis*, without prior preparation.[125] Clearly, Aristotle could use a friendly amendment here.[126] We might weaken the link between choice and deliberation, but it is chiefly by way of that link that Aristotle means to distinguish such choices from lucky hits. Alternatively, we might say that sometimes deliberation is immediate, but Aristotle thinks deliberation strongly suggests searching and pondering.[127] So, Aristotle does not seem to have had a clear view of the matter.

Even setting that side, it is at any rate too early to say whether or to what extent the nature of moral development will be illuminated by the study of skill and expertise. What does seem clear already, though, is that the current state of research both in personality theory and in the nature of skill makes the skill-based approach to moral development one of the most exciting avenues for investigation currently available. That is one sign of a promising research program. Another sign of a good program is that it can tell you when it ought to be abandoned. That program's central hypothesis is that moral personality is best understood in terms of virtues that are isomorphic to skill in both their acquisition and their structure, and that thesis is a falsifiable one. In that spirit, I want to close this chapter by looking at what I think are the chief hurdles for a research program like this one.

7. SOME HURDLES AS WE APPROACH VIRTUE VIA SKILL

Although we know a lot now about the conditions under which people must acquire a skill, those conditions seem to be greatly complicated in the case of the virtues. Psychologist Daniel Kahneman summarizes the results of research on the conditions under which people acquire a skill and he boils those results down to two main conditions:[128]

- The environment in which people learn must have enough structure that there are predictable regularities to be learned.
- The environment must afford adequate feedback for the learner to be able to learn these regularities through prolonged practice.

When you are learning to drive a car, you can quickly learn what all of the controls do because both of these conditions are met in that environment. First of all, the car's controls work in a very regular and predictable way; if you press the brake pedal, for instance, the car stops, and not otherwise. Contrast this with, say, learning to forecast the upward and downward movements of a politician's approval rating, events so complex and dependent on so many possible variables that there is very little regularity to study. And second, your experimentation with the car brings immediate and clear feedback: as soon as you press the brake pedal the car stops, so you learn very quickly how to press the brake pedal in order to stop by a certain time. It is very different with piloting a large ship in a harbor, where a pilot turns the wheel and then must wait several minutes before seeing the actual outcome.

Obviously, even if acquiring a virtue is like acquiring a skill, nobody could suppose that it is like acquiring the skill of driving a car, where these two features of learning environments are concerned.[129] The questions are, one, just how "messy" the learning environments would be in the case of the virtues in these two respects; and two, how that messiness should color our assessment of the promise of the skill approach to virtue cultivation.

Start with the structure or regularity of the learning environment. Suppose that a friend of mine finds himself in financial hardship, and I want to be generous to my friend. Now, my point in being generous is not to prove that I mean to be helpful; my point is to be helpful. Unfortunately, it is far easier to prove that I mean well than it is to do well, so now I face difficult questions about what helping would actually look like, here and now. There are some obvious dos and don'ts, but beyond those—that is, where it is really virtue rather than just ordinary common sense that is needed—there are few regularities to be found. Sometimes helping means giving a little, sometimes it means giving a lot; sometimes it means giving money, sometimes it means giving time, or just a sympathetic ear; sometimes it means offering advice, sometimes it means minding one's own business; and which of these it might mean in this case will depend on such different things as my relationship with my friend, what I am actually able to offer, why and how often my friend has problems of this kind, and so on.

The problem is not simply that my brain lacks sufficient computational power to solve a problem with this much complexity; if it were only a computational problem, then perhaps I would simply need "an app for that." The real problem is that life just does not arrange itself into the sorts of regularities that make these kinds of problems amenable to computation in the first place. This is not a special problem that arises just because we are thinking about virtues; anything recognizable as a moral theory will take outcomes seriously, so every theory of moral development must acknowledge that such development goes on in a messy environment. What is special about the virtues, though, is that on the skill model, virtues are *hexeis* in virtue of which we are adept at intelligently extracting information from such environments that is relevant to goals like helping; but it is precisely the nature of acquiring skill that reveals how difficult moral development of that sort would have to be.

The problem only gets harder as we move to the feedback in the learning environment. Suppose that in the end I decide to help my friend by lending him a little bit of money, and a week later he pays me back and is in good spirits again. That certainly looks like positive feedback; however, even though my friend feels better now, he may actually be no better off for it, all things considered. Alternatively, suppose that I decide the most helpful thing would be for me to stay out of his affairs. A week later my friend still will not speak to me; should I take that to mean my decision was a failure? My friend feels worse now, but perhaps he is also moving closer to confronting the real problems that got him into his trouble. So, by what criteria should I determine whether I have made things better or worse, and whether any good I might have done was worth what it cost? Clearly, I cannot know what to make of the feedback I receive without a fairly good idea of what success or failure would amount to here, and that means having a fairly good idea of what it is to make a person genuinely better off.

But crucially, my ideas about what makes people better off are not independent of my actual character: focusing on my friend's mood as the indicator of success or failure is itself a kind of moral immaturity—someone who naively focuses on that may be generous in a beginner's way, but is not generous in the way of those who really do know what it takes to help.[130] I think Aristotle got it right when he said, for one thing, that the virtue of practical intelligence is a virtue of deliberating under the guidance of a good overall grasp of the best things in life,[131] and for another, that having a good grasp of those things is part of what good character is.[132] In that case, part of acquiring the virtues is coming to have a good grasp of what things are really important—and that means that becoming generous involves learning both what helps based on the feedback one receives and the very criteria for interpreting that feedback in the first place. If feedback worked that way with driving, we would have to learn how to stop a car while also having to learn what counts as "stopping."[133]

These two problems—the problem of regularity and the problem of feedback—are very real, but they are nothing new. People do learn to be expert poets or painters, architects or builders, but no one would suppose that their learning environment is full of computational regularities. The problem of feedback is not unique to the virtues, either—if anything, such a problem is the rule rather than the exception. Not just poets and painters but architects and builders too must learn both when their creations are successful and what really counts as success where such creations are concerned. It takes an expert, after all, to know when a newly inserted doorway might compromise the wall that it sits in.[134]

These examples show that problems of regularity and feedback are familiar, even ordinary problems that people do manage to overcome, in the case of virtue as in the case of skill. They also suggest that overcoming them in the case of virtue is probably not a matter of starting with a comprehensive theory of well-being and translating it (miraculously) into a here-and-now proposal; that is just not how skillful problem solving works. Rather, overcoming these problems is far more likely to be yet another case of being guided by broad constraints on what counts as success or failure, and we should not expect that such constraints will always determine a unique solution any more in the case of virtue than in the case of any other skill. And these examples also remind us that we usually do not go it alone as we try to identify the salient regularities or learn the standards for success; we rely on the guidance of others who have already been where we are now.[135]

There are both psychological and philosophical lessons to be drawn here. For the psychologist, the main lesson may be that the very straightforwardness of skills like chess playing that makes them so advantageous to study is also what makes that advantage so limited. Although chess is an amazingly complex game, it is characterized by regularity of patterns and clarity of feedback, and this means that studying chess skill allows us to eliminate a lot of "noise" and just focus on how skilled observation and deliberation are oriented toward the chief goal of that skill. But it is just this feature that also makes chess skill unlike so many other skills, perhaps most other skills, and certainly unlike the sorts of skills that would offer the most relevant models for the virtues. The study of skill may well have the most light to shed on moral development. Focusing on chess has genuine value, but it does not even tell us enough about skills, much less about virtues as modeled on skills.[136]

The lesson for us philosophers is that a path-dependent approach means accepting the sort of messiness that philosophical theories of moral development have often tried to avoid. Thinking about acquiring the virtues on the model of acquiring a skill is an example of a path-dependent approach to moral development, and what we have learned about the available paths suggests that we should expect the process of becoming virtuous to be extremely messy. As we have seen, the learning environment is untidy and the feedback contestable, but the messiness does not stop there. As with skills, we should expect that what sets people on the paths to virtue is less the attraction of an ideal than recognition of their failings, or even horror at what they are capable of.[137] As with skills, people acquire virtues so that they can do better; but people face different challenges about which they need to do better, so we should expect the same virtue—courage, for example—to look different in different lives, one way for someone going to war and another for someone going to chemotherapy.[138]

Furthermore, as with skills, people do manage to learn from other people, even though no one is ever guaranteed others worth learning from. The good news is that, being social creatures, we do not have to start from nowhere; but the bad news is that where we start will never be ideal, and so moral progress is likely to be made at best in fits and starts. Individuals can be sources of cultural progress: someone takes a stand against slaveholding, and eventually the world changes.[139] It can work in the reverse direction as well: the textile industry mechanizes, and eventually children who would have spent their youth in factories get to spend it studying to become people who might change the world. At any given time within a culture, though, what passes for virtue—like what passes for good building practice—may not be much to speak of, and it is only over time that much of the progress occurs. Moral development, like the development of skill, stands on the shoulders of history, for better and for worse.

All of these things, it is safe to say, are what the available paths are like. When we learn about the available paths, we are reminded that we are not guaranteed the answers we wanted to have before we started investigating. And there is no reason to think that moral development is any less path-dependent than skills, those other sorts of getting better practically.

So, virtue is messy. In fact, one of the most valuable lessons we might learn from studying skills is just how unavoidably messy virtue is. Where does that leave us? On a path-independent approach, results like these are devastating: we begin with an idealization of the virtuous person, only to find that, by all accounts, there is no way to get to that ideal from where real persons actually have to begin. Such an approach was supposed to cast light on how we develop morally, but it turns out to have changed the topic; it was a waste of time, a distraction by an ideal that had somehow become its own point. But things are different on the path-dependent approach: there, these findings are informative, because the whole point from the outset was to discover all we can about what our options for improving actually are. And what we find is sobering: it is possible to improve our character, by all accounts, but we should expect it to be messy, piecemeal, varied, impure, culturally bounded, historically bounded, uneven, slow, and difficult. There is still room on this approach for idealized models of virtue, but only because understanding "getting better" requires having some way of saying in what direction "better" would lie.[140] But in the end, taking the skill model seriously is likely to require us to accept that sometimes getting better means getting, well, a little better.

As a research program for thinking about moral development, Aristotle's skill model does not put the virtues beyond our grasp. But it does not put them easily within our reach, either. And that is not a shortcoming. It may not be that answer we wanted, but it is precisely the sort of answer we should have expected. If we feel crestfallen, we should remind ourselves that the real defect in a theory of moral development is to suggest that the process should be simpler, easier, or more elegant than we actually know it to be. All that Aristotle's approach can offer is one picture of what "getting better" might look like for creatures like us. It offers nothing more. And it offers nothing less.[141]

NOTES

1. See *Nicomachean Ethics* [*NE*] II.1–3. All Greek translations, unless otherwise noted, are my own.
2. See *NE* II.2.
3. *NE* II.1.
4. See D. Narvaez and D. K. Lapsley, "The Psychological Foundations of Everyday Morality and Moral Expertise," in *Character Psychology and Character Education*, ed. D. K. Lapsley and F. C. Power (University of Notre Dame, 2005), 141–43.
5. L. Kohlberg, C. Levine, and A. Hewer, *Moral Stages: A Current Formulation and a Response to Critics*, vol. 10 of *Contributions to Human Development*, ed. J. A. Meacham (Basel: Karger, 1983), 17, 64–103.
6. Kohlberg et al., *Moral Stages*, 17, 81–83, 88–91.

7. D. K. Lapsley and D. Narvaez, "Moral Psychology at the Crossroads," in *Character Psychology and Character Education*, ed. D. K. Lapsley and F. C. Power (Notre Dame, IN: University of Notre Dame, 2005); Narvaez and Lapsley, "Psychological Foundations."

8. See Narvaez and Lapsley, "Psychological Foundations," 141–43; Lapsley and Narvaez, "Moral Psychology," 25–26.

9. See Lapsley and Narvaez, "Moral Psychology," 27.

10. *Metaphysics* (*Met.*) V.14, 1020b12–25.

11. See *Physics* (*Phys.*) II.7–8.

12. *Phys.* VII.3, 246a10–b3.

13. See D. S. Hutchinson, *The Virtues of Aristotle* (New York: Routledge and Kegan Paul, 1986), 34. For thorough discussions of Aristotle's account of different types of excellences, see Hutchinson, *Virtues of Aristotle*; and R. Parry, "*Episteme* and *Techne*," *Stanford Encyclopedia of Philosophy* (2007), http://plato.stanford.edu/entries/episteme-techne/.

14. *Categories* (*Cat.*) 8.

15. *Met.* V.14.

16. *Met.* V.14, 1020b12–25.

17. *Diathesis* is often translated "disposition," but in contemporary philosophy this word is far too loaded to avoid being misleading (cf. Hutchinson, *Virtues of Aristotle*, 9–10). In a technical sense, Aristotle means by *diathesis* an arrangement or ordering (*taxis*) of a complex thing (*Met.* V.19).

18. *Cat.* 8, 8b25–36, 9a10–13.

19. *Met.* V.20, 1022b10–12.

20. *Met.* V.16, 1021b20–23.

21. *Met.* V.20, 1022b10–12.

22. *NE* I.13, 1102a32–b12.

23. *NE* I.13, 1102a16–17.

24. *Met.* V.14, 1020b23–25.

25. *NE* I.13, 1102b13–1103a7.

26. *NE* I.13, 1103a7–20; see also II.5.

27. *NE* VI.3, 6.

28. *NE* VI.4.

29. *NE* VI.4.

30. *NE* II.6, VI.2.

31. *NE* II.2, 1103b26–31.

32. *NE* VI.6.

33. *NE* II.1, 1103a14–18.

34. *NE* VI.3, 7.

35. *NE* III.3, 1112a18–27.

36. *NE* VI.1, 1138b35–1139a17.

37. *NE* II.4, 1105a17–26.

38. *NE* II.4, 1105a26–33.

39. *NE* VI.5.

40. *NE* I.13; VI.12, 1144a29–b1; VI.13, 1144b14–17, 30–32.

41. *NE* VI.1, 12. See J. McDowell, "Some Issues in Aristotle's Moral Psychology," in *Companions to Ancient Thought, 4: Ethics*, ed. S. Everson (New York: Cambridge University Press, 1998); D. Russell, *Practical Intelligence and the Virtues* (Oxford: Oxford University Press, 2009), 6–11.

42. *NE* II.1.

43. *NE* II.1, 1103a17–18. H. G. Liddell and R. Scott, *Greek–English Lexicon* (Oxford: Oxford University Press, 1935) suggest that *ethos* could have originated as a mis-reading (or *falsa lectio*) of *êthos*; if so, then Aristotle is close, but has the direction of variation backwards.

44. For a thorough discussion of Aristotle on *ethos*, see T. Lockwood, "Habituation, Habit, and Character in Aristotle's *Nicomachean Ethics*," in *A History of Habit: From Aristotle to Bourdieu*, ed. T. Sparrow and A. Hutchinson (Lanham, Maryland: Lexington Books, 2013).

45. E.g., T. Irwin, ed. and trans., *Aristotle: Nicomachean Ethics* (Indianapolis: Hackett, 1985), has "virtue of character results from habit"; R. Crisp, ed. and trans., *Aristotle: Nicomachean Ethics* (Cambridge: Cambridge University Press, 2000), "virtue of character is a result of habituation"; S. Broadie and C. Rowe, eds. and trans., *Aristotle: Nicomachean Ethics* (Oxford: Oxford University Press, 2002), "excellence of character results from habituation." These are all perfectly legitimate translations.

46. *NE* II.1, 1103a18–31.

47. *NE* II.1, 1103a18–b2.

48. *NE* II.1, 1103b9–21; cp. II.2, 1104a10–27.

49. *NE* II.1, 1103b6–13.

50. *NE* II.1, 1103b2–6.

51. *NE* II.1, 1103b21–25.

52. The tendency to use cognates of *habit* here is no more than an etymological accident. *Hexis*, you will recall, is derived from the Greek verb *echein*, "to have," which when combined with an adverb is used idiomatically to say "how it is" with someone or something. The equivalent verb in Latin is *habere*, from which comes the Latin noun *habitus*—a characteristic mode—and *habitus* is the source of such English nouns as *habit*, as well as *habitat*, a living thing's characteristic place to live (the Greek noun *êthos* carries that meaning as well). See also Lockwood, "Habituation."

53. *NE* II.2, 1104a27–33.

54. *NE* II.2, 1104a33–b3.

55. *NE* II.3.

56. *NE* II.3, 1104b11–13; Plato, *Laws* II, 653a5–c8.

57. *Laws* II, 654c3–e1.

58. *Laws* II, 653b1–c4. See D. Russell, *Plato on Pleasure and the Good Life* (Oxford: Oxford University Press, 2005), 219–29.

59. *NE* I.13.

60. See *NE* VI.1, 1138b35–1139a6.

61. See R. Hursthouse, "Moral Habituation: A Review of Troels Engberg–Pedersen, *Aristotle's Theory of Moral Insight*," *Oxford Studies in Ancient Philosophy* 6 (1988): 213.

62. *NE* I.13, 1102a26–32.

63. *NE* I.7, 1098a33–b8.

64. *NE* I.4, 1095b4–8. See I. Vasiliou, "The Role of Good Upbringing in Aristotle's Ethics," *Philosophy and Phenomenological Research* 56 (1996): 775–78.

65. *NE* II.6, 1106b36–1107a2; VI.1; VI.13, 1144b21–28.

66. See Vasiliou, "Good Upbringing," 779–80.

67. Hursthouse, "Moral Habituation," 213.

68. *NE* II.1, 1103a26–32.

69. *NE* II.1, 1103a32–b2.

70. *NE* II.4, 1105a17–21.

71. *NE* II.4, 1105a21–26.
72. See J. Annas, *Intelligent Virtue* (Oxford: Oxford University Press, 2011), 16–32, for discussion.
73. *NE* II.4, 1105b12–18.
74. *NE* VI.13, 1144b1–17.
75. See *NE* VI.4. For more detailed discussions of the differences between skill and virtue in Aristotle, see Parry "*Episteme* and *Techne*"; Russell, *Practical Intelligence*, 16–17; T. Angier, *Technê in Aristotle's Ethics* (London: Continuum, 2010), 41–47.
76. *NE* II.4, 1105a26–b5.
77. *NE* VI.12, 1144a7–9. What Aristotle says, very literally, is "Moreover, the product is made complete in accordance with practical intelligence and virtue of character (*êthikê aretê*); for virtue makes the target right, and practical intelligence makes right the things towards this."
78. *NE* VI.12, 1144a20–b1.
79. *NE* VI.5.
80. *NE* III.3, 1112b11–24.
81. I discuss this function of practical intelligence further in D. Russell, "What Virtue Ethics Can Learn from Utilitarianism," in *The Cambridge Companion to Utilitarianism*, ed. B. Eggleston and D. Miller (New York: Cambridge University Press, 2014).
82. *NE* VI.4.
83. *NE* VI.5, 1140b1–4.
84. *NE* VI.1, 1138b18–34.
85. *NE* VI.5, 1140a24–31. That is why someone can be said to practice a skill either well *or badly*, whereas nothing analogous to that can be said about practical intelligence (1140b21–25).
86. *NE* VI.10–11. For discussion of the mundane nature of practical intelligence and its various component functions, see R. Hursthouse, "Practical Wisdom: A Mundane Account," *Proceedings of the Aristotelian Society* 106 (2006): 283–307; see also Russell, *Practical Intelligence*, 20–25 and references.
87. *NE* VI.10.
88. *NE* VI 10,1143a9–10.
89. *NE* VI.11, 1143a19–24.
90. *NE* VI.11.
91. *NE* VI.11, 1143a25–b5.
92. For example, *NE* VI.8, 1142a23–30; VI.10, 1143a5–b5; VI.11, 1143b13–14.
93. In the study of skill, psychologists distinguish between theories that classify basic types of expert performance (i.e., what experts are able to do that novices are not) and theories that identify the psychological mechanisms underlying these types of performance (i.e., the mental processes by which experts do what they are able to do). For discussion of this distinction, see K. J. Vicente and J. H. Wang, "An Ecological Theory of Expertise Effects in Memory Recall," *Psychological Review* 105 (1998): 33–57. It is clear, I take it, that Aristotle's primary aim in discussing practical intelligence and its various capabilities is to offer an account of the former rather than the latter sort. As Aristotle says, his aim in discussing the virtues is not to find as fine–grained a level of detail as possible, but to give an outline that subsequent inquiry and experience can fill in, just as, he says, we find in the case of skill (*NE* I.3; I.7, 1098a20–b8; II.2, 1103b26–1104a10). In fact, Aristotle takes this approach in his discussion of the virtues of theoretical intellect as well, identifying the major capacities involved in demonstrative knowledge but

not the various processes of discovery used in the demonstrative sciences (see VI.3, 6, 7).

94. *NE* VI.1, 1139a6–11.

95. *NE* VI.1, 1138b21–34.

96. J. Doris, *Lack of Character* (Cambridge: Cambridge University Press, 2002), 17.

97. See Russell, *Practical Intelligence*, chs. 4 and 11, for discussion of this very modest theoretical role for idealizations like "the virtuous person."

98. *Met.* II.1.

99. The passage in question is *Met.* I.1, 981a12–b10, where Aristotle contrasts skill with "experience" (*empeiria*), by which he means a bit of know–how about something without any deeper understanding of it; he contrasts them in terms of their relation to the ability to teach (981b7–10). D. Ross, *Aristotle's Metaphysics: A Revised Text with Introduction and Commentary* (Oxford: Oxford University Press, 1924), 118, refers the reader to *Alcibiades I*, 118d, where Plato claims that experts must be able to teach. See also Angier, *Technê*, 39.

100. See *Politics* VII–VIII. See F. Miller, *Nature, Justice, and Rights in Aristotle's Politics* (Oxford: Oxford University Press, 1995); and C. D. C. Reeve, "Aristotelian Education," in *Philosophers on Education*, ed. A. O. Rorty (New York: Routledge, 1998), for further discussion.

101. See Vicente and Wang, "Ecological Theory."

102. Narvaez and Lapsley, "Psychological Foundations," 150–51.

103. Narvaez and Lapsley, "Psychological Foundations," 153–54.

104. See esp. W. G. Chase and H. A. Simon, "The Mind's Eye in Chess," in *Visual Information Processing*, ed. W. G. Chase (New York: Academic Press, 1973).

105. See also W. G. Chase and H. A. Simon, "Perception in Chess," *Cognitive Psychology* 4 (1973): 55–81.

106. Chase and Simon, "The Mind's Eye."

107. Chase and Simon, "The Mind's Eye," 264.

108. Chase and Simon, "The Mind's Eye," 268–69.

109. M. Myles–Worsley, W. Johnston, and M. A. Simons, "The Influence of Expertise on X–Ray Image Processing," *Journal of Experimental Psychology: Learning, Memory, and Cognition* 14 (1988): 553–57.

110. This study is especially worth noting, I think, because it does not rely on any narrative from the experts; what the experts *believe* they are doing, and what they actually *are* doing, may be different things. I thank Elijah Millgram for raising this point.

111. See, e.g., N. J. Cooke, R. E. Atlas, D. M. Lane, and R. C. Berger, "Role of High–Level Knowledge in Memory for Chess Positions," *American Journal of Psychology* 106 (1993): 321–51.

112. Vicente and Wang, "Ecological Theory," 36.

113. I thank David Schmidtz for this way of putting the point.

114. Vicente and Wang, "Ecological Theory," 48.

115. N. Cantor, "From Thought to Behavior: 'Having' and 'Doing' in the Study of Personality and Cognition," *American Psychologist* 45 (1990): 735–50. See also D. K. Lapsley and D. Narvaez, "A Social–Cognitive Approach to the Moral Personality," in *Moral Development: Self and Identity*, ed. D. K. Lapsley and D. Narvaez (Mahwah, NJ: Lawrence Erlbaum, 2004), 199–201. On the importance of the social–cognitive model for virtue theory, see Russell, *Practical Intelligence*, chs. 8–10; and N. Snow, *Virtue as Social Intelligence* (New York: Routledge, 2010). On the overlap between this model and Aristotle's psychology, see K. Kristjánsson, "An Aristotelian Critique of Situationism," *Philosophy* 83 (2008): 55–76; and D. Russell, "Aristotelian

Virtue Theory: After the Person–Situation Debate," *Revue Internationale de Philosophie* 267 (2014): 37–63.

116. Lapsley and Narvaez, *Moral Development*, 200–201.
117. *NE* VI.12.
118. *NE* II.4.
119. Psychologists call this "goal–dependent automaticity"; see J. A. Bargh, "Conditional Automaticity: Varieties of Automatic Influence in Social Perception and Cognition," in *Unintended Thought*, ed. J. S. Uleman and J. A. Bargh (New York: Guilford, 1989). 10–27. See also R. M. Hogarth, *Educating Intuition* (Chicago: University of Chicago Press, 2001), 139–41, 190–933; Narvaez and Lapsley, "Psychological Foundations," 144–48; D. Kahneman, *Thinking, Fast and Slow* (New York: Penguin, 2011), ch. 22.
120. See Narvaez and Lapsley, "Psychological Foundations," 146, 150; Lapsley and Narvaez, "Moral Psychology," 30–31.
121. See Russell, *Practical Intelligence*, 11–13, for a brief discussion. See B. Finnigan, "Phronêsis in Aristotle: Reconciling Deliberation with Spontaneity," *Philosophy and Phenomenological Research* online release (2014) for a much more thorough discussion.
122. *NE* III.2, 1111b9–10.
123. *NE* III.2, 1112a15–17.
124. *NE* III.3, 112b20–24.
125. *NE* III.8, 1117a17–22.
126. See McDowell, "Some Issues," 107.
127. *NE* VI.9, 1142a31–b15.
128. Kahneman, *Thinking*, ch. 22. See Hogarth, *Educating Intuition*, for a much more thorough discussion.
129. There are other respects, nonetheless, in which the two do seem alike; see Annas, *Intelligent Virtue*, ch. 3.
130. See *NE* VI.13.
131. *NE* VI.5, 1140a24–31.
132. See *NE* VI.12.
133. See also H. Dreyfus and S. Dreyfus, "The Ethical Implications of the Five–Stage Skill–Acquisition Model," *Bulletin of Science, Technology, and Society* 24 (2004): 254.
134. I thank David Schmidtz for the example.
135. See Hogarth, *Educating Intuition*, 216–17, for this aspect of skill.
136. Here I have benefited from discussion with Elijah Millgram. Furthermore, it is worth noting that ancient philosophers tended to focus on skills involved in productive work central to their economies, like building, rather than sports or games. See J. Annas, "Virtue as a Skill," *International Journal of Philosophical Studies* 3 (1995): 229–30; see also Annas, *Intelligent Virtue*, 103.
137. See H. Fossheim, "Virtue Ethics and Everyday Strategies," *Revue Internationale de Philosophie* 267 (2014): 65–82 for an excellent discussion of this aspect of cultivating virtue.
138. See Annas, *Intelligent Virtue*, ch. 4.
139. See Annas, *Intelligent Virtue*, 58–65.
140. See Russell, *Practical Intelligence*, chs. 4 and 11.
141. I thank Nancy Snow for inviting me to contribute to this collection, and Julia Annas for steering me toward some extremely helpful literature. I thank Michael McKenna, Elijah Millgram, Carmen Pavel, Guido Pincione, David Schmidtz, and Steve Wall for their help on an earlier draft of this essay.

BIBLIOGRAPHY

Angier, T. *Technê in Aristotle's Ethics*. London: Continuum, 2010.

Annas, J. *Intelligent Virtue*. Oxford: Oxford University Press, 2011.

Annas, J. "Virtue as a Skill." *International Journal of Philosophical Studies* 3 (1995): 227–43.

Bargh, J. A. "Conditional Automaticity: Varieties of Automatic Influence in Social Perception and Cognition." In *Unintended Thought*, edited by J. S. Uleman and J. A. Bargh, 3–51. New York: Guilford, 1989.

Broadie, S., and C. Rowe, eds. and trans. *Aristotle: Nicomachean Ethics*. Oxford: Oxford University Press, 2002.

Cantor, N. "From Thought to Behavior: 'Having' and 'Doing' in the Study of Personality and Cognition." *American Psychologist* 45 (1990): 735–50.

Chase, W. G., and H. A. Simon. "Perception in Chess." *Cognitive Psychology* 4 (1973): 55–81.

Chase, W. G., and H. A. Simon. "The Mind's Eye in Chess." In *Visual Information Processing*, edited by W. G. Chase, 215–81. New York: Academic Press, 1973.

Cooke, N. J., R. E. Atlas, D. M. Lane, and R. C. Berger. "Role of High-Level Knowledge in Memory for Chess Positions." *American Journal of Psychology* 106 (1993): 321–51.

Crisp, R., ed. and trans. *Aristotle: Nicomachean Ethics*. Cambridge: Cambridge University Press, 2000.

Doris, J. *Lack of Character*. Cambridge: Cambridge University Press, 2002.

Dreyfus, H., and S. Dreyfus. "The Ethical Implications of the Five-Stage Skill-Acquisition Model." *Bulletin of Science, Technology, and Society* 24 (2004): 251–64.

Finnigan, B. "*Phronêsis* in Aristotle: Reconciling Deliberation with Spontaneity," *Philosophy and Phenomenological Research*. Online release (2014).

Fossheim, H. "Virtue Ethics and Everyday Strategies." *Revue Internationale de Philosophie* 267 (2014): 65–82.

Hogarth, R. M. *Educating Intuition*. Chicago: University of Chicago Press, 2001.

Hursthouse, R. "Moral Habituation: A Review of Troels Engberg-Pedersen, *Aristotle's Theory of Moral Insight*." *Oxford Studies in Ancient Philosophy* 6 (1988): 201–19.

Hursthouse, R. "Practical Wisdom: A Mundane Account." *Proceedings of the Aristotelian Society* 106 (2006): 283–307.

Hutchinson, D. S. *The Virtues of Aristotle*. New York: Routledge and Kegan Paul, 1986.

Irwin, T., ed. and trans. *Aristotle: Nicomachean Ethics*. Indianapolis: Hackett, 1985.

Kahneman, D. *Thinking, Fast and Slow*. New York: Penguin, 2011.

Kohlberg, L., C. Levine, and A. Hewer. *Moral Stages: A Current Formulation and a Response to Critics*. Vol. 10 of *Contributions to Human Development*, edited by J. A. Meacham. Basel: Karger, 1983.

Kristjánsson, K. "An Aristotelian Critique of Situationism." *Philosophy* 83 (2008): 55–76.

Lapsley, D. K., and D. Narvaez. "Moral Psychology at the Crossroads." In *Character Psychology and Character Education*, edited by D. K. Lapsley and F. C. Power, 18–35. Notre Dame, IN: University of Notre Dame, 2005.

Lapsley, D. K., and D. Narvaez. "A Social-Cognitive Approach to the Moral Personality." In *Moral Development: Self and Identity*, edited by D. Lapsley and D. Narvaez, 189–212. Mahwah, NJ: Lawrence Erlbaum, 2004.

Liddell, H. G., and R. Scott. *Greek-English Lexicon*. Oxford: Oxford University Press, 1935.

Lockwood, T. "Habituation, Habit, and Character in Aristotle's *Nicomachean Ethics*." In *A History of Habit: From Aristotle to Bourdieu*, edited by T. Sparrow and A. Hutchinson (Lanham, Maryland: Lexington Books, 2013).

McDowell, J. "Some Issues in Aristotle's Moral Psychology." In *Companions to Ancient Thought, 4: Ethics*, edited by S. Everson. New York: Cambridge University Press, 1998. Pp. 107–28.

Miller, F. *Nature, Justice, and Rights in Aristotle's Politics*. Oxford: Oxford University Press, 1995.

Myles-Worsley, M., W. Johnston, and M. A. Simons. "The Influence of Expertise on X-Ray Image Processing." *Journal of Experimental Psychology: Learning, Memory, and Cognition* 14 (1988): 553–57.

Narvaez, D., and D. K. Lapsley. "The Psychological Foundations of Everyday Morality and Moral Expertise." In *Character Psychology and Character Education*, edited by D. K. Lapsley and F. C. Power, 140–65. Notre Dame, IN: University of Notre Dame, 2005.

Parry, R. "*Episteme* and *Techne*." *Stanford Encyclopedia of Philosophy*. 2007. Available at http://plato.stanford.edu/entries/episteme-techne/.

Reeve, C. D. C. "Aristotelian Education." In *Philosophers on Education*, edited by A. O. Rorty, 49–63. New York: Routledge, 1998.

Ross, D. *Aristotle's Metaphysics: A Revised Text with Introduction and Commentary*. Oxford: Oxford University Press, 1924.

Russell, D. "Aristotelian Virtue Theory: After the Person-Situation Debate." *Revue Internationale de Philosophie* 267 (2014): 37–63.

Russell, D. "What Virtue Ethics Can Learn from Utilitarianism." In *The Cambridge Companion to Utilitarianism*, edited by B. Eggleston and D. Miller, 258–79. New York: Cambridge University Press, 2014.

Russell, D. *Practical Intelligence and the Virtues*. Oxford: Oxford University Press, 2009.

Russell, D. *Plato on Pleasure and the Good Life*. Oxford: Oxford University Press, 2005.

Snow, N., *Virtue as Social Intelligence*. New York: Routledge, 2010.

Vasiliou, I. "The Role of Good Upbringing in Aristotle's Ethics." *Philosophy and Phenomenological Research* 56 (1996): 771–97.

Vicente, K. J., and J. H. Wang. "An Ecological Theory of Expertise Effects in Memory Recall." *Psychological Review* 105 (1998): 33–57.

CHAPTER 2

ᴄᐯᴈ

Mill, Moral Sentimentalism, and the Cultivation of Virtue

JULIA DRIVER

[D]oes the utilitarian doctrine deny that people desire virtue, or maintain that virtue is not a thing to be desired? The very reverse. It maintains not only that virtue is to be desired, but also that it is to be desired disinterestedly, for itself. Whatever may be the opinion of utilitarian moralists as to the original conditions by which virtue is made virtue, however they may believe (as they do) that actions and dispositions are only virtuous because they promote another end than virtue, yet this being granted, and it having been decided, from considerations of this description, what is virtuous, they not only place virtue at the very head of the things which are good as means to the ultimate end, but they also recognize as a psychological fact the possibility of its being, to the individual, a good in itself, without looking to any end beyond it; and hold, that the mind is not in a right state, not in a state conformable to Utility, not in the state most conducive to the general happiness, unless it does love virtue in this manner—as a thing desirable in itself, even although, in the individual instance, it should not produce those other desirable consequences which it tends to produce, and on account of which it is held to be virtue.
—John Stuart Mill, *Utilitarianism*

Early Utilitarian philosophers such as John Stuart Mill recognized that not only is it the case that the moral virtues promote happiness, but that it is "to the individual" a good in itself. This raises the question of how, on the Utilitarian theory, virtue should be cultivated. A general answer to this question would look to (1) an account of virtue itself—for example, what makes a trait a virtue, and (2) different ways one might go about cultivating those sorts of traits, and what the effects of the different strategies would be. In this chapter I focus on the substantive views of one particular Utilitarian, John Stuart Mill, who happened to write extensively about virtue and whose views on virtue have not received adequate attention.

WHAT IS VIRTUE FOR THE UTILITARIAN?

Mill's theory of the good was hedonistic, though not a simple hedonism. He believed, as Jeremy Bentham did, that pleasure was the one intrinsic good; but unlike Jeremy Bentham, Mill distinguished between higher and lower pleasures. He believed pleasures to be distinguished from each other not simply on quantitative grounds but also on qualitative ones. Human beings are the only beings we know of capable of the higher pleasures—those associated with our capacity for rational thought, such as the pleasures of reading poetry and listening to fine music. Thus, Mill's version of hedonism has a strong perfectionist component because he believed that virtue involved the development of our higher capacities. So, in addition to experiencing higher pleasures, human beings can possess and value virtue. Of course, the perfectionism is essentially guided by the Utilitarian view that the standard for evaluating traits as virtues has to do with their contribution to overall happiness. Given Mill's views on the nature of happiness, human beings are best served by virtues that promote higher pleasures, though cultivating all virtues is important to living a good human life.

What about strategies for cultivation? Again, the general Utilitarian response to this question is to hold that we examine different strategies for cultivation by comparing consequences, choosing the strategy that best promotes happiness. But Mill himself had more specific views on this issue. In his work "Civilization" he remarks that "national institutions of education" are needed to counteract the bad influence certain features of civilization have on individual moral character.[1] Mill was worried that given the enormous growth in the size of modern communities, actions once considered shameful are not stigmatized—actions such as reckless financial speculation. Further, it becomes difficult for people to be recognized for their sensible and prudent qualities, and instead qualities such as flashiness and "quackery" are rewarded. This can have a harmful impact on the development of personal virtue. However, it can be counteracted by means of an education system that develops and rewards virtue.

Reading genuine literature—rather than the popular press—helps to develop moral character:

> But it is in literature, above all, that a change of this sort is of most pressing urgency. There the system of individual competition has fairly worked itself out, and

things can hardly continue much longer as they are. Literature is a province of exertion upon which more, of the first value to human nature, depends, than upon any other; a province in which the highest and most valuable order of works, those which most contribute to form the opinions and shape the characters of subsequent ages, are, more than in any other class of productions, placed beyond the possibility of appreciation by those who form the bulk of the purchasers in the book-market; insomuch that, even in ages when these were a far less numerous and more select class than now, it was an admitted point that the only success which writers of the first order could look to was the verdict of posterity.[2]

Statements such as this indicate an important way in which Mill believed individual character as well as that of a society could be improved: through both information and imaginative engagement with other possibilities. The exercise of putting oneself in the place of another—be it through history, documentary, or fictional literature, helps individuals position themselves in situations that encourage self-improvement. One way to develop this theme in Mill's thought is to look toward the ways he was influenced by the early sentimentalists. Mill accepts much of what they say on human nature and the significance of sympathy and sympathetic engagement to our moral lives. They, too, stress the importance of developing our aesthetic skills in developing our moral skills. Thus, I propose to fill in Mill by looking at how his work is understood in light of this influence.

MILL AND THE SENTIMENTALISTS

The broadest construal of moral sentimentalism holds that morality is "better felt than judged," in that certain affective capacities underlie both our ability to make moral judgments and the authority of those judgments. For those who hold this view, there is generally a tendency to view moral judgments as analogous to aesthetic judgments rather than to mathematical judgments. Mill was very much influenced by Hume, a sentimentalist, in his views on human nature. For example, Mill believed that moral motivation was reinforced by various sanctions, some of which were internal. Though feelings of duty are acquired, there is a basis for them in:

> powerful natural sentiment.... This firm foundation is that of the social feelings
> of mankind; the desire to be in unity with our fellow creatures, which is already
> a powerful principle in human nature, and happily one of those which tend to
> become stronger, even without express inculcation, from the influences of ad-
> vancing civilization.[3]

Only the truly pathological fail to possess any capacity for sympathy or fellow feeling, and when we identify those traits, actions, and practices that we believe to be admirable, we most often cite how those traits, actions, and practices are connected to benevolent motives, not self-interested ones.

Utilitarians need not be sentimentalists. Indeed, Jeremy Bentham was most decidedly not a sentimentalist, holding that humans are motivated solely by considerations of pleasure and pain. Thus, the claims explored in this chapter are really focused on the branch of Utilitarianism that took the sentimentalist theory of human nature (with respect to morality) as the true theory of human nature. In Utilitarianism, Mill clearly commits to the view that human beings naturally feel "a desire to be in unity with our fellow creatures."[4] He appeals to our natural sympathy in his account of our tendency to desire to punish those who commit unjust acts.[5] In Chapter 2 of *Utilitarianism*, in seeking to rebut the claim that Utilitarianism the theory turns people into cold, unsympathetic beings focused solely on producing utility, he notes that this is mistaken—Utilitarianism takes the distinction between right and wrong action seriously, but that is as it should be. And Utilitarianism does not ignore other features of a person that are morally significant. Indeed, in *Utilitarianism* Mill is clear that happiness includes virtue. In Chapter 4 of *Utilitarianism* he notes that Utilitarianism:

> maintains not only that virtue is to be desired, but that it is to be desired disinterestedly, for itself. Whatever may be the opinion of utilitarian moralists as to the original conditions by which virtue is made virtue; however they may believe (as they do) that actions and dispositions are only virtuous because they promote another end than virtue; yet this being granted, and it having been decided, from considerations of this description, what *is* virtuous, they not only place virtue at the very head of the things which are good as a means to the ultimate end, but they also recognize as a psychological fact the possibility of its being, to the individual, a good in itself, without looking to any end beyond it.... [6]

As Roger Crisp notes, Mill's view of how virtue develops intrinsic value for individuals is the result of Mill's associationist views of mind: people begin by viewing virtue in instrumental terms, but over time, associating virtue with pleasure, they come to value virtue for its own sake.[7] This would indicate that he believes that people are able to accurately judge the consequences of traits. This may be an unrealistic assumption. It seems likely that some traits that in the past were widely perceived to be virtues were not, in fact, virtues.[8]

It seems likely, too, that Mill viewed virtue as part of moral education strategy and moral progress. A feeling for one's fellow creatures can arise through society and cooperation with others, learning to view their ends as making claims on one, and over time this social feeling, which I think of as a kind of benevolence (concern for the well-being of others) "takes on a life of its own." Mill notes that "the smallest germs of the feeling are laid hold of and nourished by the contagion of sympathy and the influences of education" to the point where that feeling has its own binding force.[9] A person who has developed along these lines will see his interests served in viewing the interests of others as at least demanding his respect:

> The deeply-rooted conception which every individual even now has of himself as a social being, tends to make him feel it one of his natural wants that there should be harmony between his feelings and aims and those of his fellow creatures.[10]

At the end of Chapter 3 of *Utilitarianism*, Mill argues that we can educate people so that, over time, their interest is closely identified with the interests of others, and thus we can end up appealing to self-interest to account for why we ought to have this social feeling. The major worry about this argument is that it seems to assume a very optimistic view of human nature. Most accounts that try to bring in egoistic elements to account for the authority of morality run into fundamental plausibility problems: how likely is it—really—that my interest and that of others (all others!) coincides. Mill is probably making the somewhat more plausible claim that it can be made to coincide by proper moral education. However, that begs the authority question. That is, the authority is not reducible to considerations of self-interest since there have to be other reasons why we think we ought to try to work toward making self-interest not conflict with the interests of others.

Of course, early sentimentalists also note that human nature is not at all motivationally one-dimensional. We are also motivated by self-interest. But when it comes to understanding moral motivation and the authority of morality, early sentimentalists view it as a mistake to appeal to self-interest. What is characteristic of moral motivation is a sympathetic engagement with others. The actual feeling a person experiences may be weak. Indeed, it is even possible that it is altogether absent in a particular instance, as when someone who is clinically depressed finds it difficult to care about anything, but through force of imagination knows he should care and would care if not depressed. But even in such cases it is not self-interest that gets the person out of bed in the morning, ready to take care of others.

There may be a way of reading Mill's passage at the end of Chapter 3 differently. He is committed to the sentimentalist view that we are equipped by nature to sympathize with others. This sympathy is a crucial component in the process of developing social feeling—which he claims involves our view that the ends of others ought to be in harmony with our own. If we assume that sympathy underlies a desire for the well-being of others, and if we assume that our individual good is at least partly realized through desire satisfaction, then we can see why someone might hold that our individual good is at least partly realized by the good of others. Of course, if this is the line of argument it isn't really egoist. Desires for the well-being of others are by their nature not egoistic.

There were, therefore, differences as well as similarities between Mill and the early sentimentalists such as Hume. The affinities were also limited by the fact that, as noted earlier, Mill's view of virtue itself was rather perfectionist, whereas Hume's view of what counted as a virtue was rather modest. On Hume's view, any quality of the mind that was pleasing from the general point of view was a virtue. This led to his well-known problem of conflating what intuitively seem to be different types of virtue—some pleasing qualities are moral, but others seem more naturally to fall into the category of the aesthetic, or the prudential. Mill, on the other hand, though like Hume he viewed virtues as contributing to the good, also viewed them as constituting the good in that many of them involved the exercise of our rational or higher capacities. The lists each come up with overlap, though there will be considerable differences. Mill would not view cleanliness as a moral virtue. Still, whatever the virtues themselves were like, the developmental story is still similar in that cultivating the virtues will involve cultivating our sympathies, which in turn involves cultivating aesthetic methods of viewing the world around us. Though Hume's account of virtue itself is rather modest, like the other sentimentalists he had a more demanding view of moral agency. A moral agent must be capable of self-regulation, and self-regulation at its core involved evaluation of the self—being able to make reliable judgments about the self. In addition, being an effective agent requires being able to take someone else's perspective in order to acquire information necessary to help the other person.

Again, for Mill, in judging whether or not someone is living a good life one needs to consider the whole person, not simply the narrow scope of what he deems "moral" concern. He notes that Utilitarians who have "cultivated their moral feelings, but not their sympathies, nor their artistic perceptions, do fall into this mistake; and so do all moralists under the same conditions."[11] This, I take it, notes that to be an overall good person one must be disposed to perform the morally right actions, but also give some thought to other "beauties of character." It is clear that Mill believed that virtue was a central part of the good life and virtue itself is understood in terms of production of good and bad conduct: "[Utilitarians]...resolutely refuse to consider any mental disposition as good of which the predominant tendency is to produce bad conduct."[12] These views again raise the issues that have puzzled scholars on Mill's views on the practical realm in general, particularly in light of the rather cryptic remarks he makes in discussing the art of life. One source of possible confusion is the narrow sense in which he uses "moral" in some of his remarks—"moral" seems to only apply to our strict duties—to things like respecting the fundamental rights of others and refraining from harming them, to things like keeping our promises, and so on.

THE ART OF LIFE

In his *A System of Logic*, in discussing the "Art of Life," Mill separates three spheres: morality, prudence, and aesthetics.[13] Aesthetics is associated with virtue, morality with right. Some argue that Mill separates these three spheres as a way of rendering Utilitarianism compatible with commonsense. Thus, Wendy Donner notes that holding morality to be but one sphere of life, and holding the principle of utility to have broad scope over the other spheres as well, Mill can avoid the "moral sainthood" objection—this is basically the objection that Utilitarianism is too demanding.[14] He can avoid it because even though it is true that we ought to maximize utility, the moral ought is restricted to just one sphere of life. Elsewhere, as Donner notes, Mill also holds the distinction to be one of duty versus what we would now call supererogation. And by duty Mill means actions for which it would be appropriate to use coercion to gain compliance; virtue involves, instead, actions which "it is, on the whole, for the general interest that they should be left free."[15] This also seems similar to the realm of the imperfect duties—those duties that still have authority over our actions, but that allow wide latitude in how to fulfill them. However, my view is that Mill's considered view is to separate acting rightly and wrongly from being virtuous, though the two are connected in that one wouldn't call a trait a virtue if it leads systematically to wrong actions. Mill's categorization is awkward, given that most people view virtue as part of morality, and thus view the scope of morality as broader than the right. Keeping this in mind, it is probably more useful to view Mill's "morality" as a term of art. Our discussion will look at both what he calls morality and what he calls virtue.

There is, then, this way to conceptually distinguish the spheres. However, in this chapter I am concerned mainly with a developmental point: how are the good things in each sphere (including virtue) to be realized?

One way we cultivate a sense of duty or justice is via enlarged sympathies and enlightened self-interest. One way in which we cultivate virtue is through aesthetics. However, complicating these simple remarks is a distinction that can be drawn between cultivating something (be it a sense of duty or virtue) within oneself and cultivating one's ability to make good judgments of duty and/or virtue. In the following discussion, I treat these two as connected in the following way: in order to develop in oneself a sense of right and wrong, as well as a sense of virtue, it helps to cultivate the ability to make good judgments of right and wrong, and good or reliable attributions of virtue. I realize that this claim could be empirically contested, but it at least seems initially plausible. The initial plausibility rests on the plausibility of the view of self-regulation that was endorsed by most sentimentalists, including Shaftesbury and Hume: self-regulation required metacognition: the ability to reflect on one's own mental states and dispositions, and endorse or reject them by applying a standard.[16] This requires "judgment" if what we mean by "judgment" allows for inexplicit, not consciously accessed, judgment.

But what of the connection, if any, between virtue and aesthetic quality? One account of the connection is essentially developmental: to develop the skills needed to be virtuous and make warranted judgments of virtue, we need to develop aesthetic skills. This will aid in the "enlargement of sympathies" task. Thus, the two projects seem intertwined at the developmental level, even if not at the conceptual level. Mill believed that perspective taking is an aesthetic method, and yet it is also crucial to moral judgment. Thus, training in perspective taking is important to the development of a good character in human beings and for the ability to make proper moral judgments.[17] Perspective-taking plays many important roles: it has an epistemic role, in that it allows us to get information that is crucial to effective moral agency—one cannot help another without some understanding of what the other considers good or desirable. But there is also the function of correcting initial emotional reactions, a more affective function. This in turn proceeds via a correction of our moral judgments through perspective-taking. Sentimentalists commonly hold that moral judgment needs correction in various ways in order to be accurate. In his essay comparing the moral rationalists to the moral sentimentalists, Michael Gill notes that for the sentimentalists "in order to be worthy, a judgment may have to be based on a sentimental response toward an accurate perception of the object, and one may have to arrive at an accurate perception only through reasoning and reflection."[18] One way to do this is to get the bare facts straight; another is to get the right perspective. This is crucial in aesthetic judgment as well.

Hume was explicit: "'tis evident, a beautiful countenance cannot give so much pleasure, when seen at the distance of twenty paces, as when it is brought nearer us. We say not, however, that it appears to us less beautiful: Because we know what effect it will have in such a position, and by that reflection we correct its momentary appearance."[19] He goes on to note that the same kind of correction is needed for moral judgment.

In Hume's case, the correction was achieved by considering a person's mental quality from the general point of view. In this way, personal biases and prejudices are filtered, and one arrives at a more "just" judgment of character.

What is less appreciated is the need to have correct information, even in making aesthetic judgments. On Hume's view, the need for information in refining the sentiments gave some initial plausibility to the rationalists by making it at first appear that moral issues were really reducible to matters of fact. But rationalism does not withstand scrutiny—the importance of matters of fact actually resides instead in informing our sentiments, and in refining aesthetic judgments as well. Noting the role for aesthetic judgments is a real blow to the rationalist, since the rationalist tends to view aesthetics as quite different from morality. However, whether a work of art is appropriately deemed beautiful or grotesque may depend on what the viewer knows about the object being judged. Whether the kitten in the photograph, for example, is sleeping or dead will affect how the image is properly perceived and appreciated. If the former, it will be correctly deemed "cute"; if the latter, it will correctly be deemed "grotesque" or "macabre." More general judgments of whether the work of art is good at all, as a work of art, will also depend on certain facts. For example, the greatness of a painting may depend on when the painting was painted—where it figures in the historical development of a given technique, let's say. A later date may render what first appeared novel and interesting instead derivative and unoriginal.

Judging a person's character, and the character of the actions he or she is performing, requires knowing what is motivating the person, what sorts of reasons the person is responsive to. This is one reason why perspective-taking is important—it is very important in terms of being able to gain adequate information. When one tries to figure out a person's motive for performing a given action, one needs to take that person's perspective in the context in which the person is acting. Why did Bob have such a strong negative reaction to Alan? Maybe because Alan was flexing his muscles, and in those circumstances Bob felt threatened. One way to train people to better make judgments about motives is to teach them to engage in perspective-taking. The training may not be explicit at all. Iris Murdoch had the view that literature could develop moral sensibility by getting people to become engaged, imaginatively, in stories that presented them with novel situations. It also gets readers to see how other people might think differently from themselves. For Murdoch, to make correct moral judgments required "unselfing"—peeling away one's own distorting tendencies such as the impact even simple self-interest has on one's judgments.[20] The unselfing that Murdoch discusses is similar to the correctives that sentimentalists recommended. One can eliminate, or at least ameliorate, the distorting impact of idiosyncratic feelings by adjusting perspective on the sentimentalist view. In Murdoch's case, it was not so much switching perspective as paying careful moral attention. The attention itself can be cultivated by living it, but also through imaginative engagement with works of fiction. This serves an important epistemic role in training people to be more sensitive to factors that are morally relevant—that are relevant in making correct moral judgments.

But aside from the epistemic function of perspective-taking, it can also serve an important function is stimulating emotional responses. In Hume, sympathy is engaged also when we take the perspective of others, and this is crucial to correct moral judgment:

> Our servant, if diligent and faithful, may excite stronger sentiments of love and kindness than Marcus Brutus, as represented in history; but we say not upon that account, that the former character is more laudable than the latter. We know, that were we to approach equally near to that renown'd patriot, he wou'd command a much higher degree of affection and admiration.[21]

As mentioned earlier, our sentiments need to be corrected for the moral judgment to be accurate. All early sentimentalists considered the problem of variability a significant one. This is the problem that rationalists often raise against the approach by noting that there is a huge amount of variation between people in terms of their sympathetic responses—and not just between people but also within an individual at different times. So, which of these many disparate sympathies is the one upon which one bases judgment? Rationalists view this as a kind of *reductio*, since without a corrective standard there would be moral judgment chaos. However, sentimentalists were not in favor of chaos. The solution was to hold that a person's idiosyncratic perspective had no general authority. Instead, one needs to consider issues in light of a standard that abstracts away from the individual. The ultimate such standard was Adam Smith's impartial spectator. So, in developing sympathies appropriately one needs to train perspective-taking, and not just any perspective-taking, but taking a perspective that sheds one's idiosyncratic concerns.

But the exercise has other functions. In Hume we get a bit of an anticipation of Mill on the enlargement of sympathies, though for Hume the enlargement really has to do with the calm passions: when we engage sympathetically it is only realistic to note that our emotions may not keep up with our judgment. We still love the near and dear more. However, we rightly judge that a person such as Brutus was more admirable than any of our relations—and this is due to the sympathy we have with those who were more immediately affected by Brutus. A calmer passion, still sympathy, has "authority over our reason, and to command our judgment and opinion."[22] And this is what we need for correct, reliable, moral judgment. Further, we are able to imagine how others see us, and correct our own actions and tendencies in light of the evidence that we acquire from taking the perspective of others. To be an effective moral agent, perspective-taking greatly helps. But it also helps in developing one's own character. Again, it functions in two distinct ways: it provides information that is relevant in making practical decisions, and it excites sympathy that allows us to also make correct judgments. On the sentimentalist view, simply having the information is not enough for effective moral agency and for being a good person. Whether or not psychopaths even count as moral agents, they are not effective ones. What is lacking is the sympathetic engagement. They may be able to engage in sophisticated perspective-taking, but finding out what another person wants is only useful morally if one cares about that person.

My reading of Mill is that he tended to be expansive in his views of how sympathy is to be developed in such a way that a person properly judges and properly acts in accordance with morality. So, again, as the Brutus case illustrates, Hume in many places holds that the corrected perspective is one in which the evaluator sympathizes with those in the immediate vicinity of the character being evaluated.[23] But for Mill, the corrected perspective will be impartial, at least in one important sense: one always needs to consider the happiness of all sentient beings in determining matters of morality and virtue, not simply a small subset of those beings. To do otherwise is simply to replace one set of biases and prejudices for another.[24] However, this may itself call for cultivating dispositions to favor some in situations where that type of favoring has proved conducive to happiness.

Mill believed that the space between doing one's duty and falling into sin was flexible. Over time, as people become accustomed to going beyond their strict obligations, what was supererogatory will become obligatory. As Wendy

Donner has pointed out, this may make Mill a bit of an optimist about the benefits of cultivating virtue in the population as a whole. However, there has been some empirical support for the general phenomenon that Mill is discussing.

Since Mill includes in aesthetic education the cultivation of feelings, as well as the appreciation of beauty, it is important to the good life and it is important for individuals in realizing their personal good. A person who merely does his duty may be—in Mill's special use of the term—morally exemplary, but she will not be worthy. To broaden oneself it is helpful to view idealizations or models of human behavior and feeling. One very important feature of employing such a method in cultivating virtue or worthiness lies in the significance of the imagination. In reading history and fiction, for example, one needs to be able to imaginatively take the perspective of the historical or fictional figure and those around that figure. This is important because it allows us to move beyond a concern for ourselves and our own immediate circle. There are two strands of the "enlarged sympathies" idea that need to be distinguished: Mill discusses it mainly in the context of human beings generally, over time, enlarging the scope of what they sympathize with—who they sympathize with. But it can also refer to an individual's moral development.

In various places, Mill ties this imagination to the sort of exercises poets are noted for. Indeed, he writes that historians, who need some sympathy for those who lived in the past to understand the past, should "have some of the characteristics of the poet" who is able to extend his mind to things unknown. The study of both history and poetry are useful in cultivating the imagination and enlarging the sympathy. Considering history keeps us from focusing exclusively on our own affairs and interests. Immersing ourselves in different worlds through literature can also serve this function. In this way, some of Mill's work is reflected in themes developed later by writers such as Iris Murdoch, who believed that one of the important tasks of philosophy itself was to make us better persons, and doing so involves the use of imaginative engagement with possibilities. This is how we learn to hone moral perception. Mill was not a particularist, but shared with Murdoch the view that the study of literature—and history—could be an important route to self-improvement. Of course, there are dangers and limits: Murdoch notes that if imaginative reflection is too aesthetic it can "tempt us to be stylish rather than right."[25]

Indeed, recent studies have shown that reading literary fiction (rather than popular fiction or nonfiction) improves empathy—it improves one's ability to understand others.[26] It would be interesting to see if history is different from other forms of nonfiction.

Mill's focus on the inner life, and how important that is to the full articulation of Utilitarianism, was one of his major contributions to the development of the theory itself. It has been a grave misunderstanding on the part of some critics, particularly virtue ethicists, to hold Utilitarianism, across the board, inadequate in its account of virtue. A more developed Utilitarianism than one sees in Bentham, for example, places great weight on how sympathy underlies our desire to secure general happiness, and how, as Mill put it, feelings for the well-being of others "are laid hold of and nourished by the contagion of sympathy and the influences of education."[27] Educational practices that stimulate sympathy, then, help to develop virtue in individuals, which in turn sets an example to others—reinforcing the original round of education. "This mode of conceiving of ourselves and human life, as civilization goes on, is felt to be more and more natural.... In an improving state of the human mind, the influences are constantly on the increase, which tend to generate in each individual a feeling of unity with all the rest; which feeling, if perfect, would make him never think of, or desire, any beneficial condition for himself, in the benefits of which they are not included."[28] Morality, in Mill's narrow understanding, is only part of the picture. Full human flourishing requires virtue.

NOTES

1. John Stuart Mill, "Civilization," in *The Collected Works of John Stuart Mill*, vol. 18, ed. J. M. Robson (New York: Routledge and Kegan Paul, 1963), 117–48.
2. Mill, "Civilization."
3. John Stuart Mill, *Utilitarianism*, ed. Roger Crisp (Oxford: Oxford University Press, 1998), 77.
4. Mill, *Utilitarianism*, 77.
5. Mill, *Utilitarianism*, 95.
6. Mill, *Utilitarianism*, 82.
7. Mill, *Utilitarianism*," 25–26.
8. In *Uneasy Virtue* (Oxford: Oxford University Press, 2001), I discuss the case of romantic honor.
9. Mill, *Utilitarianism*, 79.
10. Mill, *Utilitarianism*, 79.
11. Mill, *Utilitarianism*, 67.
12. Mill, *Utilitarianism*.
13. John Stuart Mill, *A System of Logic*," in *Collected Works of John Stuart Mill*, ed. J. M. Robson (Toronto: University of Toronto Press, 1968), 950.
14. Wendy Donner, "Morality, Virtue, and Aesthetics in Mill's Art of Life," in *John Stuart Mill and the Art of Life*, ed. Ben Eggleston, Dale E. Miller, and David Weinstein (Oxford: Oxford University Press, 2011), 146–65.
15. John Stuart Mill, "Thornton on Labor and its Claims," in *The Collected Works of John Stuart Mill*, vol. 18, ed. J. M. Robson (New York: Routledge and Kegan Paul, 1963).

16. I discuss this in more detail in "Meta-cognition and Moral Agency," in *Moral Psychology and Human Agency*, ed. Justin D'Arms and Daniel Jacobsen (Oxford: Oxford University Press, forthcoming).

17. In "A Humean Account of the Status and Character of Animals" (in *Oxford Handbook of Ethics and Animals*, ed. Thomas Beauchamp and R. G. Frey [Oxford: Oxford University Press, 2012], 144–71), I argue that there is a distinction implicit in Hume between appraisability and accountability: thus, one can have a good character on his view without perspective taking skills since he has such a minimalist view of good character. But Mill's view is more demanding, and for him good character for human beings seems to definitely involve reflection and applying standards.

18. Michael Gill, "Moral Rationalism vs. Moral Sentimentalism: Is Morality more like Math or Beauty?" *Philosophy Compass* 2, no. 1 (2007): 21.

19. David Hume, *A Treatise of Human Nature*, ed. David Fate Norton and Mary Norton (Oxford: Oxford University Press, 2007), 3.3.1.

20. Iris Murdoch, "Sovereignty of the Good Over Other Concepts," in *Virtue Ethics*, ed. Roger Crisp and Michael Slote (Oxford: Oxford University Press, 1996), 99–117. However, Maria Antonaccio notes that Murdoch rejected a simple "didactic" view of art in which the purpose of art was to morally educate. That seems right. But it is an important effect of art that one's moral sensitivity can be disciplined through literature. It is just that that is not what justifies art itself. See Antonaccio's *A Philosophy to Live By* (Oxford: Oxford University Press, 2012), 157–60.

21. Hume, *Treatise* 3.3.1.

22. Hume, *Treatise* 3.3.1.

23. I have argued elsewhere that I do not believe that this is Hume's considered view. See my "Pleasure as the Standard of Virtue in Hume's Moral Psychology," *Pacific Philosophical Quarterly* 85 (2004): 173–94.

24. I have argued in "Pleasure as the Standard of Virtue in Hume's Moral Psychology," that Hume also held in places that the more impartial standard was better. Otherwise, it would be difficult to account for some of the things he said about the monkish virtues and how significant long-term consequences are to whether or not a trait counts as a virtue.

25. Iris Murdoch, *Metaphysics as a Guide to Morals* (New York: Penguin, 1994), 335.

26. David Comer Kidd and Emanuele Costano, "Reading Literary Fiction Improves Theory of Mind," *Science*, October 3, 2013.

27. Mill, *Utilitarianism*, 78.

28. Mill, *Utilitarianism*.

BIBLIOGRAPHY

Antonaccio, Maria. *A Philosophy to Live By*. Oxford: Oxford University Press, 2012.

Donner, Wendy. "Morality, Virtue, and Aesthetics in Mill's Art of Life." In *John Stuart Mill and the Art of Life*, edited by Ben Eggleston, Dale E. Miller, and David Weinstein, 146–65. Oxford: Oxford University Press, 2011.

Driver, Julia. "A Humean Account of the Status and Character of Animals." In *Oxford Handbook of Ethics and Animals*, edited by Thomas Beauchamp and R. G. Frey. Oxford: Oxford University Press, 2012.

Driver, Julia. "Meta-cognition and Moral Agency." In *Moral Psychology and Human Agency*, edited by Justin D'Arms and Daniel Jacobsen. Oxford: Oxford University Press, 2014.

Driver, Julia. "Pleasure as the Standard of Virtue in Hume's Moral Psychology." *Pacific Philosophical Quarterly* 85, no. 2 (2004): 173–94.

Driver, Julia. *Uneasy Virtue*. New York: Oxford University Press, 2001.

Gill, Michael. "Moral Rationalism vs. Moral Sentimentalism: Is Morality more like Math or Beauty?" *Philosophy Compass* 2, no. 1 (2007): 16–30.

Hume, David. *A Treatise of Human Nature*. Edited by David Fate Norton and Mary Norton. Oxford: Oxford University Press, 2007.

Kidd, David Comer, and Emanuele Costano. "Reading Literary Fiction Improves Theory of Mind." *Science*, October 3, 2013, 377–80.

Mill, John Stuart. "Civilization." In *The Collected Works of John Stuart Mill*, vol. 18, edited by J. M. Robson, 117–48. New York: Routledge and Kegan Paul, 1963.

Mill, John Stuart. *A System of Logic*. In *The Collected Works of John Stuart Mill*, edited by J. M. Robson, vols. 7 and 8. New York: Routledge and Kegan Paul, 1963.

Mill, John Stuart. "Thornton on Labor and its Claims." In *The Collected Works of John Stuart Mill*, vol. 5, edited by J. M. Robson, 631–68. New York: Routledge and Kegan Paul, 1963.

Mill, John Stuart. *Utilitarianism*. Edited by Roger Crisp. Oxford: Oxford University Press, 1998.

Murdoch, Iris. *Metaphysics as a Guide to Morals*. New York: Penguin, 1994.

Murdoch, Iris. "Sovereignty of the Good Over Other Concepts." In *Virtue Ethics*, edited by Roger Crisp and Michael Slote, 99–117. Oxford: Oxford University Press, 1996.

CHAPTER 3

 ⊘

The Roots of Empathy

MICHAEL SLOTE

1

In previous work, I have stressed the importance, the centrality, of empathy to moral education.[1] I have argued that rationalist accounts of moral education—both Kantian and Aristotelian—have a difficult time explaining the emergence and strengthening of moral motivation, and I have tried to show how a reliance on empathy can help us to do precisely that.[2] However, I now believe that my approach and my explanations have in important ways been incomplete—as have all the other explanations of moral development that I am aware of. Certain emotions have a role to play in moral education and development that has escaped our academic attention (much of what I am going to say will probably seem somewhat commonsensical to many people who have raised their own children). But these emotions play that role very early in human life, and students of moral development haven't paid much attention to how this all actually, or probably, works.

In what follows I shall try to expand upon the sentimentalist approach to moral education I have defended elsewhere. I shall assume that we can understand talk about empathy, and I shall also presuppose the truth of the widely accepted but sometimes questioned view that empathy plays a role in developing altruistic and genuinely moral motivation. Nor am I going to worry about how deontological motivation can be grounded in empathic terms, a topic I have discussed at great length in two recent books. So you can conditionalize what I say to the assumptions or point of view just indicated;

but relative to all that, I am going to try to give you a picture of how moral education or development works or may work in the earliest stages of human life.

Previous discussions of the role of empathy in moral education and moral development have tended to begin in medias res. For example, in his groundbreaking discussion of "inductive discipline" ("induction" for short), Martin Hoffman describes how a parent whose child has hurt or harmed another child can focus the child on the effects of his actions, and because of the child's general human capacity for empathy, make him feel bad (a kind of primitive guilt) about what he has done. And he argues that if enough of this occurs, then a child will develop a (generalized) resistance to harming or hurting others. I think and have argued that induction is an important tool of moral education—but this is not the place to repeat all the arguments. What is more interesting to me at this point, and in the context of the general themes of this chapter, is the fact that Hoffman and others who describe and recommend induction assume that it is being applied by a parent who (otherwise) shows love and affection toward her child. Hoffman simply assumes that parents love their children, but others (like myself and Nel Noddings) treat induction as something that will work *only if*—sometimes a big *if*—parents love their children.[3]

However, even those of us, like Noddings and myself, who explicitly recognize that some parents are unloving and that induction probably won't work with children who haven't been well loved, don't say very much about how a child gets to be in a position where induction can work. How does the child's being loved prepare the way, so to speak, for the efficacious parental use of inductive discipline? In other words, we may want to assume the child needs to be loved, but if that is all we say, then our description of the process of moral education begins in medias res, with a cherished child who is being disciplined inductively or who is consciously or unconsciously modeling himself on his parents, rather than focusing on earlier developmental/interactional processes that pave the way for such later moral learning and are thus *part of the moral learning process, part of moral education itself.*

Therefore, for the sake of completeness and a better understanding of moral development taken as a whole, I think we really need to follow moral education and learning to the source of the Nile. If at all possible, we need to say something about how early parent-child interactions make later inductive or modeling processes of moral education possible or, in some cases, make such later developments impossible. And it is this last point that perhaps explains why we have up to now been hesitant to investigate such earlier processes in our work on moral development and moral education. Most work on moral education assumes that a child (say, of eight years old)

can be morally educated. There is recognition that some adults are incapable of caring about others (intrinsically), incapable of guilt, incapable of
empathically feeling the pains and joys of others—and we label them psychopaths and sociopaths (and sometimes say that they also lack our moral
concepts). But we don't recognize sufficiently that such adult individuals
may have been shaped in that direction by the way they were parented, and
we don't therefore allow our recognition of that possibility to affect how we
describe and account for moral education and moral development. And if
some children are made incapable of morality, are turned toward psychopathy, by the ways they have interacted or failed to interact with their parents, then normal moral development—development of or toward moral
goodness and decency—may depend, or tend to depend, on an absence of
those conditions and will typically rest on child-parent interactions of a
very different, even opposite, character. If, very roughly, mistreatment and
the total absence of parental love can make for psychopathy, then love and
loving treatment of a child may (at least in most cases) be necessary if a
child is to be susceptible to later and deliberate moral education. But none
of the above has affected the ways we have written about moral education,
and it should. It is unpleasant to think that certain ways parents treat children tend to make them incapable of moral concern for others, and that
very unpleasantness may explain why we all have previously hesitated, and
more than hesitated, to describe the earliest stages of moral development
and non-development.[4] But there is in fact a great deal to say if we stop
doing moral education completely in medias res and explain—in terms relevant to moral education but also to our understanding of the way our
minds work in general—how, as a result of early parental treatment, we
become capable of moral education that will work via later processes of induction and modeling (though, as we shall see, the modeling really occurs
all along). And as part of our account of moral development, we also need
to explain how, as a result of very different treatment, some children
become incapable of such moral education and development and end up
(more or less) as sociopaths.

But does parental neglect or abuse really have any effect on psychopathy?
Much of the recent literature on psychopathy tends to assume it doesn't. A
distinction is often made between primary psychopathy of a kind that involves a lack of empathy (an inability, say, to feel another's pain or joy) and
a lack of conscience, and a secondary psychopathy that is compatible with
empathy and conscience, but that includes aggressive and anti-social tendencies. And the assumption, then, is that primary psychopathy is solely due to
genetic abnormalities and brain damage and that parental behavior can only
contribute to secondary psychopathy and is thus causally irrelevant to the

lack of empathy and conscience we standardly associate with psychopathy/sociopathy.[5] However, clinical psychology tends to disagree with this view of things. Going all the way back to the work of John Bowlby and his associates, it has been held that parental mistreatment can contribute to a child's developing a psychopathic lack of empathy and conscience. And this clinical understanding doesn't have to rule out genetic factors or brain damage as playing a substantial role in some or even many cases of full-blown psychopathy.[6] But it does insist that parental behavior and attitudes can make a major difference in these developments; and in what follows I shall not only make this assumption but also offer a specific account of the difference parents can make that helps us understand the configuration of traits involved in genuine (or primary) psychopathy better than more physically oriented explanations allow us to do. So let me proceed.

My account requires us to bring in children's need for love (which is an emotion, to be sure) and also certain emotions that are felt in reaction to how well that need is satisfied. Children are disturbed and angry if they aren't loved (let us assume), but—and this is the focal point of the present chapter—they also feel gratitude if and when they empathically register the love that some parents, good parents, feel toward them. This gratitude is the emotional basis, I shall argue, of the possibility of further moral education and development. But where rage is felt instead of gratitude, our basic capacity for empathy—something which "normal" children are often said to possess and show from infancy on—can be frozen, crushed, or nipped in the bud. So a great deal often depends on what happens emotionally very early in life—or so, at least, I shall try to show you.

Because accounts of moral education (including my own) have always begun at a point where it is assumed a child is loved by her parents and to some degree returns that love, the original need for love is never brought into the picture. And neither are the typical or frequent results of parents' *failing to satisfy* that need ever mentioned. But these are things we ought to do here. And let's begin by saying more about the need or craving for love. Needs are different from wishes and preferences, and what is I think most characteristic of that distinction is how people react to their non-fulfillment. (Desires fall somewhere in between, but don't need to be brought in for present purposes.) If I prefer or wish for vanilla, I may not react negatively if only chocolate is available, but it is a distinguishing mark of a need that one doesn't react well or happily to its non-fulfillment. And that is part of the reason why psychologists and others speak of the child's need for love. When children aren't loved (and even if their physical needs are scrupulously attended to), their development is impaired or stunted in well-known ways—and I shall assume that this is something we can all agree on. We might even consider the lack of parental love to be a kind of psychological abuse; but things, of course, can be even worse when the lack of love is accompanied by physical and/or sexual abuse. The result can be delinquency and crime or severe depression, or other conditions of mental disorder, but what seems invariably to stand behind or underlie these further and later developments is a rage at not being loved—and perhaps even greater rage, greater anger, if this is accompanied by physical abuse or neglect. I am not at this point going to try to explain how such rage could lead to depression (there is a vast literature on that topic); or how, in certain cases, it can somehow be generalized so that the child who is sexually/physically abused by his or her parents eventually takes this out on a larger class of people outside the home—most glaringly in the case of serial rapists and serial killers (not all of whom are men). All this, as I say, is fairly well known. But its relevance to moral education is usually not discussed or not discussed in sufficient detail or specificity to enable us to better understand how, in very different cases, morality and moral development are possible. Some children who are abused or neglected somehow manage to grow up fairly sane both morally and personally, but large numbers don't. And at least part of the reason is that great anger undercuts their capacity for morality by undercutting, dulling, and/or deactivating their capacity for empathy and sympathy with others.

But let me be a bit more specific. Some sociopaths are morally stunted without being incapable of empathy. Their condition may be at least partly due to abuse or a lack of love in their childhoods, but if they are intelligent enough, some of them become quite adept at getting into people's heads. The con artist and/or sadistic psychopath may be very good at reading people and seeing their weaknesses, something that obviously helps them to use or abuse some of the people they come into contact with. But this kind of empathy is what in some of the literature is called *projective empathy*, and it contrasts with the kind of *associative* or *receptive empathy* that involves feeling what another person feels (feeling their pain, for example). The sadist may deliberately get inside the head of some victim, but he doesn't feel his victim's pain but, rather, feels joy *at* his victim's pain. And when I speak of an incapacity for empathy, I shall (unless it is otherwise indicated) be talking about an incapacity for emotional receptivity and responsiveness that characterizes sociopaths and certain sadists (these are not discrete classes). Moreover, I think this lack of emotional responsiveness or receptivity to how others are feeling is often at least partially the product of childhood neglect and abuse—and, more generally, of a lack of love in childhood. When we are angry with someone, we feel less empathy for their sorrows and joys, and children who are abused or un-loved will typically feel so much rage/anger at this that their capacity for empathy with others becomes limited or withers (or is frozen) altogether. And if this happens, then the parents will have helped bring about a so-ciopath and/or sadist (or worse, if serial rapists and serial killers are considered).

But what if the child's need for love is largely met and the child doesn't have the kind of rage that leads to or constitutes a loss of the capacity for empathy, for sympathy, and for altruistic behavior? That is the kind of child we have been assuming as the subject of inductive parental discipline, a child who is capable of empathy with others and whose empathy can be en-couraged or stimulated by parents in ways that strengthen her sympathy/concern for others. But if this is all we say, then we are in effect supposing that all we need in order for a (physically normal) child to get to the point where inductive discipline and/or certain kinds of modeling can "take over" and help the child become a morally decent individual is *simply the absence of abuse and the presence of love on the part of the child's parents.* (Cases where there are non-parental guardians are somewhat different, and I won't talk about them here.) And it really isn't good enough to say just this. The process whereby a child with loving parents becomes capable of later induc-tive discipline is actually more complex, interesting, and uncharted than the ideas of non-abuse and of the presence of love allow us to understand. Love and non-abuse lead to a child capable of moral development and learning *in rather specific and complex ways that have not previously been ex-plored.* And I am going to do some of that exploration here. Once we have done that, we will see that being loved doesn't simply or immediately lead to the capacity for morality and (further) moral learning; the development of that capacity is a complex (causal) process, and though it depends on the presence of parental love, it operates via psychological mechanisms we need to describe if a full or fuller picture of human moral development (in the favorable cases) is to emerge. And at the center that picture, I believe, is the emotion of gratitude.

However, in order to understand how I think gratitude functions as a basis for moral development, you are going to need some background. The role gratitude plays is best understood within a generally sentimentalist view of how morality develops (and of what the content of morality is); and since gratitude operates, according to such philosophical assumptions, *via processes of empathy,* I need to say more here about what empathy is and how it works. But after saying some basic things about empathy, I want to go on to sketch a possible role for it in ordinary cases of adult gratitude, before going on to use this introductory discussion to illuminate the role that I believe gratitude has in early childhood as a necessary foundation stone for subsequent moral development and moral education.

Perhaps everyone knows at this point the rough difference between empathy and sympathy. Bill Clinton helped make empathy famous by saying "I feel your pain"; sympathy, by contrast, is feeling *for* someone who is in pain. Some would say that empathy is defined by a match or similarity between what one person feels or thinks and what another, via empathy, feels or thinks as a result. But this allows no room for non-veridical empathy, for empathy based on misperception or faulty beliefs (or on reading books about moving fictional characters). And our present-day usage doesn't rule out this sort of thing. So if the difference between empathy and sympathy isn't always that there is a match of (for example) feeling in the former case and not the latter, how can we distinguish them properly? Well, to begin with, doing so doesn't involve or have to involve being able to define these notions—philosophers have never succeeded in defining *any* notion accurately. But one difference between empathy and sympathy is that the former (at least in the case Bill Clinton was talking about, the case of associative as opposed to projective empathy) involves receptivity, and the latter is more reactive than receptive. If I feel the supposed pain of a character in a book or of someone who is feigning pain very realistically, I am in an emotionally receptive mode; but to feel sympathy for someone's pain is to have reacted or be reacting to what one knows or feels about that person. And, of course, the response or reaction also has to be a positive one: someone with schadenfreude responds to the pain of another with glee rather than with sympathy, commiseration, or the desire for things to improve for the person suffering the pain.

Empathy is also widely thought of as involving an identification with the other that sympathy doesn't seem to involve. But the identification doesn't require or even allow a sense or feeling of merging with or melting into another person: there is still the sense that the other is another person. And it should be added that associative empathy isn't conceptually or epistemically blind in its more mature instances. Hoffman speaks of *mediated* associative empathy in this connection, arguing that the non-deliberate/non-voluntary process of coming to feel what another feels can depend on what one knows and is able to conceive about the other. Young children, for example, lack a full idea of the reality of other people and of what is going on in other people's minds, but an adult capacity to empathize immediately and associatively with what they perceive to be someone's disappointment at losing a job will depend on their understanding what it is to lose a job, and that will require some conceptual sophistication and some knowledge about human life. So empathy can bring about real emotion in an automatic or non-deliberate fashion, but the process doesn't have to be *purely* emotional and typically involves cognitive elements as well. (These cognitive elements don't as such rest on or involve what is called practical reason, so we are still talking about sentimentalism here, not about ethical rationalism.)

Now, recent discussions of empathy have frequently focused on its (presumed or putative) role in supporting sympathy and altruistic behavior. Gratitude has been pretty much out of the picture, and the same can also be said in regard to the ethics of care. The focus in care ethics, as with most of the psychological literature on moral development, is on the origins of altruistic motivation in general. In other words, the focus is on what makes us (or is required for us to) intrinsically care about the well-being of other people—care enough to help them in cases that involve a certain degree of self-sacrifice on our part. To be sure, gratitude is a kind of altruistic motive: a grateful person typically seeks to do something nice for another person *because* of what the other person has done for him and not *in order to* get that individual to (again) do something nice for him. But a moral person, a caring person, an altruistic person is supposed to want to help others who he himself has not been helped by, and gratitude, therefore, is treated as inessential to the kind of altruistic motivation that the ethics of care values and that some of the psychology literature seeks to establish as possible on an empathic basis.

My argument here, though, is that this picture is somewhat misleading and misses out on an absolutely crucial element in the development of altruistic motivation. To be sure, the adult who helps a person in distress doesn't have to believe that person has helped *him* in order to want to help the person in question. Altruism toward a given individual clearly doesn't depend on feeling grateful toward that person in particular. And the psychologists of moral development and the care ethicists (and I consider myself a care ethicist) have been right to that extent. But what they and I haven't seen is that all this altruism may depend on a more primordial and pervasive (and inarticulate) sense/feeling of gratitude: gratitude that babies or young children who need love feel when they are given love. This gratitude is gratitude toward their parents for the love their parents show them, but I think it is also a larger and more diffuse sense of gratitude toward the whole world for having met their basic need for love. And in any event, I think that absent this sense of gratitude, the capacity for moral development and for eventual altruism will likely be stunted or destroyed. So you can see why I say that gratitude plays a larger role in adult altruism than care ethicists and developmental psychologists have thought. Even if an adult helps someone who has never helped her, she is, I believe, acting in the light and under the influence of an original and primordial sense of gratitude, and her actions, therefore, in some sense and to some degree are expressive of that original sense of gratitude.

But you may be wondering at this point what right I have to speak, as I did just a moment ago, of a diffuse sense of gratitude toward the whole world (that comes out and is expressed in all adult altruism). Why not just say that one is grateful early on to parents who love one and leave it at that? Well, my reason for the further claim has in great part to do with what I said earlier about what happens when a child's need for love and affection isn't met and when, instead, the child is abused and mistreated. I mentioned earlier—what many clinical psychologists have assumed—that such treatment can produce enough rage and anger to undercut the mistreated child's capacity for empathy and eventual altruism (or moral decency). But it would also seem that that rage has a certain tendency to generalize. The child who was severely abused by his parents may, for example, become a serial killer or con artist. This kind of thing, unfortunately, happens very often, and it shows how anger tends to generalize beyond its presumed original targets, how it tends to spread itself (so to speak) over the whole world. And I think the gratitude young children can feel toward loving parents has a similar tendency to spread beyond its original context and in effect, when it emerges eventually as altruism, spread itself over the larger world.

Perhaps similes will help. When someone who was severely abused becomes a serial killer, it is as if he is angry with and taking revenge on the whole world for what was done to him as a child. And when a child who has been loved and is grateful for that love becomes an altruist, it is as if she is grateful to the whole world, or the world as a whole, for how she was treated as (a baby and) a child. Now, I don't want to make too much of these similes: they are no part of any literal psychological explanation of how altruism develops out of gratitude, and in a moment I want to offer just such a literal explanation. But the similes may at least prepare us to some extent for what such a literal explanation will try to prove to us. The analogy between gratitude toward loving parents and anger (or hatred) toward abusive parents, and the fact that abuse can produce a con artist, say, who enjoys preying on the whole world, can ready us for the possibility that gratitude toward parents is the basis for generalized adult altruism. But it is time now to actually (and literally) explain how all this works.

2

I think we will do best if we first talk about how adult gratitude works. We understand ourselves better than we understand infants (don't we?), and once we describe the sentimental/empathic processes that I shall argue underlie and power adult gratitude, it will be easier to see how they might be instantiated in infancy or early childhood.

In typical cases of gratitude, we aren't just grateful for what has been done for us, but also for the attitude or motive of the person who has done it. There is a difference in our attitude, of course, depending on whether the other person's efforts on our behalf have been successful and on how much good or satisfaction we derive or expect to derive from the person's efforts; and this, in another guise, is the familiar problem of moral luck. Whether a negligent attitude actually has bad consequences makes or seems to make a difference to our moral assessment of the negligent person or her actions (or her attitude), and results make a difference to gratitude, too. But having said as much, I would like to drop this specific topic. Most of us philosophers find the problem of moral luck impossibly difficult to deal with, and the analogue/exemplification of that issue in the area of gratitude is no less difficult. So let me put these difficulties to one side and address those where I feel we may have some hope of making some immediate progress. In what follows, therefore, I shall assume that we are talking about gratitude for what has successfully been done for one.

So as I said, in typical cases of gratitude, one's feelings are responsive not just to what may have been done for one but also to the attitude or motive of the person or persons who did it. (One can also be grateful for what one knows will be successfully done or completed for one in the future, but I shall ignore such less standard cases.) And in the first instance, what happens when we are grateful is that we empathically "take in" the sympathetic attitude or motive that is focused in our direction. As Hume tells us, using the word *sympathy* because the term *empathy* didn't yet exist: just as we can imbibe or take in the pained or joyful feelings of another person, we can also imbibe or absorb the person's attitudes and even perhaps his beliefs. A father can pick up an interest in stamp collecting from his daughter by a kind of empathic osmosis (he is "infected" by her enthusiasm), and parental opinions/attitudes on religious or political topics can seep into children in an involuntary and often unconscious way. And so too, I think, it is with gratitude. When someone does something for us out of a sincere (and intrinsic) desire to help us, we soak up that motivation via the same associative-empathic process(es) that lead us to feel another person's joy, share the person's interest in stamp collecting, or feel as that person does about Martin Luther.

Now, the person who thus helps us has warm feelings of sympathetic concern for us, feelings that lead her to help us and that are likely based to some extent in her empathy with or for us. But when we empathically take in such feeling(s), it is our own empathy at work, and what we empathically come to feel is *her sympathy for us*. Such sympathy has (at least) two aspects: it is good will directed *toward us*, but it is also a form of *sympathy*, and by its very (conceptual) nature sympathy is always directed toward others. This is an important point. The psychology literature and common sense tell us that empathy is empathy for others, not for ourselves. One may in unusual cases feel empathy, say, for the poor, malnourished child one once was; but ongoing empathy is for others, and something similar holds for sympathy and benevolence. If I feel sorry for myself, that is *not* an example of (what we would call) feeling sympathy (benevolence) for or toward myself, and most dictionaries I have consulted in fact explicitly indicate that sympathy has to be between persons or for another person. Thus, when I say that when one feels gratitude one has empathized with, and in that sense taken in or absorbed the sympathy that another person feels toward oneself, the sympathy thus aroused or evoked in us not only involves feeling good about—or a kind of good will toward—oneself that mirrors how the other feels about us, but is also felt as a kind of (other-directed) sympathy. In other words, when someone confers a good on us out of sympathy for us and we take in or absorb that sympathy, at least part of what happens is that we become sympathetic, too; and that aroused sympathy—which I think is tantamount to gratitude—tends to focus on the person who conferred the benefit as the most salient person in the situation, as the known causal source of what one is feeling.[7]

However, I also think that when someone does something nice for us, the sympathy/gratitude that is evoked by that person's sympathy tends to spread itself around a lot and not focus entirely on the person who is most salient to us in the situation, because we know that it is that person who has brought about both the good we have received and the feeling we have in response to an intention to confer that good. This claim is of a piece with what I said just above about anger's tendency to generalize and about the analogy between anger and gratitude. And the familiar idea of "paying it forward" is also evidence for the psychological assumption(s) I am making here.[8] However, at this point one might have a further question. If gratitude spreads in the way I have just indicated, doesn't it dissipate in its force or intensity, and doesn't that mean that there isn't enough of it to enable us to account for the intense feelings of gratitude that we often feel when someone has greatly helped us?

This line of thought doesn't do justice to the psychological effects of the fact that gratitude is felt in response to what someone has done for and toward us. We can be empathically warmed by the warm sympathy an agent displays toward some third party, and what we thus feel is more naturally characterized as (emotional) approval of that agent's sympathy rather than as gratitude for it. But that is just the point. Approval, warm approval, lacks the intensity of gratitude, and the reason obviously has to do with the relation the relevant feelings of other people have toward us. We can empathize with someone's sympathy toward some third party, but in such cases we typically don't feel their sympathy as strongly or intensely as we do when their sympathy is directed toward us and results in something good for us. Other things being equal, we feel emotions directed at us much more strongly than emotions directed toward others—that is a basic fact of human psychology.

So the empathy-based gratitude that registers and responds to another person's sympathy toward us is much more strongly felt than is the empathy-based warm approval of sympathy that is directed toward other people.[9] Therefore, gratitude is much stronger, much more strongly felt, than emotional approval is; and the sympathetic, other-directed response it involves is much stronger than anything evoked or elicited by approving someone's actions toward third parties. The latter does awaken sympathy for others via empathic processes, but such sympathy is much more strongly evoked by attitudes and actions that center on us, just as, more generally, we tend to feel any emotion more strongly when it is directed toward us rather than toward others. All of this then helps us to explain how and why, in adult cases, gratitude is felt in response to what others do for us and involves not just a sheer (strong) feeling but also a sympathetic motive to help our benefactor and others. And, in addition, given that empathy is generally seen by psychologists as relating to someone other than ourselves, the fact (and readers can check their own linguistic intuitions on this) that it is odd to speak of being grateful to oneself supports what I have just been saying about the empathic character of gratitude.

What happens in early childhood can be understood in the same basic terms we have just used to describe/explain adult cases. A child who is loved by and breast-fed by his mother is often said to take in her love along with the milk, and if what I have just been saying is correct, then the love that is taken in is at least in part a form of gratitude. We might unthinkingly regard taking in love as similar to taking in a substance like milk, but the former kind of taking in is, I believe, more like the taking in of one's parents' political attitudes or the hobby interests of one's child. The taking in is an empathic taking in, and the net effect is that one develops or exemplifies something in oneself that is similar to what the person one is imbibing from has (or seems to have). This is more a matter of similarity than of (sameness of) stuff or substance—more like taking in the form of a statue than like taking in its matter. So the saying about taking in love along with mother's milk is a kind of syllepsis or zeugma (like "she arrived in a flood of tears and a new Cadillac"); but it nonetheless indicates a truth about the love received from a mother (or a father).

However, we have added to the insight here. Yes, we take in our mother's love during any period when we take in her milk (and, of course, later too); but the former taking in works via empathy, empathy with the sympathy shown us by a loving mother, and the resultant state of sympathy, which is both intensely felt and motivated benignly toward others, is what gratitude basically is. But, as happens with cases of adult gratitude, we also take in our mother's (or father's) sympathetic love in the form of the good will toward ourselves that it involves. And a child who takes in her mother's love will therefore not only feel benign sympathy toward others (especially the mother) but will also imbibe good feeling about herself—a kind of rudimentary or inchoate self-esteem. But for our purposes here, the issue of gratitude as empathically absorbed sympathy for another or others is central, so let's drop the talk of self-directed good feeling (or love) and confine our discussion to gratitude.

Young children who are grateful to their parents may have intense feelings of gratitude, but in line with their undeveloped or lesser sense of the reality and needs of others, the sympathy they feel will be inchoate, vague, and inarticulate as compared with the sympathy felt by an adult who is grateful to someone who has helped him. And, as I indicated earlier, I think the gratitude children who are loved and well cared for feel toward their parents makes later, fuller moral development and moral education possible.[10] For the child to feel gratitude toward her parents, she has to have and to have exercised (however primitively or simply) her inborn capacity for empathically taking in the attitudes of others. So I am assuming that children who are not genetically abnormal or brain damaged have the capacity for empathy from the get-go, and that is in keeping with what most writers on empathy believe. Babies in hospitals show a rudimentary form of and capacity for empathy when they start crying and show distress when some baby around them starts crying in distress. And the original capacity for and tendency toward empathic responses (and receptivity) is shown in a number of other ways as well. But that capacity is also exhibited in the gratitude very young children can feel when their desire for love is met by the love of their parents, and previous writers on early empathy haven't made this specific point. And neither have they pointed out that the gratitude amounts to a form of deeply felt, empathically derived sympathy that smoothes the way toward later altruistic/moral behavior.[11]

Moreover, if this picture is correct, then even if empathy is an inborn capacity or tendency in normal human beings, there is no need for us to say, with Hume, that sympathy with/benevolence toward others is also an "original instinct." Sympathy/benevolence can be seen, rather, as resulting (in a way that depends very much on highly contingent parental behavior) from normal inborn empathy operating on parental/maternal solicitude/ love and infusing the child or infant with a sympathy analogous to what the mother or father feels toward the child. That sympathy will be all the more intense because the mother's or father's sympathy/love is both some- thing directed at the child and something the child craves (though I won't go into all the details of this here). But in any event there is no need to posit benevolence or sympathy as a basic instinct, given the account we have of- fered, and that account not only works against Hume's assumption that benevolence is inborn but also supports Hoffman's view in *Empathy and Moral Development* that we see empathy working in childhood before we see signs of childhood sympathy, benevolence, and the like. However, what I have been saying goes beyond anything to be found in Hoffman by empha- sizing that and explaining why the transition from empathy to sympathy, caring, benevolence, and altruism isn't likely to occur if a child's funda- mental need for love (something Hoffman never mentions) isn't satisfied.

If someone's parents aren't loving, then his reaction is likely to be a kind of (generalized) rage or anger (or hatred?); and as I indicated earlier, that rage, if it is strong enough and persistent enough, undercuts the possibili- ties of later associative/emotional/receptive empathy. Since caring about and altruistic behavior toward others arguably depend on such empathy, we can say that unloving and abusive treatment of children often nullifies or deprives them of their original capacity for empathy and makes the whole process of moral development impossible.[12] But if the child has been loved and feels grateful, then her embryonic empathic tendencies and ca- pacities can be further strengthened via educative processes like induction and via immersion in an environment where she can soak up (via uncon- scious modeling) the empathic/sympathetic/altruistic tendencies of those around her. My book *Moral Sentimentalism* (hereafter, MS) describes in great detail how such (further) moral education or learning can occur, but fails to recognize or state that the later education and learning depend on and psychologically presuppose certain very specific empathic processes oc- curring in one's very early years. (Martin Hoffman, perhaps the leading writer on empathy and moral development, also neglects these specific pro- cesses.) Those processes involve a kind of empathy-induced gratitude, and in their absence there will typically be a kind of anger that is inconsistent with gratitude and that makes further moral learning impossible. And that shows that it isn't just later and earlier processes of empathy that are req- uisite to moral development, but that a certain emotion (gratitude) has to be present very early in life, and a certain different emotion (intense and persisting anger) has to be more or less absent during the same period if moral development is to occur. Moral development depends on the earliest child-hood emotions as much as or perhaps (conceptually speaking) even more than it depends on sheer empathy, and that conclusion goes beyond anything I argued for in MS and beyond what others in the field of moral education—even those with a good opinion of sentimentalism—have said about moral development.

Now, my claim that subsequent moral development depends on a child's empathically taking in parental or maternal sympathy doesn't by itself assume or presuppose that parental actions and attitude can bring about genuine psychopathy. One could say, for example, that psychopathy has strictly physical origins, yet also grant that genuine or full moral develop-ment depends on what parents do—and more particularly, on their love and sympathy toward their child or children. However, I believe what we have said above also supports the idea—contrary to much contemporary opinion—that parental neglect and/or abuse can be a primary source of full-blown psychopathy. A typical psychopath not only lacks the empathic capacity to feel what others are feeling but also actively seeks to hurt, hu-miliate, or destroy others. And on the face of it, it is difficult to see how or why a smaller amygdala or an innate genetic predisposition to stronger rage *reactions* to frustration or pain would bring about the kind of sadism, scha-denfreude, and paranoia that *compulsively originates* efforts to hurt, harm, or humiliate others just for the sake of doing so. Most distinctive psycho-paths have this constellation of character traits or psychological disposi-tions, and I believe our previous discussion can help us understand how and why better than any purely physical account.

If children (people) deeply and enduringly need love, they will react with enduring rage to abuse and total neglect, and we know that rage can un-dercut the empathy and sympathy that most of us feel toward particular others, but that psychopaths are so generally lacking in. And of course rage can lead to the kind of punitive or sadistic behavior we also find in psycho-paths, assuming that rage and anger can generalize from their original tar-gets. (And we know that that happens even with "normal" people, as when a man who has a bad day at the office comes home and kicks the family dog.) Of course, the psychopath also lacks conscience or feelings of guilt, but on any sentimentalist account (as in my MS) conscience and guilt depend on sympathy/empathy with others, so I believe our approach can also explain these other features of typical psychopaths and do so in a way purely phys-ical accounts don't allow for. But the account I have offered is certainly somewhat speculative. I have assumed a basic need for love that not all

psychologists or neuroscientists would wish to acknowledge; and I have described an empathic imbibing of parental sympathy/solicitude during early
childhood that I have no direct evidence for.[13] But there is evidence that
children have and exercise an empathic capacity in their early years, and
surely there is no reason to assume they can't or won't empathically take in
maternal/parental sympathy/love in the way they later take in parental or
other people's religious or political attitudes. In any event, what is or starts
as psychologically speculative gains some epistemic justification from its
ability to explain and tie together features of psychopathy in a way genetic
accounts don't seem capable of doing. So our overall picture here of moral
development assigns a major, though not exclusive, role to parental factors
both in the development of morality/moral virtue and in the failure of
moral development we find in psychopaths. But let me now draw some further and more wide-ranging conclusions from what I have been saying.

3

Nel Noddings and various other care ethicists have argued that care ethics
should be based on the value and importance of caring relationships, and
that the virtue of caring derives its value from such relationships rather than
having any independent moral or ethical status. I have elsewhere given
what I believe are rather strong arguments for thinking that pace Noddings
the virtue of caring does have an independent status and value. But it is
worth noting that Noddings also says that if we think of caring relationships rather than the virtue of caring as primary, that is a (theoretical)
reason to focus in the first instance on the person who is cared for rather
than the person who cares for that person.[14] However, our previous discussion shows that even someone who believes the virtue of caring has a value
independent of caring relationships has (theoretical) reason to focus on
the object of caring, the one cared for. For it is the cared-for's need for love
that helps us explain the ontogenesis of morality or virtue in its earliest
stages; and the gratitude of the one cared for is essential both to the development of virtuously caring individuals and to the possibility of good
caring relationships. The mother or father may care for the child, but if the
child, in turn, is to be become a morally good or virtuous carer, his need for
loving care has to be satisfactorily met. Until and unless we focus on the
needs and responses of the one cared for, we cannot understand or account
for his potential to become a caring individual and for the possibility of
caring dispositions and relationships generally. (If there is a chicken-and-egg
problem here, it is no more pressing than a lot of other such problems

ethics and the philosophy of mind have to face. For example, people are nowadays more preoccupied with empathy and arguably more empathic than people were two or three thousand years ago, but how did this come about? People can be educated to become more empathic and sympathetic, to be sure, but it typically takes sympathetic and empathic people to do this, so how, exactly, do social levels of empathy ever actually rise—or, for that matter, fall? We need to think more about these topics, and it would be helpful if some historian, collaborating perhaps with a philosopher and a psychologist, could write a history of empathy's origins, its spread, and its strengthening in some social contexts more than others. But we have enough to occupy us before such a history is written and before we solve our other chicken-and-egg problems.)

So, returning to Noddings and care ethics, the importance of the cared-for is independent of whether one believes the virtue of caring is derivative from caring relationships or has an independent value; and whichever way one goes on this last issue, the fact that children need love, and that their capacity for caring and sympathy for others typically depends on whether they are or can be grateful for the love that is given to them, shows that care ethics needs to focus—in its moral-psychological explanations—on the one cared for.[15] Now, Kantian and other forms of ethical rationalism (even Aristotle's) don't put emotion at the center of the moral life in the way that care ethics does. So if care ethics is correct, then emotion is much more central to this important aspect of human psychology and human life than rationalism allows for or acknowledges. But if what I have been saying here is also correct, then previous care ethics has seen the importance of emotion to morality, and to human psychology more generally, only in a somewhat limited way. Caring about others is an emotional attitude/motive, and care ethics sees that as central to the moral life in a way that ethical rationalism does not. But if the emotion of and involved in caring about others is ontogenetically based on gratitude, and precluded by anger, in relation in the desire to be loved, then these latter feelings/emotions are also important to the moral life.[16] It is not just the emotional attitude of caring, then, but anger, gratitude, and love as well that characterize morality and human psychology to the extent it underpins and supports morality. What I have said shows that both emotion and what we can see as a *variety* of emotions play a larger role in morality and our lives than ethical rationalism allows and than previous care ethics has recognized. We normally start our lives with a capacity for empathy and for becoming more empathic with time. But early certain events/situations and their emotional sequelae can undercut our capacity for (developing greater) empathy and altruistic motivation. So in some sense, the roots of adult empathy turn out to reach down to certain very powerful but typically neglected (by academics, not parents) childhood emotions.

NOTES

1. I am indebted to Yang Xiao for helpful discussion of the central issues in this paper.
2. See especially ch. 3 of my *Education and Human Values: Reconciling Talent with an Ethics of Care* (New York: Routledge, 2013).
3. See Martin Hoffman, *Empathy and Moral Development: Implications for Caring and Justice* (New York: Cambridge University Press, 2000), ch. 6; Nel Noddings, "Moral Education and Caring," *Theory and Research in Education* 8 (2010): 147; and my *Moral Sentimentalism* (New York: Oxford University Press, 2010), 20f.

    For arguments for and against the possibility of human psychological altruism (based in empathy), see, e.g., C. Daniel Batson, *Altruism in Humans* (New York: Oxford University Press, 2011); and E. Sober and D. S. Wilson, *Unto Others: The Evolution and Psychology of Unselfish Behavior* (Cambridge, MA: Harvard University Press, 1999). For a defense of psychological altruism against what I take to be the conceptual errors of those who have argued against it, see my "Egoism and Emotion," *Philosophia* 41 (2013).
4. Though, as Jane Statlander-Slote has pointed out to me, the unpleasant recognition of and sense of frustration at *our inability to ensure* that parents will love their children and not abuse them may also help to explain why moral educationists tend to avoid discussing abusive/unloving parents and what they do to their children. Let me also point out that the presumed fact that certain kinds of abuse can contribute to making some people/children incapable of developing moral motives and sentiments implies that a person's status or character as a moral being can depend on factors of luck. Various traditions (e. g., Confucianism and Kantian ethics) that stress the importance of moral self-cultivation or self-improvement play down such factors of luck, play down (in a way that Aristotle, in fact, did not) the typically crucial role that *other people* play in someone's moral education/ development. But although it would be nice to think that people can or do (successfully) take their moral development into their own hands, I believe that there are fewer realistic possibilities for or instances of this than advocates of moral self-cultivation have thought. I hope to take up this issue for fuller treatment in a future publication.
5. For this view see, for example, Linda Mealey, "The Sociobiology of Sociopathy: An Integrated Evolutionary Model," *Behavioral and Brain Sciences* 18 (1995): 523–99.
6. See, for example, John Bowlby, *Maternal Care and Mental Health* (Geneva: World Health Organization, 1952), where some of the psychological literature that connects parental neglect/abuse with psychopathy/sociopathy is (favorably) reviewed. But I believe previous work on the connection between parental behavior and psychopathy hasn't emphasized the fact that anger/rage can undercut empathy as much as I shall be doing here. Also, and as I indicated in the text above, there is no reason why genetic or physical abnormalities shouldn't play a role in causing parental neglect/abuse of children: a child who has a predisposition to rage reactions or whose smaller amygdala makes them less able to pick up on social cues may elicit harsh(er) parental treatment. And that is one way in which genetic factors or brain damage can play a role in the causation of sociopathy.

7. Since gratitude is more strongly felt than approval, our motive to help someone who has helped us will typically be stronger than our motive to help someone we see help others. Note, too, that the warm sympathetic approval we (via empathy) feel toward someone who helps another will—as a form of identification with that person—tend to make us want to help the people the person we approve of is trying to help. Thus we can, through the empathic processes that underlie approval, have sympathetic concern for the welfare of someone we approve of and also for the welfare of those they seek to help—but I have no idea at this point what to say about the relative strengths of these logically distinct motives.

8. What I am saying may be further supported by results in the psychological literature that have been used in criticism of (Aristotelian) virtue ethics and any ethics that makes a lot depend on issues about character (traditionally conceived). Decades ago, A. Isen and P. Levin did a study ("Effect of Feeling Good on Helping: Cookies and Kindness," *Journal of Personality and Social Psychology* 21 [1972]: 384–88) that showed that feeling good in certain ways (receiving a free snack of cookies, finding a small amount of change in a phone booth) seems to make people more willing to help others. Now I don't want to try to show here how these results can be accommodated within virtue ethics—though I agree, among other things, with those who point out that there are lots of reasons to think that virtuous character doesn't *require* us to stop to help someone, e.g., who has dropped a bunch of papers, however good we may or may not be feeling. But consider the people who, as the study indicated, stopped to help the person who had dropped papers after they (not the person who had dropped the papers) had found a 1972-value dime in a phone booth; or those who were more willing to help another person after they had been given free cookies by some third party. Perhaps this greater willingness to help is a sign of gratitude for what they had received and evidence for the idea that gratitude tends to spread beyond the (believed) actual source of benefits one has received (to pay itself forward, so to speak). In that case, Isen and Levin's study, far from illustrating how otiose the idea of character is, hints at the basis for moral character in the phenomenon of fundamental empathic gratitude.

9. I am assuming that the state feeling warmed by someone else's warm behavior or attitude can readily be seen as a kind of ur-approval of what that other person has done or feels. But my *Moral Sentimentalism*, chs. 2–4, defends this idea at length (and similar ideas about what moral disapproval consists in).

10. Elsewhere (e.g., in my *Education and Human Values*, ch. 3) I have argued that rationalistic (Kantian or Aristotelian) accounts of moral education fail to explain the psychological mechanisms whereby moral development/improvement occurs or is induced at a given time or during a given period of a child's or adult's life. But this is just a synchronic explanatory inadequacy, and rationalist theories also fail at a diachronic level to explain how *over a lifetime* moral development is possible and actually occurs. They fail to see the crucial role parental love plays in overall or long-term moral education or, as with Rawls, don't account for how and why such love is so crucial—and sentimentalist theorizing about moral education/development can and does allow for both these kinds or levels of explanation. All this, again, favors sentimentalism as a normative and metaethical view of morality.

Finally, Cicero in *Pro Plancio* calls gratitude the "parent" of all the other virtues, and in *De Finibus* (see *On Moral Ends* [Cambridge: Cambridge University Press, 2001], 84ff) he says that parental love is the source of all human sympathy. Both these points anticipate what I am saying here, but Cicero never talks or speculates about the empathic processes that I want to claim underlie the truth of these claims of his. It is worth noting that Darwin in *The Descent of Man and Selection in Relation to Sex* (New York: Appleton, 1871) also emphasizes the connection between parental love and general human sympathy, and there are various contemporary versions of this idea according to which human sympathy is basically just a *generalized instance* of parental instinct (see, for example, Batson, *Altruism in Humans*, ch. 2). But I believe what we are saying here gives us a more specific and causally nuanced account of how parental instinct/love and human sympathy (originally) connect than is provided by these other approaches.

11. In "Empathy: Its Ultimate and Proximate Bases," *Behavioral and Brain Sciences* 25 (2002): 7, S. Preston and F. de Waal state that: "The parent child relationship both relies on and is necessary to develop the ability of individuals to be affected by the emotional states of others." And what I have just been saying is an argument in support of this claim that is much more psychologically specific than anything these authors say. Like them, I assume that normal infants have an inborn capacity for empathy. But I argue specifically that that capacity operates on maternal empathy/sympathy to replicate such a state in the child; and I then go on to explain why that state in the child can be characterized as a kind of gratitude and is foundational to later empathy/sympathy and their role in moral development (where it isn't present we are likely to have a sociopath or anti-social personality).

12. It follows from what I am saying here that psychopaths are incapable of genuine feelings of gratitude, but I don't know of any empirical studies of this issue. It would be interesting to see whether such studies would bear out what I have been saying about the connection between (associative) empathy and gratitude (and altruism).

13. At this point in human history, the idea that children need love seems something of a commonplace, but one can find this idea explicitly defended, e.g., in John Bowlby's *Child Care and the Growth of Love* (Harmondsworth: Penguin Books, 1971), ch. 1, esp. p. 14; in Abraham Maslow's *Motivation and Personality* (New York: Harper, 1954), part I; and in Nel Noddings's *Caring: A Feminine Approach to Ethics and Moral Education* (Berkeley: University of California Press, 1984), 67ff. On the connection between aggressiveness and empathy deficits in psychopaths, see J. Decety and A. Meltzoff, "Empathy, Imitation, and the Social Brain," in *Empathy: Philosophical and Psychological Perspectives*, ed. A. Coplan and P. Goldie (Oxford: Oxford University Press, 2011), 78ff.

14. See her *Starting at Home: Caring and Social Policy* (Berkeley: University of California Press, 2002).

15. I think Noddings's insistence on and (if I may say) preoccupation with the central or foundational role of caring relationships has made her emphasize synchronic relations between individuals at the expense of those diachronic processes within individuals (as they interact with others) that turn someone cared for into someone capable of caring for others. (She does, however, talk—on a smaller diachronic scale—about how we come to take people into our circle of care.) Noddings does see children as needing love, but she doesn't bring in gratitude or any other psychological mechanism/process that might explain how we get or fail to get from such need to psychological altruism.

16. But what about phylogenesis? Why should humans and (certain) other mammals have developed a need for love? If caring ontogenetically arises out of a satisfied need for love, why shouldn't, why couldn't, evolution instead have just made us caring or benevolent independently of such a need? This is an interesting question, and as such its force breaks down into two relevant answers. First, although

caring is socially useful and evolution could conceivably have worked it into our motivational repertoire independently of any need for love, it doesn't seem to have worked caring into us in that fashion: such an all-in-one-blow change in mammalian motivation may have been too unlikely and too difficult to manage in terms of normal evolutionary forces/processes. Second, we need to understand how the evolution of caring via the instilling of a need for love would/might actually work. And let me make some initial gestures in this direction.

If caring develops in relation to children's need for love, then one way this can happen would be for the "maternal instinct" and related emotions of mammalian mothers to be ontogenetically converted from an afferent to an efferent force. The only virtue I know of that can do this is gratitude (shades of Cicero's *Pro Plancio*). And if a child can empathically feel their mother's incoming sympathetic love, that will convert to an outgoing sympathy for others that counts as gratitude and is the basis of empathic caring. (Similar, but presumably weaker, claims can be made about the parental love of fathers.) But if the child needs love and not just the physical goods a loving mother/parent provides, if what is or might be just a means is craved for its own sake, then the child will have all the more to be grateful for, will feel the sympathetic love the parent feels toward them all the more strongly, and that could then amount to or convert into stronger felt sympathy and empathic concern for others on the part of the child. So the need for love may be part of evolution's way of making us more and more capable of empathic caring. (I plan to expand on these evolutionary speculations in future work.)

BIBLIOGRAPHY

Batson, C. Daniel. *Altruism in Humans*. New York: Oxford University Press, 2011.

Bowlby, John. *Child Care and the Growth of Love*. Harmondsworth: Penguin Books, 1971.

Bowlby, John. *Maternal Care and Mental Health*. Geneva: World Health Organization, 1952.

Cicero. *On Moral Ends*. Cambridge: Cambridge University Press, 2001.

Darwin, Charles. *The Descent of Man and Selection in Relation to Sex*. New York: Appleton, 1871.

Decety, J., and A. Meltzoff. "Empathy, Imitation, and the Social Brain." In *Empathy: Philosophical and Psychological Perspectives*, edited by A. Coplan and P. Goldie. Oxford: Oxford University Press, 2011.

Hoffman, Martin. *Empathy and Moral Development: Implications for Caring and Justice*. New York: Cambridge University Press, 2000.

Isen, A., and P. Levin. "Effect of Feeling Good on Helping: Cookies and Kindness." *Journal of Personality and Social Psychology* 21 (1972): 384–88.

Maslow, Abraham. *Motivation and Personality*. New York: Harper, 1954.

Mealey, Linda. "The Sociobiology of Sociopathy: An Integrated Evolutionary Model." *Behavioral and Brain Sciences* 18 (1995): 523–99.

Noddings, Nel. *Caring: A Feminine Approach to Ethics and Moral Education*. Berkeley: University of California Press, 1984.

Noddings, Nel. "Moral Education and Caring." *Theory and Research in Education* 8 (2010): 145–51.

Noddings, Nel. *Starting at Home: Caring and Social Policy*. Berkeley: University of California Press, 2002.

Preston, S., and F. de Waal. "Empathy: Its Ultimate and Proximate Bases." *Behavioral and Brain Sciences* 25 (2002): 1–71.

Slote, Michael. *Education and Human Values: Reconciling Talent with an Ethics of Care*. New York: Routledge, 2013.

Slote, Michael. "Egoism and Emotion." *Philosophia* 41 (2013): 313–35.

Slote, Michael. *Moral Sentimentalism*. New York: Oxford University Press, 2010.

Sober, E., and D. S. Wilson. *Unto Others: The Evolution and Psychology of Unselfish Behavior*. Cambridge, MA: Harvard University Press, 1999.

CHAPTER 4

cVo

Kant on Virtue and the Virtues

ADAM CURETON AND THOMAS E. HILL

I mmanuel Kant is known for his ideas about duty and morally worthy acts, but his conception of virtue is less familiar. Nevertheless, Kant's understanding of virtue is quite distinctive and has considerable merit compared to the most familiar conceptions. Kant also took moral education seriously, writing extensively on both the duty of adults to cultivate virtue and the empirical conditions that prepare children for this life-long responsibility. Our aim is, first, to explain Kant's conception of virtue; second, to highlight some distinctive and potentially appealing features of the Kantian account of virtue; *third*, to summarize and explain Kant's prescriptions for educating young children and youth as well as the duty of moral self-improvement that he attributes to all adults; and, fourth, to respond to some common objections that we regard as misguided or insubstantial.

KANTIAN MORAL VIRTUE: A GOOD AND STRONG WILL
TO DO WHAT IS RIGHT

Although Kant mentions virtue throughout his works, his most thorough discussion of virtue is in his Doctrine of Virtue (*Tugendlehre*), which is the second part of his late work *The Metaphysics of Morals*.[1] Here Kant explains virtue as a kind of strength or fortitude of will to fulfill one's duties despite internal and external obstacles.[2] Kant distinguishes the realm of *ethics*, which concerns moral ends, attitudes, and virtue, from the realm of *justice*, which concerns rights and duties that can be coercively enforced. Although we speak of many virtues, Kant says repeatedly, there is really just one virtue.[3] To be virtuous is more than having a good will, for virtue, Kant says, is a kind of moral strength or fortitude. In other words, Kant implies that to be (fully) virtuous is to have a good will that is *firmly resolved and fully ready to overcome temptations* to immorality. This is an ideal that we can never fully achieve, though we have a duty to strive for it. To become more virtuous is not an easy task, and it requires time and practice, as well as self-scrutiny.[4] The aim is not merely to avoid wrongdoing and to pursue moral ends but also to do so for the right reasons.

What a virtuous person wills to do, more specifically, is determined by the system of ethical principles, which includes, for example, duties to others of love, respect, gratitude, and friendship, as well as duties to ourselves to avoid suicide, lying, drunkenness, and servility. Although duties in the realm of law and justice (juridical duties) are distinct from ethical duties, we have indirect ethical duties to conform to juridical duties for moral reasons.[5] We also have an indirect ethical duty to promote our own happiness and to avoid cruelty to animals.[6] Although our sentiments are not fully subject to our control and are not what make our acts morally worthy, we have a duty to cultivate certain sentiments that can help us to fulfill our other duties.[7] The highest good consists of perfect virtue and well-deserved happiness together. Kant concedes that this cannot be achieved in this life, but claims that we have reason to have faith or hope that achieving it is nevertheless possible in ways that we cannot comprehend.[8] These are some of the main themes in Kant's account of virtue.

In Kant's mature works, the ideal of virtue is to have a good will with the strength of will to do one's duty despite any opposing inclinations.[9] Let us review Kant's basic ideas about a *good will*. In the first section of the *Groundwork*, Kant presents his conception of a good will, its special value, and its basic principle. In human beings, who have inclinations and imperfect wills, a good will is a will to do one's *duty* regardless of any contrary inclinations.[10] Although we can never know for certain that anyone acts purely from a good will, Kant says, a good will would be most evident if we had no inclination to do what we knew to be morally required but nevertheless did it *from duty* or, in other words, from *respect* for moral law.[11] Kant's examples are helping others in need and refraining from suicide when one has lost the normal inclinations to help and to continue living. Kant does not rule out that one could *have* and even *act from* a good will when one also happened to have an inclination to do what was required, but he insists that morally worthy acts do not rely on inclinations. Acting on the maxim "to help others if and only if it is my duty and also serves my interests" does not have moral worth or express a purely good will. Kant contrasts a good will with a *holy will*, or an absolutely good will in a being that lacks inclinations contrary to duty and necessarily wills in accord with reason.[12] Unlike imperfect human wills, a holy will could not be morally weak, or even tempted, and so would also not be subject to moral imperatives, duty, and obligation. This contrast brings out a central feature that is also present in Kant's conception of a good will in human beings, namely that it is a will to do what is required by reason. As he explains later, our duties are specified by an unconditionally rational principle (i.e., the Categorical Imperative).[13]

Kant eloquently proclaims that a good will has the special value of being not only *good in itself* but also *good without qualification*.[14] Unlike good qualities of temperament, gifts of fortune, and even happiness, a good will is good in all contexts. The point, often misunderstood, is about what, according to reason, we should choose, given various options. Specifically, no matter what would be gained, we should never for the sake of anything else choose to abandon or sacrifice our good will *by intentionally doing ("willing") what we know to be wrong.* This claim is most plausibly understood as primarily about valuing good willing in our own present choices, and its application presupposes that our judgment about what would be wrong to do has already taken into account relevant facts and substantive moral considerations. For example, assuming that one correctly judges that it would be all-things-considered wrong for one to steal ballots to get elected to office, then one should not abandon one's good will-to-avoid-wrongdoing for the sake of power, money, and fame—or even to help the poor. The special value of a good will, then, does not entail a repugnant fixation on "keeping one's hands clean"—for example, letting innocent people suffer and die simply to maintain one's "purity" rather than to do something non-ideal and normally wrong (such as fighting) to save them.[15] To choose to fight in such a case would not be abandoning one's good will unless one has good reasons for judging that the choice to fight would be wrong. The abstract claim that a good will is good without qualification does not, by itself, determine this.[16]

Given that a good will is unqualifiedly good, what does it will? Kant argues that the principle of a good will is what he later identifies as the Categorical Imperative: "I ought never to act in such a way that I could not also will that my maxim should become a universal law."[17] Using this principle and other versions of the Categorical Imperative, Kant claimed, we can determine what our duties are, at least if we understand the relevant facts and have developed "a power of judgment sharpened by experience."[18] How more specifically the several versions of the Categorical Imperative can guide our moral judgments has been much discussed and remains controversial, but our focus here is not on how the principle of a good will determines particular duties but rather on what virtue requires above and beyond having a good will and what it takes to develop virtue.

In the *Groundwork*, Kant allows that a good will could (through some unfortunate fate) become "completely powerless to carry out its aims" despite its "utmost effort." His point is that it would still have its full worth, glistening like a jewel. We should note, however, that "powerlessness" of a good will here is not moral weakness but *lack of causal power* to bring about intended effects.[19] Imagine, for example, a person so inept, clumsy, stupid, and undermined by others that every good project fails, despite his earnest efforts. By contrast in later works Kant implies that one may fail because one *lacks the strength of will* to act as one should. We all have a "propensity" to weakness in our will to do our duty even if our fundamental will is good—that is, a basic commitment to subordinate self-love to duty.[20] We need to cultivate virtue or, in other words, to make our basically good will stronger so that we do not, weakly, yield to opposing inclinations.[21]

All this seems to fit with ordinary moral thinking, but it is philosophically puzzling. Strong and weak wills, in Kant's view, are not (like muscles) strong and weak physical capacities to exert force. We identify and explain our wills by reference to the maxims on which take ourselves to be acting— these express rationales or conceptions of what we are doing, our purpose, and (sometimes) our underlying reason for acting as we do.[22] Moral agents have wills in two senses. First, practical legislative reason (*Wille*) is our own reason which, in a sense, imposes the unconditionally rational moral law on us as our standard, even when we fail to comply with it. Second, moral agents have a power of choice (*Willkür*) which, for imperfectly rational persons like us, is an ability to choose to do what reason prescribes or choose to act otherwise.[23] In neither sense is the will an empirical entity that can be a part of a scientific explanation of bodily movements. We attribute wills to persons from a practical standpoint, as a presupposition of common morality and as capacities that are "noumenal" and ultimately beyond naturalistic explanation. We must regard our power of choice as "free" from determination by empirical forces and take ourselves to be responsible for how we use it. The person who chooses a good basic life-governing maxim (duty over self-love) has a good will; a person with a depraved (and so "evil") will is one whose basic choice is the reverse; but even a generally good will may be weak and not always in line with duty on particular occasions.[24]

One way we might understand weakness and strength of will is to think of a person whose basically good will is weak as having maxims at different levels: first, a general maxim over time to subordinate self-love to duty; but also, second, despite this a specific maxim to do something contrary to duty on a particular occasion.[25] Clearly there is a conflict in the will of such a person whose moral will is basically good but weak; in fact, there is a double conflict: the particular will to do something contrary to duty violates the rational prescriptions of the person's practical reason (*Wille*), as well as violates the good general maxim that the person chose (*Willkür*) to govern his or her life. By self-deception the weak but good-willed person may be only half aware of these conflicts, but in principle it seems that Kant can acknowledge the common belief that a person with a basically good will can sometimes knowingly and willingly do something wrong, succumbing to temptation but still making a free choice rather than being literally overpowered by the force of passions and inclinations.

We are all to some extent morally weak, lacking full *virtue*—the strength of will to do our duty always and for the right reasons. Kant implies that it is our duty to cultivate virtue in this sense, but this takes time and effort. Perfect virtue is an end to which we should aspire but cannot fully achieve (in this life at least).[26]

MORAL LUCK AND ACCOMPLISHMENTS

A distinguishing feature of Kant's theory of virtue compared to many others, including Aristotle's, is that Kant's theory holds that virtually everyone can and should become morally good and make progress toward virtue, regardless of his or her natural dispositions and feelings. At least from a contemporary point of view, this distinguishing feature may also be considered a merit of the Kantian view, for it holds that virtue is not an ideal reserved for those especially fortunate in their natural gifts, class, exemplary mentors, or social setting. In this respect Kantian ethics may be regarded as more egalitarian than some ancient theories that are more focused on perfecting an elite class of superior leaders. Kant held that whether or not a person is morally good and virtuous is basically up to that person. To be sure, a background assumption is that the human predisposition to morality has not been irreparably blocked or distorted in childhood but, instead, has been developed so that as an adult the person has the capacity to be a responsible moral agent, good or evil, innocent or culpable. In his writings on education Kant also acknowledges that having the discipline and guidance of good teachers makes it easier for a child to become a good person, but Kant does not conclude that an unfortunate early education excuses one from the adult responsibility to avoid wrongdoing and to strive to become more virtuous.[27] Innate personality traits and feelings prompted by circumstances by themselves cannot make a person essentially a better or worse moral person, for this depends on what one chooses to do given the feelings and innate tendencies that one has.[28] The point is not just that these factors fail to determine completely how we behave but, rather, that feelings and innate dispositions are not the kind of thing that constitute moral goodness because they are, as it were, aspects of ourselves that we simply find ourselves having and they do not necessarily reflect what we choose to affirm or indulge. The primary question of ethics is "What ought I to do?" and this question arises only when we have reason to believe that what we do is up to us—a choice among options that we have, not something beyond our control (as this is commonly understood). Whether to have various natural dispositions and feelings is not typically among our options for choice, and so their presence or absence is not a measure of how well we are doing what we ought to do or an essential criterion for the worth of our acts and character.

This is not to say that the fine and appropriate feelings esteemed by other virtue theorists are insignificant in the attempt to lead a morally good life. For example, failure to feel sadness when seeing innocent people suffer or indignation at their being mistreated can be a fairly reliable sign that a person lacks a genuine moral commitment to the happiness of others as an end.[29] Some feelings, such as guilt, shame, agent-regret, resentment, and indignation, may be the effects rather than the causes of moral commitment in a normal human being or they may be analyzed as dispositions that are constitutive aspects of moral commitment rather than mere affects or inclinations. Feelings of sympathy and affection, as Kant says, can help to counteract the darker and more destructive inclinations that often tempt us to make bad choices.[30] For various reasons, then, a morally good person will want to cultivate many of the feelings that other theories of virtue treat as constitutive of virtue; in other words, a morally good person will have reason to aim to become the sort of person who is disposed to have such feelings. Similarly, because vicious feelings are among the obstacles that we sometimes have to overcome, a good person will also try to eliminate these feelings so far as possible.

A related feature of Kant's theory of virtue that is not shared by all is that moral goodness and virtue do not depend on one's accomplishments or success in achieving the good results that one earnestly strives for. This too may be considered a merit of the Kantian view, even if (as Thomas Nagel argues) in our uncritical judgments we often think of someone as a better person if her good efforts are successful than if they accidentally fail due to no fault of her own. Such judgments may stem largely from our inability to know that the unsuccessful person really failed despite the best moral commitment and effort and our suspicion that the bad outcome was not due purely to luck and accident. We punish murder more severely than attempted murder, but again this does not necessarily imply that merely the difference in outcome revealed a difference in the moral worth of those convicted of murder and those convicted of attempted murder. With uncertainty of motives and intentions, there may be room to suspect that one made a more serious attempt than the other, and the threat of the more severe penalty could be supposed to deter some would-be killers from trying hard to carry out their initial plan. Alternatively, critical reflection may lead us to change our judgments and treat murder and attempted murder as morally equivalent, especially when it is stipulated that nothing but luck distinguishes the cases. It is also worth mentioning that Kant distinguishes culpability from responsibility for the consequences of one's wrongdoing, for he implies that all of the consequences of acts contrary to duty can be imputed to the agent whether or not they were intended or even foreseen.[31] This claim no doubt needs to be qualified, but it shows that the Kantian thesis that the effects of one's actions do not determine one's moral worth does not mean that one cannot be liable for the bad effects even when unintended.

UNITY OF THE VIRTUES

There is significant controversy among virtue ethicists and scholars of ancient philosophy about how, if at all, the virtues are unified, but the basic idea is that having any one of the virtues entails having them all—true courage, for example, is said to require practical wisdom to determine what is worth fighting for, justice to refrain from violating the rights of others, and temperance to avoid succumbing to frivolous desires.[32] Kant distinguishes *virtue*, which is the strength of will to fulfill all of our duties from a sense of duty, from specific virtues, which are commitments to particular moral ends.[33] Someone has the virtue of generosity, for example, if she sets the happiness of others as one of her ends, from a sense of duty, and effectively structures her choices around that commitment. It is a *duty of virtue*, according to Kant, to be generous in this sense so a *virtuous person* has the strength of will to include help for others as one of her life's projects, despite inclinations or feelings she may have to the contrary. Kant therefore holds that there is only one virtuous disposition, which is a second-order readiness to do our duty from duty, but he denies that the specific *virtues*, such as beneficence, gratitude, and self-respect, mutually entail one another.[34]

Virtues, according to Kant, involve setting specific ends.[35] Some may be surprised at the number and variety of ends that we are required to adopt on Kant's view. Self-preservation is the virtue of preserving our lives, freedom, and rational capacities; self-respect is the virtue of valuing ourselves as persons with dignity; honesty is the virtue of scrutinizing ourselves and communicating our thoughts to others; thrift is the virtue of procuring and utilizing the means necessary for cheerfully enjoying the pleasures of life; self-improvement is the virtue of striving to perfect our natural and moral powers; beneficence is the virtue of setting the permissible ends of others as our own; gratitude is the virtue of honoring a benefactor for a kindness she has done for us; sympathy is the virtue of actively sharing in the feelings of others; sociability is the virtue of associating with others and forming friendships; and forgiveness is the virtue of not seeking or hoping for vengeance for wrongs done by others.[36] In his political and historical writings, Kant describes other ends that we are required to incorporate into our life projects, including perpetual peace, enlightenment, justice, and cultural development.

If virtue is strength of a good will, then presumably vice is strength of an evil will.[37] Kant thinks it is impossible for human beings to have diabolical wills, which will evil for its own sake, but we can will to subordinate morality to self-interest for the sake of satisfying our inclinations.[38] Kant also distinguishes *vice*, which is a firm commitment to immorality, from specific *vices*, which involve refusing to adopt specific ends.[39] Some vices involve principled refusals to adopt morally required ends, such as a commitment never to help others, while other vices involve simply failing to adopt certain ends, such as allowing others to violate our rights.[40]

Kant's list of vices is more robust than is commonly recognized. Kant offers his own conception of the seven deadly sins, for example: lust is the vice of surrendering ourselves to our sexual instincts; drunkenness and gluttony are vices of impairing our rational faculties; avarice or greed is the vice of procuring the means for enjoyment but not utilizing them and leaving one's true needs unmet; laziness is the vice of refusing to develop and utilize our natural powers; vengefulness is the vice of seeking or hoping for revenge for a wrong; envy is the vice of seeking to diminish the well-being of others because it is greater than one's own; and arrogance is the vice of demanding others lose respect for themselves and respect us more.[41] Other vices, according to Kant, include suicide, asceticism, servility, destroying feelings that promote morality, tempting others to immorality, malice, contempt, defamation, and ridicule.[42]

Kant denies that the virtues are unified because he thinks that possessing any one of the virtues does not generally entail having all or most of the others.[43] We can be beneficent toward someone, for instance, but hold her in contempt.[44] He thinks that some of the virtues can be united, however. In close friendships, we are drawn together by our mutual love but kept at a distance by our mutual respect.[45] And self-improvement involves striving to develop and maintain a virtuous disposition to do all of our duties from duty. But Kant thinks that the virtues usually impose limits on one another, as when respect for others involves acting as if our generosity is owed so that we do not humiliate the person we help.[46]

All duties, according to Kant, are united by the moral law, but duties of virtue in particular are further united by the part of the Categorical Imperative, as applied to human beings, that requires each of us to "regard himself, as well as every other human being, as his end."[47] Duties of virtue prescribe "many objects that it is also our duty to have as ends," but they are brought together as various ways of treating human beings as ends in themselves.[48] Duties of right, by contrast, are merely formal. They are concerned with "the consistency of outer freedom with itself if its maxim were made universal law," and are independent of the ends we happen to have.[49] Ethical duties are a third class of duty; they include all duties of virtue along with an indirect duty to do all of our duties of right from the motive of duty.[50]

Moral perfection, according to Kant, is an ideal that human beings must strive for even though we can never fully attain it. One reason is that human nature, according to Kant, includes inclinations and desires that tempt us to immorality, and our intentions, policies, and commitments are somewhat opaque to ourselves and to one another. When we attempt to imagine a morally perfect human being, therefore, it is impossible for us to say whether she is conforming to duty only from the motive of duty or whether her inclinations are moving her as well. A further reason Kant gives for why we can never fully attain moral perfection is that it is impossible for us to imagine, in any concrete way, what it consists in, so we can never be sure that any set of specific virtues is complete and free from traits that are not virtues. For all we can know, there may be virtues we have not considered, we may be mistaken in regarding certain characteristics as virtues, and we may not understand how the virtues cohere with one another. By analogy with perfect happiness, which is an end that we all have even though we can "never say definitely and self-consistently what it really is that they wish and will," the ideal of moral perfection is an end we must set for ourselves but it is not a fully determinate goal and the best we can do is strive ever closer to moral perfection.[51]

VIRTUE AS THE FULFILLMENT OF OUR MORAL NATURE

Virtue, according to Kant, is the fulfillment of our moral nature. Following the ancients, he describes someone who possesses virtue as "free," "a king," "healthy," and "rich."[52]

Virtue would make us *free* by subjecting our desires, inclinations, and natural capacities to our own free choices rather than allowing ourselves to be involuntarily determined by habits or impulses. A virtuous person possesses self-control, she chooses whether or not to indulge her inclinations, and she decides how she will put her powers to use in service of her freely chosen ends.[53] She also strives for self-sufficiency by training herself to eliminate desires for things she cannot attain, to do without superfluous pleasures, and to endure discomfort and misfortune, all while maintaining a cheerful spirit.[54] But a virtuous person does not attempt to rid herself of all inclination, nor does she intentionally impose discomforts on herself; she simply satisfies her basic needs and enjoys the pleasures of life within the bounds of morality without allowing herself to become dependent on them.[55]

When Kant claims, in the *Groundwork*, that "it must rather be the universal wish of every rational being to be wholly free" of inclinations, he does not mean that we should actually take steps to do so, for our inclinations are part of our nature and not evil in themselves, even though they can tempt us to immorality.[56] His point may instead be that the ideal of a holy will, which necessarily conforms to reason without any inclinations to the contrary, is nonetheless unattainable for human beings who are always subject to impure motives.[57]

For all we can know, even the most innocuous inclinations can lead us astray, so we may wish to be rid of our inclinations in order to ensure that morality moves us to conform to its laws. This is impossible for us given our human nature, so the best we can do is strive for perfect virtue by governing our inclinations, refusing to be controlled by them and eliminating ones that are contrary to duty. Moreover, once we have arranged our uncritical, unreflective inclination into a system of non-moral ends, a rational person may then wish to be free of any other inclinations that remain in order to pursue her freely chosen plans and projects within the bounds of morality without influence from her distracting impulses.

Virtue would make us *a king* by bringing our desires, inclinations, and natural capacities under the control of reason.[58] As rational agents, we have the bare capacity to conform to moral principles, but as human beings our sensuous nature can lead us astray. A virtuous person has mastery over herself; she practices good self-governance by ruling her desires, inclinations, mind, and body by reason; and so strives to achieve inner unity and peace.[59] Her will is both autonomous and autocratic; it has legislative power to settle on moral principles independent of inclinations but also executive power to carry out those commands despite inclinations to the contrary.[60] A virtuous person, however, is not a fanatic about morality; she does not

necessarily devote all of her time and energy to self-improvement, beneficence, or moralizing to others, but exercises her freedom, within the
bounds of duty, to set and pursue her own plans and projects.[61]

Virtue would make us *morally healthy* because our moral nature as free
and rational human beings is fulfilled when we come close to achieving inner
peace and self-mastery by firmly committing ourselves to moral principles.[62]
Virtue would also tend to make us *physically healthy* because a virtuous
person not only fulfills her duties to preserve and perfect her body and
mind, and enjoys the pleasures of life, but her well-being is less affected by
frustrated desires for superfluous things and misfortunes she might suffer.[63]

And virtue would make us *rich* because of the moral pleasure that comes
from having and exercising our firm commitment to do our duty from
duty.[64] Virtue makes us deserving of esteem from others, which may not be
forthcoming, and it may bring external goods or great hardship, but virtue
is its own reward because of the contentment and pleasure it would give us.
A virtuous person is rewarded with a cheerful outlook by recognizing that
she does not aim to do wrong and she stands ready to resist any temptation
to do so.[65] Such a person does not feel coerced or compelled by morality, she
is not gloomy, nor does she regard morality as an extorting tyrant. Although
she is morally constrained, she does her duty easily, with a tranquil mind.
Cultivating cheerfulness and tranquillity is also an effective means to developing virtue in order to overcome the discomforts that sometimes come
from doing our duty, as well as setting an example that leads others to
admire virtue. These attitudes are not essential to virtue, however, but are
consequences of being a virtuous person or means to becoming one.

Kant faced up to the fact, however, that virtue may leave us destitute,
despised, lonely, and unhappy while vice may result in wealth, prosperity,
and prestige.[66] Although the virtuous person enjoys moral pleasures while
the vicious one suffers pangs of conscience, we cannot be sure that most
virtuous people will also be the happiest, at least in this life, so Kant argues
that we must hope that someday virtue will be matched by reward in the
form of the highest good.

MORAL EDUCATION OF CHILDREN AND ADOLESCENTS

Kant's account of the cultivation of virtue can be seen as divided into two
parts. In works on pedagogy and practical anthropology Kant describes the
empirical conditions that (he believes) help to prepare a child for moral
agency, while in the Doctrine of Virtue he presents his account of the moral
duty of every competent moral agent to cultivate virtue.

Children, according to Kant, come with natural and moral predisposi-
tions that "lie within humanity," so the primary goal of moral education is
to "unfold humanity from its germs and to make it happen that the human
being reaches its vocation."[67] Kant distinguishes two stages of moral education: discipline of children and cultivation of adolescents. Without discipline at the first stage, we are left as "savages" who are slaves to our own
passions; and without cultivation at the second stage we remain in a "raw
state" in which our natural talents and moral abilities are undeveloped.[68]

The first stage of moral education sets constraints on the "lawless freedom" of children but otherwise allows them to develop naturally.[69] Early
on, children should be subjected to rules of the family or school, along with
rules of games, so that they learn to behave and control themselves in the
face of their emotions.

These rules share striking similarities with Kant's account of the nature
of the laws of a state, which he claims are universal, necessary, unambiguous, public, and meant to protect the external freedom of all rather than
govern inner motives. All children should obey the same age-appropriate
standards, without exception, and teachers and parents must not show
preference for one child over another when administering the rules. The
rules must be treated as necessary standards, specifying age-appropriate
duties that the children must perform exactly whether they want to or
not.[70] The rules should govern external acts rather than inner desires or
motivations and they should be announced in advance.[71] The content of the
rules should be publicly designed to secure the external freedom of everyone, prevent harm, and help the children develop physically by giving
sufficient time for sleep, work, and play.[72] Children should also be given
limited choice in specifying their own rules, such as when to go to bed
within a certain period, but they must be strictly held to the rules they set
for themselves.[73] And within the legitimate constraints of the rules, children must be given free rein to make their own choices.

Kant's account of how children should be punished is similar to his conception of legal punishment, which holds that the state should punish in
proportion to the degree and kind of legal violation (*lex talionis*) without
practicing disgraceful punishments, while the system of punishment itself
is justified by the need to protect the external freedom of all.[74] The rules for
children must similarly be enforced strictly, impartially, and with punishments that are proportional to the offense, but children should not be punished for the underlying motives that led them to obey or disobey.[75] Except
in cases of lying, children at this stage lack the concepts of shame and
honor so they should not be punished by making them feel ashamed,
showing them contempt, or treating them "frostily and coldly."[76] Parents

and teachers must not punish with demeaning or degrading treatment either, or attempt to break the wills of their children, for these can lead to a servile or slavish temperament. Nor should children be punished in ways that express excessive anger or rage, which can lead them to think that the rules are merely the result of someone's whims or emotions rather than universally necessary standards that are willed by a reasonable leader. Once the punishment is over, parents and teachers must not bear grudges against children and children should not be rewarded for following the rules.[77]

A system of publicly known and enforced rules of this sort helps children develop self-control, self-confidence, and a cheerful disposition.[78] They learn that their choices face resistance from the choices of other children, who are on equal footing with them, which teaches them self-reliance, the ability to distinguish themselves through merit, and reciprocity.[79]

Once the child has learned to exercise his freedom of choice under rules, usually in early adolescence, the next stage of moral education is to help him to "make good use of his freedom" under constraints.[80] Adolescents over the course of their lives must ultimately decide for themselves to incorporate morality into their most basic life-governing maxim. Kant suggests some ways we might prepare adolescents to choose to have a good will, to develop strength of will to put their basic moral commitment into practice, and to work out for themselves what it takes to respect dignity in themselves and others.[81]

Adolescents must not be taught morality by threat, punishment, or examples, but must learn to decide for themselves to act on universally necessary principles for the sake of duty itself.[82] The desires to be honored and loved by others, however, are "aids to morality," so once an adolescent has acquired the concept of honor, she should be shamed by looks of contempt and cold treatment for violating her duty, but physical punishment should not be used as a form of moral instruction.[83]

Adolescents have a latent notion of dignity that should be "made perceptible" to them. When an adolescent brings his own "idea of humanity before his eyes" he has "an original in his idea with which he compares himself."[84] Parents should avoid displaying vanity and encouraging it in their adolescents, so that young people learn to value themselves according to their own dignity rather than by the value that others place on them, which can lead to social vices such as arrogance and envy if they fail to do so.[85] Adolescents should be reminded that others have dignity as well, by, for example, forbidding them from giving orders to servants.[86] Some commentators have doubted that Kant regarded children as having dignity and rights, yet Kant emphasizes that when, for example, an adolescent arrogantly pushes a poorer child out of the way, instead of saying "Don't do that, it hurts the other one. You should have pity! It is a poor child," parents should reprimand them with contempt for violating "the rights of humanity."[87] Adolescents should also be made aware of the fundamental equality of persons, educated to the possibility of a better, more ideal world and encouraged in their cosmopolitan spirit.[88]

Kant suggests that a Socratic method can be used to elicit from the adolescent a "dry and earnest representation of duty."[89] By presenting a series of cases that involve doing one's duty from duty, despite obstacles, as well as ones that involve failures to do so, students refine their latent idea of duty, practice exercising their moral judgment, begin to work up for themselves a system of first-order duties, and come to admire the firm and steady resolve to do one's duty from duty.[90] Students might be asked, for example, whether it is right to give away property that is owed to others or to tell white lies for the common good, or they might be presented with a case of someone who is able to overcome his fear of death in order to refrain from bearing false witness.[91] Tutors should not present examples of doing one's duty from duty as extraordinary or meritorious, and they should avoid examples of "so-called *noble* (supermeritorious) actions" because they tend to engender "empty wishes and longings for inaccessible perfection."[92] Giving adolescents illustrative moral problems encourages a habit of moral approval and disapproval as a foundation for "uprightness in the future conduct of life"; it also leads them to take pleasure in moral thinking and elicits an awareness and exaltation of their freedom over inclination, their rational disposition to do their duty from duty, and a sense of their own worth as persons with dignity.[93]

THE DUTY OF MORAL SELF-IMPROVEMENT

Once an adolescent has reached the stage of adulthood, when her rational capacities are sufficiently developed that actions can be fully imputed to her as their author, she is then under a duty to herself to continue perfecting her own moral powers. Kant's most explicit discussion of moral self-improvement is in his Doctrine of Virtue (*The Metaphysics of Morals*, Part II). The context is his discussion of ends that are duties for all morally responsible persons to adopt and pursue. Under the most general description, these are the duties to promote one's own perfection and the happiness of others.[94] The former are divided into "On a Human Being's Duty to Himself to Develop and Increase His Natural Perfection, That Is, for a Pragmatic Purpose" and "On a Human Being's Duty to Himself to Increase His Moral Perfection, That Is, for a Moral Purpose Only."[95] Kant classifies these as "duties to oneself." This implies that the responsibility to fulfill the duty lies with each person, and it is not in general the business of others to try to make a person naturally or morally better ("more perfect"). Moreover, the primary reason why one should strive to improve oneself is not to enable one to fulfill duties to others but to treat one's own humanity as an end in itself.[96]

Kant divides duties to oneself into "perfect" and "imperfect" duties. Perfect duties to oneself "as an animal being" include duties to avoid suicide, gluttony, drunkenness, and "defiling oneself by lust," and perfect duties to oneself "as a moral being" include duties to avoid lying, avarice, and servility.[97] Imperfect duties to oneself include both the duty to increase one's natural perfection and—our primary concern here—*the duty to oneself to increase one's moral perfection*.[98] Imperfect duties, Kant says, do not prescribe particular actions but only "the maxim of actions." By this Kant apparently means that imperfect duties only specify general types of attitudes and actions (e.g., "love of one's neighbor" and "love of one's parents").[99] The moral law in prescribing maxims of action "leaves a playroom (*latitudo*) for free choice in following (complying with) the law."[100] Kant hastens to add that this does not mean "permission to make exception to the maxim of actions but only to limit one maxim of duty by another," thereby widening "the field for the practice of virtue."[101] Kant evidently means at least that no one is exempt from the requirement to adopt and comply with imperfect duties, but scholars disagree about what more he means. Some have suggested that Kant means that missing an opportunity to work toward fulfilling one imperfect duty (e.g., to help one's neighbor) is impermissible unless we are instead fulfilling some other duty (e.g., helping one's parents). This reading, however, seems both implausibly rigoristic and not a position that Kant consistently affirms.[102]

Another distinguishing feature of imperfect duties, according to Kant, is this: "Fulfillment of them is merit (*meritum*) = +a; but failure to fulfill them is not in itself culpability (*demeritum*) = –a, but rather deficiency in moral worth = 0, unless the subject should make it his principle not to comply with such duties."[103] This makes sense with respect to improving one's natural capacities and promoting others' happiness, but it is puzzling with respect to moral self-improvement. Obviously Kant did not mean that we can rest content with an aim to avoid wrongdoing 90 percent or even 99 percent of the time, blamelessly indulging our vices the rest of the time. We must sincerely make it our principle to try to cultivate virtue, but arguably we are not culpable for falling short of perfect virtue *insofar as this is due to the frailty of human nature or the indeterminacy of the duty*. The duty to increase one's moral perfection is not fully analogous to the duties to promote others' happiness and develop one's natural capacities. Kant says that the duty to increase one's moral perfection "is a *narrow* and *perfect* one in terms of ... quality ... and *imperfect* in terms of ... degree, because of the *frailty (fragilitas)* of human nature."[104] The narrow and perfect duty, presumably, is to strive persistently toward moral perfection—a developed and effective will to fulfill all one's duties for the right reasons. The object of the duty (moral perfection and purity) is an uncompromised ideal, even though no exact degree of improvement toward the ideal can be specified as expected at any given time. The frailty of human nature apparently refers to the facts that we are constantly liable to inclinations contrary to duty and that a ready effective will to overcome these inner obstacles (virtue) is not innate but is something that we have a hard and unending task to cultivate. Also, "the unfathomable depths of the human heart" mean that we cannot measure our progress or know exactly what particular steps we need to take.[105] Kant suggests that scrutinizing one's motives for self-deceptive excuses, being alert to one's conscience, and keeping the basic moral law in mind are potentially helpful aids to self-improvement, but they are hardly sufficient. In Kant's view, in fact, there are no specific steps or empirical conditions that can ensure progress toward moral perfection because this ultimately is a matter of strengthening one's moral commitment and resolve so that it is more effective. What moral agents will and how they can strengthen their wills, in Kant's view, is not empirically determinable.

OBJECTIONS AND REPLIES

One common criticism of the Kantian moral agent is that she is a cold, unfeeling, emotionless, and purely rational monster. Kant's conception of rationality, however, as it applies to human agents, is not the narrow kind invoked by economists and rational choice theorists, but is closer to our common understanding of a reasonable person—someone who is sane, sensible, and fair-minded. A fully rational person, according to Kant, is not just consistent and coherent in her mental states, she is also committed to treating humanity in herself and others as an end in itself; she respects others and is genuinely concerned to promote their well-being; she is grateful, honest, forgiving, and sociable, and not just as means to promoting her own ends; and she hopes for a peaceful, just, and enlightened future. It's true that Kant downplays the role of feelings, but a commonsense understanding of emotions may involve rational commitments of the sort Kant describes along with associated feelings that tend to result in human beings who adopt such policies.[106] Love, for example, may just be a practical commitment to do good for someone; but human beings who love others in this way also tend to have feelings of various kinds even if those feelings themselves are not essential to loving someone. And, as we have suggested, Kant thinks that feelings are an aid to morality and reward us for doing our duty, they are not good or bad in themselves, and they are an important part of what a virtuous person is free to enjoy within the bounds of morality.

Another objection to Kant's conception of the virtuous agent is that she will spend her life fixated on duty and striving for moral sainthood, to the detriment of other worthy pursuits.[107] Kant is very concerned, however, to emphasize that morality affords us significant latitude to form and pursue our own aims and projects—our ability to set and pursue our own ends, after all, is part of what makes us ends in ourselves. Although we are required to incorporate various kinds of ends into our conception of the good, such as the happiness of others, Kant thinks it is important that we are free, within the bounds of perfect duty, to decide how to organize and pursue those ends and to engage with many other kinds of values over the course of our lives. Even the requirement to strive for perfect virtue is itself a wide duty that allows us, on particular occasions, to pursue various non-moral activities. Kant is also highly critical of the "fantastically virtuous," who *"allows nothing to be morally indifferent* and strews all his steps with duties, as with mantraps," for he thinks that such a person is merely concerned "with petty details" such as "whether I eat meat or fish, drink beer or wine, supposing that both agree with me."[108]

Finally, Kant's moral theory may seem to be a rigoristic and burdensome system of rules that leaves little or no room for judgment, inventiveness, or sensitivity to context and uncertainty. A virtuous person, on Kant's view, conforms to strict duties, values moral ends of various kinds, and has a firm and strong will to do all that morality requires for the sake of duty. She does not experience moral requirements as burdens that she would rather be rid of, however, and she must exercise her judgment to decide what her perfect duties require on particular occasions and how best to express her commitment to moral ends. And, Kant's absolute prohibitions on, for example, lying and certain types of suicide may not be justified by his basic ethical framework, so a suitably reconstructed set of mid-level moral requirements that interpret and apply the Categorical Imperative to persistent human conditions may allow far more exceptions, sensitivity, and room for moral judgment.[109]

The standards of morality, according to Kant, are necessary requirements of reason, but our human nature affects how we learn, experience, and act on these principles. We are predisposed to recognize morality as authoritative, but guidance from enlightened teachers helps us commit ourselves to do what is right and adopt a variety of moral values and ends. Even then morality remains a constraint on our imperfect wills because we are always tempted by our natural inclinations and desires, so we also need a firm and considered resolve to follow through on our moral commitments. A person's moral character, according to Kant, does not depend on her temperament, habits, or feelings but on whether she has committed herself to morality above all else and possesses the strength of will to put that commitment into practice.

NOTES

1. Kant's works are abbreviated with these symbols followed by volume and pages in the standard Prussian Academy Edition:

   G—*Groundwork for the Metaphysics of Morals*
   MM—*The Metaphysics of Morals*
   R—*Religion within the Boundaries of Mere Reason Alone*
   CPrR—*Critique of Practical Reason*
   CJ—*Critique of the Power of Judgment*
   LP—*Lectures on Pedagogy*
   C—Collins' Lecture Notes
   V—Vigilantius' Lecture Notes

2. See also the preface and introduction to MM 6: 205–21.
3. MM 6: 380, 383, 390.
4. MM 6: 397, 441, 484.
5. MM 6: 219–21, 394.
6. MM 6: 388, 442.
7. MM 6: 443, 457.
8. R 6: 4–7, 97–98; CPrR 5: 110–32.
9. MM 6: 380, 405–408, 477. See also Henry E. Allison, *Kant's Theory of Freedom* (Cambridge: Cambridge University Press, 1990): 162–79; Paul Guyer, *Kant on Freedom, Law, and Happiness* (Cambridge: Cambridge University Press, 2000), 303–23; and Allen W. Wood, *Kantian Ethics* (Cambridge: Cambridge University Press, 2008), 142–58.
10. G 4: 394–402. A good will in this sense is an individual's choice, resolve, or will to do one's duty, not simply the inevitable predisposition to morality that, in Kant's view, is shared by all moral agents, even the worst. At G 4: 455, however, Kant apparently uses "good will" to refer to the latter.
11. *Inclinations* are natural or acquired tendencies, dispositions to act that are, in a sense, given facts with which we must deal, not inherently rational dispositions or tendencies that we can normally control at will. *Respect for (moral) law*, by contrast, is a disposition to conform to rational moral principles because one recognizes them as rational. To say that one has no inclination to do one's duty does not mean that one has no motivating tendency (moral "interest") in doing so, for in Kant's

view recognition of a rational requirement tends to be motivating for rational agents (i.e., "pure reason can be practical").

12. G 4: 414, 439.
13. G 4: 413–21.
14. G 4: 393–94.
15. In his own moral judgments Kant sometimes allowed exceptions to norms that apply in most circumstances—for example, Kant allowed that killing in a just war or judicially prescribed execution is justified even though killing other human beings is generally wrong. His other principles, however, often allowed few if any exceptions, and so when a person with a good will held to these regardless of the consequences, that person might seem to be maintaining his good will (or "purity") at the expense of others' suffering, but if his judgment is mistaken in such cases the error is not that he overvalued a good will but that his principles of duty were too rigorous.
16. For more discussion of the point see Thomas E. Hill, "Is a Good Will Overrated?" in *Human Welfare and Moral Worth: Kantian Perspectives* (Oxford: Oxford University Press, 2002), 38–60. The abstract thesis that a good will and only a good will is good without qualification does not by itself tell us what duty requires, but it is a first step in the argument of *Groundwork* I for a principle that does enable us to determine what duty requires. G 4: 402–403.
17. G 4: 402, 420–21.
18. G 4: 389.
19. G 4: 394.
20. R 6: 29.
21. MM 6: 380, 383–84, 387, 390, 394, 404–10, 479–80.
22. G 4: 402, 421; MM 6: 225–26.
23. MM 6: 213, 18, 226. Gregor translates *Willkür* as "choice" and *Wille* as "will."
24. R 6: 29–39.
25. See Thomas E. Hill, "Kant on Weakness of Will," in *Virtue, Rules, and Justice: Kantian Aspirations*, (Oxford: Oxford University Press, 2012), 107–28. One might doubt that such conflicts of will are possible in light of Kant's discussion of good and evil wills in the *Religion*, which may suggest that each and every action must be ultimately explained or rationalized in terms of our life-governing maxim. For an alternative account of Kant's conception of weakness of will along these lines, see Adam Cureton, "Kant on Cultivating a Good and Stable Will," in *Perspectives on Character*, ed. I. Fileva (Oxford: Oxford University Press, forthcoming).
26. MM 6: 384, 405, 447.
27. CPrR 5: 97–100.
28. See, for example, G 4: 394, 398–99.
29. For more discussion, see Thomas E. Hill, "Moral Dilemmas, Gaps, and Residues," in *Human Welfare and Moral Worth: Kantian Perspectives* (Oxford: Oxford University Press, 2002), 362–402.
30. MM 6: 457.
31. MM 6: 227–28. Interpretation and problems are discussed in Thomas E. Hill, "Kant on Responsibility for Consequences," in *Respect, Pluralism, and Justice: Kantian Perspectives* (Oxford: Oxford University Press, 2000), 155–72.
32. Rosalind Hursthouse, *On Virtue Ethics* (Oxford: Oxford University Press, 1999); John McDowell, "Virtue and Reason," *The Monist* 62, no. 3 (1979): 331–50; and John M. Cooper ("The Unity of Virtue," *Social Philosophy and Policy* 15, no. 1 [1998]: 233–74) accept this thesis while Christine Swanton, *Virtue Ethics: A Pluralistic*

View (Oxford: Oxford University Press, 2003) and Robert Merrihew Adams, *A Theory of Virtue: Excellence in Being for the Good* (Oxford: Oxford University Press, 2006) do not. There are stronger and weaker versions of the unity of the virtues thesis: Gary Watson, "Virtues in excess" (*Philosophical Studies* 46, no. 1 [1984]: 57–74) suggests that having any one of the virtues entails being open to moral considerations grounded in the others; A. D. M. Walker, "Virtue and Character" (*Philosophy* 64, no. 249 [1989]: 349–62) suggests no set of characteristics counts as a virtue if it leads to violation of the minimal requirements of any other virtue; and Cooper interprets Socrates as arguing that the usual names of particular virtues all refer to the very same property, which is virtue in its entirety.

33. MM 6: 395, 406.
34. MM 6: 395, 406, 410, 447.
35. MM 6: 394, 419.
36. MM 6: 621, 435, 429–30, 452, 456, 473, 461.
37. MM 6: 384, 391, 408.
38. R 6: 35–36.
39. MM 6: 384.
40. MM 6: 390, 408, 464, 419.
41. MM 6: 404, 432; V 27–657.
42. MM 6: 485, 452, 443, 393–94.
43. In a puzzling passage Kant denies the "ancient dicta" that "There is only one virtue and one vice" (MM 6: 405) because he claims that it is a feature of his ethical framework that "For any one duty only *one* ground of obligation can be found; and if someone produces two or more proofs for a duty, this is a sure sign either that he has not yet found a valid proof or that he has mistaken two or more different duties for one" (MM 6: 403). It is unclear how Kant thinks these claims are related other than that in his rationalist framework there are distinguishable duties of virtue, and so virtues.
44. MM 6: 448.
45. MM 6: 469.
46. MM 6: 449–50.
47. MM 6: 395, 410.
48. MM 6: 410.
49. MM 6: 380.
50. MM 6: 219–21.
51. G 4: 418; MM 6: 384, 405, 447.
52. MM 6: 405.
53. MM 6: 407, 408; V 27: 626.
54. C 27: 392, 394; MM 6: 484.
55. MM 6: 484–85; R 6: 34–35.
56. G 4: 428, R 6: 21, 34–35.
57. MM 6: 383, 405.
58. MM 6: 408.
59. C 27: 368.
60. MM 6: 383; V 29: 626.
61. MM 6: 408–409.
62. MM 6: 384, 409.
63. MM 6: 484–85.
64. MM 6: 391.
65. MM 6: 485.

66. V 29: 623.
67. LP 9: 445.
68. LP 9: 440–42. The stages are divided somewhat differently in the section of the Collins lecture notes called "Of duties in regard to differences in age" (C 27: 466–71).
69. LP 9: 459; C 27: 467.
70. LP 9: 482; 488.
71. LP 9: 481.
72. LP 9: 449, 455.
73. LP 9: 481–82.
74. MM 6: 331–33.
75. LP 9: 481–84.
76. LP 9: 465, 482, 484.
77. LP 9: 481–84.
78. LP 483, 485, 491–92.
79. LP 9: 442–43, 453–54.
80. LP 9: 453, CJ 5: 431.
81. LP 9: 475.
82. LP 9: 480.
83. LP 9: 482–84.
84. LP 9: 489.
85. LP 9: 498.
86. LP 9: 486, 491.
87. LP 9: 490. See Christine M. Korsgaard, *The Sources of Normativity* (Cambridge: Cambridge University Press, 1996); Allen Wood, "Kant on Duties Regarding Nonrational Nature," *Aristotelian Society Suppl.* 72 (1998): 189–228.
88. LP 9: 447, 499.
89. CPrR 5: 157; MM 6: 411–12.
90. MM 6: 484; CPrR 5: 154; R 6:48.
91. LP 9: 490; CPrR 5: 35.
92. CPrR 5: 155, 157; R 6:49.
93. CPrR 5: 154, 160–61.
94. MM 6: 385–88, 391–94.
95. MM 6: 444–47.
96. For more regarding Kant's idea of duties to oneself, as we interpret it, see Thomas E. Hill, "Kant's Tugendlehre as Normative Ethics," in *Virtue, Rules, and Justice: Kantian Aspirations* (Oxford: Oxford University Press, 2012), 234–55.
97. MM 6: 421–37.
98. MM 6: 444–47.
99. The reference here is to "practical love" rather than feelings of affection. Practical love requires an active commitment to promote the (permissible) ends of others. See MM 6: 449–50.
100. MM 6: 390.
101. MM 6: 390.
102. See, for example, David Cummiskey, *Kantian Consequentialism* (New York: Oxford University Press, 1996), 110–11, 116; Thomas E. Hill, "Meeting Needs and Doing Favors," in *Human Welfare and Moral Worth: Kantian Perspectives* (Oxford: Oxford University Press, 2002), 219–24.
103. MM 6: 390.
104. MM 6: 446. Kant's emphasis.
105. MM 6: 447.

106. See, for example, Martha Craven Nussbaum, *Upheavals of Thought: The Intelligence of Emotions* (New York: Cambridge University Press, 2001).
107. See, for example, Susan Wolf, "Moral Saints," *Journal of Philosophy* 79, no. 8 (1982): 419–39.
108. MM 6: 409. Kant's emphasis.
109. Kant's discussions of practical issues ("applied ethics") in *The Metaphysics of Morals, Lectures,* and elsewhere often show a more subtle and qualified understanding of the implications of the Categorical Imperative than is evident in the *Groundwork.* Even so, few Kant scholars defend all of Kant's particular moral judgments as entailed by the best interpretations of the Categorical Imperative. (The most brilliant physicists are not necessarily infallible or even best at applying principles of physics to building bridges.) Some Kantians attempt to explain how the basic moral framework expressed in the Categorical Imperative can warrant more circumscribed and tenable moral judgments on practical issues than Kant himself endorsed. See, for example, Thomas E. Hill, *Virtue, Rules, and Justice: Kantian Aspirations* (Oxford: Oxford University Press, 2012), chs. 12–14; Onora O'Neill, *Towards Justice and Virtue* (Cambridge: Cambridge University Press, 1996); Wood, *Kantian Ethics.*

BIBLIOGRAPHY

Adams, Robert Merrihew. *A Theory of Virtue: Excellence in Being for the Good.* Oxford: Oxford University Press, 2006.

Allison, Henry E. *Kant's Theory of Freedom.* Cambridge: Cambridge University Press, 1990.

Cooper, John M. "The Unity of Virtue." *Social Philosophy and Policy* 15, no.1 (1998): 233–74.

Cummiskey, David. *Kantian Consequentialism.* New York: Oxford University Press, 1996.

Cureton, Adam. "Kant on Cultivating a Good and Stable Will." In *Perspectives on Character,* edited by I. Fileva. Oxford: Oxford University Press, forthcoming.

Guyer, Paul. *Kant on Freedom, Law, and Happiness.* Cambridge: Cambridge University Press, 2000.

Hill, Thomas E. "Is a Good Will Overrated?" In *Human Welfare and Moral Worth: Kantian Perspectives,* 83–60. Oxford: Oxford University Press, 2002.

Hill, Thomas E. "Kant on Responsibility for Consequences," In *Respect, Pluralism, and Justice: Kantian Perspectives,* 155–72. Oxford: Oxford University Press, 2000.

Hill, Thomas E. "Kant on Weakness of Will." In *Virtue, Rules, and Justice: Kantian Aspirations,* 107–28. Oxford: Oxford University Press, 2012.

Hill, Thomas E. "Kant's Tugendlehre as Normative Ethics." In *Virtue, Rules, and Justice: Kantian Aspirations,* 234–55. Oxford: Oxford University Press, 2012.

Hill, Thomas E. "Meeting Needs and Doing Favors." In *Human Welfare and Moral Worth: Kantian Perspectives,* 201–43. Oxford: Oxford University Press, 2002.

Hill, Thomas E. "Moral Dilemmas, Gaps, and Residues." In *Human Welfare and Moral Worth: Kantian Perspectives,* 362–402. Oxford: Oxford University Press, 2002.

Hill, Thomas E. *Virtue, Rules, and Justice: Kantian Aspirations.* Oxford: Oxford University Press, 2012.

Hursthouse, Rosalind. *On Virtue Ethics*. Oxford: Oxford University Press, 1999.

Kant, Immanuel. *Critique of the Power of Judgment*. Edited by Paul Guyer and Eric Matthews. Cambridge: Cambridge University Press, 2000.

Kant, Immanuel. *Critique of Practical Reason*. Edited by Mary J. Gregor. Cambridge: Cambridge University Press, 2007.

Kant, Immanuel. *Groundwork for the Metaphysics of Morals*. Edited by Thomas E. Hill, translated by Arnulf Zweig. Oxford: Oxford University Press, 2002.

Kant, Immanuel. "Kant on the Metaphysics of Morals: Vigilantius's Lecture Notes." In *Lectures on Ethics*, edited by P. L Heath and J. B. Schneewind, 249–52. Cambridge: Cambridge University Press, 2001.

Kant, Immanuel. "Lectures on Pedagogy." In *Anthropology, History, and Education*, edited by G. Zöller and R. B. Louden, 486–527. Cambridge: Cambridge University Press, 2007.

Kant, Immanuel. *The Metaphysics of Morals*. Translated by Mary J. Gregor. New York: Cambridge University Press, 1996.

Kant, Immanuel. "Moral Philosophy: Collins's Lecture Notes." In *Lectures on Ethics*, edited by P. L Heath and J. B. Schneewind, 37–222. Cambridge: Cambridge University Press, 2001.

Kant, Immanuel. *Religion Within the Boundaries of Mere Reason*. Edited by Allen W. Wood and George DiGiovanni. Cambridge: Cambridge University Press, 1998.

Korsgaard, Christine M. *The Sources of Normativity*. Cambridge: Cambridge University Press, 1996.

McDowell, John. "Virtue and Reason." *The Monist* 62, no. 3 (1979): 331–50.

Nagel, Thomas. "Moral Luck." In *Mortal Questions*, 24–38. Cambridge: Cambridge University Press, 1979.

Nussbaum, Martha Craven. *Upheavals of Thought: The Intelligence of Emotions*. New York: Cambridge University Press, 2001.

O'Neill, Onora. *Towards Justice and Virtue*. Cambridge: Cambridge University Press, 1996.

Swanton, Christine. *Virtue Ethics: A Pluralistic View*. Oxford: Oxford University Press, 2003.

Walker, A. D. M. "Virtue and Character." *Philosophy* 64, no. 249 (1989): 349–62.

Watson, Gary. "Virtues in Excess." *Philosophical Studies* 46, no. 1 (1984): 57–74.

Wolf, Susan. "Moral Saints." *Journal of Philosophy* 79, no. 8 (1982): 419–39.

Wood, Allen. "Kant on Duties Regarding Nonrational Nature." *Aristotelian Society Supplement* 72 (1998): 189–228.

Wood, Allen. *Kantian Ethics*. Cambridge: Cambridge University Press, 2008.

CHAPTER 5

Cultivating Virtue

Two Problems for Virtue Ethics

CHRISTINE SWANTON

1. INTRODUCTION

This collection of essays concerns an extremely important topic in virtue ethics: the idea that virtue is something learned and developed in a sustained and continuing way from early childhood through the rest of one's life. Indeed, Julia Annas goes so far as to say: "We cannot understand what virtue is without understanding how we acquire it."[1]

Yet paradoxically, this important insight is the source of persistent problems which threaten to undermine virtue ethics as a moral theory. According to virtue ethics, leading a life of virtue involves a commitment to learning to be virtuous, further developing one's virtue, and maintaining what virtues one has. Yet this very commitment allegedly gives rise to two problems internal to virtue ethics. In what follows I argue that the problems are indeed serious for a certain form of virtue ethics, but that virtue ethics need not possess the structure that generates these problems.

What are these problems? The first is the much discussed self-centeredness objection. According to the basic form of the objection, virtue ethics is committed to the view that the proper motivation for acts is the pursuit of one's own virtue, since her *own eudaimonia* (flourishing) is what a virtuous agent pursues, and since as Aristotle claims excellence of character is the finest good *for* an agent, it is the most important constituent of *eudaimonia*. The virtuous agent is thus primarily concerned with her own virtue, and thereby with cultivating and maintaining it, but surely, it is thought, she should have as her primary focus such things as caring for friends, repaying debts because that is just, being a good parent.

The second problem has also received considerable attention. In an objection to virtue ethics owed to Robert Johnson, virtue ethics cannot account for many right acts of the self-improving but not yet virtuous agent.[2] These are acts that are intuitively thought to be right (such as breaking the promise that is best in the circumstances to break when one culpably has made conflicting ones), but would not be performed by a virtuous agent (who does not culpably make conflicting promises). In particular, standard virtue ethical criteria of right action, according to the objection, are incompatible with the possibility that non-virtuous agents can perform right acts that would not be performed by virtuous agents. Such acts may be fitting for agents in the process of cultivating virtue, or who need to somehow rectify previous wrong acts.

The first of these problems is the topic of section 2–4 and the second the topic of sections 5 and 6.

2. THE SELF-CENTEREDNESS OBJECTION TO VIRTUE ETHICS

One would think that by now the self-centeredness objection has been well and truly dealt with by virtue ethicists. But the objection never seems to go away. This suggests it is more serious than virtue ethicists have taken it to be. We begin with a standard account of the self-centeredness objection. We then consider a deeper form of the objection which is not rebutted by standard replies.

The standard self-centeredness objection to virtue ethics is best described as a cluster of problems. There are in fact three related problems. Virtue ethics (at least in its eudaimonistic Aristotelian version) is vulnerable to what might be called the "narcissism objection," escape from which raises the "self-effacing objection." In order to avoid that in turn, and without re-inviting the narcissism objection in some form, it becomes vulnerable to what I shall dub the "disconnect objection."

In more detail, the problem cluster may be described as follows.

(1) Narcissism Objection

According to the *narcissism objection*, the final end of a virtuous agent is taken to be her *own eudaimonia* (usually understood as flourishing).

Since excellence of her own character is the finest good *for* an agent, and thereby the most central component of *eudaimonia*, her own virtue possession is what a virtuous (or would-be virtuous) agent pursues and is ultimately motivated by, for that is what ultimately benefits her. This motivation is intolerably narcissistic and is surely not the mark of virtue.

In reply, as virtue ethicists in the eudaimonist tradition are now tired of pointing out, the good-making or right-making features of *actions* are not characteristically features which promote or constitute the flourishing of the agent, but are the sorts of things that Bernard Williams calls the "X reasons."[3] These are reasons, associated with a virtue, which a virtuous person is characteristically motivated by, and of course they are many and varied, and circumstance dependent. For Williams (and for Hursthouse,[4] who follows him in this respect) a person who wants to do what the virtuous person would do should characteristically be motivated not by a motive under the description "promoting my own virtue or happiness" but under the description "repaying a debt," for example.

However this escape from the narcissism objection, it is claimed, lands the virtue ethicist with the self-effacing objection.[5]

(2) Self-Effacing Objection

According to the *self-effacing objection*, a theory vulnerable to the objection has the following flaw. Assume it is the case that (on that theory) what *ultimately* justifies an action as good or right is that it is conducive to or exemplifies my flourishing (as Hurka believes is a commitment of [eudaimonistic] virtue ethics).[6] Nonetheless (according to that theory) the agent in aiming at the good or right must put such an ultimate justification out of her mind when she acts, for if she does not do this, she would indeed be narcissistic. Rather, she should be motivated by the "X reasons" (as described above).

In reply, it may be claimed that even if the final end of an agent is her own flourishing, that final end does not justify actions as right for the eudaimonist virtue ethicist, not even ultimately. One's own flourishing is not part of the criterion of the right, which (on the type of virtue ethics criticized) is determined by or at least co-extensive with the choices of a virtuous agent, and is not even a *prima facie* rational or moral motivation that has to be effaced. This reply, however, makes the eudaimonist vulnerable to the *disconnect objection*.

(3) Disconnect Objection

According to the *disconnect objection*, the motivational structures appropriate to one level (the final ends of agents) do not connect with those appropriate to the other (performing right and virtuous acts). An agent's final ends pertaining to her own virtue do not connect with her everyday motivations.

In reply to the "disconnect" worry, one might point out that Annas establishes a connection by postulating that the "final end" unifies the various subordinate goals of one's life, and by claiming that this end is *eudaimonia* (one's own happiness or flourishing).[7] However, it may be argued, if the agent's final end is her *own* flourishing, then her *unifying* ultimate motivation must be egocentric for she is ultimately motivated by what benefits *her*. If, by contrast, her motivations have only to do with the "X reasons," the disconnect problem re-emerges.

It may seem that there is a way out of this problem. Why assume, as do at least many contemporary eudaimonists, that the final end of the agent is her own flourishing? If the final end (*eudaimonia*) is properly specified as "living well and finely" and "doing well," then *eudaimonia* is merely a formal notion having no necessary connection with agent *benefit*.[8] Living and acting well is a thin notion which may be thickened or interpreted in a variety of ways. A life "well lived" may be admirable, flourishing, meaningful, or successful.[9] Such a life may be admirable but unsuccessful, admirable but not flourishing, meaningful but not admirable or successful, and successful by normal standards but not flourishing. On this reply to the self-centeredness objection, unless the ultimate grounds of virtue lie wholly in agent benefit, not even the ultimate motivations of a virtuous agent (living well) are self-centered.

However, there is another form of the self-centeredness objection for which this reply does not work. According to this version of the objection, which I call, following David Solomon, the "deeper level" version of the objection, the reason for the alleged self-centeredness of the agent's moral attention and motivation lies in the logic of (eudaimonist) virtue ethics' conception of the final end of the agent.[10] Since on this view having virtue is the most important aspect of an agent's final end, I as a moral agent must hold that "having...virtue is the most important thing for me; practically I must subordinate everything else to this."[11] This "self-centered" feature, claims Solomon, is "ineliminable within virtue ethics."[12] Though the "deeper level" objection does not presuppose that what makes a trait a virtue is ultimately grounded in what benefits the agent, for virtue ethics on Solomon's view motivation is at bottom egocentric. It is as we shall call it, for short, "personal virtue motivation."

3. REBUTTING THE "DEEPER LEVEL" OBJECTION: FIRST ATTEMPT

The initial attempt at overcoming the "deeper level" self-centeredness objection assumes that Solomon is right in his view that, according to virtue ethics, for a moral agent, "having...virtue is the most important thing for me; practically I must subordinate everything else to this." I marshal arguments replying to this form of the objection and show that they fail. In the next section, I show that virtue ethics is not as such committed to Solomon's assumption.

To understand the depth of the problem of personal virtue motivation, consider the problems allegedly associated with sympathetic motivation. According to those of a Kantian persuasion, such motivation is self-centered in a problematic way, for the following reason. According to the Kantian objection, sympathetic motivation is motivation which at bottom counts as the reason for helping someone "*I* feel like it," "*I* feel moved by his plight," and so forth.[13] Call this kind of sympathetic motivation "personal sympathetic motivation." Personal sympathetic motivation is not ultimately motivation that *she* is in need and it is right on this occasion to satisfy that need, for if it were, the sympathetic nature of the motivation would be otiose. Analogously, it may be claimed, personal virtue motivation also has as one's ultimate reason for helping someone in need: "It is a virtuous action and being virtuous is the most important thing for *me*."

A reply to the problem of personal virtue motivation is analogous to that argued by defenders of sympathetic motivation. According to them, sympathetic motivation is not personal sympathetic motivation. The right way to understand sympathetic motivation is as follows:

> Sympathetic motivation does not amount to treating the consideration *that I feel like helping* as my reason for acting. A sympathetically motivated person feels like helping, but that is not itself the content of the reason she recognizes for helping. The content of her reason is *that he needs help*: the emotional state of feeling like helping is itself, at least in part, her state of recognizing this reason.[14]

I would claim further that such motivation should be understood as helping someone *out of* sympathy where the "out of" locution signifies that the action is *expressive* of one's sympathy. One's own sympathy does not feature as a state *for the sake of which* one acts, such as relieving one's discomfort, satisfying one's wants, expressing one's feelings.[15] That for the sake of which one acts when acting (virtuously) sympathetically is, for example, "satisfying her need by helping her."

Assume that Solomon is right that virtue ethics is committed to personal virtue motivation. Perhaps such motivation should be construed as motivation *expressing* a fundamental concern: that of the supreme importance of my possessing virtue. Such expression is not to be confused with the egocentric motivation of acting for the sake of expressing one's own virtue, let alone for the sake of further cultivating one's virtue. There is, however, a problem with this reply. What is it to *express* commitment to this final end when one helps another? It does not seem right to say that people who somehow express their valuing of their own virtue in helping another act *out* of this concern as if this were akin to acting out of or from an emotion such as sympathy. Rather, their actions would express that concern in a counterfactual way: if they were to succumb to temptations not to help because they would be missing out on fun or pleasure, if they felt too tired or lazy to help, or if they were indifferent to their plight, they would be ashamed and alienated from themselves.

The problem with personal virtue motivation lies deeper and has no analogue with sympathetic motivation. Those motivated by sympathy, even by personal sympathetic motivation, are not committed to the view that their sympathy is the most important thing for them, whereas those with personal virtue motivation do think that their own virtue is the most important thing for them. Is there not something deplorably narcissistic in possessing a value structure where your own virtue has greater importance to you than others being helped?

Here is a reply which might defuse the re-emergence of the narcissism objection but which is ultimately unsatisfactory. It may be said that the objection misconstrues the nature of the good to which a virtuous agent is committed. When I claim that "having...virtue is the most important thing for me," I am seeing my own virtue as a "partial good."[16] Such goods are defined as goods "constituted by attitudes of personal partiality."[17] They include one's own (worthwhile) projects, one's own friends, one's own children, one's own good character, and activities related to those goods such as working on one's philosophy papers, cultivating one's character, and relating to one's children. One may have as one's highest partial good (in the field of one's own projects) working on one's philosophy papers without being at all committed to the view that these papers have higher value than any other philosopher's papers, let alone higher value than a doctor's project in finding the causes or cure for Alzheimer's. Indeed, I would say that Annas's final end for agents, one's own *eudaimonia*, is a partial good only. The idea that one's own *eudaimonia* is a partial good only does, indeed, constitute an adequate reply to one powerful "deeper level" version of the self-centered-ness objection—that of Hare, but not, I shall ultimately argue, to Solomon's version.[18]

In his "The Self-Centredness Objection to Virtue Ethics," Christopher Toner claims that Hare "develops the clearest and most powerful version of the self-centredness objection I have seen."[19] The objection is premised on an understanding of virtue ethics as committed to eudaimonism, where the latter is taken to be "the view that makes all obligations derivative from an agent's own happiness."[20] However, the view that one's own virtue or happiness is the greatest *partial* good (for one) does not imply that all obligations are derivative from an agent's own happiness, any more than a claim that one's own worthwhile projects are the greatest partial good (for one) implies that all obligations are derived from an agent's own projects. For partial goods, whose goodness is based on partialistic bonds of various kinds generating personal commitments, are a different order of good from the impartially conceived goods of, say, people's welfare in general, the value of kauri trees in general (as opposed to the one planted by me and loved and nurtured accordingly), and so on.

Unfortunately, construing possessing virtue as a partial good does not overcome the "deeper level" version of the self-centeredness objection as presented by Solomon. A good mother would surely not consider her own virtue, even construed as a partial good, to be more important to her than the partial good of the welfare of her own children. As long as virtue ethics is held to be committed to the value structures as outlined by the "deeper level" objection described by Solomon, I see no way out.

To avoid the cluster of objections referred to as the self-centeredness objection, one needs to retain the truth in the idea of the importance of the agent's own virtue and its development, while exorcising the root of the problem, the (alleged) self -centered nature of that commitment. Commitment to the importance of one's own virtue and its development and maintenance, I shall argue, is not a commitment to the value structure at the root of the self-centeredness problem: that outlined by Solomon's "deeper level" objection. A virtue ethicist need not hold the view that a person must subordinate everything else to the possession of her own virtue. Developing a virtue ethics without this commitment lies at the foundation of my second attempt at rebutting the self-centeredness objection.

4. REBUTTING THE "DEEPER LEVEL" OBJECTION: SECOND ATTEMPT

Here I argue that virtue ethics as such is not committed to the view that the moral agent possesses fundamental motivations and values as portrayed

by Solomon. Even if Hare and Solomon are right about the core commitments of eudaimonism, those (alleged) commitments need not be those of
virtue ethics in general. A virtuous agent does not have as her greatest concern her *possessing* or *cultivating* virtue. Rather, she has as her highest commitment *living a life* of virtue—that is, acting, feeling, being motivated as
virtue demands or commends.

It is easy to equate this commitment with the view that "having...virtue
is the most important thing for me; practically I must subordinate everything else to this."

Consider this claim of James Dreier:

> according to virtue theory, each of us is to be concerned in the first instance with
> our *own* virtue. My primary moral responsibility is to live my life according to
> virtue, and yours is to live your life according to virtue. I don't mean that ac-
> cording to virtue theory, a virtuous person will spend all of his time thinking
> about how to become more virtuous. Rather, the idea is that my virtue serves as
> an endpoint in the chain of justification that virtue theory offers. In Aristotelian
> terms, it is that for the sake of which things are done.[21]

There are four different possible claims described here.

(1)   Each is to be concerned in the first instance with her own virtue.
(2)   One's primary responsibility is to live one's life according to virtue.
(3)   A virtuous person spends all his time thinking about his own virtue.
(4)   One's own virtue is that for the sake of which things are done.

Virtue ethics is committed to (2), which does not entail any of the other
three theses, all of which invite the self-centeredness objection.

How, then, do we understand (2)? What virtue commends or requires in
living a life "according to virtue" is attaining the *targets* of virtue. Targets
include such things as paying a debt and being motivated in doing so by the
justice of honoring the debt rather than fear of being prosecuted. A person
committed to leading a life of virtue is committed to attaining these targets
in various situations, even if she cannot as yet in many areas act in the *way*
a virtuous agent characteristically acts. That is, she cannot in these areas
act from a fully fledged disposition or state of virtue. As part of her commitment to leading a life of virtue, the acquisition of virtue as a stable character trait is highly important to her, since (on standard Aristotelian views
of the nature of virtue) doing what virtue demands or commends optimally
requires practical wisdom and that in turn requires virtue. Without virtue
or sufficient virtue, attaining virtuous ends—the targets of the virtues—

on a continuing, highly reliable, and sophisticated basis is impossible.[22] Thus, virtue as a character trait is indeed something to be developed and worked on, and an agent should be committed to such ongoing work.

On this understanding of the commitments of virtue ethics, the complex of problems dubbed the "self-centeredness objection" can be overcome in a virtue ethics having the following tenets.

(a) The features which *make* traits of character virtues are determined by their targets, aims, or point, as opposed to the flourishing of the possessor of the virtues (though, of course, that may be the target of some virtues). If expressing affection to one's children and promoting their welfare are the targets of parental virtue, then what makes parental virtue a virtue is that it is a disposition well attuned to such expression and promotion.

(b) Hitting the targets of (relevant) virtues is what makes actions right.[23]

(c) What fundamentally motivates a virtuous agent, and should motivate an agent aspiring to virtue, is attaining the targets of the virtues: the cultivation and maintenance of virtue is secondary to this aim.

A virtue ethics of this form is, as Kagan would put it, everywhere direct, since what makes actions right is hitting the targets of (relevant) virtues in relation to action; what makes traits virtues is determined by their targets or aims; and what should motivate an agent at both fundamental and everyday levels are these very features.[24] Admittedly, one possible implication of our understanding the commitments of the agent aspiring to virtue is the following: of all her *personal* features, good health, beauty, charm, and having a great deal of money, being virtuous is the personal feature she rates most highly.[25] However, it follows from this rating of virtue neither that she narcissistically thinks that her *own* virtue is the most important thing to her, let alone that it is more important than anyone else's, nor that she should devote most of her time or energy to *cultivating or maintaining* her virtue as a character trait. Rather, in valuing her virtuousness she is committed to *leading a life of virtue*, which as we have seen is a commitment to acting, feeling, and being motivated as virtue demands or commends.

In Aristotle's virtue ethics, this means attaining the targets of the virtues. As we see in section 6, the targets of the virtues are extremely complex, and are much more complex than in standard deontological and consequentialist theories. Far from all moral obligations deriving from the agent's own happiness or flourishing, they derive from the targets of the virtues themselves. Given that there are many virtues, there are many targets of virtues, not all of which are as important as others. These include courageous victory, excellent friendship, just outcomes, and fine conversation.

Consider an agent who both values being virtuous as her most important *personal* quality and whose fundamental commitment is to lead a life of virtue. Let us assume she realizes that to do this she needs to develop her virtue, and there is much scope for this. Assume in particular that she is rather lacking in the virtues of friendship, patience, and courage. She finds it hard to engage with friends when she is focused on her own activities, does not suffer fools gladly, becomes very impatient in queues, and finds it hard to stand up to bullies. Let us say that, though she is as usual busy, it is appropriate at this time that she engages with a friend. Since *ex hypothesi* she cannot so engage from a state of virtue, she can either act as a virtuous agent would act, meeting the target of friendship in action (though imperfectly), or fail to do so at all, concentrating her attention instead on the development of some other virtue in which she is even more seriously lacking, courage or patience. Perhaps instead of reluctantly visiting her friend, she could stay at home reading self-help books on the cultivation of courage or patience. But perhaps she should not. Nothing in our agent's commitments or values requires that she stay at home with her (admittedly fine) self-help books rather than visit her friend.

The "deeper level" version of the self-centeredness objection has misconstrued the fundamental commitments of an agent who aspires to virtue. If it were the case that her greatest concern is *having virtue,* then her fundamental commitments would be acquiring, cultivating, and maintaining her own virtue. And this seems intolerably narcissistic. If by contrast her fundamental concern is *leading a virtuous life,* then her fundamental commitments would be meeting the targets of virtue as best she can. On a virtue ethical view, this ideally requires having virtue, so having virtue is rated as the agent's most valuable personal quality.

5. THE "RIGHT BUT NOT VIRTUOUS" OBJECTION

We turn now to our second problem associated with the idea that virtue is something cultivated and developed over time. In an objection to virtue ethics owed to Robert Johnson, virtue ethics cannot account for right acts of the non-virtuous.[26] These are acts that are intuitively thought to be right (such as breaking the less important promise when one culpably has made conflicting ones), but would not be performed by a virtuous agent (who does not culpably make conflicting promises). In particular, standard virtue ethical accounts of rightness cannot account for the right acts of self-improving agents.

I overcome this objection by appeal to the "direct" kind of virtue ethics outlined above (see (a)–(c) section 4). In particular, I appeal to the target-centered conception of rightness and of what makes a trait a virtue. In overcoming the objection, I propose a virtue of excellence in striving for improvement in leading a virtuous life, a virtue of self-improvement if you will, for there can be dispositions in relation to this field, and they may be excellent or flawed in various ways.[27] One important good to be attained by this virtue is that of improving an agent's own virtue.

Before expounding my own position, let us consider a reply to Johnson from within the virtue ethics camp. Daniel Russell claims that "the proponents of "the right but not virtuous distinction" face a dilemma: either the objection overlooks the distinction between two different forms of act evaluation "ought" and "right," or it assumes without argument that "ought" implies "right."[28] According to Russell, one must distinguish what one ought to do and what it is right to do, and "ought" does not imply "right." Once that distinction is drawn, the "right but not virtuous" objection can be met.

What is the distinction? "Right" here apparently means "warranting a 'tick of approval,'" a phrase borrowed from Hursthouse,[29] but it turns out that remedial actions that would not be performed by a virtuous agent can be praiseworthy, even excellent.[30] So what does "right" mean for Russell? Here is the answer: "what the virtue ethicist does is to identify certain cases of morally excellent action as central cases, and restrict the account of right action to these."[31] So it seems that "right" means "warranting a tick of approval," and that in turn is cashed out in terms of the central cases of morally excellent actions. To my mind this is an unintuitive and unduly restrictive notion of right which could be seen as question-begging by Johnson, since this sense preserves the orthodoxy of understanding "right" in terms of the choices of the virtuous. There is, however, another prevalent notion of "right" where "right" means "correct in the circumstances" (used by consequentialists and deontologists, like Ross, alike). This notion can also be deployed by the virtue ethicist provided "correct in the circumstances" is understood through virtue notions such as meeting the targets of the virtues. If "right" is understood in virtue ethical terms as meeting the targets of (relevant) virtues *and* one of the virtues in question is a virtue of self- improvement, then self-improving actions of the non-virtuous that would not be performed by the virtuous may be right.

How does postulating a virtue of self-improvement overcome Johnson's objection? We here give a general answer to this question before (in the final section) saying more about the virtue itself. The major feature of a virtue ethical account of rightness which makes certain aspirational actions right—actions that express or are in conformity with a virtue of self-improvement but which would not performed by the virtuous—is that such a virtue ethics is dynamic. It does not assume that right actions are the province of the "already arrived" (in virtue) or necessarily conform to the actions of such persons. Now, consider the input of a virtue of self-improvement. A donation of somewhat less than average generosity may exhibit a stellar performance in the learner: she is a stingy individual who rarely gives away a cent. She has exercised the virtue of self-improvement, and as a consequence—given that as Russell allows, virtue is a *satis* or threshold concept—we may judge her to have performed a right act, all things considered.[32] It may not hit the target of generosity—"being generous for her" is not tantamount to being generous *tout court*—but it does hit the target of other relevant virtues, notably that of self-improvement, and we may judge it right overall in the circumstances. That is, it is at least permitted and we might even say admirable (given the nature of the agent: the act is *really* generous for her), but that is not to say that it is the most desirable possible action in the circumstances.

This account raises the question: What are the features of a virtue of self-improvement, and in particular, what are its targets? We answer that question in the next section.

6. THE VIRTUE OF SELF-IMPROVEMENT

To understand self-improvement as a virtue we need first to distinguish the thin from the thick account of the virtue: a distinction owed to Nussbaum.[33]

The thin conception of a virtue begins by stating a virtue's field (its domain of concern). In the case of a virtue of self-improvement, the field is aspirational. Here we focus solely on the aspiration to improve in leading a life of virtue. On the thin account, the virtue of self-improvement (in relation to a life of virtue) is a disposition of being *well* disposed with respect to striving to lead a life of virtue. The thin account does not tell us of what this consists: it merely warns us that not all such striving need be *virtuous* striving. We will need to have the substantive "thick" account to see how this can be so.

One more important feature of the thin account must be described. The virtue is fully exercised when the agent's feelings and actions hit what Aristotle calls the "mean" of the virtue. For him, all "virtue aims to hit the mean"—that is, persons of virtue have practical wisdom, including fine motivation, and that motivation constitutes the *aim* of hitting the mean.[34] But what exactly is the mean? On Aristotle's account, the mean is multi-dimensional. To fully meet the target of a virtue in action involves acting in the right circumstance, in the right manner, at the right time, to the right extent, for the right reasons, with respect to the right people, employing the right instruments.[35] Aristotle deploys the following examples (among others):

> it is easy to get angry—anyone can do that—or to give and spend money; but to feel or act towards the right person to the right extent at the right time for the right reason in the right way—that is not easy. . . . [36]
>
> But it is possible to fear these things too much or too little, and also to fear what is not fearful as if it were. One kind of error is to be afraid of the wrong thing, another to be afraid in the wrong way, and another at the wrong time, or with some other qualification. . . . [37]

The development of the thick account of a virtue consists in substantive positions on what counts, in relation to the virtue, excellence, rightness, or wrongness, on all dimensions of the mean: manner, timing, motive, extent, and so on. This is no less true of a virtue of self-improvement: ascertaining rightness here is a complex and multi-dimensional business. To see this, let us itemize the dimensions of the mean, picking out some key areas of substantive debate.

Extent

The dimension of the mean "extent" raises fascinating issues for the self-improver. In improving herself, what is the extent of improvement aimed at over a given span of time? In particular, should she follow the orthodox view (which I shall question) by directly striving to emulate the supremely virtuous, the best exemplars of virtue in her purview?

There are two main issues:

(a) Is such striving sufficient for meeting the target of the virtue?
(b) Is such striving necessary for meeting that target?

Given the multi-dimensional character of the mean, it is unlikely that it is sufficient because success on other salient dimensions may not be attained. One important kind of failure misinterprets the nature of virtue as exemplified by the supremely virtuous, so striving to emulate the supremely virtuous misses its target. Here is an example of misunderstanding in relation to the dimension of extent from Stephen Angle's *Sagehood*, where the virtue in which improvement is sought (by the physician-humanitarian Paul Farmer and Zell Kravinsky) is love in the form of *agape*.[38] Angle cites part of an interview with Farmer where the interviewer says: "Some people would say, 'Where do you get off thinking you're different from everyone and can love the children of others as much as your own?'" to which he replies: "All the great religious traditions of the world say, Love thy neighbor as thyself. My answer is, I'm sorry, I can't but I'm gonna keep on trying."[39] Kravinsky, who has a similar orientation, wishes to get rid of his "punishing ego"[40] and feels "deeply pained"[41] by his inability to do more than he already has, to the point of feeling little joy in his life and even seeing those close to him as burdens, keeping him from a truly moral life.[42]

It is clear that the longings expressed here are aspirational, but it is also clear that the virtue of self-improvement in relation to love is not expressed. Not only is there no sense of the extreme importance of partial goods, especially in relation to one's own children, but the demands of *agape* are also misconstrued, for they must be integrated (not only in reality but also in the Christian tradition) with partial loves of other and self-love, rather than displace those loves.

What about the claim of necessity? Does aspirational virtue necessarily include the requirement to directly emulate the supremely virtuous? It is possible to strive to lead a virtuous life by attempting to emulate supreme exemplars, but mistakenly overreach one's strength in emulating those paragons. A very demanding ethics is in store for us if the disposition to strive for excellence in leading a virtuous life is manifested only if we strive to directly emulate the actions, motives, and so forth of the "supremely" virtuous. The targets of virtue may include motives as well as actions, and not everyone has or is currently able to have the right motives for genuinely heroic or saintly action characteristic of the supremely virtuous. The relatively weak in their attempts at highly altruistic acts, for example, may be filled with resentment or kinds of despair. This Nietzsche saw in his warning in *Zarathustra*: "Do not be virtuous beyond your strength!,"[43] although this warning is certainly not a recipe for complacency. The warning is apt, for one may not yet have in sufficiently robust form the developmental "unifying strengths" required for the development of virtue proper.[44]

In determining the target of the virtue of self-improvement in relation to "extent," one requires a nuanced conception of what it is to avoid complacency and laziness (major vices for Nietzsche) while at the same time recognizing, as Nietzsche puts it, one's "convalescent" status.

Motive

As touched on above, some forms of attempted self-improvement, especially in leading an altruistic life, may be "pathological."[45] Nietzsche was particularly insightful on this issue, and those insights have been borne out in much recent psychology on pathological altruism.[46] Consider someone who has excessively high standards of altruism as a result of attempts to emulate an exemplar such as Jesus or a cultural paradigm such as "the dutiful wife." The latter, for example, often has motivation characteristic of personality dependence disorder, explaining the pathology of the altruism.[47] Such emulation as a strategy or attempted strategy of self-improvement may in a vulnerable personality result in pathological forms of core personality traits as identified in the Five Factor Model of Personality, the "construct validity" of which "there is considerable empirical support."[48] One such core personality trait is agreeableness, which "includes such facets as trust, straight-forwardness, compliance, modesty, tender-mindedness, and altruism."[49] Each of these facets has adaptive and maladaptive variants (in our language, virtues and vices):

> It is generally adaptive and beneficial to be trusting (high in trust), but not to the point of being characteristically gullible. Similarly it can be adaptive and beneficial to be skeptical (low in trust), but not to the point of being consistently mistrustful and paranoid.

> The same can be said for the trait of altruism. It is generally good to be giving, helpful, and even generous (high in altruism), but not to the point of suffering numerous debilitating consequences secondary to a characteristically self-sacrificing selflessness. Always placing oneself second to the interests, desires, needs, and whims of others will clearly result in mounting losses and accumulating deprivation, and at the most extreme, perhaps even victimization and abuse.[50]

We might label the maladaptive form of self-improvement perfectionistic vice, not all of which of course manifests pathological altruism. Other forms of this aspirational vice are described by Horney.[51] She distinguishes between two types of "neurotic" perfectionism: "expansionist" and "self-effacing." The former type of person

> identifies himself with his standards. This type feels superior because of his high standards, moral and intellectual, and on this basis looks down on others. His arrogant contempt for others, though, is hidden—from himself as well—behind polished friendliness, because his standards prohibit such irregular feelings.[52]

As an example of the latter type, Horney offers the following:

> Even after a good performance (perhaps in giving a party or delivering a lecture) they still will emphasise the fact that they forgot this or that, that they did not

emphasise clearly what they meant to say, that they were too subdued or too offensive, etc.[53]

Both types of perfectionism are expressive of problematic depth motivation, at the heart of which is self-condemnation. Aspirational dispositions are motivationally distorted.

Time

The issue of time has already been touched upon. The inclusion of a dynamic virtue of self-improvement in our catalogue of virtues and vices does not at all imply that an agent aspiring to lead a virtuous life should spend all or most of her time cultivating virtue. That would indeed be narcissistic, for the agent will have lost sight of meeting the "demands of the world," understood in terms of the targets of virtues *other* than one's own improvement. Remember that on our virtue ethics it is not the case that possessing virtue is the highest value or partial good for an agent.

However, there remains the issue of how exactly we should conceptualize the "time" dimension of the mean. Here Kant is very instructive, for his discussion of the nature of the "duty" to "perfect oneself morally" is sophisticated. First, he describes it as a "wide" duty, which means that the "obligatory end" of perfecting oneself morally (that is, the target of the virtue of self-improvement in relation to what he calls duties of virtue) prescribes (in relation to action) only an associated rule of the virtue (maxim).[54] That rule does not itself prescribe specific actions, let alone the time at which one should perform them. Thus, there is no specific rule such as "On a daily basis read a good self-help book on cultivating patience." "And take notes." Having visited a psychologist, however, one may be given such an instruction, or one may be asked to perform three patient acts a day, which are recorded in a diary to be discussed at the next meeting. But these are not generated by the virtue rule ("Improve oneself in virtue") itself.[55]

One must not confuse the idea of a wide duty with the idea that it is *always* permissive how one satisfies or expresses this duty. One may be required to do an act of self-improvement of a specific type on a specific occasion. (One has made a promise to one's spouse.) It is just that such a requirement cannot be specified as a duty in advance of context. The same is true of Kant's wide duty of beneficence. There may be obligations to help this person in this way here and now, but the maxim of beneficence cannot prescribe specific actions of this nature in advance of context.

Second, Kant describes the duty to perfect oneself morally as a perfect duty, unlike the duty to perfect one's talents (which is also wide, but not perfect). It is perfect because it is not constrained or limited by other duties.[56] This may seem puzzling because of the wide scope of the duty. When helping my neighbor I am not reading self-help books, so does not the duty of self-improvement conflict with the duty to help my neighbor? Not so for Kant, because in fulfilling the (wide) duty of beneficence in helping my neighbor I am not in conflict with a duty to perfect myself morally. Indeed, as Aristotle also saw, performing virtuous acts is at one and the same time training oneself into virtue.

By contrast, if I am spending all my time writing philosophy papers, developing my philosophical talents, but neglecting my children, I am violating a duty of good parenting. Similarly if I am spending all my time reading self-help books in an effort to cultivate virtue but neglecting my children, I am violating a duty of good parenting. But this does not make the duty to perfect myself morally an imperfect duty. Reading books on patience may develop the virtue of patience, but does not count as perfecting myself morally while it conflicts with my duties to my children. Such acts do not manifest the virtue of self-improvement in relation to virtue. Hence for Kant, the duty to develop one's talents is both wide and imperfect, whereas the duty to perfect oneself in virtue is wide and perfect.

To summarize, for Kant the rule of action associated with the target of the virtue of moral self-improvement does not prescribe specific actions (the duties prescribed are wide). Actions in accord with that rule do not conflict with duties associated with the targets of other virtues (the duties prescribed are perfect). By contrast, writing philosophy papers may develop my philosophical talents even while it conflicts with duties to my children. It will still count as developing my talents. So the duty to develop one's talents is an imperfect duty.

Having claimed that the duty to perfect oneself morally is a perfect duty, Kant concedes that it is only perfect "in quality" but not in "degree" because of the frailty of human nature. Hence a person's "compliance with this duty can consist only in continual progress."[57] Kant not only recognizes the aspirational quality of virtue but also tells us much about the nature of the virtues of self-improvement.

People

By definition the virtue of self-improvement has the self as its target. This is no problem for Kant, for whom the aspirational duties of cultivating virtue and sympathy are at the heart of human morality. Once we have seen that this view properly understood survives the self-centeredness objection (because the duty is satisfied and the virtue is manifested by living as well as one can a life of virtue, and leading such a life involves a characteristic focus on others), there is no problem with virtue ethics siding with Kant on the spuriousness of limiting the "moral" to the other-regarding only. Self-improvement and self-respect are indeed central to morality for Kant.

Manner

A very important dimension of the mean routinely neglected in contemporary ethics is manner. Are there vices of manner associated with self-improvement? Indeed there are, most notably self-righteousness and sanctimoniousness. The aspirant to virtue, being self-conscious about her deficiencies and even defensive about them, is prey to vices of self-righteousness.[58] This vice is marked by affective states of righteous outrage and, in action, drawing attention to others' failings of virtue, the need for them to improve, and one's own relative superiority in the improvement stakes. The psychology of the development of this particular vice of manner of self-improvement is interesting, and apparently undeveloped. In his "Self Addiction and Self-Righteousness," David Brin hypothesizes that if "neurochemical processes reinforce 'good' habits such as love, loyalty, joy in music or skill," then it is possible that "self-righteousness and indignation may sometimes be as much about chemical need as valid concerns about unfair actions."[59] Given the increasingly pernicious aspects of political ideology on Brin's view, he sees an urgent need for study of self-addictive properties of self-righteousness: a state that "can feel so intense and delicious that many people seek to return to it again and again."[60]

Instruments

What are the right instruments for the development of virtue? For Aristotle, the most potent instrument is correct upbringing, but as he recognizes, it is paramount that the upbringing be embedded in what Merritt calls the "sustaining social contribution to character": a good political structure containing good institutions with sufficiently fine traditions and culture.[61] Snow argues that we admire people's "independence of the social forces that surround them" and those who are "not at the mercy of their situations" (assuming they are virtuous in so doing), and this is undoubtedly true.[62] Being resistant to vice once *fully* virtuous is something that Aristotle recognized, but the sustaining social contribution has to do with cultivating and maintaining virtue across generations, as well as in the "virtue-fragile." And as Kant saw, we are all to some extent virtue-fragile: "Virtue is always *in progress*.... It is always in progress because, considered *objectively*, it is an ideal and unattainable, while yet constant approximation to it is a duty..., if it is not rising, [it] is unavoidably sinking."[63] It is unquestionable that corrosive institutions both undermine and make difficult the learning and sustaining of virtue. Indeed, the learning of virtue is made difficult by the disappearance or unfashionableness of virtue language and by the dominating concern with rights and entitlements, even though rights recognition as such can hardly be described as corrosive of virtue.

The claim that virtue cultivation needs a sustaining social contribution is not invalidated by our personal need for resilience (or relative "motivational self-sufficiency") in the face of loss of, for example, a loved one.[64] Resilience is after all a virtue which may itself be undermined in a culture which has gone "soft." Within the personal domain it is an empirical question what instruments (friends, relatives, self-help books, psychologists, teachers, programs) are the most efficacious in the cultivation of virtue.

7. CONCLUSION

We have accepted that virtue ethics must maintain its view that a commitment to leading a life of virtue involves, indeed necessarily involves, a commitment to learning to be virtuous, teaching others for whom you are in some way responsible to be virtuous themselves, and further developing and maintaining (in the face of pernicious influences) what virtues you already have. The problem has been that despite this commitment, virtue ethics has proceeded in an ideal- world way with concepts appropriate to a situation where agents are already perfected in virtue. There has been a neglect of the developmental strengths required for the acquisition of virtue—strengths described by psychologists such as Erik Erikson—and a consequent assumption that virtue cultivation is a matter simply of emulating the exemplars of virtue.[65] By contrast, the account of a virtue of self-improvement is extremely complex and needs much input from particularly psychology.

The admission of such a virtue with its own distinctive targets in a dynamic virtue ethics overcomes Johnson's objection to certain virtue ethical accounts of right action. An understanding of the proper targets of that virtue in terms of striving to better oneself in leading a life of virtue also overcomes the self-centeredness objection.

NOTES

1. Julia Annas, *Intelligent Virtue* (Oxford: Oxford University Press, 2011), 21.
2. Robert N. Johnson, "Virtue and Right," *Ethics* 113, no. 4 (2003): 810–34.
3. Bernard Williams, "Acting as a Virtuous Person Acts," in *Aristotle and Moral Realism*, ed. R. Heinaman (London: UCL Press, 1995), 13–23.
4. Rosalind Hursthouse, *On Virtue Ethics* (Oxford: Oxford University Press, 1999).
5. Simon Keller, "Virtue Ethics Is Self Effacing," *Australasian Journal of Philosophy* 85, no. 2 (2007): 221–31; Glen Pettigrove, "Is Virtue Ethics Self-Effacing?" *Journal of Ethics* 13, no. 3 (2011).
6. Thomas Hurka, *Virtue, Vice, and Value* (Oxford: Oxford University Press, 2001).
7. Julia Annas, *The Morality of Happiness* (Oxford: Oxford University Press, 1993).
8. Annas, *Morality of Happiness*, 44.
9. Christine Swanton, *Virtue Ethics: A Pluralistic View* (Oxford: Oxford University Press, 2003).
10. David Solomon, "Internal Objections to Virtue Ethics," In *Virtue Ethics: A Critical Reader*, ed. Daniel Statman (Edinburgh: Edinburgh University Press, 1997), 172.
11. Solomon, "Internal Objections," 172. Notice that although Aristotle claims that fineness of character is the greatest good for an agent, this does not imply that having fine character holds more importance for the agent than the welfare of her children, for example. (See further below.)
12. Solomon, "Internal Objections."
13. Garrett Cullity, *The Moral Demands of Affluence* (Oxford: Clarendon Press, 2004).
14. Garrett Cullity, "Sympathy, Discernment, and Reasons," *Philosophy and Phenomenological Research* 68, no. 1 (2004): 43.
15. See further on expressive action, Swanton, *Virtue Ethics*.
16. Cullity, "Sympathy."
17. Cullity, "Sympathy," 129–31.
18. John Hare, "Scotus on Morality and Nature," *Medieval Philosophy and Theology* 9 (2000): 15–38.
19. Christopher Toner, "The Self-Centredness Objection to Virtue Ethics," *Philosophy* 81 (2006): 595–618, at 603.
20. Toner, "Self-Centredness Objection," 603.
21. James Dreier, "Structures of Normative Theories," *The Monist* 76 (1993): 22–40, at 35.
22. On my view, practical wisdom and virtue is not sufficient for this: the expertise of *techne* may also be necessary in many areas.
23. Qualified agent conceptions of right action, such as Hursthouse's *On Virtue Ethics*, have been criticized for offering a criterion of rightness that tells us that "right action is what the virtuous person would do" as opposed to what makes actions right (see Roger Crisp, "Virtue Ethics and Virtue Epistemology," in *Virtue and vice Moral and Epistemic*, ed. Heather Battaly [Malden: Wiley Blackwell, 2010], 24). Jason Kawall ("In Defense of the Primacy of the Virtues," *Journal of Ethics and Social Philosophy* 3 [2009]: 1–21) attempts to rebut this objection by distinguishing between different notions of what makes something right. He claims that in a "meta-ethical" sense the choices of a virtuous agent make actions right in the same way that (for a utilitarian) maximizing utility makes actions right. Both would agree that in an "instantiation" sense (using Kawall's example), the suffering of the puppies would make torturing

them wrong. But the cases are disanalogous. For the utilitarian, it is not strictly the suffering of the puppies in a particular case that makes torturing them *wrong*; it is the fact that the suffering does not maximize utility, whereas in no sense do the choices of a virtuous agent make torturing the puppies wrong. Rather, it is the fact that the suffering is of a vicious nature (or so should, the virtue ethicist argue).

24. S. Kagan, "Evaluative Focal Points," in *Morality, Rules, and Consequences: A Critical Reader*, ed. B. Hooker, E. Mason, and D. E. Miller (Edinburgh: Edinburgh University Press, 2000).

25. That this is a commitment needs argument that I will not engage in here.

26. Johnson, "Virtue."

27. The inclusion of such a virtue with its own targets is in effect my reply to Johnson's argument that I (like Slote and Hursthouse) "fail to take into account that we should morally improve ourselves" (Johnson, "Virtue," 811). It is true that the inclusion of a virtue of self-improvement was not explicit in my account of right action in my 2003 book, despite my discussion of Nietzsche and the "convalescent."

28. Daniel C. Russell, *Practical Intelligence and the Virtues* (Oxford: Clarendon Press, 2009), 54.

29. Hursthouse, *On Virtue Ethics*, 51–52.

30. Russell, *Practical Intelligence*, 54.

31. Russell, *Practical Intelligence*, 55.

32. I cannot in this essay discuss the many complexities of an overall judgment of rightness relating to vagueness, the multi-dimensionality of factors contributing to rightness (see below), the fact that "right" can mean variously required, permitted, admirable but not required, and recommended, and the fact that in a given right act not all targets of all relevant virtues may be met (or fully met). See further, Christine Swanton, "Virtue Ethics and the Problem of Moral Disagreement," *Philosophical Topics* 38, no. 2 (2010): 157–80.

33. Martha Nussbaum, "Non-Relative Virtues: An Aristotelian Approach," in *Ethical Theory: Character and Virtue, Midwest Studies in Philosophy* 13, ed. P. A. French, T. E. Uehling Jr., and H. K. Wettstein (Notre Dame, IN: Notre Dame University Press, 1988), 32–53.

34. Aristotle, *The Nicomachean Ethics*, trans. J. A. K. Thomson, rev. H. Trendennick (Harmondsworth: Penguin, 1976), 1106b16–24.

35. See, e.g., Aristotle, *Nicomachean Ethics*, 1106b20–23.

36. Aristotle, *Nicomachean Ethics*, 1109a25–b15.

37. Aristotle, *Nicomachean Ethics*, , 1115a30–b19.

38. Stephen C. Angle, *Sagehood: The Contemporary Significance of Neo-Confucian Philosophy* (Oxford: Oxford University Press, 2009).

39. Angle, *Sagehood*, 91.

40. Angle, *Sagehood*, 90.

41. Angle, *Sagehood*, 90.

42. Angle, *Sagehood*, 91.

43. Friedrich Nietzsche, *Thus Spoke Zarathustra*, in *The Portable Nietzsche*, trans. and ed. Walter Kaufmann (New York: Penguin, 1976), Part 4, sect. 13, 403.

44. Erik Erikson, *Childhood and Society* (New York: W.W. Norton, 1963). See further, Christine Swanton, "Virtue Ethics," in *The Continuum Companion to Ethics*, ed. Christian Miller (London: Continuum, 2011).

45. Barbara Oakley, Ariel Knafo, Guruprasad Madhavan, and David Sloan Wilson, eds., *Pathological Altruism* (Oxford: Oxford University Press, 2012).

46. See further, Christine Swanton, "Nietzsche's Virtue Ethics," in *The Handbook of Virtue Ethics*, ed. Stan van Hooft (Durham: Acumen, 2014).
47. For case studies, see Thomas A. Widiger and Jennifer Ruth Presnall, "Pathological Altruism and Personality Disorder," in *Pathological Altruism*, ed. Barbara Oakley, Ariel Knafo, Guruprasad Madhavan, and David Sloan Wilson (Oxford: Oxford University Press, 2012), 85–93.
48. Widiger and Presnall, "Pathological Altruism," 85.
49. Widiger and Presnall, "Pathological Altruism," 86.
50. Widiger and Presnall, "Pathological Altruism."
51. Karen Horney, *Neurosis and Human Growth: The Struggle Toward Self Realization* (New York: Norton, 1970.
52. Horney, *Neurosis and Human Growth*, 196.
53. Horney, *Neurosis and Human Growth*, 317.
54. Immanuel Kant, *The Metaphysics of Morals*, trans. and ed. Mary Gregor (Cambridge: Cambridge University Press, 1996), 6: 393.
55. For more on virtue rules, see Hursthouse, *On Virtue Ethics*.
56. Kant, *Metaphysics of Morals*, 6:447.
57. Kant, *Metaphysics of Morals*, 6: 447.
58. Such vice is a core theme of Jonathan Haidt's *The Righteous Mind: Why Good People Are Divided by Politics and Religion* (London: Penguin Books, 2012). He claims that "an obsession with righteousness (leading inevitably to self-righteousness) is the core human condition." It is one, however, we must guard against, since "self-righteous" means "convinced of one's own righteousness, especially in contrast with the actions and beliefs of others; narrowly moralistic and intolerant" (xiii).
59. David Brin, "Self Addiction and Self Righteousness," in *Pathological Altruism*, ed. Barbara Oakley, Ariel Knafo, Guruprasad Madhavan, and David Sloan Wilson (Oxford: Oxford University Press, 2012), 77.
60. Brin, "Self Addition," 80.
61. Maria Merritt, "Virtue Ethics and Situationist Personality Psychology," *Ethical Theory and Moral Practice* 3 (2000): 365–83.
62. Nancy E. Snow, *Virtue as Social Intelligence: An Empirically Grounded Theory* (New York: Routledge, 2010), 6.
63. Kant, *Metaphysics of Morals*, 6:409.
64. Snow, *Virtue*, 7.
65. Erikson, *Childhood*.

BIBLIOGRAPHY

Angle, Stephen C. *Sagehood: The Contemporary Significance of Neo-Confucian Philosophy*. Oxford: Oxford University Press, 2009.
Annas, Julia. *Intelligent Virtue*. Oxford: Oxford University Press, 2011.
Annas, Julia. *The Morality of Happiness*. Oxford: Oxford University Press, 1993.
Aristotle. *The Nicomachean Ethics*. Translated by J. A. K. Thomson, revised by H. Tredennick. Harmondsworth: Penguin, 1976.
Brin, David. "Self Addiction and Self Righteousness." In *Pathological Altruism*, edited by Barbara Oakley, Ariel Knafo, Guruprasad Madhavan, and David Sloan Wilson, 77–84. Oxford: Oxford University Press, 2012.

Crisp, Roger. "Virtue Ethics and Virtue Epistemology." In *Virtue and Vice Moral and Epistemic*, edited by Heather Battaly, 21–38. Malden: Wiley Blackwell, 2010.

Cullity, Garrett. *The Moral Demands of Affluence*. Oxford: Clarendon Press, 2004.

Cullity, Garrett. "Sympathy, Discernment, and Reasons." *Philosophy and Phenomenological Research* 68, no. 1 (2004): 37–62.

Dreier, James. "Structures of Normative Theories." *The Monist* 76 (1993): 22–40.

Erikson, Erik. *Childhood and Society*. New York: W.W. Norton, 1963.

Haidt, Jonathan. *The Righteous Mind: Why Good People Are Divided by Politics and Religion*. London: Penguin Books, 2012.

Hare, John. "Scotus on Morality and Nature." *Medieval Philosophy and Theology* 9 (2000): 15–38.

Horney, Karen. *Neurosis and Human Growth: The Struggle Toward Self Realization*. New York: Norton, 1970. ·

Hurka, Thomas. *Virtue, Vice, and Value*. Oxford: Oxford University Press, 2001.

Hursthouse, Rosalind. *On Virtue Ethics*. Oxford: Oxford University Press, 1999.

Johnson, Robert N. "Virtue and Right." *Ethics* 113, no. 4 (2003): 810–34.

Kagan, S. "Evaluative Focal Points." In *Morality, Rules, and Consequences: A Critical Reader*, edited by B. Hooker, E. Mason, and D. E. Miller, 134–55. Edinburgh: Edinburgh University Press, 2000.

Kant, Immanuel. *The Metaphysics of Morals*. Translated and edited by Mary Gregor. Cambridge: Cambridge University Press, 1996.

Kawall, Jason. "In Defense of the Primacy of the Virtues." *Journal of Ethics and Social Philosophy* 3 (2009): 1–21.

Keller, Simon. "Virtue Ethics Is Self Effacing." *Australasian Journal of Philosophy* 85, no. 2 (2007): 221–31.

Merritt, Maria. "Virtue Ethics and Situationist Personality Psychology." *Ethical Theory and Moral Practice* 3 (2000): 365–83.

Nietzsche, Friedrich. *Thus Spoke Zarathustra*. In *The Portable Nietzsche*, translated and edited by Walter Kaufmann. New York: Penguin, 1976.

Nussbaum, Martha. "Non-Relative Virtues: An Aristotelian Approach." In *Ethical Theory: Character and Virtue*, Midwest Studies in Philosophy 13, edited by P. A. French, T. E.Uehling Jr., and H. K. Wettstein, 32–53. Notre Dame, IN: Notre Dame University Press, 1988.

Oakley, Barbara, Ariel Knafo, Guruprasad Madhavan, and David Sloan Wilson, eds. *Pathological Altruism*. Oxford: Oxford University Press, 2012.

Pettigrove, Glen. "Is Virtue Ethics Self-Effacing?" *Journal of Ethics* 15, no. 3 (2010): 191–207.

Russell, Daniel C. *Practical Intelligence and the Virtues*. Oxford: Clarendon Press, 2009.

Slote, Michael. *Morals from Motives*. Oxford: Oxford University Press, 2001.

Snow, Nancy E. *Virtue as Social Intelligence: An Empirically Grounded Theory*. New York: Routledge, 2010.

Solomon, David. "Internal Objections to Virtue Ethics." In *Virtue Ethics: A Critical Reader*, edited by Daniel Statman, 165–79. Edinburgh: Edinburgh University Press, 1997.

Swanton, Christine. "Nietzsche's Virtue Ethics." In *The Handbook of Virtue Ethics*, edited by Stan van Hooft, 105–17. Durham: Acumen, 2014.

Swanton, Christine. "Virtue Ethics." In *The Continuum Companion to Ethics*, edited by Christian Miller, 190–214. London: Continuum, 2011.

Swanton, Christine. *Virtue Ethics: A Pluralistic View*. Oxford: Oxford University Press, 2003.

Swanton, Christine. "Virtue Ethics and the Problem of Moral Disagreement." *Philosophical Topics* 38, no. 2 (2010): 157–80.

Toner, Christopher. "The Self-Centredness Objection to Virtue Ethics." *Philosophy* 81 (2006): 595–618.

Widiger, Thomas A., and Jennifer Ruth Presnall. "Pathological Altruism and Personality Disorder." In *Pathological Altruism*, edited by Barbara Oakley, Ariel Knafo, Guruprasad Madhavan, and David Sloan Wilson, 85–93. Oxford: Oxford University Press, 2012.

Williams, Bernard. "Acting as a Virtuous Person Acts." In *Aristotle and Moral Realism*, edited by R. Heinaman, 13–23. London: UCL Press, 1995.

CHAPTER 6

ᴄᴠᴐ

The Situationist Critique and Early Confucian Virtue Ethics

EDWARD SLINGERLAND

O ver two hundred years ago,[1] David Hume—impressed by the growing explanatory power of the natural sciences of his time—called upon philosophy to join in the trend toward empirical inquiry, abandoning armchair speculation and a priori abstraction:

> Men are now cured of their passion for hypotheses and systems in natural phi-
> losophy, and will hearken to no arguments but those which are derived from
> experience. It is full time that they should attempt a like reformation in all
> moral disquisitions; and reject every system of ethics, however subtle or ingen-
> ious, which is not founded on fact and observation.[2]

Due, no doubt, to a widespread disciplinary self-conception that relegated the empirical to the intellectually and ethically irrelevant realm of "heter-onomy," Hume's call to arms largely fell upon deaf ears, and it is only in the past decade or two that a new movement emphasizing "empirically respon-sible" philosophy has begun gaining momentum.[3] This movement—which in its latest iteration was inaugurated in the early work of Owen Flanagan and Mark Johnson[4]—has argued that philosophical speculation needs to be informed and constrained by our current best empirical accounts of how the human mind works,[5] and it encompasses positions as diverse as John-son's efforts to restore philosophical standing to embodied aesthetics,[6] the work of "neo-Humeans" such as Jesse Prinz,[7] and the experimental phi-losophy movement spearheaded by Stephen Stich and his students.[8]

Another manifestation of this empirical turn is the work of a group of philosophically minded psychologists and scientifically literate philosophers who argue that evidence about the nature of human cognition emerging from cognitive science, cognitive linguistics, neuroscience, social psychology, and primatology calls into question the psychological plausibility of the "cognitive control" models of ethics—deontology and utilitarianism—that have dominated recent Western ethical thought.[9] The apparently foundational importance of emotions, automatic and unconscious processes, and embodied, analogical reasoning has led several commentators to suggest that this body of evidence might lend weight to the proponents of the revived virtue ethics model of moral reasoning and education. Virtue ethics, which has also in the past several decades been gaining ground in academic philosophy, differs from deontology and utilitarianism in emphasizing the ethical importance of social roles, emotions, habits, and imaginative extension.[10] If deontology and utilitarianism require us to think or behave in manners that are simply not possible or sustainable in quotidian life, these modern defenders of virtue ethics contend, this should temper our enthusiasm for adopting them as moral ideals.[11]

Several proponents of empirically responsible philosophy are, however, much less sanguine about the empirical viability of virtue ethics. As far back as Flanagan's *Varieties of Moral Personality* there have been suggestions that social psychological findings concerning the apparent weakness of character traits in the face of situational pressures might call into question the very possibility of virtues as stable character traits. This criticism has become even more focused and pointed in the work of Gilbert Harman and John Doris, who argue that the very notion of moral "character"—the bedrock of any virtue ethic—has been empirically discredited.[12] It has, therefore, become quite clear that any contemporary attempt to defend virtue ethics on empirical grounds must address this "situationist critique."[13]

Several philosophical defenders of virtue ethics have risen to the challenge, questioning both the interpretation and the significance of the social psychological research cited by Harman and Doris, the notion of "character" that is under attack, and the degree to which historically accurate models of virtue ethics are, in fact, vulnerable to the "lack of character" argument.[14] Here I would like to build upon these efforts in a manner that takes on more directly the viability of the empirical claims being made, as well as the degree to which they can be seen as fatal to virtue ethics.

My argument against the situationist critique will unfold in two stages. To begin with, I will question both the empirical and the conceptual foundations of what I call the "strong" situationist position, and I will attempt to demonstrate to my colleagues in philosophy that the supposedly fatal situationist argument is not nearly as lethal as advertised. Personality traits are alive and well, which means that the cognitive foundation of virtue ethics is, in fact, in rather good shape. In the second part, I will go on to suggest that, even if we acknowledge that traditional notions of character set an extremely high bar for the virtues, there are features of the early Confucian virtue ethics tradition that can be seen as effective and empirically plausible responses to even this more significant challenge.[15] Framed in terms of the high-bar metaphor, section 1 argues that people do, in fact, have the natural capacity to jump (that is, character traits do exist), while section 2 explores the manner in which early Confucian moral training simultaneously boosts this natural capacity through training and lowers the bar several notches by means of situational controls. It is this combination of enhanced jump and lowered bar that may—and I leave this as an open empirical question—make something like Confucian ethics a psychologically realistic model of virtue cultivation, and therefore a potentially valuable resource for contemporary ethical theorists and educators.

1. PERSONALITY TRAITS ARE ALIVE AND WELL

The entire person vs. situation debate was kicked off in 1968 by Walter Mischel, with his landmark study *Personality and Assessment*, and the decade or so that followed saw an explosion of the sorts of classic studies— Darley and Batson's study of Princeton Theological Seminarians, or Isen and Levin's study of the effect of finding a dime in a pay phone on subsequent helping behaviors—that feature so prominently in the work of Harman and Doris.[16] The demise of the public pay phone and depreciation of the dime is not, however, the only thing that has changed since the 1970s: personality psychologists, spurred on and informed by the situationist critique, developed more nuanced models of what a trait might be, as well as more sophisticated methods for exploring the connection between personality traits and behavior. The result has been a massive body of evidence documenting the existence of a robust and diverse set of personality traits. In an important special issue summarizing the state of the person–situation debate, David Funder declares that it "ended as a serious scientific conversation decades ago."[17]

This is partially because the dichotomous nature of the debate has been recognized as fundamentally mistaken: persons and situations are no more separable than genes and environments, and a strong form of the person-situation contrast is as conceptually muddled as a strong form of the nature–nurture debate. In this regard, the work of Mischel and others has performed a valuable service in debunking early, naïvely strong views of character as invariant and immune to situational effects.[18] Of course, as with gene–environment interactions, much hangs on the relative causal efficacy one attributes to the two factors, and the thrust of Funder's argument is that the causal efficacy of personality traits can no longer be plausibly denied.

Strong Situationism: The Anti-Globalist Argument

The one fundamental disagreement that still remains, and the crux of the position that I will be calling "strong situationism," is whether relatively broad personality traits can be seen as having any predictive efficacy, or if it is rather best to see persons as characterized by a motley collection of quite narrow, local, extremely situation-sensitive traits. In his recent commentary on the person–situation debate, Mischel maintains as the central thrust of his work a critique of "the classic assumption of high cross-situational consistency in trait-relevant behavior,"[19] and his current position is that individual consistency in character consists of a relatively stable "signature" of quite narrow "*if...then...*" dispositional tendencies, such as the tendency of a given child to be verbally aggressive when chastised by an adult on the playground, but unaggressive when approached by a peer.[20] This version of situationism forms the backdrop of Harman's claim that local traits "do not count," as well as Doris's "anti-globalist" position that local traits are ethically "fragmented," cohering only in "evaluatively disintegrated" loose associations.[21] There are at least two sets of problems with this critique of the classic conception of character, one involving the empirical data on broad character traits and the other a conceptual confusion about the local–global distinction.

Empirical Issues

The vast bulk of the situationist literature demonstrating that broad character traits have negligible predictive power is based upon one-off assessments of subjects' behaviors in a particular experimental environment. The problem with this approach is that it misses the aggregation effect: the extent to which a clear correlation between character traits and behavior may only begin to emerge over repeated observations over a long period of time. In the 1970s and '80s, when the situationist literature had its heyday, there were few large-scale longitudinal studies of the sort that could pick out aggregation effects, primarily because such studies are difficult and quite expensive to pull off. However, in part as a reaction to situationism, personality psychologists in the last few decades have accumulated a wealth of evidence from longitudinal studies demonstrating the reality of broad character traits. For instance, few now would dispute that the so-called "Big Five" personality traits—openness, conscientiousness, extraversion, agreeableness, and neuroticism—are "real" in the sense that they are stable over time, although not entirely unalterable or context insensitive;[22] appear to have a considerable genetic component;[23] and predict substantive life outcomes, such as mortality, health, marital satisfaction, divorce, and occupational success.[24]

To his credit, Doris addresses the aggregation effect, but dismisses its importance on the grounds that "observers want to predict and explain not only general trends but also particular behaviors," and that the sorts of predictions given by personality traits leave us "completely in the dark" about what a particular person's behavior might be on any given specific occasion.[25] This brings us to another major problem with the strong situationist critique, one that straddles the empirical and conceptual: a severe underestimation of the power and pragmatic usefulness of relatively small correlations.

One of the key arguments in Mischel's groundbreaking 1968 work was that the correlation between broad personality traits (such as "conscientiousness") and behavior, and within broad personality traits (such as "honesty") across a variety of trait-relevant situations, never seems to exceed 0.3 in any given observation—a degree of correlation dismissed by Mischel as "weak."[26] This 0.3 figure became famous, or infamous, as the so-called "personality coefficient," and the essence of the argument against broad character traits hangs on the claim that a correlation coefficient of 0.3 is of negligible significance.[27]

It is not, and unfortunately philosophers who are simply told that it is often lack the formal knowledge of statistics or intuitive understanding of probability to critically evaluate the claim. To begin with, it is important to see that correlation coefficients in the 0.3 range are not a unique feature of personality research. Gregory Meyer et al. point out in an important meta-analysis that few correlations in psychology exceed 0.3, and that this is not even a particular weakness of psychology as a discipline: comparing psychological studies with correlations established in a wide variety of fields, they found that effect sizes in psychology are similar to, for instance, those used to justify medical interventions in the health sciences.[28] Indeed, the link between consuming aspirin and warding off heart attacks, or between chemotherapy and positive outcomes in breast cancer, hover around 0.02 or 0.03 (that's an extra zero), and yet this is deemed significant enough by the medical community to make recommendation of these interventions standard practice. Moreover, other large-scale meta-analyses[29] have found that the "situation" effects obtained in the situationist literature, when translated into a common metric, give a correlation coefficient of 0.2 to 0.3—that is, as "weak," if not weaker, than the supposed "personality coefficient."[30] If a correlation of 0.3 is genuinely so weak as to be negligible, then *nothing* predicts behavior.

Fortunately, 0.3 is actually quite good. Robert Rosenthal and Donald Rubin, for instance, observe that a 0.3–0.4 correlation is enough to predict dichotomous outcomes 65 to 75 percent of the time.[31] Perhaps most helpful for the statistically challenged (including this author) is an example that helps spell out the significance of correlation coefficients in terms of an everyday baseball analogy.[32] Ted Williams is considered the greatest batter who ever lived, whereas Bob Uecker, while widely admired for his later efforts as a color commentator, is generally regarded as one of the worst hitters to ever play in the Major Leagues. Williams's lifetime batting average was.344, as compared to Uecker's.200—a difference of only.144. As Robert Abelson points out, the supposedly "weak" correlation of 0.3 is actually three to twenty-seven times more predictive of whether, say, a conscientious person is likely to behave in a conscientious fashion on any given occasion than the difference between Williams's and Uecker's lifetime batting averages would predict the likelihood of their getting a hit when at bat. And yet, with two out and the bases loaded in the bottom of the ninth, only a fool would want Bob Uecker rather than Ted Williams coming up to bat for their team. In contemporary Major League baseball, differences in batting averages (or earned run averages for pitchers) much less than.144 dictate enormous variations in salary and prestige of players—hard economic evidence suggesting that even quite small correlation effects can have very significant practical implications.

Conceptual Issues

This debate about the significance of correlation coefficients of a particular magnitude, of course, begins to straddle the empirical and the conceptual. On a more purely conceptual level, there are additional points upon which the strong situationist position can be criticized.

To begin with, the philosophical bite of the anti-globalist critique derives from the claim that local traits, whose existence no one would dispute, are not really traits at all—that is, as Harman puts it, that "narrow dispositions do not count"—or that they are so ethically and evaluatively fragmented that they cannot perform any of the conceptual lifting that virtue ethics would require of them.[33] This point, in turn, is entirely dependent on the implicit assumption that we know what we are talking about when we contrast "local" with "global" traits: that is, that there is a clear, principled distinction between the two.

This is not at all the case. When offered as an analytic dichotomy, the "local" vs. "global" distinction is simply not tenable because any truly "local" trait would not be a trait at all, but merely a single occurrence: John performed behavior *X* in situation *Y* at this particular time and place. The sorts of local traits that Doris thinks worthy of our attention count as "traits" because they are already abstract to various degrees: it is not merely that John behaved in an honest or extroverted fashion in the presence of Joe on April 24, 2009, at 3:45 P.M., but also that he reliably behaves honestly on tests or is extroverted with friends. Looked at in contrast to a truly one-off report of behavior, local traits are already quite broad in their predictive claims. Anything that we can call a "trait" or a "disposition" is already more or less global or broad, which seriously undermines the blanket dismissal of "local traits" or "narrow dispositions" as ethically irrelevant.[34]

It is thus clear that "local" and "global" mark off opposite ends of a spectrum of abstraction rather than the sort of analytic dichotomy that the anti-globalist critique needs to have any real traction. Once we realize this point, it becomes equally clear that what degree of locality or globality "counts" fundamentally depends on one's pragmatic needs: the range of behavior one is interested in making predictions about and the degree of predictive reliability one feels comfortable with. As David Funder argues, extremely fractionated traits do give us high fidelity, but "at the cost of narrowing the bandwidth" to the point that they are often pragmatically useless.[35] The degree of abstraction in trait formulation that strikes one as desirable depends, in the final analysis, on what kind of trade-off between fidelity and broad usefulness one is willing to accept, an observation that leads Richard Lucas and Brent Donnellan to conclude that the local vs. global trait debate is best seen as a debate *among* personality psychologists with different pragmatic goals, not between personologists and situationists.[36]

To understand the force of this point, it is helpful to consider the study by Hugh Hartshorne and Mark May that is often cited as the *locus classicus* of the local vs. global critique.[37] Following the behavior of 8,000 school-children over a variety of situations involving what they perceived as "honesty," the authors found a very high degree of correlation (in the 0.7 range) within specific behaviors such as

- Cheating on written or puzzle test
- Cheating on homework, faking a record in athletic competition, faking or cheating in party games

- Stealing from a box of money left out
- Lying about any of the above

In contrast, they found "little" correlation—0.227, to be precise—between these four local tendencies. In other words, if one views 0.227 as an unacceptably weak correlation, the conclusion is that the children in this study exhibited local "honesties" ("honest when taking a test"), but no such thing as "honesty" in the way we would normally use the term.

As I hope I have established in the discussion of correlation coefficients, there is no reason to embrace this conclusion—0.227 can do quite a bit of work for us. While it is wonderful, and potentially quite useful, to know that we can predict with great certainty that little Sarah is going to cheat on a test, what we are often interested in doing is extrapolating from one specific type of behavior to another that is perceived as relevant. Assume that I am a youth camp counselor, and that all that I have at my disposal at the moment is information about which kids tend to cheat on tests and which kids tend to cheat in games. I now have to decide whom to leave in charge of the donation jar at an important fundraising event. I am an underpaid counselor at an underfunded youth camp, quite concerned about making sure that none of this badly needed money goes unaccounted for, rather than an academic psychologist interested in achieving extremely high correlations to impress journal referees. I do not see how it can be denied that 0.227 is good enough for me: I'm going to pass over little Sarah, whom I saw cheating on the exam, and little Johnny, who habitually cheats at Monopoly, when I choose my donation jar monitor, and this is an entirely rational decision given my available information and pragmatic needs. It is quite reasonable to assume that the origin of global-trait terms like "honest" or "brave" arose precisely out of this pragmatic need for broad predictions: over time, correlations in the .02 to .03 range are extremely significant, and we would expect that people interested in extrapolating from one behavioral tendency to another related one would latch onto such significant connections and invent labels for them.

It is, nonetheless, the case that if we could follow Hartshorne and May's children into adulthood, we are likely to find genuinely weak correlation between their broad "honesty" with regard to their professional behavior and their honesty with regard to, say, displaying fidelity to their spouse. The idea that this is a problem for virtue ethics hinges on another conceptual misunderstanding—one that begins to nudge us toward our final historical case example because it revolves around the intended scope of traditional virtue terms.

At one point in *Lack of Character*, Doris makes the helpful observation that "if your mechanic is honest in working on your car, you can commend her honesty to potential customers without worrying that she cheats on her taxes."[38] We could note that Doris fails to emphasize how global this attribution of professional honesty already is—an "honest" mechanic not only refrains from adding spurious items and services to your bill, but also refrains from stealing valuable objects from your car, replacing parts that still have some useful life in them, and in general putting her own financial interests above those of her clients. Nonetheless, he is probably correct that even a quite robust attribution of "honest" to a mechanic would fail to helpfully predict, for instance, the degree to which she refrained from cheating sexually on her spouse.

When presented as a critique of traditional virtue ethics, however, this observation fails to take into account the fact that traditional virtue terms, such as "honesty" or "bravery," were actually used in a relatively narrow context when compared to their modern folk usage. Consider the closest thing we could find to a term for "honesty" in Warring States (6th–3rd century BCE) China: the virtue term *xin* 信, usually translated as "trustworthiness" or "reliability." There is always a bit of debate concerning the precise connotation of traditional virtue terms such as this, and their usage also varied somewhat from thinker to thinker and over time, but what is beyond dispute is that the scope of *xin* 信 is confined to a gentleman's *professional* behavior toward his colleagues,[39] superiors, and/or inferiors, and the idea that it should also encompass an elite male's sexual fidelity to his wives and concubines would have been incomprehensible to the early Chinese.

What is true for *xin* 信 is also true for other traditional Confucian virtue terms: because the concerned actors form a relatively small subset of the population, and the social realities involved are much more clearly structured, Confucian virtue terms inevitably have a narrower scope than their English translations do in contemporary usage. I suspect that this is also true of virtue terms derived from Aristotle or later Western virtue ethicists, although I am not qualified to assert this with any confidence. In any case, the broader issue here is that a small set of virtue words inherited from traditional, highly structured societies are now arguably being asked to bear too much weight in the sort of unstructured, complex environments that characterize modern life in the industrialized world. The idea that the social psychology literature demonstrates that "there is no empirical support for the existence of character traits" picked out by such words as "honesty" or "courage" really depends on one's personal predilection regarding trade-offs of accuracy versus usefulness.[40] In any case, even if defensible, such a claim should be seen not so much as an indictment of traditional virtue ethics as a symptom of a problem with modern English: it has failed to innovate linguistically as the structure of society has radically changed.

However, even this more limited critique is probably overblown. It is not at all clear to me—and this is something that could and should be empirically investigated—that the actual, contemporary "folk" have any real expectation that there would be a correlation between their "honest" mechanic's professional behavior and the degree of sexual fidelity she observes in her private life. When we talk about "cheating" spouses we are talking about something quite different from "cheating" one's customers; the fact that the same word is used in both cases is conceptually interesting and requires explanation, but it in no way proves that the two domains have equivalent moral valence or structure in folk psychology.[41] Critiques of the predictive usefulness of such labels as "honest" or "courageous" might then be seen, not as a fatal blow to our fundamental concept of character but, rather, as an indication of how loosely we use virtue terms in contemporary discourse—a looseness that is permissible because our implicit, shared background knowledge allows us to call up the appropriate social and ethical frameworks required for comprehending any particular use of a term.

2. EARLY CONFUCIANISM VIRTUE ETHICS AND THE "HIGH BAR" ARGUMENT

There is another important feature of traditional virtue terms such as "honest" or "courageous," however, that may present more of a hurdle for virtue ethics. Even if we grant that traditional virtue terms had a relatively narrow scope of application, they nonetheless seem to demand more than even the most robust current conception of personality traits can provide. In characterizing a correlation coefficient on the magnitude of 0.3 as "negligible," situationists such as Doris are not denying it *any* predictive power but, rather, are contrasting it with the closer to 1.0 correlation that traditional notions of the virtues seem to require.[42]

For instance, Ted Williams's formidable batting prowess was not diminished by the fact that he occasionally failed to make a hit or even struck out. On the other hand, we would be hard-pressed to characterize as "faithful" a spouse who manages to resist extramarital sexual temptations only much of the time, or to laud as "courageous" a warrior who drops his weapons and flees from the enemy only somewhat less frequently than his peers. The core claim of the situationist critique—what we might call the "high bar" argument—is that virtue ethics demands a correlation between virtue possession and actual behavior of close to 1.0, and anything short of that is a fatal problem.

One way around this problem is to argue that the early Confucians had a much weaker notion of the virtues than, say, Aristotle, and that the "high bar" argument therefore simply does not apply to them. Unfortunately this does not seem to be the case, at least when it comes to moral exemplars. The *Analects*, for instance, portrays the perfected Confucian gentleman as impervious to the influence of reputation or material temptations. This internal moral autonomy is perhaps best expressed in Confucius's famous declaration that he could go and live among the Eastern barbarians and not only maintain his moral perfection but, in fact, transform his social environment through his moral influence.[43] It would thus seem that the early Confucian notion of virtue—like the Aristotelian and modern folk notion—is of a more or less 100 percent reliable, environmentally impermeable character trait, which would mean that it faces the same "high bar" challenge as posed by the situationist critique.

I wish to argue that the early Confucian model of virtue education gets them over this hurdle, but not entirely in the manner that the early Confucians themselves envisioned.[44] To begin with, their emphasis on intensive, life-long, highly regimented training gives them a higher jump, as it were: the virtues that they ask the gentleman to rely upon are not untutored natural gifts but, rather, intensively cultivated dispositions, which can be expected to be much more reliable than the traits typically studied by social psychologists. In addition, the manner in which they continuously bolster these cultivated traits with a host of situational buffers—ranging from strict social regulations to careful modulation of one's physical and interpersonal environment—effectively lowers the bar several notches. I will address both of these points in turn.

Moral Training and Dispositional "Extension"

To begin with, although there are occasional suggestions that some extraordinary individuals may come into the world with already well-developed and fully robust character traits,[45] the dominant position in early Confucianism is that whatever positive traits we may possess "naturally" at the beginning of the process of self-cultivation are relatively weak, and they require long-term, intensive training in order to become genuinely reliable—that is, in order to become true *virtues*. Relating this to some of the empirical literature reviewed above, we can observe that, even if one would want to insist that the sort of local "honesties" that characterize the children in Hartshorne and May's study are not correlated to a degree that would warrant the global label "honest" as a predictive term, a perfectly reasonable response would be that perhaps this is because they are *children* and have not yet learned to integrate these local traits into a broad and reliable disposition. Looked at this way, local traits remain ethically fragmented only to the extent that they remain untutored. Most, if not all, traditional virtue ethics envision some sort of cultural training as a necessary prerequisite to the acquisition of virtue, and one way to understand this training is that it involves the extension and integration of ethically related, but naturally fragmented, local traits.

Several responses to Doris's critique have made this point, but one of the most intriguing is that of Nancy Snow, because it draws upon current research in social psychology to demonstrate the plausibility of local trait extension and modification.[46] For instance, Snow takes the example of a negative local trait, such as an undesirable racial stereotype—a "deep-seated psychology construct...whose activation often occurs automatically and outside of the agent's conscious awareness"[47]—and discusses research suggesting that a process of self-regulation can lead to some degree of conscious control over the otherwise automatic activation of social stereotypes.[48] The same is presumably true in the case of positive behavioral tendencies. Snow remarks that this body of research suggests that "it is possible, with effort, to inhibit and control negative traits and cultivate and extend desired ones,"[49] which means that "though our virtues might start out by being local, they need not remain so."[50]

Interestingly, she also speculates about how one would go about extending a positive behavioral tendency limited to a very small domain of objective triggering conditions—say, compassion for small, cuddly animals—to a broader domain of sentient beings including, for example, one's friends, relatives, and even unrelated strangers. This process of modifying or extending, under the guidance of an expert, various naturally given but overly local traits is in fact the central strategy of early Confucian moral education. The process of compassion-extension that Snow envisions recalls a famous dialogue in the early Confucian text, *The Mencius* (4th century BCE), which describes precisely this sort of identification of a desirable, but overly local trait, and a strategy for extending this trait through reflection and imaginative work. Because this passage, *Mencius* 1:A:7, is such a masterwork of psychological insight and displays so paradigmatically the manner in which virtue ethical training might proceed, I would like to describe it in some detail, informed by the considerable body of scholarship that has formed around it, especially regarding the concept of "extension" (*tui* 推; lit. "pushing") that it introduces.

The passage open with Mencius in dialogue with a notoriously selfish and brutal king, King Xuan of Qi, who oppresses his people and shows no apparent concern for traditional Confucian morality. When Mencius suggests to the king that he can change his ways and become a true, compassionate Confucian ruler—one who protects and nourishes his people rather than oppressing them—the king is dubious: "What makes you think that a person like myself could be capable of this?" Mencius replies by relaying a story that he heard from one of the king's retainers:

> The King was sitting up upon his elevated throne in the Great Hall when an ox was led past him. The King saw it and asked, "Where is that ox being taken?" The reply was, "It is being taken to be ritually slaughtered so that its blood can be used to consecrate a newly-forged bell." The King said, "Let it go! I cannot bear its look of terror, like that of an innocent man being led to the execution ground." "Should we then abandon the consecration ritual?" "How could we abandon the ritual? Substitute a sheep in its place."

"Did this really happen?" Mencius slyly inquires. The king admits that it did, and Mencius then proceeds to lead him through the process of identifying the emotion that he felt—one that "is sufficient in and of itself to make one a true King"—and to distinguish it from other possible motivations. He first mentions that some of the king's subjects, noting the substitution of the sheep for the ox, speculate that the king was simply trying to economize on ritual expenditures, sheep being considerably cheaper than oxen. The king indignantly denies this—Qi is a small state, but he can certainly afford an ox—and repeats that he was motivated solely by the look of terror on the ox's face.

> "The King should not be surprised that the common people took him to be cheap," Mencius replied, "You exchanged a small animal for a large one, what were they to make of it? If the King were truly pained by the expression like that of an innocent man headed to the execution ground, then why spare the ox and sacrifice the sheep?"
>
> The King smiled uncomfortably, saying, "What, indeed, was my feeling at that moment? I certainly was not worried about the expense, and yet I did put the sheep in the ox's place. It is no wonder that the people think me cheap."
>
> Mencius replied, "There is no harm in this—in fact, it is precisely the feeling that you had that is the method of benevolence. You saw the ox, but had not yet seen the sheep. The gentleman's attitude toward animals is thus: having seen them alive, he cannot bear to see them killed; having heard their cries, he cannot bear to eat their flesh. This is why the gentleman keeps his distance from the kitchen."

This injunction for the gentleman to keep his distance from the kitchen has been understood as an expression of monumental hypocrisy, but the basic sentiment is quite understandable, and seems to be as follows.[51] Human beings universally react with compassion to the sight of a suffering animal. In a society where vegetarianism was not even a notional possibility, this means that those who wish to preserve this feeling must avoid exposure to the slaughter and processing of animals—a clear instance of situational management. Presumably those charged by society with performing these necessary functions, such as butchers and tanners, will learn to suppress this sort of compassion, or will simply become desensitized to animal suffering, which is why they were accorded a lowly status in Confucian society. In any case, Mencius holds up as the "method of benevolence" this isolated expression of compassion for an animal that the king had actually seen and heard—a very local and certainly extremely ethically fragmented trait, considering that the king had no compunction about having some anonymous sheep slaughtered in its place, and of course behaves in a notably nonbenevolent manner toward his subjects.[52]

Mencius's task as a moral educator is to get the king to see the ethical relevance of this narrow and isolated feeling of compassion for the ox—to understand its nature, and to begin to see how it might be relevant to broader ethical life. This next step begins after the king admits that Mencius has seen into his own heart and "taken its measure" better than the king himself had been able to do. He had indeed felt a twinge of compassion, motivated by the sight of suffering. However, in what way, he asks Mencius, is this momentary feeling relevant to the task of becoming a truly benevolent king?

> Mencius replied, "If someone came to you and said 'My strength is sufficient to lift five hundred pounds, but not sufficient to lift a single feather,' or 'My eyesight is sharp enough to distinguish the tip of an autumn hair, but unable to perceive a cartful of wood,' would you accept such words?
>
> The King said, "No."
>
> "Now, your compassion is abundant enough to reach even a lowly beast, and yet your bounty does not even extend to the common people of the realm. How is this any different?"

In other words, the king is apparently capable of a relatively difficult task (having compassion for a lowly sacrificial animal, in Mencius's mind not an obvious object of compassion) and yet has shown himself to be incapable of what should be a much easier task, showing compassion and kindness toward the common people—generally conceived of in early Chinese political discourse as the metaphorical children of the ruler, and thus natural objects of compassion.

There is considerable debate in the literature about what Mencius thinks he has accomplished by pointing out this apparent inconsistency to the king,[53] but it seems most likely that his goal is, as P. J. Ivanhoe has argued, to set up an "analogical resonance"—involving "emotional resonance not cognitive similarity"—between the "local" feeling of compassion for a suffering animal, which the king acknowledges having experienced, and another "local" feeling, that of compassion for his suffering people, which the king has for some reason yet to experience.[54] Arguably, it is precisely this sort of cross-situational resonance that is captured in global terms such as "compassion" or "honesty."

Having gotten the king to see, by examining his own emotional reactions, that he has the "sprout" of true benevolence (*ren* 仁) within him, and that there is some analogical relation between suffering animals and suffering commoners, Mencius's task is then to turn the king's quite narrow— and to Mencius's mind, at least, ethically irrelevant—disposition to feel empathy for an animal into a broader disposition to feel empathy for suffering humans.[55] This is to be accomplished through gradual strengthening or "extension" (*tui* 推) of the local disposition, a process of sympathetic projection and emotional training guided by metaphor and analogy:

> Treat the aged of your own family in a manner that respects their seniority, and
> then cause this treatment to reach the aged of other families. Treat the young
> ones of your family in a manner appropriate to their youth, and then cause this
> treatment to reach the young of other families. Once you are able to do this, you
> will have the world in the palm of your hand.

The passage in question, 1:A:7, is actually quite thin when it comes to spelling out precisely how "extension" is to be accomplished—Mencius immediately moves on to another argumentative tack with King Xuan— but the remainder of the text, and the early Confucian cultural context, helps us to flesh this out. It clearly involves imaginative work and emotional analysis, directed at previously experienced emotions, as in the case of King Xuan, or imagined emotions, as when Mencius famously invites all of us to consider the feeling of "alarm and distress" we would experience, at least for a moment, upon seeing a baby about to experience immanent physical harm.[56] This emotional analysis is to occur under expert guidance, such as that of Mencius himself, which serves to highlight for the novice as yet unperceived analogical resonances and nuances of the emotion, as well as offer suggestions about how "fragmented" local responses might be integrated into more coherent, broad and ethically useful dispositions.[57]

Two points need to be made in conclusion to this section. To begin with, it may certainly be the case that, even with extensive training, nothing anywhere near a 1.0 correlation between character traits and behavior is attainable. If it turns out that even intensely cultivated character traits cannot break through the 0.3 correlation coefficient barrier, this may very well end up being a fatal problem for virtue ethics of any stripe. This, however, is emphatically *not* what is demonstrated by the existing situationist literature, which looks only at completely untutored character traits. The degree of reliability in character traits attainable through deliberate training is a mostly unexplored and promising topic for future empirical inquiry, and one that must be pursued by anyone interesting in establishing the empirical plausibility of the virtue ethical model.

Second, it is important to realize that the entire process of Confucian character training was portrayed as occurring in a context of intense environmental manipulation, accomplished through immersion in and submission to traditional cultural forms. It is, moreover, not at all clear that—whatever the rhetoric about perfected sages and illustrious gentlemen—it was envisioned that even a fully trained individual was expected to function reliably outside of this buffer of environmental control. We might thus conclude that the function of such environmental buffering was to take up any slack between the reliability of even fully trained virtues and the close to 1.0 reliability expected of a true gentleman—to lower the bar just enough notches to allow the trained jump of the Confucian gentleman to clear it. This leads us to our next point, the role of the "situation" in Confucian self-cultivation.

Confucian Self-Cultivation as Manipulation of the Situation

The most important of the traditional cultural forms advocated by the early Confucians is ritual (*li* 禮). In the Warring States Confucian context, *li* referred to a set of cultural scripts governing a broad range of behaviors, from ancestral sacrifice and diplomatic ceremonies to details of one's personal comportment, such as the manner in which one dresses, takes one's meal, enters a room, or takes one's seat. Confucius himself was the first to argue that, by submitting to and internalizing these ritual forms, an aspiring gentleman would be able to restrain improper inborn tendencies, acquire the means to "take his place" (*li* 立) among other adults in society, and thereby acquire full virtue and win the favor of heaven. As P. J. Ivanhoe notes, although Mencius, with his faith in the potential goodness of human nature, appeared to have viewed ritual forms more as guidelines or supports to help direct incipient moral tendencies, both Confucius and his late War-ring States follower Xunzi conceptualized ritual as a tool for reshaping oth-erwise crude innate dispositions.[58] As Xunzi puts it:

> [Sorrow and joy] are emotions that are firmly rooted in the nature that people have at birth.[59] If these emotions can be trimmed or stretched, broadened or narrowed, augmented or decreased, categorized and thereby put to their full use, embellished and beautified, so that the root and branch, beginning and end match together seamlessly, and are worthy to serve as a model for ten thousand generations—this, then, is ritual.[60]

Training in ritual was to proceed alongside other forms of behavioral modification, including the appreciation and performance of music and dance, archery, riding, and calligraphy. The product of this immersion in cultural forms was to be the perfectly culturally refined (*wen* 文) gent-leman, who in every aspect of his physical deportment would reflect the aesthetic-moral ideals of the past Golden Age.[61] This sort of fully culti-vated gentleman would then, in turn, exert an influence on others by his mere physical presence, an idea expressed most strongly by Confucius in the passage mentioned above, *Analects* 9.14. Frustrated by his failure to be recognized by the rulers of his day, Confucius expresses a desire to go live among the barbarian tribes of the Eastern seaboard. When someone asks him how he—such an eminently cultured man—would be able to endure the uncouthness of barbarian life, Confucius replies, "If a true gentleman were to dwell among them, what uncouthness would there be?" The early Confucians had a specific term of art for this type of per-sonal, often unconscious influence of the gentleman upon others: *de* 德, or "charismatic Virtue." Metaphorically compared to the power of the Pole Star to attract the other stars in the sky and keep them in their proper orbits (2.1), or the ability of the wind to bend the grass below it (12.19), *de* might be seen as a form of interpersonally exerted situational control par excellence.[62]

Finally, an account of Confucian sensitivity to the situational effects cannot neglect their attention to one's conceptual environment. For in-stance, the literature on social stereotype priming highlights the manner in which specific social role terms can automatically and unconsciously impact behavior. Subjects who unscrambled a word jumble with words that evoke old people ("Florida," "gray," "wrinkle") walked more slowly when they left the laboratory, and those primed by concepts of politeness waited longer before interrupting. Subjects who unscrambled sentences about helpfulness were more likely to pick up objects dropped by an experimenter. Subjects primed by the social role "professor" performed significantly better on a general-knowledge task than nonprimed subjects, while subjects primed with the "soccer hooligan" role performed more poorly.[63] Similarly, alternative verbal framings of situations can significantly alter subjects' behaviors: higher levels of generosity in economic games, for instance, can be obtained simply by framing the exercise as a "community game" as opposed to a "Wall Street game."[64]

One way to view the Confucian practice of "learning" (*xue* 學)—a process of intensive study and memorization of textual classics, which describe in great detail the exemplary thoughts and conduct of the ancient sages—was that it served as a form of ever-present conceptual priming. A fully learned Confucian would have always at the forefront of his mind the exemplary behavior and words of ancient paragons, and it is not too great a stretch to see this as designed to increase the probability that he would act in accordance with these models. In *Analects* 2.2, Confucius remarks of the *Book of Odes*, a collection of poetry that records the sentiments of the ancients and the deeds of the ancient sage-kings, that "its poems number several hundred, but can be judged with a single phrase: 'They will not lead you astray.'" Moreover, the early Confucians were also very much concerned with the regulation of language use: while there is some scholarly disagreement concerning the exact nature of the Confucian practice of "rectifying names" (*zhengming* 正名),[65] it was clearly intended to provide normatively desirable frames for behavior. In *Analects* 13.3, Confucius is asked by a disciple what his first priority would be if he were given control of a state, and Confucius replies, "I would rectify names." The disciple is surprised by this answer, and Confucius elaborates:

> If names are not rectified, speech will not accord with reality; when speech does not accord with reality, things will not be successfully accomplished. When things are not successfully accomplished, ritual practice and music will fail to flourish; when ritual and music fail to flourish, punishments and penalties will miss the mark. And when punishments and penalties miss the mark, the common people will be at a loss as to what to do with themselves. This is why the gentleman only applies names that can be properly spoken, and assures that what he says can be properly put into action.

In another related passage, 12.11, a certain Duke Jing of Qi asks Confucius about how best to govern a state, and Confucius replies simply, "Let the lord be a true lord, the ministers true ministers, the fathers true fathers, and the sons true sons." This advice appears to be two-sided. Words should be applied only to their proper objects: someone who is not a true son, for instance, should not be called "son"—a message that many commentators feel is specifically directed to the Duke of Qi, who had passed over his elder son for succession and caused discord among his children. At the same time, words such as "father" or "ruler" bring with them certain positive social norms, and their very invocation should inspire a certain type of model emulation. The power of such words is, in turn, linked to the broader conceptual training provided by textual study: it is the paradigmatic behavior of the ancients as recorded in the classics that set the standards for what a "son" or "father" is, and that provide the idealized cultural models that are to be activated by proper language use.

The early Confucians clearly believed in the possibility of developing robust, global character traits that could endow an individual with a degree of independence from situational forces. The perfected Confucian gentleman is thought to possess an expansive compassion that would reliably produce benevolent behavior with regard to his inferiors and people in his charge; a degree of moral rectitude and inner strength that would convey stoic invulnerability to external temptations and vicissitudes such as social reputation, wealth, or sickness; a degree of wisdom and ritual propriety that would allow him to stand apart from and judge the cultural practices of his contemporaries; and a forthright courage in the face of corruption or immorality that would allow him to speak out against social superiors and those in power. To put this another way, the early Confucians seemed to believe that fully cultivated virtues should produce a close to 1.0 correlation with behavior. To the extent that even intensive, extended training is incapable of producing something in the neighborhood of such a correlation—something that remains to be examined empirically—we might therefore be forced to conclude that the early Confucians were as deluded as the Aristotelians about the power of character.

However, whatever their explicit claims, the specific social practices and institutions prescribed by Confucian thinkers suggest that—consciously or not—early Confucianism saw the need to bolster even fully trained dispositions with situational support. It is important to note that immersion in carefully designed cultural forms was not seen as coming to an end when the individual "finished" his training and attained the status of gentleman—indeed, the Confucians arguably saw the process of training as *never* coming to an end.[66] In their rhetoric concerning the incorruptible, lofty gentleman or sage, the early Confucians may have been as vulnerable as Aristotle to the "fundamental attribution error."[67] In fact, work in social psychology suggests that this attribution error is a basic, deeply engrained human cognitive tendency. What I hope to suggest here is that, whatever their explicit claims or assumptions, Confucian practices as envisioned by early thinkers did not rely entirely upon fully internalized, 100 percent reliable, and environmentally impervious character traits. At some level, the Confucians were exquisitely aware of the power of the situation, and their methods of self-cultivation—their techniques for producing relatively independent character traits—thus focused heavily on the manipulation of all aspects of the learner's physical, linguistic, and social environment.

In his response to Doris's work, Eric Hutton has also focused on this aspect of Confucianism, and he concludes by citing a passage from the *Xunzi* that captures quite well this attention to—even anxiety about—situational factors, conceptualized metaphorically as an external surface that one "rubs up against" (*mi* 靡):[68]

> Even if you possess a fine nature and character, as well as a discerning and well-informed mind, you still need to find a worthy teacher and devote yourself to his service, as well as a group of noble friends to befriend. If you obtain a worthy teacher to serve, then what you hear will be the ways of [the sages] Yao, Shun, Yu, and Tang. If you obtain a noble friend to befriend, then what you see will be conduct that is dutiful, trustworthy, respectful, and deferential. In this way, you in your own person will make daily progress toward benevolence and rightness without even being aware of it. This is because it is what you are rubbing up against that is making it so. Now, if you live among those who are not good, then what you hear will be trickery, deception, falseness, and hypocrisy, and what you see will be conduct that is foul, arrogant, perverse, deviant, and greedy. In this way, you in your own person will come to suffer punishment and execution, without you even being aware of what is happening. This is because it is what you are rubbing up against that is making it so. A saying goes, "If you do not know your son, observe his friends. If you do not know your lord, observe his companions." It is simply a matter of what you rub up against! It is simply a matter of what you rub up against![69]

I lack the expertise to judge whether or not the Aristotelian version of virtue ethics was based upon an empirically unjustifiable confidence in the robustness of character traits, independent of situational forces. What I hope to have suggested here is that the early Confucians, at least, combined a quite reasonable faith in trained, culturally modified, somewhat stable and independent character traits with a profound sensitivity to the power of "the situation."[70] Their example not only provides us with a picture of what an empirically defensible virtue ethic might look like, but also gives us a wealth of insights into how situational effects can be drawn upon and utilized in the process of moral education.

CONCLUSION

Over the past decade or so, one of the areas of research upon which Walter Mischel and his colleagues have been focusing attention is the interaction of the "hot," automatic, emotional "know how" systems and the "cool," conscious, "knowing that" systems, demonstrating that "willpower"—that is, the ability to resist adverse situational influences—can be enhanced through various forms of conceptual priming and training.[71] Mischel concludes:

> The French philosopher Descartes a few hundred years ago famously proclaimed "cogito ergo sum," I think, therefore I am, opening the way to what a few hundred years later became modern psychology. With what is now becoming known about personality, we can change his assertion to say: "I think, therefore I can change what I am. Because by changing how I think, I can change what I feel, do, and become."[72]

This observation might serve as a nice expression of the essence of Confucian virtue ethics. To be sure, early Confucian thinkers clearly perceived the ethical importance of rationality and willpower. For instance, they emphasized the importance of willpower when it comes to choosing one's general life priorities, as well as the role of the "heart-mind" (*xin* 心)[73] as the proper "ruler" of the self, charged with moral decision making and the enforcement of those decisions on the rest of the self. However, the education system that they established reveals a recognition—conscious or not—of the limits of what contemporary cognitive scientists would call on-line cognitive control. Although the decision to devote oneself to the Confucian Way was often portrayed as a momentary act of will, the actual process of following this Way involved the development of stable, gradually broadened dispositions, proper perceptual habits, and culturally constructed moods—all to be trained and maintained in a carefully controlled physical, conceptual, and social environment.

This progression of internalization of desirable moral norms is best exemplified by Confucius himself. In *Analects* 2.4, he describes his spiritual journey as beginning when he set his heart on learning at age fifteen, and finally ending at age seventy, where he can follow his spontaneous responses without ever transgressing the bounds of proper behavior.[74] That is, after a lifetime committed to the Confucian Way, having subjected himself to the rigors of learning and ritual practice until these traditional forms have become completely internalized, Confucius's hot cognition has been so thoroughly harmonized with the demands of culture that he behaves properly and yet completely spontaneously. Having reached this stage,

Confucius is described as "affable yet firm, awe-inspiring without being severe, simultaneously respectful and relaxed."[75] He is so immersed in Confucian culture that it even penetrates his dream life. "How seriously I have declined!" he says at one point, "It has been so long since I last dreamt of meeting the Duke of Zhou."[76] The Duke of Zhou was a great cultural hero for Confucius, the model of everything refined and virtuous. The fact that he became worried about not seeing the duke in his dreams every night gives a sense of how profoundly the Confucian Way was to get inside and transform the individual.[77]

One way to look at Confucian virtue ethics is as a kind of "time-delayed" cognitive control that functioned by embedding higher-level desires and goals in lower-level emotional and sensory-motor systems. The strength of this approach—and its great advantage over models of ethics such as deontology and utilitarianism that have dominated recent philosophical ethics in the West—is that it avoids the sharp limitations of on-line cognitive control that recent work in social psychology and cognitive science have made clear.[78] There is, moreover, a nascent but growing body of empirical evidence that this kind of dispositional education actually works. In addition to Mischel et al.'s work on the "agentic, proactive self," one might also consider the review by Jonathan Cohen of the relationship between emotions and prefrontal-cortex–mediated cognitive control in human behavior.[79] Cohen notes that, for instance,

> The specialized training given to doctors and soldiers involves the cultivation of mechanisms for averting or overcoming strong emotional responses that may interfere with their professional functions. These mechanisms may not rely directly on the prefrontal cortex; instead, they may involve the training of other lower-level mechanisms specific to the particular circumstances involved. Importantly, however, the social structures that devised and support the training procedures almost certainly did rely on the prefrontal cortex.[80]

The sort of training undergone by doctors and soldiers—designed to instill specific forms of courage and calmness under pressure as stable character traits—employs a set of strategies designed by the prefrontal cortex in order to overcome its own limitations in on-line, "hot" cognition situations: in other words, time-delayed cognitive control. Moreover, at least with regard to a subset of professionally relevant situations, this medical and military training seems to do its job.

With regard to more conceptual virtues, Nancy Snow, as noted above, argues that recent work on stereotype modification gives us reason to believe that even quite automatic and unconscious conceptual habits can, through gradual training, be brought into conscious attention and thereby modified in socially desirable directions. Similarly, Patrick Hill and Daniel Lapsley survey a set of contemporary approaches aimed at developing moral personality in ways not dissimilar to the early Confucian strategy, and this remains a very promising direction for future research on the empirical viability of virtue ethics.[81]

One of the great contributions of the situationist research agenda has been to make clear the immense power of subtle, and often unnoticed, aspects of situations and environments to shape human behavior. Like many scientific insights, it is somewhat counter-intuitive. It certainly presents a challenge to the models of ethics that have recently dominated modern Western philosophy, deontology and utilitarianism, which rely on rational agents making explicit decisions grounded in a transparent chain of reasoning under fully conscious control. It also exposed deep problems with early, naïve models of personality traits as rigid, situation-insensitive, and invariant, forcing personality psychologists to develop much more nuanced models of personality traits that take into account situational cues and developmental change. As championed in philosophical circles by scholars such as Harman and Doris, it has also forced defenders of virtue ethics—which, since at least the time of Mencius (4th century BCE), have seen psychological realism as their unique strength—to confront an important body of empirical data that calls into questions basic folk assumptions about the nature of the self.[82]

However, philosophers need to recognize that reports of the death of character have been greatly exaggerated. *Pace* observers such as Harman and Doris, recognizing the importance of the situation, could actually strengthen the empirical plausibility and appeal of virtue ethical models of moral reasoning and moral education, at least in something resembling their traditional Confucian forms. Unlike most modern Western ethicists, the early Chinese Confucians paid a great deal of attention to the power of the embodied situation—social role, dress, ambient color and sound—to effect human dispositions and behavior. They designed a sophisticated set of technologies to structure such environments in a way that would be conducive to morality, as well as a body of self-cultivation techniques to integrate potentially "fragmented," untutored dispositions into more robust ones that would—automatically and largely unconsciously—produce reliable, ethically desirable behaviors across a broad range of situations. The combination of the higher jump given by training and the lower bar provided by situational supports might very well be enough to allow the early Confucians to clear the main situationist hurdle—something close to a 1.0 correlation between virtue and behavior—albeit at the expense of bracketing some of the Confucians' own explicit claims.

Such bracketing will always be necessary when adapting ancient modes of thought to the modern world. No contemporary advocate of Confucianism would endorse their undeniable misogyny or their particular historical or metaphysical views. Adopting anything even remotely resembling the Zhou rituals endorsed by Confucius or Xunzi would of course be absurd, and the hierarchical and patriarchal society envisioned by the early Confucians would not seem to sit well with any sort of modern, liberal democracy. Moreover, we have to admit that these may be fatal problems: it is an open question whether or not one could achieve an effective enough combination of virtue training and situational control within the context of modern, secular democracy.

I will therefore keep my conclusion fairly modest: the early Confucian form of virtue ethics seems as if it could survive even the strongest and most plausible form of the situationist critique, which means that proclamations of the death of virtue ethics are rather premature. We can frame this a bit more strongly by observing that our current understanding of human cognition suggests that rationalist, cognitive-control–based models of ethics, such as deontology or utilitarianism, appear profoundly psychologically unrealistic. This, in turn, suggests that *some* form of virtue ethics is our best hope—if, that is, empirical plausibility is deemed a desirable feature when it comes to ethics. At the very least, we can say that, as we learn more about how the human mind works, ethical traditions such as early Confucianism help us to fill in enormous blind spots—the importance of the body, emotions, cultural training, the unconscious, and the social environment—that have hindered modern Western ethical thinking for the past several hundred years. They are thus of more than merely antiquarian interest, and can potentially help us in developing an ethic that will meet the challenges of the twenty-first century.[83]

NOTES

1. This is a modified version of a journal article that originally appeared in *Ethics* 121, no. 2 (2011): 390–419, © 2011 University of Chicago Press. I am very much indebted to Toni Schmader, Jess Tracy, Nancy Snow, John Doris, the *Ethics* editorial board, and especially one of the anonymous referees from *Ethics* for assistance and feedback that substantially improved that article; and would also like to thank Stephen Angle, Matt Bedke, Owen Flanagan, Eric Hutton, Hagop Sarkissian, Stephen Stich, and audience members at the 2009 Pacific APA meeting for helpful conversations on the topic. Work on both the original project and this revision was supported by the Social Sciences and Humanities Research Council of Canada and the Canada Research Chairs program.

2. David Hume, *Enquiries Concerning Human Understanding and Concerning the Principles of Morals*, 3rd ed. (Oxford: Clarendon, 1777/1976), 174–75.
3. This attitude is well exemplified in Kant's indignant rejection of the "slack, or indeed ignoble, attitude which seeks for the moral principles among empirical motives or laws," as well as his claim that the purity of moral philosophy depends upon its being "the authoress of her own laws" rather than "the mouthpiece of laws whispered to her by some implanted sense or by who knows what tutelary nature." *Groundwork of the Metaphysic of Morals*, trans. H. J. Paton (New York: Harper Torchbooks, 1785/1964), 93.
4. Owen Flanagan, *Varieties of Moral Personality: Ethics and Psychological Realism* (Cambridge, MA: Harvard University Press, 1991); Mark Johnson, *Moral Imagination: Implications of Cognitive Science for Ethics* (Chicago: University of Chicago Press, 1993).
5. Most succinctly and famously expressed in Flanagan's "Principle of Minimal Psychological Realism": "Make sure when constructing a moral theory or projecting a moral ideal that the character, decision processing, and behavior prescribed are possible...for creatures like us" (Flanagan, *Varieties*, 32).
6. Mark Johnson, *The Meaning of the Body: Aesthetics of Human Understanding* (Chicago: University of Chicago Press, 2008).
7. Jesse Prinz, "Passionate Thoughts: The Embodiment of Moral Concepts," in *Grounding Cognition: The Role of Perception and Action in Memory, Language and Thinking*, ed. D. R. Z. Pecher (Cambridge: Cambridge University Press, 2005); *The Emotional Construction of Morals* (New York: Oxford University Press, 2007).
8. A recent, representative collection of this work can be found in Joshua Knobe and Shaun Nichols, eds. *Experimental Philosophy* (New York: Oxford University Press, 2008).
9. See especially Antonio Damasio, *Descartes' Error: Emotion, Reason, and the Human Brain* (New York: G.P. Putnam's Sons, 1994); and Jonathan Haidt, "The Emotional Dog and its Rational Tail: A Social Intuitionist Approach to Moral Judgment," *Psychological Review* 108 (2001): 814–34; a helpful review of this literature can be found in Haidt, "The New Synthesis in Moral Psychology," *Science* 316 (2007): 998–1002.
10. Paul Churchland, "Toward a Cognitive Neurobiology of the Moral Virtues," *Topoi* 17 (1998): 83–96; William Casebeer, *Natural Ethical Facts: Evolution, Connectionism and Moral Cognition* (Cambridge, MA: MIT Press, 2003); Edward Slingerland, "'Of What Use are the *Odes*?' Cognitive Science, Virtue Ethics, and Early Confucian Ethics," *Philosophy East & West* 61 (2011): 80–109.
11. Of course, more recent proponents of both deontology and utilitarianism have acknowledged an important role for intuitive, implicit cognitive processes, sometimes confining explicit, algorithmic reasoning to a critical meta-level, which may only be invoked when conflicts arise or justifications need to be provided. While certainly more psychologically realistic, this still begs the question of how the behavioral *desiderata* arrived at through deontological or utilitarian reasoning are to be built into automatic, everyday cognition, which is an issue that I would argue virtue ethics uniquely and explicitly addresses.
12. Gilbert Harman, "Moral Philosophy Meets Social Psychology: Virtue Ethics and the Fundamental Attribution Error," *Proceedings of the Aristotelian Society* 99 (1999): 315–31; John Doris, *Lack of Character: Personality and Moral Behavior* (New York: Cambridge University Press, 2002).
13. It is worth noting the Flanagan's original cautions were relatively mild, and he has since become quite critical of what he refers to as "a small band of mischievous hyperbolists, really just two" (i.e., Harman, "Moral Philosophy"; and Doris, *Lack of*

Character) who "have had their fun for too long making ontological mischief" (55) among psychologically and statistically underinformed philosophers. See Flanagan "Moral Science? Still Metaphysical After All these Years," *Personality, Identity, and Character: Explorations in Moral Psychology*, ed. D. Narvaez and D. Lapsley (Notre Dame, IN: University of Notre Dame Press, 2009), 54–65, for a critique of situationism that resonates with the arguments that I will be making below, as well as the contribution by Russell to this volume (chapter 1).

14. See, e.g., Joel Kupperman, "Naturalness Revisited," *Confucius and the Analects*, ed. B. Van Norden (New York: Oxford University Press, 2002); Rachana Kamtekar, "Situationism and Virtue Ethics on the Content of Our Character," *Ethics* 114 (2004): 458–91; John Sabini and Maury Silver, "Lack of Character? Situationism Critiqued," *Ethics* 115 (2005): 535–62; Diana Fleming, "The Character of Virtue: Answering the Situationist Challenge to Virtue Ethics," *Ratio* 19 (2006): 24–42; Eric Hutton, "Character, Situationism, and Early Confucian Thought," *Philosophical Studies* 127 (2006): 37–58; and Nancy Snow, *Virtue as Social Intelligence: An Empirically Grounded Theory* (New York: Routledge, 2010).

15. For a defense of Confucianism as "virtue ethic," see Stephen Wilson, "Conformity, Individuality, and the Nature of Virtue: A Classical Confucian Contribution to Contemporary Ethical Reflection," *Journal of Religious Ethics* 23 (1995): 263–89; Philip J. Ivanhoe, *Confucian Moral Self Cultivation*, 2nd ed. (Indianapolis/Cambridge MA: Hackett, 2000); Edward Slingerland, "Virtue Ethics, the *Analects*, and the Problem of Commensurability," *Journal of Religious Ethics* 29 (2001); and Bryan Van Norden, *Virtue Ethics and Consequentialism in Early Chinese Philosophy* (New York: Cambridge University Press, 2007). I take early Confucian thought as my model of virtue ethics both because it is the only form of virtue ethics that I am qualified to responsibly discuss and because, as I will argue in this second section, it may be less vulnerable to the situationist critique than the Aristotelian form that has played a more prominent role in the revival of virtue ethics.

16. John Darley and C. Daniel Batson, "From Jerusalem to Jericho: A Study of Situational and Dispositional Variables in Helping Behavior," *Journal of Personality and Social Psychology* 27 (1973): 100–19; Alice Isen and Paula Levin, "The Effect of Feeling Good on Helping: Cookies and Kindness," *Journal of Personality and Social Psychology* 21 (1972): 384–88.

17. Brent Donnelan, Richard Lucas, and William Fleeson, eds., *Journal of Research in Personality* 43, no. 2 (April 2009). M. The reader is referred to this issue for a much more detailed account of the state of the field than can be provided here. Although one might feel that *JRP*'s hosting a survey of the personality vs. situation debate is a bit like *Pravda* at the height of the Cold War devoting an issue to the relative merits of capitalism vs. communism; the editors of this special issue made a concerted effort to be even-handed, and the full spectrum of opinions on the topic is represented. David C. Funder, "Persons, Behaviors and Situations: An Agenda for Personality Psychology in the Postwar Era," *Journal of Research in Personality* 43 (2009): 120–26. Also see the comment in this volume by Dan P. McAdams (chapter 12) that "whereas the situationist critique offered useful corrective points for the field of personality psychology, it ultimately lost the intellectual war."

18. See Brent Roberts, "Back to the Future: Personality and Assessment and Personality Development," *Journal of Research in Personality* 43 (2009): 139–40, on "what are personality traits, anyway?"

19. Walter Mischel, "From *Personality and Assessment* (1968) to Personality Science, 2009," *Journal of Research in Personality* 43 (2009): 284.

20. Walter Mischel, Yuichi Shoda, and Rodolfo Mendoza-Denton, "Situation-Behavior Profiles as a Locus of Consistency in Personality," *Current Directions in Psychological Science* 11 (2002): 50–54.
21. Doris, *Lack of Character*, 64.
22. Jack Block and Jeanne H. Block, "Venturing a 30-Year Longitudinal Study,"*American Psychologist* 61 (2006): 315–27; D. P. McAdams and J. L. Pals, "A New Big Five: Fundamental Principles for an Integrative Science of Personality," *American Psychologist* 61 (2006): 204–17.
23. Auke Tellegen et al., "Personality Similarity in Twins Reared Apart and Together," *Journal of Personality and Social Psychology* 54 (1988): 1031–39.
24. Paul Costa and Robert McRae, "Personality in Adulthood: A Six-Year Longitudinal Study of Self-Reports and Spouse Ratings on the Neo Personality Inventory," *Journal of Personality and Social Psychology* 54 (1988): 853–63; Robert Hogan, "In Defense of Personality Measurement: New Wine for Old Whiners," *Human Performance* 18 (2005): 331–41; Daniel Ozer and Verónica Benet-Martinez, "Personality and the Prediction of Consequential Outcomes," *Annual Review of Psychology* 57 (2006): 401–21; Brent Roberts, Nathan Kuncel, Rebecca Shiner, Avshalom Caspi, and Lewis Goldberg, "The Power of Personality: The Comparative Validity of Personality Traits, Socioeconomic Status, and Cognitive Ability for Predicting Important Life Outcomes," *Perspectives on Psychological Science* 2 (2007): 313–45.
25. Doris, *Lack of Character*, 73–74.
26. In another of the early situationist classics, Lee Ross and Richard Nisbett granted that the correlations might be as high as 0.4. (Lee Ross and Richard Nisbett, *The Person and the Situation: Perspectives of Social Psychology* [Philadelphia: Temple University Press, 1991]).
27. As always sensitive to potential counterarguments (a character trait?), Doris does acknowledge that one person's "weak" correlation is another person's "suggestive" one (*Lack of Character*, 38), but fails to further question this dismissal of 0.3 as insignificant.
28. Gregory J. Meyer et al., "Psychological Testing and Psychological Assessment: A Review of Evidence and Issues," *American Psychologist* 56 (2001): 128–65.
29. David Funder and Daniel Ozer, "Behavior as a Function of the Situation," *Journal of Peronality and Social Psychology* 44 (1983): 107–12; F. D. Richard, Charles Jr. Bond, and Juli Stokes-Zoota, "One Hundred Years of Social Psychology Quantitatively Described," *Review of General Psychology* 7 (2003): 331–63.
30. Richard, Bond and Stokes-Zoota, "One Hundred Years," a massive meta-study of a century of social psychology literature encompassing 25,000 studies of 8 million subjects, concluded that social psychological effects averaged a "Pearson product-moment coefficient" (*r*)—which measures the linear dependence between two variables—of.21, with a standard deviation of. 15.
31. Robert Rosenthal and Donald Rubin, "A Simple, General Purpose Display of Magnitude of Experimental Effect," *Journal of Educational Psychology* 74 (1982): 166–69.
32. From Robert Abelson, "A Variance Explanation Paradox: When a Little is a Lot," *Psychological Bulletin* 97: 129–33 (cited in Sabini and Silver, "Lack of Character?").
33. Harman, "Moral Philosophy"; Doris, *Lack of Character*, 64. As Nancy Snow observes, Doris's strong anti-globalist view of local traits is even more extreme than the model currently embraced by Walter Mischel and his colleagues, the "cognitive-affecting processing system (CAPS)," which encompasses the individual's subjective interpretation of situations as well as objective situational features, and

thus is much more amenable to modification or extension (Snow, *Virtue as Social Intelligence*).

34. To be fair, for all his dramatic talk of "lack of character," the argument of Doris, at least, is not based upon a blanket denial of global traits, or an absolute distinction between local and global, but merely the claim that empirically defensible traits are not global *enough* to do the work that virtue ethics requires of them. I will address this "high bar" argument—the claim that nothing short of a nearly 1.0 correlation between traits and behavior is adequate to get a virtue ethical system off the ground—in section 2.

35. Funder, "Persons," 122.

36. Richard E. Lucas and M. Brent Donnellan, "If the Person-Situation Debate Is Really Over, Why Does it Still Generate so Much Negative Affect?," *Journal of Research in Personality* 43 (2009): 146–49.

37. Hugh Hartshorne and Mark May, *Studies in the Nature of Character. Volume 1. Studies in Deceit* (New York: Macmillan, 1928).

38. Doris, *Lack of Character*, 115.

39. It was pointed out by an anonymous reader that *xin* is a crucial virtue in interactions with one's *you* 友, a term typically translated as "friends," which might seem to undermine my claim that *xin* is restricted to one's professional behavior. It is important to realize that, in the Confucian context, *you* refers not to random acquaintances or childhood buddies but, rather, to a subset of the *professional* colleagues of a given "gentleman"—the cultivated scholar-politician who is the target of Confucian education—who are more or less of the same rank/seniority, and with whom the gentleman, to borrow a concept from Aristotle, shares a vision of the "Good." *You* marks out those colleagues whom one finds personally amenable and who also share one's moral aspirations.

40. Harman, "Moral Philosophy."

41. My first-run guess would be that it involves a perceived metaphorical resonance between the financial harm caused by professional compact with a client and the emotional harm caused to one's spouse by violating a social compact.

42. As mentioned in a note above, this can be seen as the core of Doris's argument against virtue ethics, and I thank both Doris (in conversation with author, April 2009) and one of the anonymous readers of my original *Ethics* submission for clarifying this point and focusing my attention upon it.

43. Confucius, *Analects* 9.14. See *Xunzi*, ch. 2 ("Cultivating the Self") for a more extended expression of this sentiment (John Knoblock, *Xunzi: A Translation and Study of the Complete Works*. Vol. 1. (Stanford, CA: Stanford University Press, 1988, 154–55).

44. This chapter is intended more as a response to the situationist critique than a full introduction to early Confucian ethics, so I will do no more here than briefly sketch out a few relevant aspects of the early Confucian picture of self-cultivation. For more in-depth discussions, the reader is referred to Ivanhoe, *Confucian Moral Self-Cultivation*; Edward Slingerland, *Effortless Action: Wu-wei as Conceptual Metaphor and Spiritual Ideal in Early China* (New York: Oxford University Press, 2003); and Van Norden, *Virtue Ethics*, as well as the Confucian response to situationism described by Eric Hutton, "Character, Situationism," 37–58.

45. Confucius declares in *Analects* 16.9 that "those who are born understanding it are the best," and the portrayal of the disciple Yan Hui in that text suggests that he was such a person (see especially 2.9, 5.9, 6.7, and 11.4); cf. the portrayal of the sage-king Shun in *Mencius* 7:A:16.

46. See, for instance, Kamtekar's observation ("Situationism and Virtue Ethics") that narrow dispositions can be extended cross-situationally through analogical reasoning. Snow, *Virtue as Social Intelligence.*

47. Snow, *Virtue as Social Intelligence,* 34.

48. E.g., Patricia Devine and Margo Monteith, "Automaticity and Control in Stereotyping," *Dual-Process Models and Themes in Social and Cognitive Psychology,* ed. S. Chaiken and Y. Trope (New York: Guilford, 1999).

49. Snow, *Virtue as Social Intelligence,* 38.

50. Snow, *Virtue as Social Intelligence,* 37.

51. A roughly contemporaneous text that is very critical of Confucian morality, the *Zhuangzi,* contains a passage where a butcher cutting up an ox in front of his ruler, presumably for just such a sacrifice, is presented as a perfected sage, and his butchering as a model for proper living. It is possible that this story is partially intended to mock the fastidious hypocrisy of *Mencius* 1:A:7.

52. For Mencius, "benevolence" (*ren* 仁), although only one of four cardinal virtues, is the most important, and often stands in metonymically for the other three, which accounts for his eagerness to demonstrate its existence in even such as figure as King Xuan.

53. See Ivanhoe, *Confucian Moral Self Cultivation,* for an overview of this literature.

54. P.J. Ivanhoe, "Confucian Self-Cultivation and Mengzi's Notion of Extension," *Essays in the Moral Philosophy of Mengzi,* ed. Xiusheng Liu and P. J. Ivanhoe (Cambridge, MA: Hackett, 2002): 226; cf. David Wong, "Reasons and Analogical reasoning in *Mengzi*," in Liu and Ivanhoe, *Essays*; and Van Norden, *Virtue Ethics,* 234–38.

55. This account of Mencian self-cultivation is derived from Ivanhoe, *Confucian Moral Self Education,* to which the reader is referred for a more complete account.

56. *Mencius,* 2:A:6.

57. See D. Narvaez, "The Co-Construction of Virtue: Epigenetics, Development, and Culture," chapter 10 this volume, for parallels with this Mencian technique.

58. See Ivanhoe, "Confucian Self-Cultivation," for an outline of the various strategies found in early Confucian self-cultivation.

59. In this passage, "sorrow and joy" are standing in metonymically for all innate human emotions.

60. Knoblock, *Xunzi,* ch. 19, *Discourse on Ritual.*

61. For more on the moral significance of "style" for the early Confucians, see Nicholas Gier, "The Dancing Ru: A Confucian Aesthetics of Virtue," *Philosophy East & West* 51 (2001): 280–305; Joel Kupperman, "Naturalness Revisited"; and Amy Olberding, "The Educative Function of Personal Style in the *Analects*," *Philosophy East & West* 57 (2007): 357–74.

62. On this topic, see also the discussion of Hagop Sarkissian on the apparent importance of "agent-introduced situational effects" in Confucius's *Analects* (Hagop Sarkissian, "Minor Tweaks, Major Payoffs: The Problems and Promise of Situationism in Moral Philosophy," *Philosopher's Imprint* 10, no. 9 (2012): 1–15. For contemporary discussions on the importance of situational factors for virtue ethics, see Maria Merritt, "Virtue Ethics and Situationist Personality Psychology," *Ethical Theory and Moral Practice* 3 (2000): 365–83, on virtues as local traits sustained by social relationships and settings; or Steven Samuels and William Casebeer, "A Social Psychological View of Morality: Why Knowledge of Situational Influences on Behavior Can Improve Character Development Practices," *Journal of Moral Education* 34 (2005): 73–87, on the role of proper training environments in facilitating virtue acquisition.

63. Ap Dijkhuizen and A. Van Knippenberg, "The Relation Between Perception and Behavior or How to Win a Game of Trivial Pursuit," *Journal of Personality and Social Psychology* 74 (1998): 865–77. For a review of some of this literature, see Ap Dijkhuizen and John Bargh, "The Perception-Behavior Expressway: Automatic Effects of Social Perception on Social Behavior," *Advances in Experimental Social Psychology*, ed. M. P. Zanna (San Diego: Academic Press: 2001). Quite recently controversy has arisen because of repeated failed attempts to replicate previously published results (e.g., Harold Pashler, Noriko Coburn, and Christine Harris, "Priming of Social Distance? Failure to Replicate Effects on Social and Food Judgments," *PLoS One* 7, no. 8 (2012): e42510); and there are now calls to rigorously review the entire priming literature (Ed Yong, "Nobel Laureate Challenges Psychologists to Clean up Their Act," *Nature News* 490 [2012]: 7418). Some of the failed replication attempts suggest that priming does, in fact, work, although not quite in the way suggested by earlier work. For instance, a very interesting recent study (Stéphane Doyen, Olivier Klein, Cora-Elise Pichon, and Axel Cleeremans, "Behavioral Priming: It's All in the Mind, but Whose Mind?" *PLoS ONE* 7, no. 1 [2012]: e29081) failed to replicate Bargh et al 1996's precise results, except in a condition where the "old person" primes were delivered in the presence of an experimenter who *expected* the subject to walk more slowly as a result (John A. Bargh, Mark Chen, and Lara Burrows, "Automaticity of Social Behavior: Direct Effects of Trait Construct and Stereotype Activation on Action," *Journal of Personality and Social Psychology* 71, no. 2 [1996]: 230–44); this suggests that conceptual priming has a causal effect on behavior when accompanied by subtle interpersonal clues. This combination of conceptual priming and interpersonal cueing would, of course, be characteristic of Confucian education.

64. Lee Ross and Andrew Ward. "Naive Realism in Everyday Life: Implications for Social Conflict and Misunderstandings," in *Values and Knowledge*, ed. E. Reed, E. Turiel, and T. Brown (Mahwah, NJ: Lawrence Erlbaum, 1996).

65. For more on *zhengming*, see Hui Chieh Loy, "*Analects* 13.3 and the Doctrine of 'Correcting Names,'" *Monumenta Serica* (2003): 19–36.

66. To take merely a few examples from the *Analects*, Confucius himself was reluctant to declare himself perfected, noting that "what can be said about me is no more than this: I work at it without growing tired and encourage others without growing weary" (7.34); on a similar note, he warned his disciples to "learn as if you will never catch up, and as if you feared losing what you have already attained" (8.17). Master Zeng in 8.7 notes that the journey of the gentleman ends "only with death," and even the supposedly "good-by-birth" disciple Yan Hui is portrayed in *Analects* 9.11 as lamenting of the Confucian Way, "the more I look up at it the higher it seems; the more I delve into it, the harder it becomes. Catching a glimpse of it before me, I then suddenly find it at my back."

67. Harman, "Moral Philosophy."

68. Hutton, "Character, Situationism."

69. Knoblock, *Xunzi*, ch. 23 ("Human Nature if Bad"), adapted from Hutton's translation, with an additional line cited at the beginning.

70. As one anonymous *Ethics* referee observed, one might argue that such an ethic should be seen as "situationism with a touch of virtue theory thrown in," rather than a genuine virtue ethic. However, since situationism as it has typically been formulated leaves essentially *no* causal room for character traits, it would seem that, when it comes to early Confucian ethics, we are still clearly under the ambit of "virtue ethics," although the relative roles being played by enhanced character traits and situational controls is an open question.

71. See Walter Mischel, "From *Personality and Assessment*," for a helpful overview of this work on the "agentic, proactive self."
72. Mischel, "From *Personality and Assessment*," 288.
73. *Xin* refers to the organ of the heart, which by mid-Warring States was perceived as the locus of distinction making, language use, reasoning, and free will, as well as the locus of certain moral emotions. It thus does not correspond neatly to either "mind" or "heart."
74. Edward Slingerland, *Effortless Action*, 9.
75. Confucius, *Analects* 7.38; Slingerland, *Effortless Action*, 77.
76. Confucius, *Analects* 7.5; Slingerland, *Effortless Action*, 65.
77. One of the primary debates in early Confucianism concerned the extent to which moral norms are something already present in human nature, only needing to be strengthened and extended by training (the position of Mencius), or something external to the individual needing to be internalized through training. See Slingerland, *Effortless Action*, for more details on this debate.
78. On this topic, see Slingerland, "Toward an Empirically-Responsible Ethics: Cognitive Science, Virtue Ethics, and Effortless Attention in Early Chinese Thought," in *Effortless Attention: A New Perspective in the Cognitive Science of Attention and Action*, ed. Brian Bruya (Cambridge, MA: MIT Press, 2010); and Slingerland, "Of What Use?"
79. Jonathan D.Cohen, "The Vulcanization of the Human Brain: A Neural Perspective on Interactions Between Cognition and Emotion," *Journal of Economic Perspectives* 19 (2004): 3–24.
80. Cohen, "The Vulcanization," 19.
81. Patrick Hill and Daniel Lapsley, "Persons and Situations in the Moral Domain," *Journal of Research in Personality* 43 (2009): 245–46; also see the discussion by McAdams (chapter 12, this volume) of the importance of cultivation and training in the Aristotelian scheme.
82. One of Mencius's primary critiques of the consequentialist, rationalist Mohist school was that their ethical demands and extreme voluntarism went against basic human cognitive and emotional capacities, and were therefore psychologically infeasible; Xunzi similarly criticized Mohism for ignoring basic human emotional tendencies and the ability of cultural forms to reshape these tendencies in an ethically desirable way.
83. For more on this topic, see Donald Munro, *A Chinese Ethics for the New Century: The Ch'ien Mu Lectures in History and Culture, and Other Essays on Science and Confucian Ethics* (Hong Kong: The Chinese University of Hong Kong Press, 2005); and Slingerland, "Of What Use?"

BIBLIOGRAPHY

Abelson, Robert. "A Variance Explanation Paradox: When a Little is a Lot." *Psychological Bulletin* 97 (1985): 129–33.
Bargh, John A., Mark Chen, and Lara Burrows. "Automaticity of Social Behavior: Direct Effects of Trait Construct and Stereotype Activation on Action." *Journal of Personality & Social Psychology* 71, no. 2 (1996): 230–44.
Block, Jack, and Jeanne H. Block. "Venturing a 30-Year Longitudinal Study." *American Psychologist* 61 (2006): 315–27.

Casebeer, William. *Natural Ethical Facts: Evolution, Connectionism and Moral Cognition.* Cambridge, MA: MIT Press, 2003.

Churchland, Paul. "Toward a Cognitive Neurobiology of the Moral Virtues." *Topoi* 17 (1998): 83–96.

Cohen, Jonathan D. "The Vulcanization of the Human Brain: A Neural Perspective on Interactions Between Cognition and Emotion." *Journal of Economic Perspectives* 19 (2004): 3–24.

Confucius. *Analects, With Selections from Traditional Commentaries.* Translated by Edward Slingerland. Indianapolis: Hackett, 2003.

Costa, Paul, and Robert McRae. "Personality in Adulthood: A Six-Year Longitudinal Study of Self-Reports and Spouse Ratings on the Neo Personality Inventory." *Journal of Personality and Social Psychology* 54 (1988): 853–63.

Damasio, Antonio. *Descartes' Error: Emotion, Reason, and the Human Brain.* New York: G.P. Putnam's Sons, 1994.

Darley, John, and C. Daniel Batson. "From Jerusalem to Jericho: A Study of Situational and Dispositional Variables in Helping Behavior." *Journal of Personality and Social Psychology* 27 (1973): 100–19.

Devine, Patricia, and Margo Monteith, "Automaticity and Control in Stereotyping." In *Dual-Process Models and Themes in Social and Cognitive Psychology*, edited by S. Chaiken and Y. Trope, 339–60. New York: Guilford, 1999.

Dijkhuizen, Ap, and John Bargh. "The Perception-Behavior Expressway: Automatic Effects of Social Perception on Social Behavior." In *Advances in Experimental Social Psychology*, edited by M. P. Zanna, 1–40. San Diego: Academic Press, 2001.

Dijkhuizen, Ap, and A. Van Knippenberg. "The Relation Between Perception and Behavior or How to Win a Game of Trivial Pursuit." *Journal of Personality and Social Psychology* 74 (1998): 865–77.

Donnelan, M. Brent, Richard Lucas, and William Fleeson, eds. *Journal of Research in Personality* 43, no. 2 (April 2009): entire issue.

Doris, John. *Lack of Character: Personality and Moral Behavior.* New York: Cambridge University Press, 2002.

Doyen, Stéphane, Olivier Klein, Cora-Elise Pichon, and Axel Cleeremans. "Behavioral Priming: It's All in the Mind, but Whose Mind?" *PLoS ONE* 7, no. 1 (2012): e29081.

Flanagan, Owen. "Moral Science? Still Metaphysical After All these Years." In *Personality, Identity, and Character: Explorations in Moral Psychology*, edited by D. Narvaez and D. Lapsley, 54–65. Notre Dame, IN: University of Notre Dame Press, 2009.

Flanagan, Owen. *Varieties of Moral Personality: Ethics and Psychological Realism.* Cambridge, MA: Harvard University Press, 1991.

Fleming, Diana. "The Character of Virtue: Answering the Situationist Challenge to Virtue Ethics." *Ratio* 19 (2006): 24–42.

Funder, David C. "Persons, Behaviors and Situations: An Agenda for Personality Psychology in the Postwar Era." *Journal of Research in Personality* 43 (2009): 120–26.

Funder, David C., and Daniel Ozer. "Behavior as a Function of the Situation." *Journal of Peronality and Social Psychology* 44 (1983): 107–12.

Gier, Nicholas. "The Dancing Ru: A Confucian Aesthetics of Virtue." *Philosophy East & West* 51 (2001): 280–305.

Haidt, Jonathan. "The Emotional Dog and its Rational Tail: A Social Intuitionist Approach to Moral Judgment." *Psychological Review* 108 (2001): 814–34.

Haidt, Jonathan. "The New Synthesis in Moral Psychology." *Science* 316 (2007): 998–1002.

Harman, Gilbert. "Moral Philosophy Meets Social Psychology: Virtue Ethics and the Fundamental Attribution Error." *Proceedings of the Aristotelian Society* 99 (1999): 315–31.

Hartshorne, Hugh, and Mark May. *Studies in the Nature of Character. Volume 1. Studies in Deceit.* New York: Macmillan, 1928.

Hill, Patrick, and Daniel Lapsley. "Persons and Situations in the Moral Domain." *Journal of Research in Personality* 43 (2009): 245–46.

Hogan, Robert. "In Defense of Personality Measurement: New Wine for Old Whiners." *Human Performance* 18 (2005): 331–41.

Hume, David. *Enquiries Concerning Human Understanding and Concerning the Principles of Morals,* 3rd ed. Oxford: Clarendon, 1777/1976.

Hutton, Eric. "Character, Situationism, and Early Confucian Thought." *Philosophical Studies* 127 (2006): 37–58.

Isen, Alice, and Paula Levin. "The Effect of Feeling Good on Helping: Cookies and Kindness." *Journal of Personality and Social Psychology* 21 (1972): 384–88.

Ivanhoe, Philip J. *Confucian Moral Self Cultivation,* 2nd ed. Indianapolis/Cambridge MA: Hackett, 2000.

Ivanhoe, Philip J. "Confucian Self-Cultivation and Mengzi's Notion of Extension." *Essays in the Moral Philosophy of Mengzi,* edited by Xiusheng Liu and P. J. Ivanhoe. Cambridge, MA: Hackett, 2002.

Johnson, Mark. *The Meaning of the Body: Aesthetics of Human Understanding.* Chicago: University of Chicago Press, 2008.

Johnson, Mark. *Moral Imagination: Implications of Cognitive Science for Ethics.* Chicago: University of Chicago Press, 1993.

Kamtekar, Rachana. "Situationism and Virtue Ethics on the Content of Our Character." *Ethics* 114 (2004): 458–91.

Kant, Immanuel. *Groundwork of the Metaphysic of Morals.* Translated by H. J. Paton. New York: Harper Torchbooks, 1785/1964.

Knobe, Joshua, and Shaun Nichols, eds. *Experimental Philosophy.* New York: Oxford University Press, 2008.

Knoblock, John. *Xunzi: A Translation and Study of the Complete Works,* vol. 1. Stanford, CA: Stanford University Press, 1988.

Kupperman, Joel. "Naturalness Revisited." In *Confucius and the Analects,* edited by B. Van Norden, 39–42. New York: Oxford University Press, 2002.

Loy, Hui Chieh. "*Analects* 13.3 and the Doctrine of 'Correcting Names.'" *Monumenta Serica* 60 (2003): 19–36.

Lucas, Richard E., and M. Brent Donnellan. "If the Person-Situation Debate Is Really Over, Why Does it Still Generate so Much Negative Affect?" *Journal of Research in Personality* 43 (2009): 146–49.

McAdams, D. P. "Psychological Science and the *Nicomachean Ethics*: Virtuous Actors, Agents, and Authors." Chapter 10 in *Cultivating Virtue: Multiple Perspectives,* edited by Nancy E. Snow. New York: Oxford University Press, 2014.

McAdams, D. P., and J. L. Pals. "A New Big Five: Fundamental Principles for an Integrative Science of Personality." *American Psychologist* 61 (2006): 204–17.

Merritt, Maria. "Virtue Ethics and Situationist Personality Psychology." *Ethical Theory and Moral Practice* 3 (2000): 365–83.

Meyer, Gregory J., et al. "Psychological Testing and Psychological Assessment: A Review of Evidence and Issues." *American Psychologist* 56 (2001): 128–65.

Mischel, Walter. "From *Personality and Assessment* (1968) to Personality Science, 2009." *Journal of Research in Personality* 43 (2009): 284.

Mischel, Walter, Yuichi Shoda, and Rodolfo Mendoza-Denton. "Situation-Behavior Profiles as a Locus of Consistency in Personality." *Current Directions in Psychological Science* 11 (2002): 50–54.

Munro, Donald. *A Chinese Ethics for the New Century: The Ch'ien Mu Lectures in History and Culture, and Other Essays on Science and Confucian Ethics.* Hong Kong: The Chinese University of Hong Kong Press, 2005.

Narvaez, D. "The Co-Construction of Virtue: Epigenetics, Development, and Culture." Chapter 10 in *Cultivating Virtue: Multiple Perspectives*, edited by Nancy E. Snow. New York: Oxford University Press, 2014.

Olberding, Amy. "The Educative Function of Personal Style in the *Analects.*" *Philosophy East & West* 57 (2007): 357–74.

Ozer, Daniel, and Verónica Benet-Martinez. "Personality and the Prediction of Consequential Outcomes." *Annual Review of Psychology* 57 (2006): 401–21.

Pashler, Harold, Noriko Coburn, and Christine Harris. "Priming of Social Distance? Failure to Replicate Effects on Social and Food Judgments." *PLoS One* 7, no. 8 (2012): e42510.

Prinz, Jesse. *The Emotional Construction of Morals.* New York: Oxford University Press, 2007.

Prinz, Jesse. "Passionate Thoughts: The Embodiment of Moral Concepts." In *Grounding Cognition: The Role of Perception and Action in Memory, Language and Thinking*, edited by D. R. Z. Pecher, 93–114. Cambridge: Cambridge University Press, 2005.

Richard, F. D., Charles Bond Jr., and Juli Stokes-Zoota. "One Hundred Years of Social Psychology Quantitatively Described." *Review of General Psychology* 7 (2003): 331–63.

Roberts, Brent. "Back to the Future: Personality and Assessment and Personality Development." *Journal of Research in Personality* 43 (2009): 139–40.

Roberts, Brent, Nathan Kuncel, Rebecca Shiner, Avshalom Caspi, and Lewis Goldberg. "The Power of Personality: The Comparative Validity of Personality Traits, Socioeconomic Status, and Cognitive Ability for Predicting Important Life Outcomes." *Perspectives on Psychological Science* 2 (2007): 313–45.

Rosenthal, Robert, and Donald Rubin. "A Simple, General Purpose Display of Magnitude of Experimental Effect." *Journal of Educational Psychology* 74 (1982): 166–69.

Ross, Lee, and Richard Nisbett. *The Person and the Situation: Perspectives of Social Psychology.* Philadelphia: Temple University Press, 1991.

Ross, Lee, and Andrew Ward. "Naive Realism in Everyday Life: Implications for Social Conflict and Misunderstandings." In *Values and Knowledge*, edited by E. Reed, E. Turiel, and T. Brown, 103–35. Mahwah, NJ: Lawrence Erlbaum, 1996.

Russell, Daniel C. "Cultivating Virtue: The Aristotelian Tradition." Chapter 1 in *Cultivating Virtue: Multiple Perspectives*, edited by Nancy E. Snow. New York: Oxford University Press, 2014.

Sabini, John, and Maury Silver. "Lack of Character? Situationism Critiqued." *Ethics* 115 (2005): 535–62.

Samuels, Steven, and William Casebeer. "A Social Psychological View of Morality: Why Knowledge of Situational Influences on Behavior Can Improve Character Development Practices." *Journal of Moral Education* 34 (2005): 73–87.

Sarkissian, Hagop. "Minor Tweaks, Major Payoffs: The Problems and Promise of Situationism in Moral Philosophy." *Philosopher's Imprint* 10, no. 9 (2012): 1–15.

Slingerland, Edward. *Effortless Action: Wu-wei as Conceptual Metaphor and Spiritual Ideal in Early China.* New York: Oxford University Press, 2003.

Slingerland, Edward. "'Of What Use are the *Odes*?' Cognitive Science, Virtue Ethics, and Early Confucian Ethics." *Philosophy East & West* 61 (2011): 80–109.

Slingerland, Edward. "Toward an Empirically-Responsible Ethics: Cognitive Science, Virtue Ethics, and Effortless Attention in Early Chinese Thought." In *Effortless Attention: A New Perspective in the Cognitive Science of Attention and Action*, edited by Brian Bruya, 247–86. Cambridge, MA: MIT Press, 2010.

Slingerland, Edward. "Virtue Ethics, the *Analects*, and the Problem of Commensurability." *Journal of Religious Ethics* 29 (2001): 97–125.

Snow, Nancy E. *Virtue as Social Intelligence: An Empirically Grounded Theory*. New York: Routledge, 2010.

Tellegen, Auke, et al. "Personality Similarity in Twins Reared Apart and Together." *Journal of Personality and Social Psychology* 54 (1988): 1031–39.

Van Norden, Bryan. *Virtue Ethics and Consequentialism in Early Chinese Philosophy*. New York: Cambridge University Press, 2007.

Wilson, Stephen. "Conformity, Individuality, and the Nature of Virtue: A Classical Confucian Contribution to Contemporary Ethical Reflection." *Journal of Religious Ethics* 23 (1995): 263–89.

Wong, David. "Reasons and Analogical reasoning in *Mengzi*." In *Essays in the Moral Philosophy of Mengzi*, edited by Xiusheng Liu and P. J. Ivanhoe, 187–200. Cambridge, MA: Hackett, 2002.

Yong, Ed. "Nobel Laureate Challenges Psychologists to Clean up Their Act." *Nature News* 490 (2012): 7418.

CHAPTER 7

It Takes a Metaphysics

Raising Virtuous Buddhists

OWEN FLANAGAN

All experience is preceded by mind,
    Led by mind.
    Made by mind.
Speak or act with a corrupted mind,
    And suffering follows
As the wagon wheel follows the hoof
of the ox.
All experience is preceded by mind,
    Led by mind.
    Made by mind.
Speak or act with a peaceful mind,
    And happiness follows
Like a never departing shadow.
    —*Dhammapada* 1–2[1]

THE TOPIC

In the *Matrix Trilogy*, the second and third installments of which I strongly discourage anyone from seeing, Buddhists are presented as pretty much the only decent souls left on earth. This fits the popular imaginary sense according to which, even in our pre-apocalyptic world, Buddhists are thought to be above average in the morality department, on the kind and gentle side; naïve perhaps, but at least not big troublemakers; admirable, possibly—odd as it might sound—virtuous. How, if it is so, is there such a thing as Buddhist virtue in this red in tooth and claw world? How, if indeed it is so, do Buddhists reliably produce virtue in their charges? We can put the question in Plato's way: Can Buddhist virtue be taught or otherwise acquired? How, if they are, are the distinctively Buddhist virtues of compassion and loving-kindness, seeking to alleviate the suffering of all sentient beings and to bring happiness and well-being in its stead, taught, activated, or otherwise put in place in the hearts, minds, and lives of Buddhists?

This is my topic.[2] Buddhism is philosophically interesting and unusual as living ethical systems go, or so I claim, in that it is explicit in seeing that training in virtue involves teaching about more than virtue. Becoming virtuous Buddhist style requires a certain understanding of reality and the human predicament, even a metaphysics, according to which everything, including your self, is understood to be interdependent and impermanent. The metaphysics can, or so I'll say, be taught to the youth. Indeed, many Buddhists teach it to the youth.[3] It is possible that it, or something like it, must be taught in order to motivate Buddhist ethics. There is also in Buddhism recognition that not all the relevant truths necessary for or constitutive of an enlightened mind and an excellent person are conceptual. Some very deep truths or aspects of the deep truths (impermanence, suffering, no-self) must be grasped non-conceptually.

But even all the truths of Buddhist philosophy, conceptual and non-conceptual, are insufficient to warrant rationally the vow Buddhists take to alleviate suffering for all sentient beings. According to Buddhist logic, like our own, ordinary "oughts" (I ought to eat) do not follow from ordinary facts (I am hungry), nor do vows, vocations, duties (I will, I must, I promise) follow from beliefs, nor even do our deepest or highest moral commitments (to be compassionate to all sentient beings) follow logically from the deepest metaphysical facts, that we are impermanent or no-self. This central feature of Buddhist ethics is, I think, best understood as involving a vow, a decision, a calling, a compelling attitude, a conviction that a Buddhist person finds natural to adopt and accept as her own after—or as she is—absorbing Buddhist metaphysics. She feels called to alleviate suffering for all sentient beings and to bring happiness in its stead in a distinctive human ecology where certain metaphysical and logical beliefs and certain attitudes, feelings, and judgments are perceived to go well together. Together they make sense in and of the Buddhist form of life. I'll try to explain all this.

THE BUDDHIST FORM OF LIFE

Buddhism is a comprehensive form of life, a complex way of being that exemplifies the ancient idea of a philosophy as way of life.[4] Seeing the way reality is and seeing the way I exist or subsist, or unfold in reality, helps ground and motivate a certain way of being-in-the-world that we, from a Western perspective, would say is virtuous, good, and moral, but that, from a Buddhist perspective, is intended to be much more than that. Buddhism is not a kind of morality for its own sake. Buddhism is intended as a way of being fully awakened or enlightened, not simply or only being good.

Buddhists clearly care about virtue in the sense that they care about goodness, about good people, about people with good values who behave in a morally decent and upstanding manner. Whether and to what extent Buddhism is committed to virtues—conceived as internal dispositions of character—as the psychological equipment by way of which good persons are good is a different and more complicated question.

Compassion and loving-kindness are distinctive Buddhist traits, but they are described in multifarious ways inside Buddhism. Consider three familiar ways that compassion is described: (1) *disposition* to alleviate suffering for all sentient beings; (2) *desire* to alleviate suffering; (3) *belief* that suffering ought to be alleviated. Likewise, loving-kindness is described as a disposition or habit of a well-developed person to bring well-being where there is ill-being, or a desire to do so, or a belief that this ought to be done. The descriptions point in three non-incompatible directions: to a behavioral disposition, to a conative or affective state, and to a cognitive state. And thus one can see how virtue theoretical, non-cognitivist, and cognitivist theories might all claim allies in Buddhism. In principle, Buddhist compassion and loving-kindness could be all three or have elements from all three at once (as they might be on some expansive conception of virtue); or perhaps these "traits" or "states" are configured differently in different people, different kinds of people, people of different ages, and so on.

Traditional Buddhist philosophy provides abundant resources for normative ethics. There are expressions of value, norms of behavior, abundant rules, absolute prohibitions, long lists of wholesome and unwholesome states of the heart and mind, self-cultivation techniques, rules of thumb, antidotes to vice, aids to virtue, and all sorts of stories about the Buddha's past lives to instruct the youth. But there is nothing in the way of meta-ethics. Meta-ethics is under-theorized, as the French would say. This has led to controversy among Western philosophers as to whether Buddhist ethics is a virtue theory, a kind of consequentialism, possibly act- or rule-consequentialism, perhaps virtue consequentialism, a kind of religious ethics with deontic structure, and so on.[5]

My tactic here is to leave Buddhism be. It has all these elements, and this may serve as a good lesson for us. That is, it need not be seen as a weakness of Buddhist ethics that it can't be corralled into one of our familiar kinds.

Moral life perhaps eludes systematicity, in part because the domain of the moral is not a well-behaved kind. One might take our failure to find any of the familiar flavors of ethical theory adequate to the task of ethics as lived as inspiration to pay more attention to traditions that don't fetishize systematicity and unification. The way I recommend understanding Buddhist ethics and moral psychology involves treating three elements as inextricably interwoven (I call it the NYC pretzel picture), where certain philosophical views, as well as multifarious mindfulness skills and a complex moral tool kit akin to a Swiss army knife, are all required to live a good human life.

THE CORE OF BUDDHISM

There is no Buddhism, only Buddhisms,[6] a plethora of related traditions that emerged, along with Jainism, on the Indian subcontinent in the fifth century BCE,[7] as both a reaction to and a development of a host of indigenous threads that came eventually to be called Hinduism.[8] Buddhism is now a dominant form of life throughout much of Southeast Asia, Thailand, Cambodia, Myanmar, and Sri Lanka, as well in parts of East Asia, China, Korea, and Japan. And, there are many Westerners who now self-describe as Buddhists. Most Buddhists believe in reincarnation or rebirth, but some don't. Many Buddhists think that the best state is nirvana and conceive of it as similar to heaven; others conceive of it as a state of bliss or rapture; others as a state of dissolution where one is dissolved back into the bosom of the universe, akin to annihilation. Most Buddhists believe that it takes many lives to achieve enlightenment; others that it can happen in one life. Most Buddhists are atheists by Abrahamic standards, but many believe in ghosts and evil spirits. Some Buddhists believe that the best human life is one of solitary, hermetic meditation; others that such a life is narcissistic and that the best human life is dedicated to saving others from suffering by teaching them the way, the *dhamma*, *dharma*, the *dao*. Some Buddhists sects recommend meditation; others favor chanting and ritualized hand movements. Some varieties of Buddhism are very intellectual, conceptual, philosophical (Tibetan); others less so (Japanese Pure Land). There is no pope of Buddhism so such debates are left unresolved, or better, left to communities to work out according to local rules and antecedent traditions.[9]

Despite the diversity among the Buddhisms, there is a common core, a common denominator. All Buddhist sects agree that the "Four Noble Truths," the "Noble Eightfold Path," and the "Four Immeasurables" constitute a core philosophy, a minimal set of commitments that is shared across the Buddhisms. This much yields a very clear conception of Buddhist ethics. I provide a gloss that will be understandable by contemporary philosophers and moral psychologists:

The Four Noble Truths
1. *Suffering (Dukkha)*: There is a lot of unsatisfactoriness and suffering in the world. There is sickness, pain, loss, and death. There are things—the finest cuisine, perfect beauty, beachfront property—that I want but can't have, get, or keep.
2. *Causes of Suffering in Ego.* There are two main kinds of suffering, distinguished by their causes. The first kind has causes that are external and largely outside human control—earthquakes, tsunamis, plagues, and childhood leukemia. The other kind of suffering has causes that are in us, in our grasping egos—anger, envy, disappointment, resentment, fear.
3. *Cessation of Suffering.* If we could control the suffering caused by our grasping egos, we could diminish the unsatisfactoriness we cause to ourselves and to others.
4. *The Noble Eightfold Path.* We can control the suffering we cause by our grasping egos (and even at the limit become indifferent to and accepting of the naturally caused suffering) by following the eightfold path that consists of: Right View/Understanding, Right Thought/Intention, Right Speech, Right Action, Right Livelihood, Right Effort, Right Mindfulness, and Right Concentration.

The Noble Eightfold Path consists of more than moral recommendations. It is usually understood this way: steps 1 and 2—Right View/Understanding and Right Thought—pertain specifically to understanding three or four key truths of Buddhist philosophy, to wisdom (*panna*; Skt: *prajna*):

(i) *Impermanence (anicca)*: Everything is impermanent. Nothing lasts forever. Good things pass; bad things happen (*dukkha*).[10]

(ii) *Dependent Origination* and *Dependent Being*: everything is interdependent; there is no such thing as independent being; everything is becoming, an unfolding in a field of causes and effects.

(iii) *No-self*: A person is one of the dependently originating things, one of the constituents of the ever-changing flux that is the world, the sum of everything that is changing.[11] A person, like all other things that seem to exist as independent substances (think diamonds that are said to last forever but came from coal and don't last forever), has only conventionally or pragmatically endowed stability. And thus personal identity is not an all-or-nothing matter; it is a matter of psycho-biological continuity and connectedness. There is no permanent diamond in the rough that is me, that makes me exactly the same person over time.

(iv) *Emptiness*: There are no things that are as they seem, indeed there are no things at all. Because of (i–iii), it is a mistake to think that at the ultimate level, as opposed to the conventional level, there are any independent, non-relational entities that exist or subsist on their own, outside of relations with other "things," events, and processes. In our terms this would mean that neither science nor first philosophy discovers or uncovers essences.[12]

Steps 3, 4, and 5, Right Speech, Right Action, and Right Livelihood, pertain to *sila*, to what we would call "morality" or "ethics." Right Livelihood encourages work that alleviates suffering and prohibits work for firms that make weapons. Right Speech demands truthfulness and honesty, and prohibits gossip, slander, teasing, and bullying. First pass, these steps do not ask that people possess any particular virtues; they simply require that one do or refrain from doing certain kinds of actions. That is compatible, of course, with thinking that, in their mature forms, acting, living, and speaking well will most reliably and smoothly and wisely emerge from a person of virtuous character. In either case, the actions that are endorsed and prohibited in steps 3, 4, and 5 constitute a familiar conventional morality. Except for the familiar Indian virtue of *ashima*, non-violence, most everything endorsed will be judged good or right across the unconnected Abrahamic, Confucian, pan-African, Australasian aboriginal, and Amerindian traditions.

Steps 6, 7, and 8, Right Effort, Right Mindfulness, and Right Concentration, all pertain to aspects of what we have come to call "mindfulness" and "meditation," but that are much broader and consist (eventually) of literally thousands of practices to help keep one's intentions and purposes aligned with one's aims, to cultivate one's character, and generally to keep one's eyes on the prize.

The main thing to understand is that the eightfold path is like a New York City pretzel or a complex spider web. It is a threefold chord, an interconnected set of rings or a wheel (it is symbolized by Indian Buddhists as an eight-spoke wheel *Dharmachakra*). The three aspects of wisdom (*panna*; Skt: *prajna*), virtue (*sila*), and mindfulness (*samadhi*) can be analytically separated, but they only co-occur in their mature forms interwoven with each other.

THE PATH AND THE FOUR IMMEASURABLES

Steps 3, 4, and 5, Right Speech, Right Action, and Right Livelihood, pertain, as I have said, to conventional morality. Some aspects of Buddhist conventional morality are different from twenty-first-century American conventional morality or Aristotelian morality or classical or contemporary Confucian morality. For example, Right Action is often understood to require not moderation but refraining from *all* intoxicants. Not killing, familiar to us from the Sixth (sometimes Fifth) Commandment, is understood by Buddhists to prohibit killing animals.[13] Neither of these prohibitions go well with familiar practices associated with America college life or with traditional French cuisine. It is worth noting that a common feature of conventional moralities is that, whereas virtues may differ in range, scope, and extent, it is rare that what one group (Confucians, Aristotelians, Buddhists) thinks is a general virtue type is conceived a vice by some other group.[14]

That said, the conventional morality endorsed as virtuous does not consist, not obviously at least, of recommendations that people possess or cultivate certain virtues, where virtues are conceived as traits, as reliable dispositions to perceive, feel, judge, and act in the right ways. What are endorsed are performing certain actions or refraining from certain actions, doing or not doing certain things. This behaviorist reading changes, however, when we look at the entire path, especially at the wisdom and mindfulness aspects that take us to see the higher, nonconventional values and virtues. The ideal, even as far as Right Action, Right Speech, and Right Livelihood go, is that an agent does the right things because she has developed deep-seated dispositions that have cognitive, emotional, conative, and behavioral aspects. She tells the truth and resists gossip because she is disposed to be honest and kind. She is that kind of person. Not simply continent, but virtuous.

The *Dhammapada*, a part of the *Khuddaka Nikaya* in the *Pali Canon*, is a collection of poetic sayings of the Buddha. Buddha clearly marks the distinction between virtue and continence:[15]

> The one who keeps anger in check as it arises,
>> As one would a careening chariot,
> I call a charioteer.
>> Others are mere rein-holders.[16]

The immeasurables or divine abodes (*brahmavihāras*) are introduced and endorsed in the *Metta Sutta* in the *Pali Canon*, although they have long roots in Indic philosophy as the virtues possessed by a saint or sage who is on the verge of achieving liberation (*moksa, moksha, mukti, nibbana, nirvana*).[17] These immeasurable virtues are:

- Compassion—the disposition to alleviate suffering for all sentient beings.
- Loving-kindness—the disposition to bring happiness to all sentient beings.
- Sympathetic joy—the disposition to experience joy at the successes of all others including in zero-sum games.
- Equanimity—the disposition to want the well-being of all sentient being equally.

These traits involve dispositions to perceive, feel, think, and act in ways characteristic of the virtue in question. They develop slowly and much of the work of development involves self-work, self-cultivation, and mindfulness. Buddhists often use the language of skill to describe what we might call a virtue. Developing the relevant skills or virtues involves self-cultivation.

The work of self-cultivation involves getting your head around the core truths that constitute wisdom and, if possible, gaining non-conceptual insight that can only be achieved through certain unusual meditative states (*jhanas*; Skt: *dhyana*); for example, understanding the doctrine of no-self and possibly, if one is gifted and lucky, experiencing one's self as no-self.

Several connected issues deserve attention: the role of philosophical wisdom in developing these virtues; the role of non-conceptual knowledge or mindfulness in developing and perfecting these virtues; the relative roles of the individual and the community in developing and perfecting these virtues; and whether all this taken together is enough to ground or warrant Buddhist ethics of compassion are loving kindness for all sentient beings.

THE ROLE OF PHILOSOPHICAL WISDOM

Wisdom (Pali: *panna*; Skt: *prajna*) in Buddhism involves seeing reality as it is, not as it seems or appears. Philosophy is required to see things as they are, and the relevant philosophical wisdom is available to anyone who is willing to reflect on and absorb some basic truths about the nature of persons and the world.

There are three poisons in human nature that make us prone to act wrongly and to understand things incorrectly. The first two poisons are tendencies to moral vice, the third is to epistemic vice: (1) acquisitiveness exemplified by avarice, craving, covetousness, and thirst (*lobha*) for all that we want (which is a lot); (2) anger, resentment, jealousy, and envy (*dosa*) for all that we want but don't get, or get but don't keep; (3) wishful, superficial, and false beliefs (*moha*), especially ones that pertain to what we need to be really happy.

The first poison disposes us to be egoists, to be selfish; the second poison disposes us to be disappointed, angry, resentful, rageful, and possibly violent, when we don't get what we want. The third poison disposes us to project our desires onto reality and to believe that we both need and deserve everything we want and that our happiness depends upon acquiring what we desire.

Eliminating or overcoming the poisons in us requires Buddhist wisdom, seeing, for example, that, as the Noble Truths teach, we contribute to our own suffering and that of others by making a mistake, several mistakes. We believe that short-term sensual pleasures and money, for example, will bring happiness; but they won't. How do we know this? The Buddha said so. But the reason to believe it is not that he said so, but because what he said is true. This is a discovery that has been made again and again over world historical time by other buddhas, bodhisattvas, arhats, sages, and saints, and that has been detected by many of us less worthy or advanced in minimally reflective moments. The people who don't suffer, who flourish and are happy, are those who reliably get out of the way of their egos and who are virtuous, who stop grasping, and who stop being angry when they don't get what they want.[18]

Buddhist ethics—the Buddhist form of life, generally—is empiricist. The claims made about overcoming suffering and enlightenment are put forward as discoveries, not as inventions or revelations. In principle, at least, they can be tested.[19] Indeed, one might think that one task of comparative philosophy is to compare various ethical conceptions in terms of whether and how well they produce flourishing as it is conceived by the tradition and then, insofar as there are commonalities among conceptions, across traditions to see how well other traditions produce flourishing as we conceive it.[20]

It helps if one starts to understand the way things really are. How's that? They are impermanent. "Things" arise and pass in fields of relations that encompass all that is unfolding, the mother of all unfoldings, Unfolding Itself. The unfolding unfolds. What there is, and all there is, is unfolding. Therefore, it is a fiction to think that I am a stable thing, especially that I am or possess a special eternal aspect, an essence that the unfolding, the universe, reality cares especially, or at all, about preserving.[21]

Deflating myself, my diachronic and even my synchronic swath (the latter is the work or emptiness, *sunyata*),[22] seeing that whether conceived horizontally or vertically I am not a substantial thing but, rather, relationally

constituted, as are you and as are all other things; and also that we all suffer
the slings and arrows, as well as the pleasures and treasures, of the unfolding
might make me care less about my own satisfactions and sufferings and more
about yours. "Might." Many Buddhists say these recognitions "should" make
me more compassionate. Maybe. One might wonder why seeing or understanding this much should warrant virtue and unselfishness rather than
nihilism or hedonism. This is a good question, a pressing one for Buddhists
to answer.[23] I return to it at the end.

THE ROLE OF MEDITATION AND MINDFULNESS

But, one says: "It is very hard to understand this, to comprehend that I am
no-self" (*annata*; Skt: *anatman*); it is also very hard to understand what
reason there is for me to care about others as much as about my self. So one
idea, one answer to the question I just posed is that further cognitive and
affective work is required to motivate virtue. Here is where meditation and
mindfulness come in. "Systematic meditation on the four Holy Truths, as
on the basic facts of life, is a central task of the Buddhist life."[24] The "basic
facts" include such truths as that I do not want to suffer, nor do others."
We, Hume's progeny, will be quick to remind ourselves that nothing normative follows from these facts unless we add norms to the effect that we
ought to be logically consistent or that we ought to care about others.
Buddhism adds these "oughts." In the *Dhammapada*, we read:

> All tremble at violence;
>> All fear death.
> Seeing others as being like yourself,
>> Do not kill or cause others to kill.[25]

And later:

> Doing no evil,
>> Engaging in what's skillful,
> And purifying one's mind:
>> This is the teaching of the buddhas.[26]

Some kinds of mindfulness are straightforwardly practical. If one is riven
with lust toward an inappropriate person, Shantideva recommends
thinking of the individual as old and decrepit, or if that doesn't work,
thinking of the person covered with excrement. A famous Buddhist teacher

in the Netherlands explained that he had found another more Dutch and twenty-first-century technique than Shantideva's for such unwholesome lust. He recommended that, when aroused, you immediately try to imagine that you are in post-coital mode with the object of your lust. This, he explained, makes the urge seem less urgent, possibly over, satisfied (and perhaps makes you want a cigarette).

This sort of practice involves the use of antidotes that are straightfor- wardly psychologically incompatible with the unwholesome impulses, thoughts, and desires. So, for example, one will hear Buddhists ask a person with vengeful thoughts to think of the person—the murderer, or of Hitler or Stalin—as your mother or your child. The idea is that love is incompat- ible with vengeance.[27] Related techniques involve meeting disappoint- ments that lead to feeling pity for oneself by making a list of things for which one is grateful; or by working on arrogance and conceit by making a list of one's weaknesses—depending on the situation, one's physical, intel- lectual, or moral weaknesses. This might make one less complacent, more inclined to want to do some work on improving oneself.

This much sounds like an emergency first-aid kit, consisting of good tricks of a cognitive-behavioral sort. But the work of meditation and mind- fulness is meant to go much deeper, and it consists, as I said above, of nu- merous practices designed to cultivate one's character so that one comes to feel the truths of Buddhist philosophy in one's blood and bones, and to act in wholesome ways because of one's well-honed virtue, not simply because one knows what one is supposed to do, not simply out of continence. The continent person merely holds the reins.

There are several other kinds of Buddhist mindfulness that need emphasizing, Most every kind of meditation comes from earlier Indian traditions, from yoga practices. The general term for meditation is *sa- madhi*, which means something like "concentration." It comes in varieties. The aim is to become skilled at attention, at laser-like attention. Techniques include one-pointed attention to the breath (one of my teachers said that no one has ever been able to follow a full in-and-out breath, only the in or the out part; but still, attending to the full breadth is the aim); to the weal and woe of others; to one's aches and pains (really focus on where it hurts). In these ways, one starts to benefit from close attention, from seeing what is there as it is. One might start to see one's states as imper- manent (that breath is done, gone forever; that pain in my right lower back has yielded to one on the left side). One aim of *samadhi* is to pro- duce a calm and tranquil mind, and especially the skill at returning to it when attention seems fractured, when one seems overwhelmed, discom- bobulated, frantic. Once the meditator achieves a strong and powerful

concentration, an ability to see things as they are, she is ready to pene-
trate and see into the ultimate nature of reality, to eventually obtain
release from suffering through enlightenment. *Vipassana* (Skt: *Vipasanya*)
is insight meditation, and it marks meditation on the truths of impermanence, dependent origination, no-self, and (in Mahayana) emptiness.

Taken together, the various kinds of mindfulness and meditation produce detachment from the ego, release from the poisons in our nature, and
according to many, offer non-conceptual knowledge of truths that cannot
be fully grasped in ordinary ways—say, by perception or understanding.
Which truths are these? Well, the ideas that things are impermanent and
that everything that arises does so in relation to other things, which also
dependently arise, seem like truths that can be captured conceptually, in
ordinary language, as just the truths they are, namely impermanence and
dependent origination.

The same can be said for the truth of suffering (*dukkha*). Getting *dukkha*
requires attention and acceptance, rather than Pollyanna-ish denial, but
once one faces facts, as we say, one sees how many things that we seek or
grasp elude us. And we get how this is a source of much disappointment.
But truths such as no-self (*annata*; *anatman*) and the emptiness (*sunyata*)
of all things, as well as truths about deep pure wells of goodness in each of
us (Buddha-nature), are truths than cannot be (fully) captured conceptually.[28] We cannot express or say them in a way that fully captures them; but
perhaps they can be seen, shown, grasped, or revealed. Truly enlightened
souls, arhats, bodhisattvas, buddhas "grasp that," rather than "know that"
in the usual sense: we are no-self, that all things are empty, and that there
is in each of us a pure consciousness undefiled by the poisons.

Although there is a debate in philosophy about whether non-conceptual
knowledge is possible, there is no debate in animal ethology and child psychology about the topic. Babies, toddlers, and all nonhuman animals have
mostly—possibly only—non-conceptual knowledge. What is more interesting philosophically is this epistemic question: Do the various kinds of
meditation designed to help us grasp the truths of Buddhist philosophy
actually do that? Do they lead to the "grasping" of these truths? Or, are
they better described as inculcating belief in these truths (that are possibly
not true) by something like self-hypnosis, encouraged by previously hypno-
tized members who have drank from the same vat of Kool-Aid? This matters because Buddhism, along with Jainism, and for similar reasons,
supports the most demanding ethic of compassion and loving-kindness on
earth, and it does so on grounds that relate to seeing the truths of philosophy as Buddhists see them.[29]

INDIVIDUAL AND COMMUNAL WORK

This brings me to the question: What is the role of the community versus the individual in becoming a good, even an excellent, Buddhist person, where a good Buddhist person is understood in the wide way that involves possessing Buddhist wisdom, as well as virtue and mindfulness?

Much of the literature on the development of excellent Buddhist persons focuses on the development of saints and sages—arhats, bodhisattvas, and buddhas. There is also focus on the training of monks and, to a lesser extent, of nuns. (The largest by far of the three books of the *Pali Canon* is devoted to rules for monastics.) In part, this is because they uniquely preserve the tradition and because the life of a monk or nun is most conducive to the development of advanced skills in wisdom, virtue, and mindfulness. In many Buddhist countries, especially in Southeast Asia, it is as common for young men to do a stint as a monk (often a signal that they are ready for marriage), as it is for youth in other countries to serve for a period in the military. This makes it surprisingly difficult to say what canonical views are on the education of ordinary Buddhist youth.

There is no text I know of that provides, for example, anything like an Aristotelian theory of habituation in virtue. But here are some surmises: Buddhist children are raised into the Buddhist form of life in all the usual ways, by direct instruction in do's and don'ts, and in the norms and values that one would expect in socio-moral ecologies we think of as Buddhist. The methods of developing as a good Buddhist person are all the familiar ones, including Aristotelian virtue education. The reason to think this is that Aristotle did not put forward his theory of moral learning as a theory only about how Greek youth develop but also about how all youth develop. If Aristotle's theory is true, then it is also true of Buddhist youth. That said, Buddhist moral education calls attention to the multifarious ways that a life form is passed on in addition to habituation or practice in virtue.

Two common ways that do not always get noticed in discussions about virtue are worth noting. First, there is the use of exemplars—the Buddha, first and foremost. The *Jakatas* are stories of many of Buddha's later reincarnations. Once Buddha became a bodhisattva, he vowed to keep returning to earth (this is what bodhisattvas do) to help all sentient beings achieve enlightenment and eventually be released from conditioned existence (nirvana). Some of Buddha's reincarnation are as animals, but normally they are as humans, and always they contain moral lessons, sometimes of what it is like to display virtue generally but often of particular virtues—patience, compassion, loving-kindness. The *Jakatas* are not about children, but they form the basis for the Buddhist versions of moral lessons that are often told to children orally or in picture books (previously in cave drawings). The lives of the Buddha are almost all exemplary, and they clearly depict him as a person of virtue, and not simply as someone who always, or almost always behaves well.[30]

One feature that emerges in Buddhism, and that is different from principle-based theories or divine-law ethics, is that the Buddha practices what Buddhists call "skillful means"; he reveals his compassion and loving-kindness in the ways that particular situations call for. There are elements of particularism in Buddhism. The widespread use, and possible importance, of exemplars is worth thinking about. It is not incompatible with virtue theories, or utilitarianism or Kantianism, but it is not often emphasized in discussions in these traditions.

The other feature of Buddhism that I want to emphasize takes me back to my claim that it is a deeply philosophical ethic. If this is true, then it would be good for my argument if, then and now, Buddhist kids are taught such truths as impermanence, dependent arising, no-self, and emptiness. They are. For example, the *Dhammapada*, the *Jakata* stories, and the everydayness of talk of the Four Noble Truths puts these ideas in the air for everyone to breath. We do not speak these ways, but among Buddhists such talk is ubiquitous.

Do all Buddhists meditate? Insofar as meditation and mindfulness involve hearing, repeating, and knowing such things as the Four Noble Truths, Buddhist children—then and now—hear these about as often as, say, Christian children hear the Ten Commandments. That is, it is highly variable. If the question is about life-long practice of what in the West we think of as meditation—for example, sitting *Samadhi* or *Vipassana*, or even chanting ("Namu Amida Butsu")—then the best answer is that Buddhist children— outside of monasteries—meditate about as often as Jewish, Muslim, and Christian people pray. That is to say, again, that how much is highly variable, but the worldwide average is in the vicinity of not-very-much, or mainly at communal rituals and public celebrations. Monks, nuns, and individuals who are hoping for enlightenment soon—in the next few thousand lives—are encouraged to do so, and this is the aspect of Buddhism that strongly emphasizes the importance of self-cultivation, where an individual works with the wisdom and methods of the tradition to seek perfection.

In the *Dhammapada*, we read again and again about how the work of enlightenment requires "removing impurities" from oneself and "taming" oneself.

> The gift of Dharma surpasses all gifts.
> The taste of Dharma surpasses all tastes.

The delight of Dharma surpasses all delights.
> The destruction of craving conquers all suffering.
> As a smith does with silver,
>> The wise person
> Gradually,
>> Bit by bit,
>>> Moment by moment,
> Removes impurities from herself.[31]

Eventually one becomes virtuous.
Irrigators guide water;
> Fletchers shape arrows;
Carpenters fashion wood.
The well-practiced tame themselves.[32]

But here's the rub. I have been arguing that Buddhism offer a deeply philo-sophical vision of the good life, where excellence involves a three-note chord where goodness (virtue, *sila*), philosophical wisdom (*panna*; Skt: *prajna*, which we would think of as metaphysical), and mindfulness work together to create good persons. Buddhism (at least many varieties of Buddhism) is more deeply philosophical in the colloquial sense than I have indicated so far, but also in a way that might make it objectionable to con-temporary philosophers. This objectionable philosophy involves its soteri-ology, its eschatology, its salvific vision. Most forms of Buddhism are committed to the belief in rebirth and to the belief that the quality of rebirths—cockroach, owl; criminal, saint—involves the elaborate working out of a largely impersonal system of karma. Even if there is no omniscient God who keeps track of moral goodness and badness, and who offers eternal reward or punishment in the hereafter, the universe does.[33]

A legitimate question is whether Buddhist philosophy (the sort of Buddhist philosophy that contains the wisdom of impermanence, dependent origination, no-self, and emptiness) can be separated from the soteriology that involves belief in karma[34] and rebirth, and still make sense of the immea-surables of compassion, loving-kindness, empathetic joy, and equanimity.

This is a controversial question. I'll assume that Buddhism can be natu-ralized[35] and that certain forms of naturalized Buddhism already exist— some say that some early forms of Buddhism did without both karma and rebirth.[36] But that aside, there is this question, which I raised at the start: How do Buddhists get from "is" to "ought"? If I am right that Buddhist ethics is unusual in being deeply philosophical in the sense that, the twin beliefs in karma and rebirth aside, goodness requires belief in impermanence, dependent origination, no-self, and emptiness, then the question remains how these philosophical beliefs ground or (what is different) motivate the demanding virtues of compassion and loving-kindness. These philosoph-ical facts, despite being metaphysical and thus deep, are still just facts, whereas compassion and loving-kindness are not facts—they are values, norms, almost certainly, and in their mature forms, virtues.

Let me briefly review where we are in order to motivate the question. Suppose one asks what grounds conventional Buddhist morality—hon-esty, no gossip and no backstabbing, sexual propriety, temperance, worthy work, and so on? Prudence seems an obvious answer, where prudence is conceived as the desire for safety, security, and acceptance, and the belief that acting well conventionally secures these goods. Reciprocal altruism can also be grounded in prudence.[37]

But how can compassion and loving-kindness for all sentient beings be grounded or (again, what is different) how can these great (maha) virtues actually gain motivational bearing? One answer for the version of Buddhism that includes karma and rebirth is prudence. One gains moksha or nirvana if and only if one achieves enlightenment, where that enlightenment involves deep comprehension or absorption of the truths of impermanence, no-self, and so on, and also if one lives as a maximally virtuous person, a sage, a saint, eventually a bodhisattva, in the last in a series of many lives that yield Buddhahood, and then—and only then—release, nirvana.[38]

But if one subtracts belief in karma and rebirth from Buddhism, then there is no prudential basis for a life of great compassion and loving-kind-ness. So why would we want or aim to be that virtuous?

One might think that what I have said about the non-conceptual knowl-edge required by Buddhism, and promised in the work of meditation (where, for example, grasping the full truth of no-self [annata; anatman] would just yield or be an insight that is not linguistic but that yields some-thing like the thought that my desires are no more important than anyone else's), provides the answer and solves the problem. But it doesn't if the grasping (despite being a grasp of something that is ineffable, something that can only be seen not shown) is still grasping a fact, if it is still a cogni-tive grasping even if it is non-conceptual cognitive grasping.[39]

Here is another possibility: What one grasps in the work of meditation, what one experiences, is a calling—something akin to an overpowering desire, which, thanks to the prior work of philosophical preparation in no-self and its suite, one sees no reason to refuse. One has already both un-derstood and seen that we are all interrelated, that my good is tied up with the good of all other creatures, my ego's guard is down (and it is down for principled reasons), and I am called upon to attend to the suffering of all sentient beings.[40] There are different ways to express what happens: I experience a powerful call; I experience myself as having a duty to all sentient beings; I feel drawn to a life of great compassion (*maha-karuna*).

One might think that the situation is similar to what Kierkegaard calls the "teleological suspension of the ethical," where one is called by God to do something that cannot be rationalized. But here the Buddhist is better off than Abraham, who truly cannot explain to the rest of us why he thought it was justified to sacrifice his son Isaac upon hearing God's weird demand. The Buddhist can reply to anyone who wonders why he believes in and tries to live a life of compassion and loving-kindness for all sentient beings: I saw that my egoism leads to suffering, I saw that I am impermanent, dependently originating, no-self, empty, and part of the flux; this much made me open to feeling my solidarity with all beings who suffer, I began to comprehend myself as less bounded; I started to see my fate as a shared fate; and then I felt it—my solidarity, the calling. It all started to add up, to make sense.

This sort of explanation doesn't yield anything like a deductive grounding of Buddhist ethics. Nothing does that for any ethical form of life.[41] What this sort of explanation does, though, is make sense of how a certain set of Buddhist philosophical beliefs might help create fertile soil for certain feelings and motivations to take hold and to seem like the right fruits to grow in that soil. Again, the truths are ones that can be taught even to the youth.

CONCLUSION

I've offered a rational reconstruction of education in Buddhist virtue. It would be ideal if the sociology aligned with the reconstruction. I have some confidence based on informants in East, South, and Southeast Asia and my own reading and observation that it does. Like almost every ethical tradition, Buddhists use every available resource to convey to the youth the content of their form of life and the specific ways that it is to be enacted. There is direct instruction in do's and don'ts. There are encouragements and sanctions. There are stories of exemplars, arhats, bodhisattvas, and buddhas. And there is a philosophical and ethical theory that is explicitly taught, and that is then always there for those in the know as penumbra, as the surround or background that sets the conditions for what it means to be a Buddhist, one of our kind, and at the same time offers justifications for the Buddhist form of life. It includes instruction in a metaphysic that includes learning what Buddhists mean by the Four Noble Truths, the Noble Eightfold Path, and the immeasurable virtues of compassion, loving-kindness, sympathetic joy, and equanimity—and how they are connected to wisdom about impermanence, interdependence, no-self, and emptiness.

Like every other ethical form of life, Buddhist morality is taught and then enacted inside a web of mutually reinforcing associations and implicatures. At the center of the web are certain distinctive Buddhist metaphysical assumptions about the nature of the self and the human predicament. "Getting" Buddhism involves getting the metaphysics, and "conveying" Buddhism involves conveying the metaphysics. The metaphysics doesn't entail the ethics. As with every other great philosophical tradition, the ethics do not logically follow from the metaphysics, but they gain some considerable support from it.

If one starts with the metaphysic of no-self and massive cosmic interdependence, then an ethic of great compassion and loving-kindness is a sensible place to build toward. It is one plausible way to build the web out from that particular metaphysical architecture. It happens often enough so that the stereotype of Buddhists who are on the chilled side, not chasing their own tail in the hamster wheel of acquisitiveness, and who tend toward being kind and considerate, is not totally unwarranted. How the Buddhist form of life will fare as it meets other ways of being human in our increasingly cosmopolitan world remains to be seen. Because it is patient, not brash, it will need advocates who speak on its behalf. One can hope.

NOTES

1. This theme repeats. See Jack Kornfield and Gil Fronsdal, trans. *Dhammapada* (Boston: Shambhala, 2012), ch. 3, esp. 33–36.
2. Roger Jackson was helpful at the beginning stages of this essay, and Nancy Snow at all stages. I am grateful to members of the Columbia University Comparative Philosophy Seminar for continuous inspiration and support over the years, especially Chris Kelley, Jonathan Gold, Chris Gowans, Georges Dreyfus, Mark Siderits, Marie Friquegnon, Raziel Abelson, and Tao Jing. I also thank P. J. Ivanhoe and Eirik Harris at City University Hong Kong, as well as an audience at Hong Kong University, especially Chris Fraser, Max Deutsch, Johanna Wolff, and Andrea Sauchelli.
3. See Vanessa R. Sasson, ed. *Little Buddhas: Children and Childhoods in Buddhist Texts and Traditions* (Oxford: Oxford University Press, 2013), for one of the first books on the moral education of Buddhist children in several different contemporary Buddhist societies. In her Introduction, Sasson addresses the fraught question: Is Buddhism unfriendly to family? One reason to worry is that Siddhartha Gotama himself abandons his wife and newborn son Rahula to seek enlightenment; and throughout the history of the tradition, the life of monks, sometimes of nuns, is prized as the kind of life most congenial to enlightenment. One reason it is so prized is principled: attachment causes suffering and a monk or nun is detached from the primal zone of attachment, the family.

4. Michel Foucault, Pierre Hadot, Martha Nussbaum, and Alexander Nehamas have each emphasized recently this way of thinking of philosophy, as involving *techniques de soi*, the therapy of desire, spiritual exercise, and self-fashioning. Hadot writes: "Philosophy then appears in its original aspect: not as a theoretical construct, but as a method for training to live and to look at the world in a new way. It is an attempt to transform mankind" (Pierre Hadot, *Philosophy as a Way of Life*, ed. Arnold Davidson, trans. Michael Chase [Oxford: Blackwell, 1995], 107). See Matthew Kapstein *Reason's Traces: Identity and Interpretation in Indian and Tibetan Buddhist Thought* (Boston: Wisdom, 2001) for profitable application of this "philosophy as spiritual exercise" hermeneutic to understand Buddhist texts and debates.

5. Damien Keown, *The Nature of Buddhist Ethics* (London: Palgrave, 2001) assimilates Buddhist ethics, at least structurally, to an Aristotelian style virtue ethics; Charles Goodman (*Consequences of Compassion: An Interpretation and Defense of Buddhist Ethics* [Oxford: Oxford University Press, 2009]) emphasizes the consequentialist aspects of Buddhism, what he calls "compassionate consequentialism." Despite relevant similarities with virtue theory and consequentialism, neither Keown nor Goodman claims that the theories are the same. Christopher Gowans judiciously describes ways in which Buddhist ethics has aspects reminiscent of Aristotelian virtue ethics, classical utilitarianism, and Kantian deontology, but is clear that he thinks it can't be assimilated to any of our main contender moral theories (*Philosophy of the Buddha* [New York: Routledge, 2003]). Among comparative ethics, the almost universal view is that Buddhist ethics is a *sui generis* kind, possibly several *sui generis* kinds.

6. A common demarcation is between the Southern Schools and the Northern (and Eastern) Schools, which also aligns relatively well with the Theravada-Mahayana distinction. Theravada Buddhists claim to follow primarily and to stick close to the early teachings contained in the *Pali Canon*, and to emphasize the life of an arhat, one who realizes enlightenment by self-cultivation and extraordinary spiritual discipline. Mahayana also normally takes the *Pali Canon* as its root texts but especially as it exports to lands (Tibet, China, Japan), where *Pali* is not well known, depends more on commentaries and elaborations (often intertwined with indigenous religions). "The Mahayana is characterized, on the one hand, by devotion to a number of holy savior beings, and on the other by several sophisticated philosophies, developed by extending the implications of the earlier teachings. The savior beings are both heavenly *Bodhisattva's* (Skt; Pali: *Bodhisatta*), 'beings for enlightenment' who are near the end of the long *Bodhisattva* path – much elaborated and emphasized by the Mahayana – that leads to Buddhahood" (Peter Harvey, *An Introduction to Buddhist Ethics* [Cambridge: Cambridge University Press, 2000], 6).

7. Buddha has been getting younger recently. Consensus is now that he died around 400 BCE (Charles S. Prebish, "Cooking the Buddhist Books: The Implications of the New Dating of the Buddha for the History of Early Indian Buddhism," *Journal of Buddhist Ethics* 15 [2008]): 1–21). This is almost one hundred years later than most scholars believed a century ago. To make things easier for philosophers to remember, I choose 399 BCE for his death, which allows him and Socrates to have crossed the five rivers of Hades or to achieve nirvana together.

8. Hinduism certainly has deontic elements. Its founding texts, for example, the *Vedas* 1000 BCE and the *Mahabharata* 500 BCE have much to do with duties that override personal inclinations and particularistic loyalty. Buddhism comes from

the same roots, and the apple doesn't fall too far from the tree. In 2000, I was asked by Tibetan Buddhists to explain what makes a Christian a Christian. Try it. It is very hard. Jesus is God? Jesus is the Son of God? Jesus is god-like, a great prophet, a very good person? Trinity or not? Faith versus works? Are Quakers and Unitarians and Mormons Christians? Up close, the Buddhisms vary in similar ways.

9. Buddhism's root text is the *Pali Canon,* compiled in the first couple of centuries of the common era. But there are also early but less complete texts in Sanskrit and various Indian languages. Generally, Buddhists agree that texts that are the word of Buddha and his close disciples are *Buddhavacana.* God does not dictate the canon—there is no creator, omniscient God of the sort familiar from the Abrahamic traditions. Thus the canon is not infallible. It is the source book for Buddhists and contains many stories of the Buddha's lives, his last one in which he reaches enlightenment and then passes to final nirvana, as well as many previous reincarnations. It contains rules for monks and a fair dose of Buddhist metaphysics. Beyond the *Buddhavacana* there are commentaries on the canon and on previous commentaries. The rules governing acceptable commentaries and commentaries on commentaries are determined by local rules inside the abundant—non-shared—linguistic communities across many countries where Buddhism has assimilated and been accommodated.

10. One could put suffering/unsatisfactoriness (*dukkha*) on the list of elemental Buddhist truths along with impermanence, dependent origination, no-self; or one can, as I am doing here, treat *dukkha* as a corollary or obvious logical consequence in this world (although perhaps not in every logically possible one) of impermanence.

11. No-self (*annata*; Skt: *anatman*) is (technically or originally) not human or person specific. In the first instance it is the claim no-things have selves, *ipseity*; nothing is an independent thing. Nothing has an essence. Understood this way, and not in person-specific terms, one can see how this thesis (*anicca*) yields eventually the doctrine that all things are empty (Pali: *sunnata*: Sanskrit: *sunyata*). Gombrich says that we need be careful not to assume that what the Buddha denies in no-self is a conception of self that we have or understand. "Once we see what the Buddha was arguing against, we realise that it was something very few westerners have ever believed in and must have never heard of. He was refusing to accept that a person had an unchanging essence" (Richard F. Gombrich, *How Buddhism Began: The Conditioned Genesis of the Early Teachings* [New Delhi: Munishiram Manoharial Publishers, 1997], 16). Gombrich is no doubt right to caution assimilating an Indian conversation to our own, but the idea of the self or soul as an essence is a familiar one in the West, especially in the Abrahamic traditions (Owen Flanagan, *The Problem of the Soul: Two Visions of Mind and How to Reconcile Them* [New York: Basic, 2002]).

12. One might object: surely the periodical table of elements reveals essences. Reply: In cosmology and astrophysics, no one thinks that any member of that esteemed periodic table, not helium, not hydrogen, etc., existed at the Big Bang. So, these "essences" are simply sightings of certain stabilities that occur over certain large swaths of space-time, but not forever. One would have to see whether and how far one could take this sort of reply—for example, to the laws of nature itself, to the bosons and fermions, or whatever there was, at the time of the Big Bang, etc. I am agnostic.

13. Not all Asian Buddhists are vegetarians. Some restrict the kinds of animals that can be eaten (e.g., no elephants or hyenas); others think that animals killed humanely are edible (in the moral sense); still others, that there are different rules for monks and laypeople. Jainism, which emerges at the same time as Buddhism, is categorically and universally vegetarian.

14. Killing is bad; but who is an innocent (a range or scope issue) differs; Marriage is a virtue; but whom you can marry and how many of them (a range or scope issue) differs; and so on.

15. The so-called Path Texts are also excellent resources for short(ish) versions of the path, the road, the way, the dharma, the way to pure mind *bodhicitta*. For Theravadas there is Buddhaghosa's, fifth-century CE, *The Path of Purification* (*Visuddhimagga*); for Mahayana, there is Shantideva's, seventh-century CE, *Guide to the Bodhisattva's Way of Life* (*Bodhicaryāvatāra*). They introduce the Noble Truths and are handbooks of methods for the cultivation of beneficial or wholesome ideas and practices.

16. The *Dhammapada*, a part of the *Khuddaka Nikaya* in the *Pali Canon* (222).

17. *Brahmavihāras* means something like "abodes of Brahma." Buddhism rejects the idea of a hereditary Brahmin class (which is ordained by Brahma, the god of creation, which they also typically reject or at least see no need for), but maintains the idea of great spiritual achievement that is brahamic. See also the *Dhammapada* chapter "The Brahmin," where the language that organizes caste, hierarchy, and privilege is reappropriated, reconfigured, and redesigned. Practically, Buddhists are taught more mundane but distinctive practices of offering oneself to the service of others and of gratitude. Here are some anecdotes from recent trips. Thailand (from a female 32-year-old college graduate tour guide): "I was taught to wake up every day and ask what can I give today." Cambodia (from a 42-year-old taxi driver whose father was killed when he was a baby by Pol Pot and who never went to school—there were none—on receiving his taxi fare): "Thank you, from me, my family, and my country."

18. Then there are various carrots and sticks that are part of the background soteriology or eschatology:

> Some are reborn in a womb;
> Evildoers are reborn in hell.
> People of good conduct go to heaven;
> Those without toxins
> Are fully released in Nirvana. (126)

19. Of course, since only the few, not the many, have experienced enlightenment and have been released from the suffering caused by craving and attachment, those of us who choose to follow the path as beginners (as stream-enterers) must rely on their expert testimony plus perhaps our own nascent belief in the truth of what they say and our trust that they do live or did live excellent lives. One might worry that Buddhism is unsatisfactory, a failure, because like every other extant ethical theory it fails to find a metaphysics of morals that grounds morality outside of morality. Naturalists and pragmatists typically do not think that this can be done, for two reasons: first, we are creatures who naturally value certain goods and ends and thus our nature comes with certain ends, values, and oughts (which is not to say that all these ends, values, and wants cannot be adjusted or modified if there is reason to do so); second, worries about deriving "oughts" from "is's" are of no concern as long as

no claims of demonstration or deduction are made. If ethics is concerned with defensible ends and means, and inferences to the best practices, ends, values, and norms, then we are doing the best we can do. The hope for a metaphysics of morals that grounds morality in a completely a priori way is a fatuous fantasy.

20. Owen Flanagan, *The Really Hard Problem: Meaning in a Material World* (Cambridge, MA: MIT Press, 2007); Owen Flanagan, *The Bodhisattva's Brain: Buddhism Naturalized* (Cambridge, MA: MIT Press, 2011).

21. In one Indic tradition that Buddhism is reacting to, Brahmanism, this involved the puffed-up view that for certain special people, the priestly caste, one's soul, one's essence, one's *atman* is both a mirror image of and to be reunified with Brahma, the God of Creation, or Brahman, the sum of all there is, that it in some sense already is or partakes. Importantly, on the apple doesn't fall too far from the tree principle, this tradition like Buddhism and Jainism did think that is was a mistake, an illusion, to grant one's ego or self great significance. The sum of all things of which we partake is ultimately impersonal, although quite possibly directed toward the good (impersonally conceived).

22. The doctrine of emptiness (*sunyata* comes from the Sanskrit word that means "hollow") can be understood this way: First, start with the doctrine of no-self and think of it as a doctrine about horizontal-diachronic decomposition or reduction. My boundaries, conceived as the being-in-time that I am, are not clear. My identity or personhood today is different from my identity yesterday and tomorrow. Conventionally, I am the same guy I was yesterday and will be tomorrow, but ultimately (really) I'm not. Likewise, conceived at this moment in time, synchronically, I am a composite being. I am made up of organic parts. My organs are composite as well. The cells that compose the organs too, and so on possibly, ad infinitum, or even if not ad infinitum, at least until the whole seems to dissolve into radically unfamiliar "things," events, and processes to lose its substantiality. Buddhist reductionism (Mark Siderits, *Personal Identity and Buddhist Philosophy: Empty Persons* [Aldershot: Ashgate, 2003]) is the view that the self really completely dissolves ultimately; it is not there at all. Contrast that with the punctual self, the neo-Lockean view that I am a series of self-stages that have some sort of phenomenal reality over certain short swaths of time (length to be determined). The Buddhist reductionist denies this. Ultimately, there are not really even short-lived phenomenal states—the refreshing quality of a cool drink of water. There seem to be such states, but there aren't. So both horizontally and diachronically (no-self), and vertically and synchronically (emptiness), my self-hood (indeed, the self-hood of all relational and composite things) dissolves into something less substantial, something insubstantial, something not really there at all, or into some "things" that reveal what we started with to be not the thing it seemed, no thing at all. I'll let the reader explore the existential and process philosophical resonances of what I have just said. See Owen Flanagan, "Non-Narrative, Non-Forensic Dasein: The First and Second Self," in *Self Consciousness*, ed. Jee Loo Liu and John Perry (Cambridge: Cambridge University Press, 2011); Owen Flanagan, "Phenomenal and Historical Selves," special issue on Facets of Self-Consciousness, ed. Katja Crone, Kristina Musholt, and Anna Strasser, *Grazer Philosophische Studien* 84 (2012): 217–40.

23. Roger-Pol Droit, *The Cult of Nothingness: The Philosophers and the Buddha* (Chapel Hill: University of North Carolina Press,1997/2003) explains how the original audience of Buddhism in Europe, especially Germany, in the nineteenth century found the nihilistic reading attractive.

24. Edward Conze, *Buddhism: Its Essence and Development* (Mineola, NY: Dover, 1951/2003), 43.
25. Kornfield and Fronsdal, *Dhammapada*, 130.
26. Kornfield and Fronsdal, *Dhammapada*, 183.
27. *Eternal recurrence*: I have met some neo-Confucians—this is Buddhism mixed with Confucianism in Korea and China, for example—who think that each and every one of us actually was and will be Hitler's mother and child (as well as Jeffrey Dahmer's and Jesus's) because there is an infinite amount of time for every possible configuration of persons, worlds, and relations to take place an infinite amount of time. This idea of eternal recurrence appears among Indian, Pythagoreans, and Stoics, and was resurrected by Nietzsche.
28. In my experience, Buddhists think that you can speak falsely or truly about all the philosophical truths it endorses; it isn't as if the truths are totally ineffable, but a select few truths are esoteric and ineffable in the sense that they can only be seen or grasped fully in a non-conceptual way.
29. The Golden Rule ethic of Jesus is demanding, but asks only than we love our human neighbor as much as ourselves, not all sentient beings, as is the ethic of utilitarianism, especially act-utilitarianism, which may also extend to all sentient beings. One spots a similar ethics in ancient China in Mozi, fifth-century BCE, who recommended, impartial love (*jian ai*) in contrast to the graded family first love of classical Confucianism.
30. *Shantideva's The Bodhicaryavatara* and *The Questions of King Milinda* are other important teaching texts.
31. Kornfield and Fronsdal, *Dhammapada*, 239.
32. Kornfield and Fronsdal, *Dhammapada*, 145.
33. In my experience visiting Buddhist countries and communing with Buddhists, many well-educated Buddhists will say that they give money or food to monks to gain merit, where they (say) they conceive merit as credit for better rebirth.
34. In my *Really Hard Problem* and *The Bodhisattva's Brain*, I distinguish between tame and untame conceptions of karma. Tame karma is the commonsense belief that in actual worlds goodness usually pays and badness typically catches up to you. Untame karma involves the beliefs that (1) ultimately, *sub specie aeternitatis*, no good person suffers and no bad person flourishes, and (2) the impersonal cosmos orchestrates the scheme that provides ultimate justice.
35. I'll assume that Buddhism can be naturalized (Flanagan, *The Bodhisattva's Brain*).
36. So in the *Dhammapada* we read this lesson about perfectly tame karma:

> Don't' disregard evil, thinking
> "It won't come back to me!"
> With dripping drops of water.
> Even a water jug is filled.
> Little by little
> A fool is filled with evil. (121)
> Don't disregard merit, thinking,
> "It won't come back to me!"
> With dripping drops of water
> Even a water jug is filled.
> Little by little,
> A sage is filled with merit. (122)

37. Kin altruism is even easier: it is grounded in a small and rational extension of egoism to those with whom I share genes and a household.

38. One might wonder how many rebirths one needs before one is released from the cycle of suffering. Here is an answer a Tibetan lama once gave me: Imagine a mountain range 84,000 times the size of the Himalayan mountain range. And imagine that each day you touch the closest piece of rock with a soft cloth, where that touch is the equivalent of one life. It will take as many lives as it would take to erode that entire range by your effort.

39. Derek Parfit (*Reasons and Person* [Oxford: Oxford University Press, 1986]) and Mark Johnston (*Surviving Death* [Princeton: Princeton University Press, 2010]) discuss whether a deconstructive view of the self or identity, which they rightly see as similar to certain Buddhist views, entails or bears any moral consequences— for example, favors, say, utilitarianism or Christian *agape*. My view is that it doesn't unless the relevant insights about the metaphysics of personhood are paired with the grasping of a calling or something more motivationally powerful than even a deep philosophical truth.

40. Schopenhauer gets this. Schopenhauer criticized Kant for thinking that pure practical reason can ground morality. At some point the feeling of compassion is required. Schopenhauer was influenced by the Indic idea of Vedanta, where the thought is that the apparent boundaries between things are illusory (*maya*). Ultimately, our individual selves and souls (*atman*) are absorbed into *Brahman*— the ultimate reality, the sum of all that there is and that we partake. Although Buddhism is a reaction to certain aspects of this tradition; it shares this idea that the boundaries of ego are an illusion and evaporate upon reflection.

41. Paul Grice (*Studies in the Way of Words* [Cambridge, MA: Harvard University Press, 1987]) developed the idea that in different linguistic communities certain ideas are understood to be "implicatures" of other ideas. "Good son" means different things in contemporary America than in a classical Confucian culture. "Implicatures" are not logical implications; they are implications inside a form of life (part of "pragmatics"). I think this is a useful way to think of ethics in the broad sense. Ideas, feelings, and motivations go together because they are endorsed historically inside that form of life, they reach and maintain an equilibrium inside that form of life— quite possibly if they are long-lived because they do go well together—and they create the conditions for flourishing as conceived inside that form of life. Ideas and feelings that marinate together thrive together.

BIBLIOGRAPHY

Conze, Edward. *Buddhism: Its Essence and Development*. Mineola, NY: Dover, 1951/2003.

Crosby, Kate, and Andrew Skilton, trans. *Shantideva's The Bodhicaryavatara: A Guide to the Buddhist Path to Awakening*. Oxford: Oxford University Press, 1998.

Droit, Roger-Pol. *The Cult of Nothingness: The Philosophers and the Buddha*. Chapel Hill: University of North Carolina Press, 1997/2003.

Flanagan, Owen. *The Bodhisattva's Brain: Buddhism Naturalized*. Cambridge, MA: MIT Press, 2011.

Flanagan, Owen. "Non-Narrative, Non-Forensic Dasein: The First and Second Self." In *Self Consciousness*, edited by Jee Loo Liu and John Perry. Cambridge: Cambridge University Press, 2011.

Flanagan, Owen. "Phenomenal and Historical Selves." In special issue on Facets of Self-Consciousness, edited by Katja Crone, Kristina Musholt, and Anna Strasser, *Grazer Philosophische Studien* 84 (2012): 217–40.

Flanagan, Owen. *The Problem of the Soul: Two Visions of Mind and How to Reconcile Them.* New York: Basic, 2002.

Flanagan, Owen. *The Really Hard Problem: Meaning in a Material World.* Cambridge, MA: MIT Press, 2007.

Goodman, Charles. *Consequences of Compassion: An Interpretation and Defense of Buddhist Ethics.* Oxford: Oxford University Press, 2009.

Gombrich, Richard F. *How Buddhism Began: the Conditioned Genesis of the Early Teachings.* New Delhi: Munishiram Manoharial Publishers, 1997.

Gowans, Christopher W. *Philosophy of the Buddha.* New York: Routledge, 2003.

Grice, Paul. *Studies in the Way of Words.* Cambridge, MA: Harvard University Press, 1987.

Hadot, Pierre. *Philosophy as a Way of Life.* Edited by Arnold Davidson, translated by Michael Chase. Oxford: Blackwell, 1995.

Harvey, Peter. *An Introduction to Buddhist Ethics.* Cambridge: Cambridge University Press, 2000.

Johnston, Mark. *Surviving Death.* Princeton: Princeton University Press, 2010.

Kapstein, Matthew T. *Reason's Traces: Identity and Interpretation in Indian and Tibetan Buddhist Thought.* Boston: Wisdom, 2001.

Keown, Damien. *The Nature of Buddhist Ethics.* London: Palgrave, 2001.

Kornfield, Jack, and Gil Fronsdal, trans. *Dhammapada.* Boston: Shambhala, 2012.

Muller, Friedrich Max, trans. *The Questions of King Milinda. Volume 35: The Sacred Books of the East.* Facsimile Reprint Elibron Classics. Oxford: Clarendon Press, 1890/2005.

Prebish, Charles S. "Cooking the Buddhist Books: The Implications of the New Dating of the Buddha for the History of Early Indian Buddhism." *Journal of Buddhist Ethics* 15 (2008): 1–21.

Sasson, Vanessa R., ed. *Little Buddhas: Children and Childhoods in Buddhist Texts and Traditions.* Oxford: Oxford University Press, 2013.

Shaw, Sarah, trans. *Jatakas: Birth Stories of the Bodhisattva.* New York: Penguin, 2006.

Siderits, Mark. *Personal Identity and Buddhist Philosophy: Empty Persons.* Aldershot: Ashgate, 2003.

CHAPTER 8

Islam and the Cultivation
of Character

Ibn Miskawayh's Synthesis
and the Case of the Veil

ELIZABETH M. BUCAR

"The most perfect of you in faith is the one who attains excellence in character and is most kind to his kin."
—The Prophet Muhammad

G iven that over 80 percent of the world's population is religiously affiliated, the study of religious ethics has much to add to our understanding of virtue.[1, 2] Religious traditions entail their own assumptions about human nature and human flourishing and thus have something at stake in the discussion of which virtues are valued and how best to cultivate these virtues. Arguably the best known work in religious ethics on character formation is produced by scholars working within Christian traditions[3] or Chinese philosophy and Confucianism.[4] However, it would be wrong to presume that the moral theorization of virtue is primarily something done by Christian or Chinese thinkers. In truth, scholars of other traditions have also given substantial attention to virtue, and this work has insights for the ethical study of virtue more generally.[5] In this chapter, my goal is to introduce to the reader one exemplary Islamic figure: the tenth-century thinker Ibn Miskawayh. Specifically, my focus is on the theory of virtue in the ethics of Ibn Miskawayh and its contemporary applications to Islamic everyday practices like veiling.

It is helpful to keep in mind two fundamental facts about the study of ethics in Islam as we move forward. First, in Islam, revelation, recorded in the Qur'an and hadith, provides specific moral content. However, this content is limited: it does not cover every possible moral dilemma a Muslim may encounter nor do these sacred sources articulate a theoretical framework for the elaboration of a fully robust Islamic ethics (such as a full moral anthropology or theory of ethical reasoning). This is not to say that individual Islamic thinkers did not develop systematic theories of moral philosophy, because theologians like al-Ghazali (d. 1111) and Ibn Sina (d. 1037) certainly did. My point is that in the Islamic tradition, ethical concerns are not exhausted in the sacred texts but instead have been discussed in various specialized "sciences" focused on *akhlaq* (morals), *tasawwuf* (spirituality), *tafsir* (exegesis, especially of the Qur'an), *fiqh* (legal jurisprudence), *falsafa* (philosophy), *adab* (etiquette), and so on.[6]

Second, Islamic legal thought (*fiqh*), which focuses on the forms of reasoning, abstract values, and codes of conduct, is often perceived to be the dominant form for reflection on moral matters, and most work that we call "Islamic ethics" produced in the West (Europe and the United States) in the last fifty years is properly categorized as *fiqh*. Classically the complementarity among all of the Islamic sciences was more evident. Moreover, extralegal concerns with spiritual development have deep roots in the tradition, as seen in its founding narratives and texts. For instance, the actions and sayings of the Prophet Muhammad and his early companions, as recorded in hadith collections, provide important examples of how character is formed and how a virtuous Muslim behaves. One hadith report records Muhammad linking faith to virtue in an intimate way: "The most perfect of you in faith is the one who attains excellence in character and is most kind to his kin."[7]

Virtue ethics is a synthesis of moral psychology, casuistry, epistemology, sociology, law, and the like. The fact that a full account of virtue pulls together so many different areas of scholarship poses a problem not only for Islamic ethics but also for any intellectual tradition that recognizes separate disciplines. Given the organization of distinct, if complementary, Islamic sciences, and the fact that the majority of work on ethics has been in Islamic legal jurisprudence (*fiqh*), this is a particular challenge for contemporary Islamic studies of character formation. Moreover, while it is deeply problematic to separate any one Islamic discipline and call it "ethics," if we do so for the sake of study, it is not *fiqh* but *adab* discourse that is the closest to current philosophical and religious discussions of virtue. *Adab* is concerned with Islamic etiquette, or more specifically for our purposes, with how to acquire good manners, morals, and character. Recent scholarship in Islamic ethics has begun the work of reclaiming and reviving *adab* as an academic discipline.[8] I hope here to contribute in a small way to this effort.

To expose the reader of this volume to the sorts of contributions Islamic *adab* literature makes to our understanding of character formation, I have organized my discussion into two sections. In the first section, I introduce the work of Ibn Miskawayh, arguably the founding father of what could be called Islamic virtue ethics. He reformulates Greek philosophy to infuse it with spiritual virtues and to balance personal and political dimensions of character formation, which has implications beyond Islamic studies. In the second section, in order to show Ibn Miskawayh's theory in action, I turn to the case of the Islamic veil, as a specific practice aimed at character formation. Although Ibn Miskawayh does not explicitly address the role of veiling in character formation, he does discuss frames and concepts that we can apply to this case study, such as the role of bodily actions for character formation, the importance of habituating desires, and the social dimension of virtue acquisition.

IBN MISKAWAYH'S THEORY OF VIRTUE

Ibn Miskawah's *Tahdhib al-akhlaq* ("The Refinement of Character") is an example of a specific genre of *adab* whose purpose is to bring together two sources, Islamic revelation and the Greek philosophical canon, and it is one of the earliest examples of this type of *tahdhib* we have.[9] In this work, Ibn Miskawayh develops a practical theory of virtue ethics that draws selectively from Greek philosophy to make it consistent with an Islamic ethos and worldview. He holds a central place in Islamic ethics for his summary and explication of existing basic elements of practical philosophy, especially those arising from Neoplatonism.[10]

Ibn Miskawayh was born Abu 'Ali Ahmad ibn Muhammad ibn Ya'qub ibn Miskawayh around 932/940 AD in Rayy, near modern Tehran, Iran. In his various appointed positions until his death in 1030, such as his seven-year service as Ibn al-'Amid's librarian, he was part of a class of intellectuals who flourished under Buwayhid patronage in the tenth and eleventh centuries. These positions allowed him to live in vibrant intellectual centers of the time—Baghdad, Isfahan, and Rayy—and afforded him ample time to pursue his own research and writing.

Ibn Miskawayh has a good understanding of the diversity of Greek thought, and he understands that some strands are more naturalistic and less inclined toward theology, while other strands are much more inclined toward theology. He uses Greek philosophy in the service of Islamic thought about morality accordingly. For instance, Ibn Miskawayh adopts Plato's metaphysics of the soul as a self-subsisting entity or substance in order to build his ethics.[11] As Ibn Miskawayh puts it, character is a two-part state of the soul, involving both natural and moral virtue. On the one hand, there is the natural temperament of an individual that determines her character. On the other hand, there is the part of character that is "acquired by habit and self-training. This training may have its beginning in deliberation and thought, but then it becomes, by gradual and continued practice, an aptitude and a trait of character."[12]

Anyone familiar with Aristotle's *Nicomachean Ethics* will recognize Ibn Miskawayh's debt to this work in *Tahbdhib Al-Akhlaq* well before he mentions the Greek philosopher by name in the second discourse. He draws heavily from Aristotle in his formulation of what virtue is and what the process of moral development looks like.[13] Like Aristotle, for Ibn Miskawayh virtues are dispositions related to faculties of the soul. Virtues are acquired through a process of training, which begins as a struggle, requires the repetition of moral acts, and the formation of a habit (*malaka*). Good habits, in turn, help cultivate virtues. Virtues are character traits, which are permanent parts of a state of the soul that "go all the way down," so that to have a virtue is to be a certain sort of person.[14] Moreover a virtue, as opposed to a habit, effects multiple actions and causes a person eventually to perform a variety of moral actions without deliberation. Following Aristotle's doctrine of the mean, the virtues are conceptualized by Ibn Miskawayh as a form of moderation (*i'tidal*) or proportion (*nisba*) between two extremes so that acting virtuously is acting moderately:

> Virtues are means between extremes. . . . Putting it in general terms: The center of a circle is at the extreme distance from the circumference, and if a thing is at the extreme distance from something else, then it should, from this point of view, fall on the diameter. In this way, we should understand the meaning of a virtue as a mean, for it lies between vices and at the extreme distance from them.[15]

Ibn Miskawayh's ethics, however, is not a perfect adoption of Neoplatonic or Aristotelian theory. One fundamental difference is the nature of humans assumed by the respective thinkers. For Ibn Miskawayh, "the art of character training . . . is concerned with the betterment of actions of man *qua* man," and since we are fundamentally religious beings, the cultivation of our character is about discovering and then following a divine plan as

revealed in the Qur'an and the Sunna of the Prophet (the action and sayings of the Prophet recorded in the hadith).[16] In contrast, Aristotle is not
necessarily a theological thinker, even if recently Christian moral philosophers have gone out of their way to reclaim the place of the divine in Aristotle's philosophy.[17] For Aristotle, like all Greek thinkers, humans have the
ability to be moral because of our rational capacities, not our relationship
to God.

Ibn Miskawayh solves this problem by simply asserting that all Greek
philosophy affirms the existence and unity (*tawhid*) of God. It is not a typo-
graphical error that Ibn Miskawayh misquotes Aristotle's pagan conception of "Gods" (*theon*) as a monothestic "God" in his Islamic application:
this is necessary because within the Islamic worldview good character is
not only about intellectually discerning the right thing and acting on this
but also, and more importantly, being in right relationship with God as
vice-regents on earth. Character formation for Muslims is a process of perfecting the soul for God, who is *the* perfection.

There are three tenets of Ibn Miskawayh's ethics that are important to
grasp in order to understand character as cultivated in his view: the centrality of bodily practices, the possibility of habituating sexual appetites,
and the social dimensions of virtue. These same three tenets will in turn be
helpful in analyzing the contemporary practice of public veiling.

1. Bodily Practices

Religions are not concerned only with right beliefs but also with right
action. Islam is no exception, and Muslims believe that completing certain
bodily actions—such as prayer, fasting, alms-giving, and so on—are the
"pillars" of a pious Muslim life. In religious ethics this is formulated along
the following lines: belief, understanding, discussion, or persuasion are not
enough to transform a person; repetitive behavior and physical habits are
also part of moral development.[18] As Ibn Miskawayh put it, a disposition to
do the right thing "may have its beginning in deliberation and thought, but
then it becomes, by gradual and continued practice, an aptitude and a trait
of character."[19]

When religious ethicists talk about the ways actions affect the people
who do them we almost always reference French philosophers like Michel
Foucault or Pierre Hadot. These thinkers help us describe and explain
how bodily actions, categorized as "technologies of the self"[20] and "spiritual exercises,"[21] affect who a person is. The core idea is that practices
modify and transform the person who does them. In this way the prostration

of daily prayer cultivates humility and submission in the person who prays; fasting during Ramadan cultivates devotion; alms-giving cultivates generosity.

Ibn Miskawayh considers bodily actions central to the cultivation of character, a role he discusses in the following passage of *Tahdhib al-akhlaq*:

> Now, as the soul is a divine, incorporeal faculty, and as it is, at the same time, used for a particular constitution and tied to it physically and divinely in such a way that neither of them can be separated from the other except by the will of the Creator ... you must realize that each one of them [i.e., the soul and the constitution] is dependent upon the other, changing when it changes, becoming healthy when it is healthy, and ill when it is ill. . . . Thus we must inquire into the origin of the diseases of our souls. If it lies in the soul itself ... we should try to remedy these diseases in the way which is appropriate to them. But if, on the other hand, their origin lies in the [physical] constitution or in the senses ... then we should attempt to remedy it in the way which is appropriate to these diseases.[22]

Here the importance put on bodily action for virtue is grounded in part in a dual conception of the human. Using the analogy of health and disease for virtue and vice, Ibn Miskawayh points out that some vices originate in our physical constitution, and thus we should expect their treatment to have a physical component. He goes on to discuss how bodily practices are an integral part of character formation just like physical activity is part of a healthy lifestyle:

> Another obligation incumbent on the person who seeks to preserve the health of his soul is to apply himself to a duty relating to the theoretical part [of knowledge] as well as to the practical—a duty, which he should not, under any circumstances, be allowed to neglect, so that it may serve the soul as physical exercise is pursued to preserve the health of the body. Physicians ascribe great importance to exercise in the preservation of the health of the body, and the physician of the soul attributes even greater importance to it in the preservation of the health of the soul.[23]

Some virtues can only be formed through proper bodily practice, just like some aspects of bodily health can only be acquired through exercise. Exercise that raises one's heart rate strengthens the heart. Lifting weights builds bone density. Physical corrections, while necessary, might not be sufficient, but they are part of a "healthy/moral" lifestyle. In other words, to become a more virtuous person we must do certain things.

This is slightly different from how many Christian thinkers, as well as some Islamic thinkers, view the role of practice in moral development. For example, the Christian tradition emphasizes both (1) God as agent in our cultivation of character (the role of grace); and (2) the radical interiority of virtue as seen in the use as "heart."[24] This is not to say that Christian ethics does not have a role for right action, because it does, but there is a tendency to make the morality of such action dependent on receiving God's gift of grace, or at the very least on the individual's intention.

"Heart" (*qalb*) is featured as the focus of our moral development in some Islamic ethical thought as well, especially those working out of the Sufi tradition of *tasawwuf*. A prominent example is al-Makki's *Qut al-qulub* ("The Nourishment of Hearts").[25] However, by my reading, God is not the facilitator in our process of character formation in Ibn Miskawayh's account of character formation. He writes "that the existence of the human substance is due to the power of his Maker and Creator ... but that the betterment of this substance is entrusted to man and depends upon his will."[26] In addition, Ibn Miskawayh's view of bodily practices means that the right actions are understood sometimes to be necessary to create virtue independently of the intent or "heart" of the believer. In fact, the action itself sometimes seems to be what cultivates the correct intent. There is still a sense in which intent is valued, and certainly other Islamic thinkers, but at least for Ibn Miskawayh, a "good heart" does not necessarily need to precede physical actions as part of the cultivation of character. In this view, the idea that one might need to "fake it until you make it" is not ethical insincerity but, rather, a natural part of the process of character formation.

The underlying issue here is both whether there is a potentiality within the agent for goodness (much like a patient for health) and how this potentiality is developed.[27] One option is that dispositions can be seen as potentialities that are awakened through things like physical repetition, social pressure, the will of God, and the like. A second option is that dispositions are somehow *created* by these same forces. Ibn Miskawayh seems to prefer the first option in this text. For example, at the outset of the second discourse of *Tahdhib al-akhlaq*, he discusses the manner in which one type of character "is acquired by habit and self-training. It may have its beginning in deliberation and thought, but then it becomes, by gradual and continued practice, an aptitude and a trait of character."[28]

A related issue is whether individuals (1) are simply born good or bad; or (2) have a greater natural potentiality or aptitude for goodness. Here Ibn Miskawayh sides with the ancients who argue, "no part of character is natural to man, nor it is non-natural. For we are disposed to it, but it also changes as a result of discipline and admonition either rapidly or slowly."[29] In other words, there are not "good individuals" versus "bad individuals." However, our receptivity to change is different. Following Aristotle, Ibn Miskawayh asserts "that the repetition of admonitions and discipline and the good and virtuous guidance of people cannot but produce different results on different people: some are responsive to discipline and acquire virtue rapidly, while others are also responsive but acquire it slowly."[30]

2. Habituating Sexual Appetites

In the context of the physical health of the soul, Ibn Miskawayh also discusses human sexuality. He begins with the assumption that sexual appetites, which he refers to as "passionate love"[31] and "concupiscent and irascible faculties,"[32] are not in and of themselves problematic. This highlights another difference between early Islamic and Christian concerns with bodily practice—this time, explicitly sexual acts.

For instance, scholars have pointed out a tendency of some Apostles (e.g., Paul) and some early church thinkers (e.g., Augustine) to see human sexuality as fundamentally flawed because of the biblical account of the Fall. As a result, there is a strand of Christian thought that makes celibacy the ideal sexual virtue and sexual acts between spouses tolerated only when aimed at procreation.[33] Islam has a very different ethical understanding of sex. While a narrative about creation of man and woman and their disobedience to God is found in the Qur'an that is similar to the one in Genesis, the Qur'anic version is not interpreted by Islamic thinkers as resulting in an "original sin" that affects the state of human sexuality.[34] Instead, like the Greeks, Islamic ethicists have often treated sexual appetites alongside other physical ones, such as hunger and thirst, as a drive that needs to be kept within bounds, but also is necessary for human life.[35] Medieval Islamic thinkers addressed the importance of sexual satisfaction, both men's and women's, and encouraged specific practices for that end, such as foreplay. Celibacy is a way to emulate Christ, but the Prophet Muhammad not only had multiple wives but also multiple children. In Islam, sexual activity is assumed to be an important part of any fully human life, and thus celibacy is not encouraged or judged as virtuous.

However, human sexuality is also highly regulated in Islam because sexual appetites are considered very powerful. Part of this regulation occurs through stringent legal codes, which severely punish illicit sexual acts (defined in *fiqh* as genital acts between anyone except married spouses or a master and his female slave). Regulation also occurs at the level of character formation: improper sexuality activity is to be both avoided and, ultimately, to be not desired. Ibn Miskawayh describes this as learning how to "refrain from stirring" our sexual appetites, and suggests that we should instead "leave them alone until they are stirred by themselves."[36] He wants to make sure we do not dwell on our memories of pleasures: "this is like the one who arouses beasts of prey and excites wild, rapacious animals and then seeks to appease them and to be delivered from them. The intelligent man does not choose to be in such a condition."[37] Thus, sexual desire is a natural desire that should be habituated in order to be controlled, but it is not a vice that needs to be eradicated.

To help us understand this more precisely, we can consider what sorts of things Ibn Miskawayh does consider vices, such as vanity. "As for vanity, when we come to define it, [we find that] it is, in fact, a false belief in one's self whereby that self is held to belong to a rank which it does not deserve."[38] Vanity is a complex state that incorporates both an erroneous belief (independence of the self) and an erroneous valuation (superiority of the self). It is a vice because it rejects a fundamental fact of human existence, namely our dependency on others.

> He who knows his own self should be aware of the many vices and defects which blemish it, and [should realize] that virtuousness is divided among men and that no one can attain perfection without the virtues of others. Consequently, when one's virtues depend upon others, it is one's duty not to be vain.[39]

Vanity is at its foundation a mistake in self-perception. Human sexuality and thus sexual appetites and actions, on the contrary, affirm our humanness, and our job in character formation is to create habits and dispositions so that we have specific types of desires (e.g., lust for our spouse), as opposed to others (e.g., lust for someone else's spouse), and thus act in specific ways (e.g., engage in genital acts with our spouse), as opposed to others (e.g., flirt, sexually touch, or engage in genital acts with an inappropriate sexual partner).

3. Virtue as Social

One objection to virtue ethics is that it can support forms of egoism when it focuses on character formation as a process of personal cultivation.[40] Ibn Miskawayh's theory of virtue is an important challenge to this critique, and it is a model for how this problem might be avoided in future work, because of the way he emphasizes the social, communal, and political aspects of the cultivation of character.

It is true that much of Ibn Miskawayh's theory of virtue is focused on self-formation. While this seems to formulate the moral life as a personal journey, for a thinker like Ibn Miskawayh, this personal spiritual journey is only part of the story. He understands the training of the soul to occur in public, with others, and ideally resulting in a form of corporate virtue. Another way to put this is to say that in Ibn Miskawayh's virtue theory, character formation is not merely an individual process aimed at merely an individual result. In fact, he devotes the entire fifth discourse of *Tahdhib al-akhlaq* to love and friendship:

> We have already spoken of the need which people have for one another, and it has become clear that every one of them finds his completion in his friend and that necessity requires that they should seek one another's assistance. The reason is that men are born with deficiencies which they have to remedy and, as we have explained before, there is no way for any single individual among them to become complete by himself. There is, then[,] a genuine need and a demanding necessity for a condition in which diverse persons are brought together and combined so that they become, by agreement and harmony, as one single person all of whose [bodily] organs associate in the performance of the single act which is useful to him.[41]

This emphasis on friends is not surprising, given that Ibn Miskawayh understands humans to be "civic beings" by nature.[42] It is also another place we can clearly see him drawing from Aristotle, for whom friendship is an external good needed for human flourishing.[43]

Ibn Miskawayh's view of community involvement in the cultivation of character can be broken down into four levels. First, *becoming* virtuous requires support from and interaction with others. Ibn Miskawayh rejects ascetic life: "Man, of all the animals, cannot attain his perfection by himself alone. He must have recourse to the help of a great number of people in order to achieve a good life and follow the right path."[44] This is more than just observing others as possible moral exemplars. Ibn Miskawayh describes a multifaceted process in which our efforts at character formation are supported and reinforced by our interpersonal relationships and political context:

> To achieve perfection, the individual's own efforts must be reinforced by those of others. The good man must have good friends to help guide him to good thoughts and deeds. The example of a good ruler and the restraints of a well-governed society are also important.[45]

Thus, the ideal is not withdrawal from the world for the sake of spiritual formation, "The ideal is of a person ... who is involved in the world but not at its mercy."[46]

Second, we need others to *act* virtuously insofar as interpersonal spheres of activity create occasions to be virtuous. In other words, true virtue requires not only dispositions but also an opportunity to act virtuously. Ibn Miskawayh writes,

> For he who does not mingle with other people and who does not live with them in cities cannot show temperance, intrepidity, liberality, or justice. On the contrary, all the faculties and aptitudes with which he is equipped are nullified, since they are not directed towards either good or evil. And when they become nil and cease to perform their own distinctive actions, those who possess them are reduced to the rank of inanimate objects or dead people.[47]

This passage emphasizes the moral danger of withdrawal from society: when we do not practice virtuous action with others, the value of our correct cultivation is nullified. Later in the text Ibn Miskawayh describes how our social interactions also provide us an opportunity to share what we have learned. Quoting al-Kindi (d. 873), he analogizes from the moon and the sun to describe this process.[48] The light reflected from the sun makes the moon shine, although not as brightly as the sun itself. Likewise our public performance of virtue can transmit virtue to others, even if in a lesser degree. This "shining" of our virtue on others is itself a virtuous act, which is impossible without having others to "shine" upon.

Third, our community and our social institutions help us *see* (or reflect on) our own process of character formation. Again quoting al-Kindi, although reminiscent of Aristotle as well,[49] Ibn Miskawayh suggests that an individual who seeks virtue should consider others as mirrors in which to view the success and failures of his own character cultivation:

> The seeker of virtue should look at the images of all his acquaintances as if these images were to him mirrors in which he can see the image of each one of these acquaintances as each of them undergoes the pains which produce misdeeds. In this way, he will not fail to notice any of his own misdeeds, for he will be looking for the misdeeds of others. Whenever he sees a misdeed in some one, he will blame himself for it as if he had committed it and will reproach himself exceedingly on its account.[50]

Ibn Miskawayh's premise is that it is easier to seek and find the moral failings of others.[51] Once we perceive a moral defect in someone else, we should turn the blame onto our selves and set about correcting the error of character as if it were our own. This process gets us used to looking for misdeeds and we can apply this to ourselves as well. Thus, others help us to see and reflect on our own attempts to acquire virtue and act virtuously.

Finally, although Ibn Miskawayh is concerned with the perfection of the individual insofar as he tries to provide a theoretical and practical road map for character formation, the ultimate goal of virtue ethics is a just society with a sort of *corporate virtue*. It is in this level of virtue as social that we can see Ibn Miskawayh incorporating *fiqh* into his ethics so that virtue becomes the ultimate form of social justice. According to Ibn Miskawayh, if character formation begins with an individual's process of cultivation,

> it ends with civic organization, in which actions and faculties are properly regulated among the people in such a way that they attain the same kind of harmony [as in the individual] and the people achieve a common happiness, like that which takes place in the individual person.[52]

Character formation becomes part of articulating and sustaining the distinctive Muslim morality, which becomes the necessary basis for political action within our contemporary pluralistic social contexts.

THE VIRTUE OF THE VEIL

The Islamic veil continues to be one of the most contentious Islamic practices—both because of disagreements among Muslims over its necessity and because of its meaning and non-Muslim judgments of it—and thus it is one of the most studied by academics. When ethicists consider the veil, it is most often to assess whether veiling is good or bad within a specific framework (e.g., international law, feminism). In my view, however, the best scholarship on the virtue of veiling has been written, ironically, by non-ethicists, and it focuses on how as a performance, veiling creates specific attributes.[53]

When asked why they cover their head, body, or face, most Muslim women reply that they are following a written directive in Islamic scripture and do so in order to make themselves into good Muslim women. Three verses are commonly cited as Qur'anic evidence of the Islamic veil—33:53, 33:59–60, and 24:30–31. However, there is enormous diversity among these verses as well. The terms that get translated as "veil" are different: *hijab* (curtain), *jilbab* (cloak), *khimar* (kerchief). Who is asked to veil, for what reasons, and in front of whom differ in these verses, which complicates what norms are at stake in the practice. Various virtues are related to women's dress, including modesty, purity, honor, righteousness, and faith. But one thing these verses share is that Muslims have interpreted them as requiring specific bodily actions of Muslim women in order to become and be pious.[54]

The verse that connects veiling most explicitly to the cultivation of modesty is 24:30–31, often referred to as the verse of the *hijab*. We have very few reports in the canonical hadith collections providing us with the context for this revelation, and those we do have appeared later, in the fourteenth and fifteenth centuries, when veiling practices had already been established in Muslim communities. Complicating things further, the specific Arabic terms used in the verse have various and contentious meanings.

Verses 24:30–31 read as follows:

> Say to the believing men that they should lower their gaze and guard their modesty [*furujahun*]: that will make for greater purity for them: and God is well acquainted with all that they do. And say to the believing women that they should lower their gaze and guard their modesty; that they should not display their beauty and ornaments [*zina*] except what (must ordinarily) appear thereof; that they should draw their veils [*khumur*, sing. *khimar*] over their bosoms [*juyub*] and not display their beauty [*zina*] except to their husbands, their fathers, their husband's fathers, their sons, their husband's sons, their brothers or their brother's sons, or their sister's sons, or their women, or the slaves whom their right hands possess, or male servants free of physical needs, or small children who have no sense of the shame of sex ['*awra*]; and that they should not strike their feet in order to draw attention to their hidden ornaments. And O you Believers! You turn all together toward God, that you may attain Bliss.[55]

Throughout history, Qur'anic commentators have disagreed over what verse 24:31 requires women to cover. In some legal opinions, even a woman's voice is found to be '*awra*.[56] But for other scholars, only her bosom, neck, and head should be covered; and for still others, only her genitals.[57]

Despite these important interpretative debates, there is a majority opinion that verses 24:30–31 are instructing Muslims how to be good Muslims—that is, how to properly cultivate their character. Ibn Miskawayh's framework can help us understand more precisely what this process looks like. Instead of beginning with the question "Should Muslim women veil?," I use Ibn Miskawayh's virtue theory to answer the question "What does veiling ethically *do*?," or "What role does the veil have in character formation?" Specifically I will consider how veiling is part of the cultivation of character, versus merely a *symbol* of fundamentalism or identity, as is often claimed. Understanding the role of virtue in veiling will help explain why veiling has continued to be a popular practice in Islamic communities, despite the ways in which it clashes with other local social norms, such as secularism and feminism: many Muslims claim the practice is the necessary means to creating virtue, as well as a virtuous action in and of itself. In other words, Islamic virtue theory helps explain why veiling might be an ethical practice integral not only as the display for virtue but also for the cultivation of virtue.

1. Bodily Practices: Looking and Dressing

In verse 24:30, men and women are asked to *do* certain things in order to *be* a certain way, specifically to "lower their gaze," an action "that will make for greater purity for them." Qur'anic commentators have tended to interpret averting the eyes metaphorically as avoiding desiring what is forbidden. But Muslims also interpret this quite literally so that modesty understood at its most fundamental level is about how one physically interacts with others. Physical submission[58] (lowering the gaze) is recommended in interpersonal interactions in order to prevent intimacy and to cultivate the virtue of modesty.[59] By not looking at someone directly we not only do not "flirt," we also maintain bodily distance despite physical proximity. The more a person does this practice, the more it becomes automatic, and the more successful she will be in cultivating the virtue of modesty.

Lowering one's gaze is a bodily action suggested for both men and women, but verse 24:31 requires a second category of bodily actions for women: they should not display their "ornaments." This is most often interpreted as requiring a specific sartorial practice. Since the meanings of both *zina* and *'awra* are up for debate, it is not particularly helpful that in verses 24:30–31 the things a woman must cover with clothing are defined by these terms. Luckily, we are given a few other hints about what proper dress entails in the verse itself. For one, we are told Muslim women should cover their *juyub* with *khimar*. The root of *juyub* means an "opening" or "space between." Although it is often translated as bosom, it is technically a woman's cleavage. *Khimar*, a term some commentators gloss as "veil," refers to a specific type of clothing, mainly a kerchief. In other words, the verse tells us that cleavage is part of hidden *'awra* and thus should be covered by something a woman wears. The implication is that in addition to a specific form of physical interaction that is required of men and women (lowering the gaze), women should dress in a manner that covers parts of their body (at least their bosom) in order to cultivate modesty.

Just as described by Ibn Miskawayh, many veiling Muslim women report that in the beginning the bodily practice of veiling is difficult. It takes a conscious effort. But after time, a woman acquires a habit (*malaka*) so that she wants to veil and then unveiling is what feels uncomfortable. For instance, the anthropologist Saba Mahmood's well-received book on the Egyptian piety movement includes the following often-cited exchange with one of her informants describing her experience with veiling:

> It's just like the veil. In the beginning when you wear it, you're embarrassed and don't want to wear it because people say that you look older and unattractive, that you won't get married and will never find a husband. But you must wear the veil, first because it is God's command and then, with time, because your inside learns to feel shy without the veil, and if you take it off, your entire being feels uncomfortable about it.[60]

This woman describes a successful formation of character through bodily practice. Veiling feels unnatural to her in the beginning because she is concerned with looking unattractive, indicating she has some measure of vanity. But after repetition it is unveiling that feels unnatural, an indication that the dispositions associated with veiling such as modesty, or in her words, shyness, have been successfully cultivated.

2. Habituating Sexual Appetites: Avoiding Illicit Desires

Of the many verses cited as supporting Muslim women's veiling, only 24:31 connects veiling to a concern with sexual modesty (versus concerns with privacy and security in 33:53 and 33:59–60, respectively). Depending on how you translate *'awra* (genitals or simply vulnerable parts), sexuality might not be mentioned explicitly in this verse at all. Nevertheless there are other clues that tell us the modesty at stake here has to do with properly ordering the interactions of men and women. For one, the act of covering is assigned to women, not men. In addition, several categories of men in front of whom women do not need to cover are mentioned, mainly her close male relatives (her father, father-in-law, son, stepson, brother, nephew), male servants (both slaves and eunuchs), and young boys. These are the cases in which it is assumed a woman and a man will not desire each other in a sexual way and thus there is no danger of improper sexual desires or illicit genital acts.

Ibn Miskawayh does not specifically discuss veiling in *Tahdhib al-akhlaq*, but his understanding of sexuality can help explain why this practice is so important to many Muslims. As we saw, Ibn Miskawayh considers lust among a class of human appetites, which while potentially problematic, are not vices that need to be eradicated. Sexual appetites, so hardwired into human beings, must be trained so that they do not dictate our actions. This can help explain *"the why"* of verse 24:31—that is, why women are told to lower their gaze, guard their modesty, refrain from ornaments, cover their bosoms. These are explicit directions, a guidebook of sorts, for character formation. By repeating these practices women remind themselves not to arouse their own sexual appetites, as well as to prevent the arousal of men around them.

Finally, if we take verse 24:31 as our point of departure, women's bodies are assumed to be more problematic in terms of their ability to evoke strong sexual desires. The concern is not with female beauty per se but, rather, with what the tradition refers to as hidden beauty and adornment— that is, the aspects of physical beauty and enhancement that sexually entice others. If veiling is about cultivating sexual modesty, then the goal of this practice is to (1) change the way women look to men (2) in order to change the way men look at women, and ultimately, (3) so that women cease to be and be perceived as sexual objects.

3. Virtue as Social: Veiling in Public

I highlighted four ways in which character cultivation requires others in Ibn Miskawayh's ethics, mainly by providing an arena (1) to become virtuous, (2) to act virtuously, (3) to see our own virtue, and (4) to create communal virtue. We can use these to think about veiling as a moral practice that occurs in the public space.

First, women can only use veiling to become virtuous and act virtuously if this sartorial practice is performed within a social context. Of the two actions related to cultivating modesty discussed in verses 24:30–31, lowering one's gaze and dressing a certain way, both are meaningless unless performed in front of others. Modesty is not a virtue we cultivate alone or in our homes. It is not even a virtue we can cultivate with friends or family, a fact highlighted by the list of men a woman does not need to dress modestly in front of, including her family members and servants. Instead, modesty requires the cultivation of habit through interaction with strangers. The public sphere is the place where this occurs.

Second, given the textual ambiguity about what to wear when veiling, society provides necessary examples of how to veil for a woman to imitate. As mentioned above, three different Arabic words are used in the Qur'an that might be translated as the Islamic veil: *hijab, jilbab, khimar. Jilbab* and *khimar* at least refer to articles of clothing, but not the same ones. *Jilbab* is most often translated as a cloak, but we have no way of knowing what the tenth-century version of *jilbab* referenced in verse 33:59 looked like. *Khimar* is a kerchief, and in verse 24:31 it specifically covers a woman's cleavage, but this gives no guidance about what style of headscarf a Muslim woman should wear. The common Qur'anic meaning of *hijab*, which is used in 33:53 in reference to protecting the privacy of the Prophet's wives, might not refer to clothing at all but, rather, to a separation. This ambiguity means that the sacred text does not provide practical guidance about what to wear to a Muslim woman who wants to dress modestly. She can only learn this by observing other Muslim women. Simona Tersigni uses the concept of "horizontal pedagogy" to talk about the adoption of the veil in European contexts.[61] In Indonesia, for example, veiling is becoming increasingly popular among young women in the last ten years, but it is often the case that their mothers and grandmothers do not veil. In these cases, girls learn from observing and admiring their peers.

Third, society, and specifically our social interactions with others within society, can help us gauge our own character. Ibn Miskawayh believes it is easier to judge others, so our goal is to judge the morality of others' actions and then apply this judgment to ourselves. A practice like public veiling is especially well suited for engaging in public assessment because it is a visual practice. As we begin to dress modestly, the sartorial practices of those around us act as a mirror within which we gauge our own success and thereby where we are in our process of character cultivation.

Finally, Ibn Miskawayh's idea of a corporate dimension of virtue can also be used to help explain the role of public veiling in the contemporary world. For Ibn Miskawayh, the cultivation of an individual's character was the first step to virtue acquisition, but he understood the ultimate goal of this cultivation was to have a community in which individuals, acting cooperatively out of habit, create a virtuous society. In the case of public veiling, the veil not only forms the character of the woman who wears it but also helps to create a "public virtue zone" that works to habituate all individuals, men included, to have proper sexual desires. Take the case of Iran, where veiling is mandatory for all women in public, including non-Muslim Iranians and non-Iranian visitors. Iranian leaders have decided it is not enough for most women to veil publicly; all women must veil. It is not enough for a woman to veil in front of others; she must veil *with* others. That is why the Iranian authorities require me to veil when I am in Iran doing fieldwork. My veiling is just as integral to the corporate virtue of modesty as the veiling of the most pious Iranian Muslim.

CONCLUSIONS

Ibn Miskawayh provides a complex theory of virtue acquisition as dependent on bodily action, habituation of desires, and public interaction. When applied to veiling, his framework counters the flattening, popular in media and political discourse, that the veil is merely *a symbol* and encourages us to see it instead as *the means by which* virtues are made. Further, the case of the modern veil demonstrates how the cultivation of virtue involves transformation not only at the personal level but also at the interpersonal and social levels. First, this reflects a deep interest in the tradition about how right action can make virtuous Muslims, strengthen relationships, and contribute to a just and stable society. Second, it is why bans on the veil are so egregious to many Muslims: they are interpreted as taking away a woman's, a family's, and even a community's ability not only to *be* but even to *become* pious. Third, framing the veil as a part of a social ethical project helps us to understand why it is so contentious in some national contexts. For veiling supporters, outlawing the public veiling of women prevents the cultivation of a corporate form of virtue. For veiling opponents, public veiling influences civic ethics so that the public space is not purely secular. Both sides agree that this sartorial practice influences the shared ethos of the nation.

One of the important ways in which ethical theories and practice are related in scholarship is that not only does theory illuminate practice—in this case, Ibn Miskawayh's understanding of virtue helping to explain the importance of veiling to character formation—but practice can also point out the unstated assumptions or limitations of any particular theory. Veiling does this for Ibn Miskawayh's theory of virtue and in doing so suggests two important future directions for research.

Assumption: Virtue as Gendered

Reading the Islamic veil as part of character formation highlights the gendered assumptions in Islamic virtue ethics, since the specific acts required for men and women to cultivate modesty are different. In verses 24:30–31, for instance, both men and women are directed to be modest; however, the text treats men and women quite differently in that it devotes substantially more time to discussing women's modesty. Men and women are told to lower their gaze, but additional actions are required for women (such as covering bosoms and *'awra*) and others are forbidden (such as drawing attention to themselves). The text also conceives women's beauty as a particular obstacle to realizing modesty norms.

Barbara Metcalf, a historian of Islam who has written extensively on the role of character formation in religious movements in India, has argued that, in principle, virtue ethics in Islam is radically equalizing: anyone can cultivate an excellent moral character. Formal training, social status, gender, and race do not preclude or ensure successful cultivation. Character formation properly conceived is formation "away from habits of false hierarchy and pride."[62] While this holds true for Ibn Miskawayh's theory of attaining moral perfection, so does one major exception: gender difference. In Islam, the very process of character formation is gendered: men and women are expected to perform different bodily actions to obtain similar virtues. Not only are these actions assigned to specific genders but also the virtues themselves are gendered. It would be interesting to try to parse this out further—for example, through comparing *adab* written for a general audience with *adab* written specifically for Muslim girls and women, instructing them in proper conduct of their everyday lives.

The classic example of the latter is Maulana Ashraf 'Ali Thanawi's (1864–1943) *Bihishti Zewar* ("Perfecting Women"), a text written in Urdu in northern India in the early 1900s and well known in the West through Metcalf's excellent English translation.[63] Contemporary versions of this advice literature exist as well, including some aimed specifically at how Muslim women should wear their headscarf. Questions we might ask include: Do these texts discuss a form of modesty that is specific to women, entailing, for example, a shy demeanor and specific sartorial practices? If so, is there a different version of modesty for men? If some Islamic virtues are gendered, does this mean there is something we might call a virtue of femininity, that only women should cultivate?

Islam is certainly not the only tradition with deeply embedded assumptions of differences between men and women. The philosopher Julia Annas asserts that every society has "two actual norms for human life" and that your sex "always makes a difference to what your options are over your life as a whole."[64] These two norms are not necessarily unjust, but we will want to pay close attention to what ideals of human nature they assume and how they affect the quality of individual lives.[65] Comparative attention to this issue is especially important for reasons similar to those Ibn Miskawayh gives for the role of social interaction for seeing our own moral failures: when we get used to judging others, we can become better at judging ourselves. Annas describes how it is easier to view the injustice of the two norms in other, more "traditional" societies: "It is, of course, easier to appreciate the injustices that the norms of a society give rise to if we do not have to live with the norms ourselves. It is much harder to stand back from, and criticize, the injustices arising from the differentiated norms that are part of our own society's current way of thinking."[66]

This suggests another possible future area of research, especially given that virtue ethicists aspire to capture the details of everyday life often missed by other forms of ethical inquiry. With careful investigations into how character is cultivated by men and women in different ways, either in their actual practices or in the ways religious thinkers talk about this formation as gendered, we can gain a greater insight into the cross-cultural complexity of sexual difference in ethical life. The result may not be a simple assessment of gender differences as socially or politically problematic for women: we have evidence that when religious communities or individuals try to implement strict gender distinctions, the result is often a shift in these distinctions and their underlying logic.[67] Attention to the two-track system of virtue ethics will help identify assumptions about gendered forms of subjectivity and thus spaces of gendered-based activism.

Limitation: Cross-Cultural Diversity of Virtue

When Ibn Miskawayh wrote *Tahdhib al-akhlaq*, it was not his intention to describe virtue for only eleventh-century Muslims living in Baghdad. His theory is meant to apply universally to Islam, and in fact, we have seen it is still applicable to contemporary character formation. But specific practices engaged in by Muslims as part of character formation, such as veiling, demonstrate that there is actually enormous cultural diversity in regard to specific virtues.

What counts as proper veiling and modesty, for example, is not the same across time and space. A Turkish, an Iranian, and an Indonesian woman who all decide to veil agree that this practice is important for character formation. It is likely they also agree that the practice is related to the virtue of modesty. But what they wear will radically differ because what counts as modest Islamic veiling differs from one social context to another. In Iran, belts and other forms of clothing that show a woman's curves are improper, but in Indonesia modest dress is understood as literally covering skin. In Turkey, where the new upper-middle class of Muslim women are veiling in increasing numbers, modesty is defined by some as not wearing expensive name-brand clothing.

On one hand, this diversity demonstrates the status of virtue within an Islamic ethics.[68] I don't mean to get into a metaphysical discussion of virtue here. Instead, my point is that in the case of modesty we see that even when there is agreement within the tradition that modesty is a virtue, the content of that virtue might be still open to debate. In addition, within the same location, what counts as modesty can shift over time as local norms about dress and fashion change.

On the other hand, this diversity is a reflection of the significance of Aristotle's claim that virtue is a mean, or, as it is expressed by Ibn Miskawayh, virtue is a form of moderation (*i'tidal*) or proportion (*nisba*) between two extremes. In Aristotle's thought, this is often explained in terms of his assertion in the *Nicomachean Ethics* that a virtue is "the mean relative to us."[69] Ibn Miskawayh formulates a virtue similarly as "the means of these extremes should be sought separately for each individual person."[70] In other words, one person's courage is another person's timidity; it depends on the character of the agent. But some aspects of virtue are also means relative to our social context. For a virtue like modesty and a practice like veiling, how others perceive one is important. The same outfit that reads as modest on a U.S. college campus reads as immodest on the streets of Riyadh. Likewise, the variability of modesty is to be expected given the dependency of virtue on social context.

Virtue ethicists will likely find the cultural relativism of my presentation of Islamic modesty unsatisfying, and wonder if there is a common core to the virtue of modesty in Islamic ethics, which, if lacking, disqualifies a trait from counting as modesty. I continue to resist trying to define some core essence to this virtue, which is temporally and geographically universal. I find more accurate the proposition that Islamic modesty is defined through an ongoing dialectic between interpretation and implementation within various visual, social, and political contexts. However, I am able to offer the following, qualified, response to the question "what currently counts as modesty" in this tradition.

If we take a snapshot of modest sartorial practices in various Muslim communities—I am most familiar with Turkey, Iran, Indonesia, and to a lesser extent the United States and France—there are a couple of shared aspects of modesty. First, there is certainly more discussion about and attention to women's bodies than men's bodies in discussions about the cultivation of modesty. There are a number of historical factors for this, including a pattern of legal reasoning in medieval *fiqh* (jurisprudence) that linked female *'awra* (genitals) to *fitna* (worldly disorder). This idea continues to be used to explain why the covering of women's bodies is required: it prevents the chaos of sexual desire outside of marriage. In terms of what should be covered, interpretations differ radically, from only the top of her head (and thus some hair), to her entire body (including her eyes). However, the majority of these discussions are concerned with what women, and not men, wear.

Second, in general there is an assumption that modesty goes beyond dress or interpersonal interactions (such as appropriate gaze): it entails a disposition that affects the person all the way down. For instance, much of the discussion of veiling today references the concept of "inner beauty" that is connected to an external, aesthetic value. In this way modesty entails a cluster of behaviors and dispositions: dress, maintaining interpersonal distance, and acting on others—especially God's—behalf.

Finally, Islamic modesty has something important to say about the relationship between virtue and visual culture. When a Muslim woman in the United States, for example, decides to wear a headscarf, she is making a choice to dress noticeably different from her non-Muslim friends and neighbors. Her decision to be visibly Muslim contributes to the visual culture of her community, and is based on the assumption that shared images and perceptions by others contribute to the construction of subjectivity, identity, and personal virtue.[71]

I end with a note of caution. The account of virtue I present should not be understood as a universal or exhaustive Islamic ethical theory. I happen to believe that such a project would fundamentally misunderstand the dynamic nature of Islamic ethics. My intent here is simply to show how aspects of Muslims' practice of virtue can be understood by referring to Islamic religious texts and traditions. I have tried to show that Ibn Miskawayh's views open important perspectives on the place of virtue and its cultivation in the Islamic worldview. In particular, they provide a framework within which to revisit the Muslim practice of veiling, thereby allowing us to understand veiling as integral to the development of the virtue of modesty, as well as afford us a nuanced glimpse into Islamic religious theories and practices, and aid our understanding of an important and frequently misconstrued tradition.

NOTES

1. The author would like to thank Jamie Schillinger, Kirsten Wesselhoeft, Jung Lee, and the participants of Brown University's Religion and Critical Thought Workshop for their comments and critical engagement with earlier versions of this essay. This paper was made possible in part through the support of a grant from The Character Project at Wake Forest University and the John Templeton Foundation. The opinions expressed in this publication are those of the author and do not necessarily reflect the views of The Character Project, Wake Forest University, or the John Templeton Foundation.
2. According to the Pew Forum, 84 percent of the world population, of 5.8 billion adults and children are religiously affiliated. *The Global Religious Landscape: A Report on the Size and Distribution of the World's Major Religious Groups as of 2010.* Part of the Pew-Templeton Global Religious Futures Project (Washington, DC: Pew Forum on Religion & Public Life, 2012).

3. E.g., Stanley Hauerwas, *A Community of Character: Toward a Constructive Christian Social Ethic* (Notre Dame, IN: University of Notre Dame Press, 1991); Stanley Hauerwas, *Vision and Virtue: Essays in Christian Ethical Reflection* (Notre Dame, IN: University of Notre Dame Press, 1981); Nancey Murphy et al., eds., *Virtues and Practices in the Christian Tradition: Christian Ethics after Macintyre* (Harrisburg: Trinity International, 1997); Alasdair MacIntyre, *After Virtue: A Study in Moral Theory* (Notre Dame, IN: University of Notre Dame, 1984); Jennifer Herdt, *Putting on Virtue: The Legacy of the Splendid Vices* (Chicago: University of Chicago Press, 2008).

4. E.g., Bryan van Norden, *Virtue Ethics and Consequentialism in Early Chinese Philosophy* (New York: Cambridge University Press, 2007); P. J. Ivanhoe, *Confucian Moral Self-Cultivation* (Indianapolis: Hackett, 2000); Lee Yearley, *Mencius and Aquinas: Theories of Virtue and Conceptions of Courage* (Albany: SUNY Press, 1990); Thomas A. Lewis, Jonathan W. Schofer, Aaron Stalnaker, and Mark A. Berkson, "Anthropos and Ethics: Categories of Inquiry and Procedures of Comparison," *Journal of Religious Ethics* 33, no. 2 (2005): 177–85; Aaron Stalnaker, *Overcoming Our Evil: Human Nature and Spiritual Exercises in Xunzi and Augustine* (Washington, DC: Georgetown University Press, 2006); Aaron Stalnaker, "Spiritual Exercises and the Grace of God: Paradoxes of Personal Formation in Augustine," *Journal of the Society of Christian Ethics* 24, no. 2 (2004): 137–70.

5. See, for example, the excellent work of Jonathan Wyn Schofer, *Confronting Vulnerability: The Body and the Divine in Rabbinic Ethics* (Chicago: University of Chicago Press, 2010); and Jonathan Wyn Schofer, *The Making of a Sage: A Study in Rabbinic Ethics* (Madison: University of Wisconsin Press, 2004) on rabbinic ethics; and Anand Pandian, *Crooked Stalks: Cultivating Virtue in South India* (Durham, NC: Duke University Press, 2009) on cultivation of character and land in South India; and Damien Keown, *The Nature of Buddhist Ethics* (New York: Palgrave, 2001); and Donald Swearer "Buddhist Virtue, Voluntary Poverty, and Extensive Benevolence," *Journal of Religious Ethics* 26, no. 1 (1998): 71–103, on Buddhist virtue.

6. My thanks to Jamie Schillinger for pushing me to clarify this point.

7. Al-Tirmithi, as translated by Abdullahi Hassan Zaroug, "Ethics from an Islamic Perspective: Basic Issues," *American Journal of Islamic Social Sciences* 16, no. 3 (1999): 54.

8. Full-length English-language studies of ethics and *adab* are limited, especially when compared to those dealing with *fiqh*. Notable exceptions include the following work by Barbara Metcalf: *Moral Conduct and Authority: The Place of Adab in South Asian Islam* (Berkeley: University of California Press, 1983); *Perfecting Women: Maulana Ashraf 'Ali Thanawi's Bihishti Zewar* (Berkeley: University of California Press, 1990); "'Remaking Ourselves': Islamic Self-Fashioning in a Global Movement of Spiritual Renewal," in *Accounting for Fundamentalisms*, ed. Martin Marty and Scott Appleby (Chicago: University of Chicago Press, 1994). See also Kamran Karimullah, "Rival Moral Traditions in the Late Ottoman Empire, 1839–1908," *Journal of Islamic Studies* 24, no. 1 (2013): 37–66. But the field seems to be changing. For example, there were a number of presentations on *adab* at the 2013 Society for the Study of Muslim Ethics, including those by Kamran Karimullah, Kirsten Wesselhoeft, and Brannon Ingram.

9. The Greek philosophical canon Ibn Miskwayh would have had access to was handed down and somewhat transformed via Neoplatonic mergings of Aristotle and Plato, as well as Christian theological interpretation. It is worth noting in passing that in Ibn Miskawayh's text, the reflection on the Qur'an and hadith is implied rather than stated. In fact there are few to no direct references.

10. For a more detailed biography of Ibn Miskawayh, including his influence on Islamic thought, see Constantine Zurayk, "Preface" in *The Refinement of Character* (Beirut: Kazi, 2002); and Oliver Leaman, "Ibn Miskawayh, Ahmad ibn Muhammad (c. 940-1030)," in *Muslim Philosophy*, 1998, www.muslimphilosophy.com/ip/rep/H042. For an account of the context within which Ibn Miskawayh worked and the influence of his views on Islamic philosophy, see Oliver Leaman, "Ibn Miskawayh," in *History of Islamic Philosophy*, ed. S. H. Nasr and O. Leaman (London: Routledge, 1996), 252–57. For an account of Ibn Miskawayh's metaphysics and ethics, see Majid Fakhry, "The Platonism of Miskawayh and its Implications for his Ethics," *Studia Islamica* 43 (1975): 39–57; and Mohammed Arkoun, "'Deux épîtres de Miskawayh' (Two Treatises of Miskawayh)," *Bulletin d'Études Orientales* (Institut Français de Damas) 17 (1961–62): 7–74.

11. Leaman, "Ibn Miskawayh."

12. Ibn Miskawayh, "Ahmad ibn Muhammad," *Tahdhib al-akhlaq* (The Refinement of Character), trans. Constantine Zurayk (Chicago: Kazi, 2002), 29.

13. This borrowing is to be expected in a work of Islamic philosophy, because Aristotle is referred to as simply "the philosopher" (*al-hakim*) or "the first teacher" (*al-mu`allim al-awwal*) in classical Islamic thought.

14. Rosalind Hursthouse, "Virtue Ethics," in *The Stanford Encyclopedia of Philosophy* (Fall 2013 Edition), ed. Edward N. Zalta, http://plato.stanford.edu/archives/fall2013/entries/ethics-virtue/.

15. Miskawayh, "Ahmad," 22.

16. Miskawayh, "Ahmad," 33.

17. E.g., John Hare, *God and Morality: A Philosophical History* (Oxford: Blackwell, 2007).

18. Metcalf, "Remaking Ourselves," 710.

19. Miskawayh, "Ahmad," 29.

20. Michel Foucault, *The Use of Pleasure*, vol. 2 of *The History of Sexuality*, trans. R. Hurley (New York: Vintage, 1990).

21. Pierre Hadot, *Philosophy as a Way of Life: Spiritual Exercises from Socrates to Foucault*, ed. A. Davidson, trans. M. Chase (Oxford: Blackwell, 1995).

22. Miskawayh, "Ahmad," 157–58.

23. Miskawayh, "Ahmad," 159–60.

24. See Jennifer Herdt's chapter 9, this volume.

25. For an analysis of this work in English, see Yazaki Saeko, *Islamic Mysticism and Abu Talib al-Makki: The Role of the Heart* (New York: Routledge, 2012).

26. Miskawayh, "Ahmad," 35.

27. My thanks to Jamie Schillinger for raising this issue.

28. Miskawayh, "Ahmad," 29.

29. Miskawayh, "Ahmad," 29.

30. Miskawayh, "Ahmad," 31.

31. Miskawayh, "Ahmad," 158.

32. Miskawayh, "Ahmad," 165.

33. For persuasive Christian counter-narratives that support sexual pleasure see, for example, Mark Jordan, *The Ethics of Sex* (Malden: Blackwell, 2002); and Christine Gudorf, *Body, Sex and Pleasure: Reconstructing Christian Sexual Ethics* (Cleveland: Pilgrim, 1994). I should note that Ibn Miskawayh also believes that procreation is an important goal of sexual activity. In *Tahdhib al-akhlaq* he asserts "in the matter of sexual intercourse, his practice of it should go only as far as will preserve his kind and perpetuate his image" (Miskawayh, "Ahmad," 44). This implies that the best sort of sexual activity is aimed as procreation. However, unlike some Christian

thinkers, Ibn Miskawayh does not go as far as to argue that sex that is not aimed at procreation (e.g., contraceptive use) is immoral.

34. For a more in-depth comparative treatment of Christian and Islamic creation narratives and their implications for sexual ethics, see Elizabeth Bucar, "Religious Diversity and the Ethics of Sex," in *The Blackwell Companion to Religious Diversity*, ed. K. Schilbrack (Oxford: Blackwell, forthcoming).

35. Martha Nussbaum, "Non-relative Virtues: An Aristotelian Approach," in *The Quality of Life*, ed. Martha Nussbaum and Amartya Sen (Oxford: Clarendon, 1993), 253.

36. Miskawayh, "Ahmad," 165.

37. Miskawayh, "Ahmad."

38. Miskawayh, "Ahmad," 174.

39. Miskawayh, "Ahmad."

40. Julia Annas, "Virtue Ethics and the Charge of Egoism," in *Morality and Self-Interest*, ed. Paul Bloomfield (Oxford: Oxford University Press, 2009); Thomas Hurka, *Virtue, Vice, and Value* (Oxford: Oxford University Press, 2001); Christopher Toner, "The Self-Centeredness Objection to Virtue Ethics," *Philosophy* 81 (2006): 595–618.

41. Miskawayh, "Ahmad," 123.

42. Miskawayh, "Ahmad," 25. For a larger discussion of Ibn Miskawayh's notion of friendship, see Lenn Goodman, "Friendship in Aristotle, Miskawayh and al-Ghazali," in *Friendship East and West: Philosophical Perspectives*, ed. O. Leaman (Richmond: Curzon, 1996), 164–91; and Oliver Leaman, "Secular Friendship and Religious Devotion," in *Friendship East and West: Philosophical Perspectives*, ed. O. Leaman (Richmond: Curzon, 1996), 251–62.

43. For example:

> It is also surely paradoxical to represent the man of perfect happiness as a solitary being; for nobody would choose to have all the good things in the world by himself because man is a social creature and naturally constituted to live in company. Therefore the happy man also has this quality, because he possesses everything that is naturally good; and it is clearly better to spend one's time in the company of friends and good men than in that of strangers and people of uncertain character. It follows, therefore, that the happy man needs friends (Aristotle, *The Ethics of Aristotle: The Nicomachean Ethics*, trans. J. A. K. Thomson, ed. Jonathan Barnes [New York: Penguin, 1976], 1169b16–21).

44. Miskawayh, "Ahmad," 25.

45. Miskawayh, "Ahmad," 44.

46. Miskawayh, "Ahmad," 45. This social dimension applies to legal (both religious and secular) understandings of ethics as well, since fulfilling the law requires support from and interaction with others.

47. Miskawayh, "Ahmad," 26.

48. Miskawayh, "Ahmad," 170.

49. See, for example, Aristotle's reference to friends as mirrors in *Magna Moralia*, 1213a13–26 (*The Complete Works of Aristotle*, vol. 2, ed. Jonathan Barnes, trans. St. George Stock [Princeton: Princeton University Press, 1984]).

50. Miskawayh, "Ahmad," 169.

51. Aristotle makes a similar point in regard to the importance of others to our self-knowledge: "we are better able to observe our neighbors than ourselves, and their actions than our own" (Aristotle, *Ethics: NE*, 1169b33–35).

52. Miskawayh, "Ahmad," 37.

53. Saba Mahmood, *Politics of Piety: The Islamic Revival and the Feminist Subject* (Princeton: Princeton University Press, 2005); Carla Jones, "Images of Desire: Creating Virtue and Value in an Indonesian Islamic Lifestyle Magazine," *Journal of Middle East Women's Studies* 6, no. 3 (2010): 91–117; Banu Gökarıksel andAnna Secor, "'Even I Was Tempted:' The Moral Ambivalence and Ethical Practice of Veiling-Fashion in Turkey," *Annals of the Association of American Geographers* 102, no. 4 (2012): 847–62; and Banu Gökarıksel and Anna Secor, "The Veil, Desire, and the Gaze: Turning the Inside Out," *Signs: Journal of Women in Culture and Society* (in press, 2014): .

54. For further discussion of references to veiling in Islamic sacred texts, see ch. 2 of Elizabeth Bucar, *The Islamic Veil: A Beginner's Guide* (Oxford: Oneworld, 2012), 28–48.

55. A.Yusuf. Ali, trans., *The Holy Qur'an* (Hertfordshire: Wordsworth, 2001), 261–62.

56. Khaled Abou El Fadl, *Speaking in God's Name: Islamic Law, Authority and Women* (Oxford: Oneworld, 2001), 185.

57. Al-Tabari (d. 932), one of the earliest interpreters of the Qur'an, allows faces and hands to show, even faces with makeup and ringed fingers, but includes bracelets, anklets, and necklaces as hidden adornment that should be covered. Al-Zamakh-shari (d. 1144) argues that a woman's face and hands may always show because to cover them causes difficulty in everyday life (V. J. Hoffman, "Qur'anic Interpretation and Modesty," in *The Shaping of an American Islamic Discourse:A Memorial to Fazlur Rhaman*, ed. E.Waugh and F. Denny [Atlanta: Scholars Press, 1998], 92). On the strictest end of the spectrum are Islamic scholars who want all of a woman's natural beauty to be covered. Ibn Taymiyya (d. 1328) and al-Baydawi (d. 1282), for instance, allow women's faces and hands to be uncovered only during prayer (Hoffman, "Qur'anic Interpretation," 94). For an interesting contemporary interpretation, see the work of Soraya Hajjaji-Jarrah, "Women's Modesty in Qur'anic Commentaries: The Founding Discourse," in *The Muslim Veil in North America*, ed. S. S. Alvi, H. Hoodfar, and S. McDonough (Toronto: Women's Press, 2003). She argues that this directive to cover does not apply to a woman's hair, face, arms, or legs, as "these parts of the female body are neither unessential, nor extraneous, nor fundamentally intended to enhance the appearance of a woman...they are essential parts of the human anatomy" (188).

58. It is important to note that in Islam, submission is not seen as in conflict with an individual's freedom; rather, in a way that will be familiar to those who work on Christian conceptions of virtue, our submission to God is the very condition of our true freedom.

59. Elsewhere in the Qur'an (e.g., 33:33), modesty is juxtaposed against *tabarruj*, an overt form of flirtation that involves prancing, flaunting, and embellishing with the goal of attracting attention.

60. Mahmood, *Politics*, 157.

61. Simona Tersigni, "La pratique du hijab en France," in *La Politisation du Voile: l'affaire en France, en Europe, et dans le monde arabe* (Paris: L'Harmattan, 2005).

62. Metcalf, "Remaking Ourselves," 708.

63. Metcalf, *Perfecting Women*.

64. Julia Annas, "Women and the Quality of Life: Two Norms or One?," in *The Quality of Life*, ed. Martha Nussbaum and Amartya Sen (Oxford: Clarendon, 1993), 279.

65. Elizabeth Wolgast, *Equality and the Rights of Wome*. (Ithaca, NY: Cornell University Press, 1980), 108 and 110; Mary Midgley and Judith Hughes, *Women's Choices* (London: Weidenfeld and Nicholson, 1983), 185.

66. Annas, "Women," 281.

67. See, for example, Elizabeth Bucar, *Creative Conformity: The Feminist Politics of U.S. Catholic and Iranian Shi'i Women* (Washington, DC: Georgetown University Press, 2011); R. Marie Griffith, *God's Daugthers: Evangelical Women and the Power of Submission* (Berkeley: University of California Press, 1997); Mahmood, *Politics*.
68. My thanks to the participants of the April 2013 Religion and Critical Thought Workshop at Brown University for their help in thinking through this issue.
69. Aristotle, *Complete Works*, vol. 2, 1106a28.
70. Miskawayh, "Ahmad," 22. This is interesting in light of Lesley Brown's argument that Aristotle's point about the mean relative to us has been widely misunderstood by ethicists. Brown argues that "'the mean relative to us' should be explained not as 'relative to individual agents'... but as 'relative to us as human beings,' and that Aristotle uses the phrase to convey a normative notion, the notion of something related to human nature, needs or purposes, and which is the object of a certain kind of expertise and judgment" (78). If Brown is correct, and applying this mean to each agent is indeed a misreading, it is a misreading shared by Miskawayh who is actually more explicit than Aristotle that the relativity of the mean requires special attention to "each individual person." (Lesley Brown, "What Is 'The Mean Relative to Us' in Aristotle's "Ethics"? *Phronesis* 42, no. 1 [1997]: 77–93.)
71. Emma Tarlo, *Visibly Muslim: Fashion, Politics and Faith* (Oxford: Berg, 2010).

BIBLIOGRAPHY

Ali, A.Yusuf, trans. *The Holy Qur'an*. Hertfordshire: Wordsworth, 2001.
Annas, Julia. "Virtue Ethics and the Charge of Egoism." In *Morality and Self-Interest*, edited by Paul Bloomfield, 205–21. Oxford: Oxford University Press, 2009.
Annas, Julia. "Women and the Quality of Life: Two Norms or One?" In *The Quality of Life*, edited by Martha Nussbaum and Amartya Sen, 279–96. Oxford: Clarendon Press, 1993.
Aristotle. *The Ethics of Aristotle: The Nicomachean Ethics*, translated by J. A. K. Thomson, edited by Jonathan Barnes. New York: Penguin, 1976.
Aristotle. *The Complete Works of Aristotle*, vol. 2. Edited by Jonathan Barnes, translated by St. George Stock (Princeton: Princeton University Press, 1984), 1213a13–26.
Arkoun, Mohammed. "'Deux épîtres de Miskawayh' (Two Treatises of Miskawayh)." *Bulletin d'Études Orientales* (Institut Français de Damas) 17 (1961–62): 7–74.
Brown, Lesley. "What Is 'The Mean Relative to Us' in Aristotle's Ethics"? *Phronesis* 42, no. 1 (1997): 77–93.
Bucar, Elizabeth. *Creative Conformity: The Feminist Politics of U.S. Catholic and Iranian Shi'i Women*. Washington, DC: Georgetown University Press, 2011.
Bucar, Elizabeth. *The Islamic Veil: A Beginner's Guide*. Oxford: Oneworld, 2012.
Bucar, Elizabeth. "Religious Diversity and the Ethics of Sex." In *The Blackwell Companion to Religious Diversity*, edited by K. Schilbrack. Oxford: Blackwell, forthcoming.
El Fadl, Khaled Abou. *Speaking in God's Name: Islamic Law, Authority and Women*. Oxford: Oneworld, 2001.
Fakhry, Majid. "The Platonism of Miskawayh and its Implications for his Ethics." *Studia Islamica* 43 (1975): 39–57.
Foucault, Michel. *The Use of Pleasure*. Vol. 2 of *The History of Sexuality*, translated by R. Hurley. New York: Vintage, 1990.

Gökarıksel, Banu, and Anna Secor. "'Even I Was Tempted:' The Moral Ambivalence and Ethical Practice of Veiling-Fashion in Turkey." *Annals of the Association of American Geographers* 102, no. 4 (2012): 847–62.

Gökarıksel, Banu, and Anna Secor. "The Veil, Desire, and the Gaze: Turning the Inside Out." *Signs: Journal of Women in Culture and Society,* in press.

Goodman, Lenn. "Friendship in Aristotle, Miskawayh and al-Ghazali." In *Friendship East and West: Philosophical Perspectives,* edited by O. Leaman (Richmond: Curzon, 1996), 164–91.

Griffith, R. Marie. *God's Daughters: Evangelical Women and the Power of Submission.* Berkeley: University of California Press, 1997.

Gudorf, Christine. *Body, Sex and Pleasure: Reconstructing Christian Sexual Ethics.* Cleveland: Pilgrim, 1994.

Hadot, Pierre. *Philosophy as a Way of Life: Spiritual Exercises from Socrates to Foucault,* edited by A. Davidson, translated by M. Chase. Oxford: Blackwell, 1995.

Hajjaji-Jarrah, S. "Women's Modesty in Qur'anic Commentaries: The Founding Discourse." In *The Muslim Veil in North America,* edited by S. S. Alvi, H. Hoodfar, and S. McDonough, 181–213. Toronto: Women's Press, 2003.

Hare, John. *God and Morality: A Philosophical History.* Oxford: Blackwell, 2007.

Hauerwas, Stanley. *A Community of Character: Toward a Constructive Christian Social Ethic.* Notre Dame, IN: University of Notre Dame Press, 1991.

Hauerwas, Stanley. *Vision and Virtue: Essays in Christian Ethical Reflection.* Notre Dame, IN: University of Notre Dame Press, 1981.

Herdt, Jennifer. *Putting on Virtue: The Legacy of the Splendid Vices.* Chicago: University of Chicago Press, 2008.

Hoffman, V. J. "Qur'anic Interpretation and Modesty." In *The Shaping of an American Islamic Discourse:A Memorial to Fazlur Rhaman,* edited by E. Waugh and F. Denny, 89–121. Atlanta: Scholars Press, 1998.

Hurka, Thomas. *Virtue, Vice, and Value.* Oxford: Oxford University Press, 2001.

Hursthouse, Rosalind. "Virtue Ethics." In *The Stanford Encyclopedia of Philosophy* (Fall 2013 Edition), edited by Edward N. Zalta. Available at http://plato.stanford.edu/archives/fall2013/entries/ethics-virtue/.

Ivanhoe, P. J. *Confucian Moral Self-Cultivation.* Indianapolis: Hackett, 2000.

Jones, Carla. "Images of Desire: Creating Virtue and Value in an Indonesian Islamic Lifestyle Magazine." *Journal of Middle East Women's Studies* 6, no. 3 (2010): 91–117.

Jordan, Mark. *The Ethics of Sex.* Malden: Blackwell, 2002.

Karimullah, Karman. "Rival Moral Traditions in the Late Ottoman Empire, 1839–1908." *Journal of Islamic Studies* 24, no. 1 (2013): 37–66.

Keown, Damien. *The Nature of Buddhist Ethics.* New York: Palgrave, 2001.

Leaman, Oliver. "Ibn Miskawayh." In *History of Islamic Philosophy,* edited by S. H. Nasr and O. Leaman, 252–57. London: Routledge, 1996.

Leaman, Oliver. "Ibn Miskawayh, Ahmad ibn Muhammad (c. 940–1030)." In *Muslim Philosophy* (1998). Available at www.muslimphilosophy.com/ip/rep/H042.

Leaman, Oliver. "Secular Friendship and Religious Devotion." In *Friendship East and West: Philosophical Perspectives,* edited by O. Leaman, 251–62. Richmond: Curzon, 1996.

Lewis, Thomas A., Jonathan W. Schofer, Aaron Stalnaker, and Mark A. Berkson, "Anthropos and Ethics: Categories of Inquiry and Procedures of Comparison." *Journal of Religious Ethics* 33, no. 2 (2005): 177–85.

MacIntyre, Alasdair. *After Virtue: A Study in Moral Theory.* Notre Dame, IN: University of Notre Dame Press, 1984.

Mahmood, Saba. *Politics of Piety: The Islamic Revival and the Feminist Subject.* Princeton: Princeton University Press, 2005.

Metcalf, Barbara, ed. *Moral Conduct and Authority: The Place of Adab in South Asian Islam*. Berkeley: University of California Press, 1983.

Metcalf, Barbara. *Perfecting Women: Maulana Ashraf 'Ali Thanawi's Bihishti Zewar*. Berkeley: University of California Press, 1990.

Metcalf, Barbara. "'Remaking Ourselves': Islamic Self-Fashioning in a Global Movement of Spiritual Renewal." In *Accounting for Fundamentalisms*, edited by Martin Marty and Scott Appleby, 706–25. Chicago: University of Chicago Press, 1994.

Midgley, Mary, and Judith Hughes. *Women's Choices*. London: Weidenfeld and Nicholson, 1983.

[Ibn] Miskawayh, Ahmad ibn Muhammad. *Tahdhib al-akhlaq* (The Refinement of Character), translated by Constantine Zurayk. Chicago: Kazi, 2002.

Murphy, Nancey, et al., eds. *Virtues and Practices in the Christian Tradition: Christian Ethics after Macintyre*. Harrisburg: Trinity International, 1997.

Nussbaum, Martha. "Non-relative Virtues: An Aristotelian Approach." In *The Quality of Life*, edited by Martha Nussbaum and Amartya Sen, 242–69. Oxford: Clarendon, 1993.

Pandian, Anand. *Crooked Stalks: Cultivating Virtue in South India*. Durham, NC: Duke University Press, 2009.

Saeko, Yazaki. *Islamic Mysticism and Abu Talib al-Makki: The Role of the Heart*. New York: Routledge, 2012.

Schofer, Jonathan Wyn. *Confronting Vulnerability: The Body and the Divine in Rabbinic Ethics*. Chicago: University of Chicago Press, 2010.

Schofer, Jonathan Wyn. *The Making of a Sage: A Study in Rabbinic Ethics*. Madison: University of Wisconsin Press, 2004.

Stalnaker, Aaron. *Overcoming Our Evil: Human Nature and Spiritual Exercises in Xunzi and Augustine*, 197–245. Washington, DC: Georgetown University Press, 2006.

Stalnaker, Aaron. "Spiritual Exercises and the Grace of God: Paradoxes of Personal Formation in Augustine." *Journal of the Society of Christian Ethics* 24, no. 2 (2004): 137–70.

Swearer, Donald. "Buddhist Virtue, Voluntary Poverty, and Extensive Benevolence." *Journal of Religious Ethics* 26, no. 1 (1998): 71–103.

Tarlo, Emma. *Visibly Muslim: Fashion, Politics and Faith*. Oxford: Berg, 2010.

Tersigni, Simona. "La pratique du hijab en France." In *La Politisation du Voile: l'affaire en France, en Europe, et dans le monde arabe*. Paris: L'Harmattan, 2005.

Toner, Christopher. "The Self-Centeredness Objection to Virtue Ethics." *Philosophy* 81 (2006): 595–618.

Van Norden, Bryan. *Virtue Ethics and Consequentialism in Early Chinese Philosophy*. New York: Cambridge University Press, 2007.

Wolgast, Elizabeth. *Equality and the Rights of Women*. Ithaca, NY: Cornell University Press, 1980.

Yearley, Lee. *Mencius and Aquinas: Theories of Virtue and Conceptions of Courage*. Albany: SUNY Press, 1990.

Zaroug, Abdullahi Hassan. "Ethics from an Islamic Perspective: Basic Issues." *American Journal of Islamic Social Sciences* 16, no. 3 (1999): 45–63.

Zurayk, Constantine. "Preface." *The Refinement of Character*. Beirut: Kazi, 2002.

CHAPTER 9

༺

Frailty, Fragmentation, and Social Dependency in the Cultivation of Christian Virtue

JENNIFER A. HERDT

Any reflection on the theme of the cultivation of virtue in relation to Christianity must attend to two distinct phenomena. First, Christians have always been concerned not just with a correct understanding of reality but also with how to live, individually and collectively, in relation to this reality. Christian convictions about how to live in relation to a finite reality grasped as God's creation, and a divine reality revealed in Jesus Christ, have consistently been expressed in practices for the formation of character. Christianity is a living tradition of ethical formation. Because of this, it provides a resource for anyone interested in reflecting on the social conditions for the cultivation of the virtues. But it is not just that Christians have consistently been engaged in processes of moral formation. It also happens to be the case that Christianity was from its inception deeply shaped by pagan reflection on the virtues. Thus—and this is the second phenomenon of note—Christianity has in fact been, and continues to be, a vital context for theoretical reflection on the virtues and their development. Moreover, this theoretical reflection has been the primary historical carrier for the traditions of ancient Greek and Roman ethics, from which contemporary virtue theory derives. Thus, while Confucianism, say, may have a strong claim to being best construed as a virtue ethics, the categories of virtue and vice, and specific virtues such as courage and justice, are applied by *analogy* to concepts within the Confucian

tradition. With Christianity, things are different; these concepts from ancient Greek and Roman thought were themselves woven into the tradition
from its inception, even if in ways that sometimes dramatically transformed them.

If we attend either only to practices within Christian communities for
the cultivation of virtue or only to Christian theoretical reflection on the
formation of virtue, we miss half the picture. But attending to both is important for a further reason: practice and theory have not always been related in straightforward or complementary ways. A rich set of practices for
the cultivation of Christian character has in some contexts coexisted with
an outright hostility to virtue theory, seen as incorporating a hubristic denial of human sinfulness, a refusal of dependency on divine grace, and a
corrupting concern for the agent's own happiness. Christian ambivalence
concerning the possibility of humanly acquired virtues may fit the Christian
tradition especially well to respond to contemporary empirically grounded
concerns about the frail, fragmented, and socially dependent character of
the virtues.

DIVINE EXEMPLARITY AND CONFORMITY TO CHRIST

Within the Christian tradition, practices for the formation of virtuous
character have been intrinsically bound up with faith convictions about
God acting to redeem and perfect a beloved but fallen creation. The primary focus of attention here has been on how to follow Christ, how to live
as a Christian; the question of how and whether this might be distinct or
separable from the task of cultivating virtue has been secondary. A central
feature of the teachings of Jesus as related in the gospels was the summons
to emulate the character of God: "Be perfect, therefore, as your heavenly
Father is perfect."[1] The requirement of enemy-love is also tightly linked
with divine exemplarity: "Love your enemies and pray for those who perse-
cute you, so that you may be children of your Father in heaven."[2] This became a common element in early Christian ethical teaching: to realize one's
identity as a child of God by emulating God, and in particular (since what it
could mean for finite, mortal, embodied, creatures to imitate the Creator of
the universe is far from an unproblematic or obvious matter) by emulating
divine love.[3] Christians looked to Jesus as divine love incarnate, as the un-
surpassable exemplar for life as a child of God.[4] The heart of Christ's exemplarity was the cross; to suffer, like Jesus, for fidelity to God's ways in an
unjust world was to be assimilated to Christ.[5] Here, Christians argued,
God's love for a sinful world was most fully revealed. But Christians did not

simply affirm that by following Jesus's teachings, or living as Jesus had lived, one would flourish or live well. They claimed that Jesus was savior; by coming into the right relationship with Jesus, one of trusting faith in his saving power, one could be freed from both sin and death.

A productive tension thus lay at the heart of the Christian tradition: between faith on the one hand and virtuous activity (or, in the classic formulation, works) on the other, between reliance on Christ's saving power on the one hand and striving for excellence on the other. Since the scriptural basis for both themes was strong, it was rare for one to be elevated at the total expense of the other. There were various ways of relating the two together. Divine grace might be seen as making up the difference between human moral strivings and the inadequate results of those strivings, such that human moral agency, capable of acquiring some virtue on its own, achieves more when it cooperates with supernatural grace. Alternatively, the development of virtue might be seen as utterly impossible so long as sin reigns; grace frees persons from the burden of sin and guilt so that progress in virtue becomes possible for the first time. Or, the effects of sin might be seen as such that any progress in virtue is attributable to divine agency alone. In any case, Jesus is not for the Christian tradition simply an example of good character, but is also the source of power to emulate that example. Christians speak not simply of imitating Jesus, but of assimilation to Christ, conformity with Christ—terms that place a question mark over independent human agency.

PRACTICES OF CHRISTIAN FORMATION

Christian practices for the cultivation of virtue were thus from the outset also practices for the formation of Christians, of followers of Christ, and practices of worship. The early Christians regarded the martyrs as figures of exemplary—that is, Christlike—virtue. While the martyrs were literally witnesses to their faith in Christ, some Christians in the second through fourth centuries believed that imitating Jesus's death through martyrdom was the only sure way to salvation. Ignatius, Bishop of Antioch, in letters written circa 113 CE to churches that received him as he traveled to Rome to be put on trial for being a Christian, evidences this widespread desire for martyrdom. "It is not that I want merely to be called a Christian, but actually to *be* one," he writes.[6] Even if persecution of Christians was a scattershot phenomenon, the idealization of martyrs was not.[7]

Ascetic spiritual practices, including fasting, vigils, sleeping on bare ground, prayer, and virginity, were also central to Christianity from the earliest decades of its existence.[8] To some extent, Christianity simply took over ascetic practices common in various philosophical schools in the ancient world. But a distinctive feature of Christianity was the fact that asceticism was interpreted in relation to the exemplarity of the cross, as a form of spiritual martyrdom.[9] Asceticism, like martyrdom, was regarded not simply as a way to cultivate virtue but also as a way to emulate Christ. After the Edict of Milan in 325 and the Christianization of the Roman Empire, martyrdom became a remote possibility. Asceticism, however, remained open as a new source of sainthood, a new form of spiritual heroism, a martyrdom of the senses and of one's physical being. The flesh and its vicious passions—of pride, covetousness, and lust, were seen both as enslaving persons to sin and as tying them down to the material world; heavily influenced by Neoplatonism, Christians viewed ascetic practices as putting the flesh to death in order to allow the spirit to rise freely into intimacy with God. Communally practiced asceticism became early monasticism.

Even as some viewed martyrdom and asceticism as necessary to being a Christian, to being "united with Christ in a death like his," others held that another path was open, one that did not require a monastic or anchoritic existence. The initiation ritual of baptism, in which believers were submerged in water, was itself interpreted as dying with Christ. Those who have thus ritually died with Christ are Christians, freed from sin for a newly Christlike life: "Therefore we have been buried with him by baptism into death, so that, just as Christ was raised from the dead by the glory of the Father, so we too might walk in newness of life."[10] This perspective focused less on extreme forms of spiritual gymnastics and more on practices open to those in all walks of life. The Didache, a brief early Christian treatise that has been traced back to early second-century Syria, reflects this emphasis on distinctive ethical markers of the Christian community. These are framed by a strong emphasis on love as "the way of life": the Didache brings together a statement of the twofold love commandment (love God, and love your neighbor as yourself, given by Jesus in Mark 12:30–31 as a summary of the divine law), a negative statement of the Golden Rule common in the Torah (do not do unto others what you do not want to have done to yourself), and the command to love enemies.[11]

The ethical teaching of the Didache consists of a list of precepts, not a table of virtues. But the commandment to love is a commandment, among other things, to cultivate certain dispositions, certain patterns of perception and response, not simply to perform prescribed actions. This demand is deeply rooted in the prophetic strand of the Hebrew Bible: Yahweh rejects the sacrificial offerings of the people and demands that they "hate evil and love good," refusing to enrich themselves at the expense of others, championing the rightful claims of the poor, ferreting out judicial corruption.[12] The concern is not simply that certain actions be performed, but that persons with certain sorts of character, intentions, and motives be formed.

After foregrounding love as the core of the way of life, the Didache enumerates other features of the "way of life": generous giving to those in need, avoiding anger and lust, eschewing astrology and magic, being meek and quiet and humble, and not seeking glory. Offering very little by way of theological explication or justification of its enumeration of the characteristics of the "way of life," the Didache nevertheless offers a glimpse into a Christian community that saw itself as distinguished from the "way of death" of the culture around it by way of a communal character of humble loving kindness. The first centuries of Christianity thus present us with a diverse set of aspirations. The sober way of life inculcated by the Didache may seem to have little in common with the spiritual heroism of martyrdom and asceticism. But by the fourth century shared features have emerged: a widespread set of common practices for Christian spiritual formation, and an emphasis on two virtues, love and humility, interpreted in ways that drew together the ideals of martyrdom, asceticism, and ordinary Christian life.

Some spiritual practices were primarily confined to the monastic context: voluntary poverty, communal ownership of property, virginity, and celibacy. Others were more easily adaptable to those who remained within the ordinary structures of family and community life: alms-giving, fasting, prayer, self-examination, meditative study of scripture, confession of sins, singing of psalms, listening to preaching, penance, catechesis, baptism, and partaking of the Eucharist.[13] Many of these were taken over from pagan philosophical schools or pagan cultic life. Others have more distinctly Jewish roots. All have persisted in recognizable forms up to the present. Pierre Hadot has fruitfully argued that we identify them as "spiritual exercises"—that is, "exercises designed to ensure spiritual progress toward the ideal state of wisdom, exercises of reason that will be, for the soul, analogous to the athlete's training or to the application of a medical cure."[14] *Ascesis* is, after all, literally exercise, even if we tend to think of it as rigorous self-denial. Hadot's primary focus is on Hellenistic and Roman philosophical schools, and on features of these that were absorbed into Christianity by patristic thinkers such as Clement of Alexandria, Origen, the Cappadocians, and many others who conceived of Christianity as a philosophical school devoted to *paideia* and the cultivation of wisdom.[15] This analysis is particularly illuminating of practices related to self-control and meditation; one arrives at a state of transcendent wisdom (which Socrates had identified with virtue) via a highly developed capacity for self-command, and exquisite attention to one's thoughts and character. Practices for developing self-command taken over from pagan philosophical schools into Christianity range from exercises for controlling anger, curiosity, the desire for food, love of wealth and luxury, excessive speech, to exercises for controlling patterns of thought and attention. Meditation was understood as beginning with memorizing dogmas and rules for life associated with a particular philosophical school and proceeding to imaginative visual exercises, meditation on death, and cultivating attention to the present moment.[16]

LOVE AND HUMILITY: "CARDINAL" VIRTUES

Even as they took over spiritual exercises from Hellenistic philosophy, and even as a spiritual elite within the Christian community thought of Christianity itself as a school of philosophy, there were distinctive features both of Christian understanding of the character of the wisdom or virtue to which they aspired and of their understanding of the path that led to it. These were evident in practice, and they were also thematized in explicit reflection on the virtues. While Christian thinkers took over the scheme of the four Platonic virtues (and it was only with Ambrose in the fourth century that they were dubbed "cardinal"), and complemented these with the three theological virtues of faith, hope, and charity, it is the virtues of love and humility that were particularly central to Christian identity.[17]

We have already seen how love is foregrounded in the New Testament and central to Christian conceptions of God and of Jesus Christ. The Christian insistence that love of God, love of neighbor, love of enemy, love of self, and God's own love for creation are all properly spoken of as love has had profound implications for the cultivation of virtue in the Christian tradition. For if love of God and love of neighbor do not compete but, rather, complement and express one another, then prayer, participation in worship, and the like do not detract from but, rather, are integral elements in the cultivation of love of neighbor. And if a cup of water given to one who thirsts is seen as given to Jesus Christ, God incarnate, care for neighbor becomes an expression of fidelity to God.

To be thus perfected in love is cause, not for pride in one's moral achievements, but for gratitude; honor is not to be basked in, but to be reflected on to God, its proper object, just as persecution for the sake of fidelity to God's ways is to be seen as an opportunity to honor God rather than as an occasion for worldly shame. So the development of love was seen as requiring the accompaniment of humility. But what accounts for the valorization of humility in the Christian tradition? We can gesture to elements of Jesus's teaching: that the meek shall inherit the earth, that the kingdom of heaven belongs to little children.[18] Jesus's Passion is also key: if a man humiliated on a cross can be recognized as God incarnate, then ordinary conceptions of honor and glory are being overturned. And again, the roots go deep into the Hebrew Bible: Moses may have led the Hebrew people out of slavery in Egypt, but only through God's power, only with the words that God provided him to speak.[19] On Augustine's enormously influential account, humility has centrally to do with acknowledging dependency on God, not with belittling one's own abilities.[20]

Hadot regards this as a key differentiating feature of Christian spiritual exercises, and as defining "the overall spirit in which Christian and monastic spiritual exercises were practiced. They always presupposed the assistance of God's grace, and they made of humility the most important of virtues."[21] And Augustine's unrelenting attack on what he regarded as the empty façade of pagan virtue was fundamentally a critique of pride as a denial of dependency on God. This emphasis introduced a self-critical element into heroic conceptions of martyrdom and asceticism. All such exceptional accomplishments could be an occasion for praising God's enabling power—or occasions for self-aggrandizement.

The ideal of humility informed Christian appropriations of practices for the cultivation of self-control in several ways. First, as already suggested, the accomplishment of self-control was seen as grace-enabled, rather than as an independent achievement. Second, the ideal of humility expressed a strong egalitarian thrust. If the world's foolishness is God's wisdom, and the meek will inherit the earth, if the weakest and most ignorant can be empowered by God, then it was no longer simply to be accepted that since, as Hellenistic culture accepted, a proper education from an early age is crucial to the development of virtue and leisure is required for the philosophical life, only the fortunate and favored have any chance of progressing to wisdom.[22] Christianity offered a way to wisdom, to virtue, to salvation, open to all. Third, there was a chastening of expectations: grace does not erase the effects of sin, and this life remains for Christians one of ongoing struggle; virtuous action is not easy and pleasant in the way envisioned by Aristotle; continence displaces temperance.

The ascetic practices of a spiritual elite were thus transformed in order to make them available to the masses. Augustine's preaching eschewed rhetorical virtuosity and employed a simple style in an act of humility designed to reach and welcome ordinary people.[23] Those unable to enact a Neoplatonic spiritual ascent by way of long hours of disciplined meditation could still assemble in worship, undergo baptism, partake of the Eucharist, listen to preaching, and sing psalms. They could refrain from taking in the spectacles of the gladiatorial arena and scandalous theater, and could instead feed their imaginations on scripture and on the stories of the saints and martyrs. They could give to the poor. These acts of charity took on a distinctive character; they were not to be identified either with the voluntary poverty of the monastic life or with pagan traditions of civic beneficence on the part of the wealthy. The focus was on attending and responding to need and suffering responsiveness to need, as a primary avenue for both the cultivation and the expression of neighbor-love.[24]

Moreover, given convictions regarding the ongoing reality of sin, practices for the formation of Christian character were joined by practices for the acknowledgment of sin and failure and the need for forgiveness and reconciliation. These incorporate aspects of the exercise of self-examination, identifying daily episodes of anger, for instance, but go beyond this to the cultivation and expression of emotions of regret and to rituals of individual and communal healing. So while monasticism clearly represented an elite spirituality for the cultivation of Christian virtue, it developed hand in hand with practices of Christian formation that were open to all Christians, but which nevertheless aimed at the cultivation of character and not simply at the correct performance of ritual.[25]

CHRISTIANITY AND THE DEVELOPMENT OF CLASSICAL VIRTUE ETHICS

Given that there were patristic thinkers who understood Christianity as a philosophical school, and given the fact that the spiritual exercises of pagan schools of philosophy provided an influential model both for Christian asceticism and for broader practices of Christian formation, it is no surprise that Christian thinkers would also reflect explicitly on the virtues as these were conceived by the various schools of ancient philosophy. The influence on patristic authors of Platonism and Stoicism (particularly Seneca and Cicero) was especially pronounced.[26] Aristotle became central in the scholastic period, particularly from the thirteenth century onward, as the full text of the *Nicomachean Ethics* became available in Latin translation.[27] Christian thinkers thus took over and transformed pagan debates concerning the interconnection of the virtues and the unity of virtue, temperance and continence, and *eudaimonia*.

Christian conceptions of human agency as dependent on God in order to reach its own proper telos or end held significant implications for understandings of the cultivation of virtue. Patristic thinkers tended to regard all virtue as both acquired by human effort and infused by divine grace. Medieval scholastics sought to develop more systematic accounts, which differentiated between natural, acquired virtues and supernatural, infused virtues. Aquinas's take on the issue was particularly sophisticated.

The virtues are for Aquinas dispositions to act well, dispositions that perfect their possessor and that person's actions, directing her to happiness.[28] Some virtues are acquired by habituation; repeated actions dispose the appetitive powers to be moved easily in accord with reason's grasp of what is good.[29] But since reason cannot on its own grasp the perfect good to which humankind is ordained, which is God, other virtues are required in order to direct their possessors to this perfect happiness, and these must be infused by God.[30]

The acquired virtues render action in accordance with them easy and pleasant. Virtuous dispositions may be acquired even by those who lack supernatural grace. Unlike Augustine, who judged that in the absence of love of God any virtue was merely apparent, Aquinas held that genuine pagan virtue was possible. Pagans could acquire real but imperfect virtues, imperfect because they were directed only at the last end insofar as this is graspable by human reason, rather than as that end that can be grasped through grace.[31] Acquired virtues are relatively stable; they develop gradually over the course of repeated action and can also be either corrupted or preserved in the same way. They render action in accordance with reason easy and pleasant and thus become a sort of second nature.[32]

The infused virtues, as their name implies, cannot be acquired via habituation, although repeated action in accordance with an infused virtue can strengthen that disposition.[33] They are given directly by God through the sacraments of the church, notably baptism and the Eucharist. Aquinas argued that it was not simply the theological virtues of faith, hope, and charity that were divinely infused, but moral virtues as well, complementing the full array of acquired moral virtues. Infused moral virtues are needed so that each of the moral virtues may be directed appropriately to the final end of fellowship with God, and not simply to the end of happiness as grasped by human reason.[34] It might seem surprising that infused virtues could be regarded as virtues in any proper sense at all, since we tend to think of a virtue as a kind of habit, a tendency acquired through repeated actions.[35] The scholastics, however, due in part to Stoic influences, understood a *habitus* (properly translated as "disposition," rather than "habit") as an inner state that might or might not be expressed in action.[36] There was therefore no conceptual barrier to conceiving of an infused *habitus*. Something akin to habituation occurs through the process of repeated action in accordance with infused virtues; concupiscible and irascible passions become trained to follow the will's adherence to the good grasped by faith, hope, and charity. Such action does not, in the case of infused virtues, *cause* the virtuous disposition but, rather, *strengthens* an already existing disposition, gradually rendering action in accord with the infused virtues easy and pleasant, like that expressing acquired virtues.[37]

Technical as scholastic discussions of the virtues became, they continued to reflect the core concerns I have already flagged. Humankind's final end is not achievable by human effort, but only through divine gift. Hence even an infant, vulnerable and unformed in character, can be saved, as can the most vicious offender; neither an ideal upbringing nor leisure for reflection is necessary.[38] Grace levels the playing field. Humility, as the recognition of virtue's fundamentally dependent character, is thus central.[39] It is love, though, that has pride of place. Infused charity makes possible the love of God for the sake of God's own goodness, not for the sake of God's gifts to oneself.[40] This charity enables its recipient to love as God loves, and thus to seek the neighbor's good as God seeks that neighbor's good.[41] For Aquinas, charity directs the acts of all the other virtues to their final end and is thus said to be the form of the virtues;[42] while he rejects the strong Socratic thesis of the unity of virtue, he thus affirms the interconnectedness of the virtues. Jesus Christ is the perfect exemplar of the virtues, and "demonstrates to us the way of truth" by which we can arrive at the ultimate end of human life.[43] But what Christ demonstrates is not independently acquired virtues, but the humble reception of divine grace; hence Christ is not simply the exemplar of perfected virtue, but the exemplar of dependency on grace. In this way Christ serves both as exemplar and savior, whose saving grace others may now receive. While human beings can reach their final end only through divine grace, they are not puppets. They act according to their own intrinsic dispositions, their own grasp of what is good, their own affective orientation toward those goods, and the acquired virtues that are needed if virtuous action is to become easy and pleasant.

THE REPUDIATION OF VIRTUE AND ITS RECOVERY

In Aquinas's thought we witness a high point of Christian theoretical reflection on the virtues and their cultivation. Yet as I mentioned at the outset, significant strands of the theological tradition have rejected virtue theory, have regarded it as intrinsically pagan and incompatible with core Christian convictions. This tendency is particularly evident within early modern Augustinian thought, including the Protestant reformers; picking up on Augustine's critique of the ostensibly prideful character of pagan virtue, some went on to regard virtue itself as a tainted category.[44] Martin Luther is the poster child for the Augustinian rejection of virtue. To Luther, Aristotle's "book on ethics is the worst of all books," since "it flatly opposes divine grace and all Christian virtues."[45] It encourages us to think that a good character can be acquired through works, through human effort, through imitating virtuous exemplars. In fact, though, we must relinquish all reliance on human agency, admit our own utter bankruptcy, and accept the gift of justification, allowing God alone to work in us and doing nothing on our own.[46] Rather than aspiring to imitate Christ, Christians are "clothed in" Christ's perfect righteousness, which becomes theirs despite their own inherent sinfulness, which is never eradicated in this life. Freed from the futile aspiration to acquire virtue, and united with Christ by faith, Christians become capable of genuine neighbor-love.[47]

While the concerns that separate Luther from Aquinas and, more generally, from Christian appropriations of pagan virtue ethics are not insignificant, and much more could be said about them, two points are central for our purposes here. First, Luther protests against virtue-discourse not because he rejects the core features of Christian virtue ethics as identified above—the rejection of elitism, the centrality of humility (acknowledged dependency) and love, the interconnectedness of love of God and love of neighbor, the perfection of Christ, the ongoing difficulties Christians experience in acting well—but precisely because he seeks to defend these.

Second, however firmly Luther rejects pagan virtue-theory and the language of virtue, practices for the cultivation of good character continued in the communities that embraced his way of thinking. He did reject monasticism and clerical celibacy, arguing against any sort of a higher Christian ethic that could be realized only by a few. He attacked certain forms of medieval spirituality, such as the veneration of saints' relics and the selling of indulgences. But he certainly envisioned Christian character as nourished by the traditional practices of prayer, corporate worship, listening to preaching, study and meditation on scripture, practices of recalling one's faults and God's mercy and forgiveness, and fasting and corporal discipline aimed at curbing bad habits and thus enabling freer service to neighbor.[48] He speaks of faith as an infused gift rather than as a virtue, and separates the growth of this gift from the grace of justification, which is given all at once to transform Christians' standing before the judgment seat of God.[49] He does, though, consider the gift of faith as something that can be cultivated and grow, and that can gradually transform the character of those in whom it is found into the likeness of Christ: "everything is forgiven through grace, but as yet not everything is healed through the gift. The gift has been infused, the leaven has been added to the mixture."[50]

Given the broad influence of this early modern Augustinian critique of the language of virtue, virtue ethics became more closely associated with Catholic rather than Protestant thought.[51] While the language of virtue was more fully sustained within the Catholic tradition, post-Reformation Catholic moral theology shifted its focus from the cultivation of virtue to the permissibility or impermissibility of actions and the development of manuals for confessors, so that appropriate penances could be assigned for every infraction.[52] The separation of spirituality, devoted to the cultivation of faith, from moral theology, focused on conformity to obligation, rendered reflection on the virtues marginal within the Catholic tradition as in the Protestant churches. Nevertheless, even when theoretical reflection on the virtues languished or was repudiated, practices formative of character continued, in forms recognizably continuous with the earliest strands of the tradition.

The philosophical retrieval of virtue ethics in the last century was accompanied by a theological retrieval by both Catholic and Protestant thinkers. Among Catholics, the retrieval was fed by a broader *Ressourcement* movement that sought to reach back behind the perceived encrustations of neo-Scholasticism to the sources of the faith in scripture and patristic theology, and to scholastic thought as informed by this recovery.[53] Among Protestants, the turn to virtue was associated with the rise of "narrative theology." This movement emphasized the ways in which a holistic Christian identity and character are formed through historically extended communal activities, notably the interpretation of scripture and other liturgical practices.[54] Catholic and Protestant thinkers alike were influenced by mid-twentieth-century philosophical work on the virtues, including that of Elizabeth Anscombe, Alasdair MacIntyre, and Bernard Williams.[55] Like philosophical virtue theorists, they often critiqued the formalism of modern moral theory and evinced new interest in moral psychology and the emotions. In this context, features of Christian ethics that had long been viewed as liabilities— its thick particularism, woven into identity-forming narratives, communal practices, rituals, and exemplary figures— began to be seen as strengths. If MacIntyre was right, and the virtues require for their sustenance not just the pursuit of goods internal to practices but also the pursuit of a good life understood in relation to a tradition of reflection on the good life, those conditions were fulfilled in the Christian tradition.[56]

CULTIVATING VIRTUES?

The Christian tradition offers a living context for the formation of character. But how successfully? Can we say precisely what dispositions are cultivated by its practices? Do they succeed in cultivating those virtues that are regarded within the tradition as particularly significant, or do they perhaps do more to form quite other dispositions? David Hume was famously of the opinion that the monastic life cultivated traits of character that were more worthy of being dubbed vices than virtues: "Celibacy, fasting, penance, mortification, self-denial, humility, silence, solitude...serve to no manner of purpose; neither advance a man's fortune in the world, nor render him a more valuable member of society.... [T]hey cross all these desirable ends; stupify the understanding and harden the heart, obscure the fancy and sour the temper."[57] Today we are more receptive to the possibility that ascetic practices and meditation indeed form character in positive ways that are reliably expressed in action. For instance, recent studies in social psychology have indicated that persons who meditate regularly are more likely to respond compassionately to others, even in situations in which the so-called "bystander effect" normally dampers helping responses.[58] At the same time, situationists offer evidence that purportedly calls into question stable dispositions of character or suggests that they exist only as highly local traits.[59] Seemingly insignificant features of situations can swamp characterological differences in behavior; whether or not you have just found a dime in phone booth can have a dramatic effect on whether or not you help someone who has dropped an armload of papers; whether seminary students stop to help someone in distress depends on how great a hurry they are in.[60] So what can be said about Christianity and the cultivation of virtue in light of such studies and the claims made about them?

One point, already made by numerous critics of situationism, is that social psychologists focus on behavior, not directly on disposition or character trait. Thus it is problematic for such studies to draw conclusions about the existence (or lack thereof) of virtues.[61] On the other hand, while a virtue can exist even if it is not in some particular instance expressed in action, and even if a virtue is not simply a disposition to act but also to attend and feel in particular ways, typically we are not in a position to attribute a virtue to someone unless it makes a reliable difference in how they act. It is helpful here to recognize that we attribute virtues in different ways; we do not withhold the term even from a young learner, but a child's generosity may be rather limited and inflexible. By the same token, the generosity even of the saint will fall short of perfection. If virtues are helpfully thought of on analogy with skills, rather than as automatic and routine, we will be in a position to note that "there are very different ways of being virtuous, ranging from the beginner to the truly virtuous, analogously to development in a practical skill."[62] Another productive line of response emphasizes the subjective meaning that situations have for participants, rather than simply the objective features of situations, as situationists have done. In judging whether a person's behavior evidences stable character traits across a variety of situations, it is the subjective meaning of a situation that is relevant, and social-cognitivist experiments designed to attend to how individuals perceive a situation do find evidence of stable character traits.[63]

It is worth noting several distinctive ways in which those in the Christian tradition might respond to this set of issues. First, while virtues are typically considered robust and resistant to change, within the Christian tradition, attributions of virtue come together with the affirmation that all human persons are sinners, prone to repeated moral failure and able only through grace to sustain virtue.[64] Hence, the frailty of human virtues, the fact that they can be overcome by situation, particularly by social pressures, should come as no surprise. Second, Christians have traditionally attributed some virtues to persons even where these are never expressed in action. So, for instance, in the Catholic tradition a baptized infant can be affirmed to possess the infused virtues of faith, hope, and charity even if she or he dies as an infant. And, third, Christians affirm that only Christ, as fully human and fully divine, is a sage, perfected in every virtue. In various ways, then, the Christian tradition has simultaneously emphasized and relativized the significance of the acquired moral virtues, summoning Christians to moral perfection, but not expecting that perfection and not deeming the current state of one's moral character ultimately decisive for one's acceptance by God.

It might further be argued that if the repeated activation of clusters of ideals, beliefs, desires, and goals can build relatively stable personality traits, then reading scripture, hearing preaching, singing hymns, participating in bible studies, involvement in outreach activities, examining one's own actions and failures in family life, at work, and so on contribute to the development of such clusters, such that commonalities of subjective meaning come to overlay what might otherwise be perceived as significant objective differences of situation. Individuals formed within a church community might, say, interpret a call out of the blue from a distant family member in trouble, a chance encounter with a stranger in need, and a fundraising letter from a local service organization all as opportunities to respond in gratitude to the self-giving love of God. If I begin to worship in a community that affirms that Christians are required to love whatever "neighbor" I happen to encounter in need, I may well still scurry by a homeless person on the street with feelings of fear or disgust, but I am also likely to experience this as a "neighbor-relevant" situation and respond to my own action with a sense of guilt. If I do identify my responses as deficient, that renders it more likely, some studies suggest, that in my future such responses will be immediately interrupted and new cognitive and affective patterns slowly will begin to develop.[65] This process takes place through a complex interplay of conscious reflection and effort, on the one hand, and "automatic goal activation"—in situations in which individuals unconsciously perceive situations as relevant to their goals and ideals—on the other.[66]

Holocaust rescuers have been found by multiple studies to have exhibited a distinctive moral outlook, characterized by feelings of "shared humanity" and a heightened sense of "extensivity."[67] While one certainly cannot claim that mere participation in any Christian practices of prayer and worship reliably cultivates such dispositions, the research on meditation and compassion mentioned above suggests that those who do regularly call to mind the needs of others, who dwell on their common humanity, who idealize caring responses to the marginalized and disempowered, and do so in the context of communities that prize and practice these same forms of attention and responsiveness, will be more likely than those who do not to develop robust virtues of compassion and generosity. The virtues cultivated by Christian practices, and the degree to which they are consistent across situations, will likely depend on a host of factors. Notably, the concrete local community will count, not just common scriptural, ritual, and/or doctrinal features, since it will matter how scripture is interpreted, what concerns are expressed in prayer, how that community commits itself in local and global ministries.

Beyond this, if it is true that the expression of character traits is highly context dependent, as situationists argue, it makes sense for us to anticipate and provide for that context dependency by constructing social environments that reinforce the kind of dispositions we hope reliably to possess.[68] Given that we act for the most part in situations with which we are familiar, even situationists concede that we exhibit for the most part reliable *local* dispositions, reliable not so much because of strength of character but because of stability in social situation.[69] This is another way in which to view the characterological significance of Christian churches and their many liturgical and paraliturgical practices—as offering social sustenance for the practice of virtue.[70] Christians surround themselves with others who expect them to be loving, generous, forgiving, faithful, and look to God as the ever present "bystander" who, rather than reinforcing their lack of intervention, calls them to account for failures to intervene, to assist, to respond to those in need, while always finding them lovable. One might worry that the virtues so construed, as situation-specific virtuous dispositions supported by specific social settings, might be too confined and too poorly internalized to be worthy of the name. If practicing being nice to folks at coffee hour following worship cultivates nothing more than a reliable disposition to be nice to folks at coffee hour, it isn't much to brag about. But then, Christians have been taught that virtue is nothing to brag about, anyway. Maria Merrit comments that "once we admit into reflective self-awareness a conception of such dispositions as socially sustained, we must reckon with the understanding of our own ethical character as dependent, in an ongoing way and in maturity (not just during early development), upon our involvements in social life."[71] And this is in fact just how Christians have consistently regarded their virtues—as sustained by the church and, even where that social contribution is corrupt or otherwise lacking, by divine grace.

CONCLUSION

Christian practices powerfully bring together a constellation of features conducive to the cultivation of the very virtues most cherished by Christians. We can identify four general features of particular importance. First, there are the meditative practices of various sorts, including forms of self-examination, meditative prayer and attention to the present moment, and reflection on exemplary persons, acts, narratives, and virtues. These are far from purely cognitive, engaging patterns of emotional response, habits of attention, and modes of perception. Second is the fact that these take place in a social context and have the broadest possible social reference. One's own concerns, needs, and aspirations are placed in a context that relates them to others—the human others of one's own community and those encountered as "neighbors," and also God, the source and destiny of all things. In this way, one's own perspective, one's own dispositions and habitual modes of action, are supported by one's community—the "cloud of witnesses" that lends resistance to the "bystander effect." At the same time, the practices and assumptions of that community are also seen as always potentially in question and capable of correction, given their responsibility to God. The dependency of Christian virtue, rather than being denied, is thus underscored in practice, as it is theoretically in the valorization of humility. The virtues are never regarded as individual achievements or possessions. Third, practices of coping with frailty are prominent within these communities—practices for identifying failure, for holding community members responsible, for offering forgiveness, and for seeking reconciliation. Frailty is not simply theoretically recognized; it is integrated into the community's practices of moral formation. Practices for the cultivation of virtue are thus merged with practices for healing and starting over in the face of the frailty of human virtues. Finally, practices of meditation, of reflection, of prayer and formal worship are inseparably joined with practices of outreach and ministry in the "world"—that is, beyond the formal worship context. Practicing the virtues is regarded as just as integral to the Christian life as prayer. Hence, the tradition incorporates its own forms of internal correction for any theory–practice dichotomy.

As I emphasized at the outset, the Christian tradition has not only been the primary historical carrier for classical virtue ethics, it also remains a living tradition of ethical formation. Even those strands of Christian tradition most suspicious of pagan ethics, and thus of the discourse of virtue, carried on traditional practices for the cultivation of the virtues, some of which are rooted in schools of ancient philosophy. Christianity has never been simply a virtue ethics, not even simply a school for the cultivation of the virtues. But the very features that might seem extraneous turn out to be those that render it particularly responsive to the challenges of cultivating the virtues in frail and socially dependent creatures such as ourselves.

NOTES

1. Matt. 5:48.
2. Matt. 5:44–45.
3. Dale C. Allison, *The Sermon on the Mount: Inspiring the Moral Imagination* (New York: Herder & Herder, 1999), 105. Other New Testament passages articulating this theme include Eph. 5:1–2, 1 Pet. 1:13–25, and 1 John 4:7–12. See my "Rain on the Just and the Unjust: The Ethical Implications of Indiscriminate Divine Love," *Studies in Christian Ethics* 22, no. 1 (2009): 34–47.
4. On puzzles surrounding the emulation of Jesus, given Christian doctrinal affirmations concerning the incarnation, see Gene Outka, "Following at a Distance: Ethics and the Identity of Jesus," in *Scriptural Authority and Narrative Interpretation*, ed. Garrett Green (Philadelphia: Fortress Press, 1987), 144–60.
5. See Jerome H. Neyrey, *Honor and Shame in the Gospel of Matthew* (Louisville, KY: Westminster John Knox Press, 1998); and Bruce J. Malina and Jerome H. Neyrey, "Honor and Shame in Luke-Acts: Pivotal Values of the Mediterranean World," in *The Social World of Luke-Acts: Models for Interpretation*, ed. Jerome H. Neyrey (Peabody, MA: Hendrickson, 1991), 25–65.
6. Bart D. Ehrman, ed., *Letter of Ignatius to the Romans* (New York: Oxford University Press, 1998), 329.
7. See, e.g., G. W. Bowersock, *Martyrdom and Rome* (Cambridge: Cambridge University Press, 1995); Candida Moss, *The Other Christs: Imitating Jesus in Ancient Christian Ideologies of Martyrdom* (Oxford: Oxford University Press, 2012).
8. Elizabeth A. Clark, "Asceticism, Pre-Augustine, in *Augustine Through the Ages*, ed. Allan D. Fitgerald (Grand Rapids, MI: Eerdmans, 1999).
9. Alfred C. Rush, "Spiritual Martyrdom in St. Gregory the Great," *Theological Studies* 23, no. 4 (1962): 569–89.
10. Rom. 6:4.
11. A translation of the document is included in Bart D. Ehrman, ed., *The New Testament and Other Early Christian Writings*, (Oxford: Oxford University Press, 1998), 313–17.

12. Amos 5:15–22; cf. Isa. 1:11–17.

13. Aaron Stalnaker helpfully explores the spiritual practices advocated by Augustine, in terms of Hadot's concept of spiritual exercises, in "Spiritual Exercises and the Grace of God: Paradoxes of Personal Formation in Augustine," *Journal of the Society of Christian Ethics* 24, no. 2 (2004): 137–70; and *Overcoming Our Evil: Human Nature and Spiritual Exercises in Xunzi and Augustine* (Washington, DC: Georgetown University Press, 2006), 197–245.

14. Pierre Hadot, *Philosophy as a Way of Life*, trans. Michael Chase (Oxford: Blackwell, 1995), 59.

15. Hadot, *Philosophy as a Way of Life*, 128.

16. Hadot, *Philosophy as a Way of Life*, 59.

17. Augustine, following the strong Socratic position on the unity of virtue, argued that the multiple cardinal virtues were all to be understood as manifestations of one. This one, however, was not Socratic wisdom but rather love of God, *De moribus* 1.15, PL32.

18. Matt. 5:5; Mark 10:14.

19. Exod. 4:10–12.

20. Augustine, *City of God* V19, trans. Henry Bettenson, (London: Penguin, 1972, 1984), 213.

21. Hadot, *Philosophy as a Way of Life*, 139.

22. Paul particularly develops the theme of worldly wisdom and divine foolishness; see, e.g., 1 Cor. 1:18–31, 3:19.

23. See John Cavadini's illuminating analysis in "Simplifying Augustine," in *Educating People of Faith: Exploring the History of Jewish and Christian Communities*, ed. John Van Engen (Grand Rapids, MI: Eerdmans, 2004), 63–84.

24. Peter Brown, *Poverty and Leadership in the Later Roman Empire* (Hanover, NH: Brandeis University Press, 2002), 3.

25. See my "The Theater of the Virtues: Augustine's Critique of Pagan Mimesis," in *Augustine's City of God: A Critical Guide*, ed. James Wetzel (Cambridge: Cambridge University Press, 2012), 111–29; and *Putting on Virtue: The Legacy of the Splendid Vices* (Chicago: University of Chicago Press, 2008), 56–58. Augustine is deeply critical of the way in which the Neoplatonist Porphyry reserves for philosophers what he regards as the true way of salvation, and offers to the public theurgic practices, ritual invocations of the gods that he himself regards as unable to purify the highest part of the soul; Christianity, he insists, offers a single way of salvation to all (Theater of the Virtues, 118).

26. Servais Pinckaers, *The Sources of Christian Ethics*, trans. Mary Thomas Noble (Washington, DC: Catholic University of American Press, 1995), 203.

27. Istvan Bejczy, ed., *Virtue Ethics in the Middle Ages: Commentaries on Aristotle's Nicomachean Ethics, 1200–1500* (Boston: Brill, 2008), 2.

28. Thomas Aquinas, *Summa Theologiae* I–II.56.3; 62.1. Translations are taken from *Summa Theologica*, trans. Fathers of the English Dominican Province (Westminster, MD: Christian Classics, 1981), hereafter *S.T.*, with references to part, question, and article. Further citations are given parenthetically.

29. *S.T.* I–II.51.2.

30. *S.T.* I–II.62.1.

31. *S.T.* I–II.63.2; I–II.65.2; II–II.23.7.

32. *S.T.* I–II.53.1, 78.2.

33. *S.T.* I–II.51.4.

34. *S.T.* I–I.65.3.

35. For a fascinating account of why scholastics, even prior to Aristotle's widespread influence, assumed God-given virtues to be dispositions in the soul, see Bonnie Kent, "Augustine's *On the Good of Marriage* and Infused Virtue in the Twelfth Century," *Journal of Religious Ethics* 41, no. 1 (2013): 112–36.

36. Marcia Colish, "*Habitus* Revisited: A Reply to Cary Nederman," *Traditio* 48 (1993), 80–82.

37. *S.T.* I–II.52.4 ad 3.

38. *S.T.* II–II.47.14 ad 1.

39. For a fuller discussion of Aquinas's account of humility, see Herdt, *Putting on Virtue*, 77–80.

40. *S.T.* II–II.23.6.

41. *S.T.* II–II.25.1–2.

42. *S.T.* II–II.23.8.

43. *S.T.* III, *pro.* See Joseph Wawrykow, "Jesus in the Moral Theology of Thomas Aquinas," *Journal of Medieval and Early Modern Studies* 42, no. 1 (2012): 13–33; and Brian Shanley, "Aquinas's Exemplar Ethics," *The Thomist* 72 (2008): 349–50.

44. Herdt, *Putting on Virtue*, 173–96.

45. Martin Luther, "Treatise on Good Works (1520)," in *D. Martin Luthers Werke* (Weimar: Herman Boehlhaus Nachfolger, 1897), 6:458; translation in *Luther's Works*, ed. Helmut T. Lehman, vol. 44 (Philadelphia: Fortress Press, 1966), 201. Further references are given to the volume and page from the Weimar (WA) edition, followed by the volume and page from the English translation (LW).

46. Luther, WA 6:244; LW 44:72.

47. Luther, *Freedom of a Christian*, WA 7:64; LW 31:359.

48. Luther, *Against Latomus*, WA: 8:114, LW 32:239; *Freedom of a Christian* WA 7:60; LW 31:358.

49. Wilfried Joest, *Gesezt und Freiheit*, 4th ed. (Goettingen: Vandenhoeck & Ruprecht, 1951), 24–26.

50. Luther, WA 8:107; LW 32:229.

51. Although there are important exceptions to this generalization, such as the Reformed philosophical theologian Jonathan Edwards, whose eighteenth-century engagement with British sentimentalist ethics was carried out in terms of reflection on virtue.

52. Pinckaers, *Sources of Christian Ethics*, 230–33; John Mahoney, *The Making of Moral Theology* (Oxford: Clarendon, 1987), 251–52.

53. See, e.g., Matthew Levering and Reinhard Huetter, eds., *Ressourcement Thomism: Sacred Doctrine, the Sacraments, and the Moral Life* (Washington, DC: Catholic University of America Press, 2010).

54. See, e.g., Stanley Hauerwas and L. Gregory Jones, eds., *Why Narrative? Readings in Narrative Theology* (London: Wipf & Stock, 1997).

55. Elizabeth Anscombe, "Modern Moral Philosophy," *Philosophy* 33 (1958): 1–16; Alasdair MacIntyre, *After Virtue* (Notre Dame, IN: University of Notre Dame Press, 1981); Bernard Williams, *Ethics and the Limits of Philosophy* (Cambridge, MA: Harvard University Press, 1986).

56. Stanley Hauerwas, *Vision and Virtue* (Notre Dame, IN: University of Notre Dame Press, 1986); Nancey Murphy, et al., eds., *Virtues and Practices in the Christian Tradition: Christian Ethics after MacIntyre* (Harrisburg: Trinity International, 1997).

57. David Hume, *Enquiry into the Principles of Morals*, ed. L. A. Selby-Bigge, rev. P. H. Nidditch from the 1777 ed. (Oxford: Clarendon, 1975), 270.

58. The research on the topic is exploding, but here is a striking recent example: in a study at Northeastern University, researchers found that 50 percent of subjects who had just completed an 8-week course in meditation offered to help a person on crutches and in evident pain, compared with 15 percent of non-meditators—and even though others in the room ignored the person in need, setting up classic conditions for the bystander effect. P. Condon, G. Desbordes, W. Miller, and D. DeSteno, "Meditation Increases Compassionate Responses to Suffering," *Psychological Science* 24, no. 10 (October 2013). Discussed in Northeastern Press release, http://www.northeastern.edu/cos/2013/04/release-can-meditation-make-you-a-more-compassionate-person/, accessed 5/25/13.

59. Many of the relevant studies are discussed in detail in John Doris, *Lack of Character: Personality and Moral Behavior* (Cambridge: Cambridge University Press, 2002).

60. A. M. Isen and P. F. Levin, "Effect of Feeling Good on Helping: Cookies and Kindness," *Journal of Personality and Social Psychology* 21 (1978): 145–54; J. M. Darley and C. D. Batson, "From Jerusalem to Jericho: A Study of Situational and Dispositional Variables in Helping Behavior," *Journal of Personality and Social Psychology* 27 (1973): 100–108. Both are discussed in Doris, *Lack of Character*, 30–34.

61. See, e.g., John Sabini and Maury Silver, "Lack of Character? Situationism Critiqued," *Ethics* 115 (2005): 535–62; Robert M. Adams, *A Theory of Virtue* (Oxford: Oxford University Press, 2006), 120–22; Nancy E. Snow, *Virtue as Social Intelligence: An Empirically Grounded Theory* (New York: Routledge, 2010); Julia Annas, *Intelligent Virtue* (Oxford: Oxford University Press, 2011), 173.

62. Annas, *Intelligent Virtue*, 65.

63. W. Mischel and Y. Shoda, "A Cognitive-Affective System Theory of Personality: Reconceptualizing Situations, Dispositions, Dynamics, and Invariance in Personality Structure," *Psychological Review* 102, no. 2: 246–68. The significance for virtue ethics of Mischel and Shoda's research on personality is developed in Snow, *Virtue as Social Intelligence*, 17–38.

64. Adams makes this point in conceding a measure of frailty to human virtue, *Theory of Virtue*, 157.

65. P. G. Devine and M. J. Monteith, "Automaticity and Control in Stereotyping," in *Dual-Process Theories in Social Psychology*, ed. S. Chaiken and Y. Trope (New York: Guilford, 1999), 352–53. I am indebted to Snow's discussion of this research, which focused on the psychology of prejudice (34–38).

66. J. A. Bargh, P. M. Bollwitzer, A. Lee-Chair, K. Barndollar, and R. Trotschel, "The Automated Will: Nonconscious Activation and Pursuit of Behavioral Goals," *Journal of Personality and Social Psychology* 81 (2001) 1014–27; T. L. Chartrand and J. A. Bargh, "Automatic Activation of Impression Formation and Memorization Goals: Nonconscious Goal Priming Reproduces Effects of Explicit Task Instructions," *Journal of Personality and Social Psychology* 71 (1996): 464–78. These studies and more are discussed by Snow, *Virtue as Social Intelligence*, 43–45.

67. See, e.g., S. P. Oliner and P. M. Oliner, *The Altruistic Personality: Rescuers of Jews in Nazi Germany* (London: Collier Macmillan, 1988), 173, 249, 299; K. R. Monroe, *The Heart of Altruism: Perceptions of a Common Humanity* (Princeton: Princeton University Press, 1996), 213–16.

68. Maria Merritt suggests that the sort of virtues that we can realistically attribute depend for their stability on stable social conditions, calling this the "sustaining social contribution" ("Virtue Ethics and Situationist Personality Psychology," *Ethical Theory and Moral Practice* 3 (2000): 374–81.

69. Even situationist John Doris argues for this conclusion; *Lack of Character*, 65.
70. Christians will, of course, want to affirm that the significance of the church, as the Body of Christ, is not merely characterological.
71. Merritt, "Virtue Ethics and Situationist Personality Psychology," 374.

BIBLIOGRAPHY

Adams, Robert M. *A Theory of Virtue*. Oxford: Oxford University Press, 2006.
Allison, Dale C. *The Sermon on the Mount: Inspiring the Moral Imagination*. New York: Herder & Herder, 1999.
Annas, Julia. *Intelligent Virtue*. Oxford: Oxford University Press, 2011.
Anscombe, Elizabeth. "Modern Moral Philosophy." *Philosophy* 33, no. 124 (1958): 1–19.
Aquinas, Thomas. *Summa Theologiae*. Translated by Fathers of the English Dominican Province. Westminster, MD: Christian Classics, 1981.
Augustine, *City of God*. Translated by Henry Bettenson. London: Penguin, 1972.
Bargh, J. A., P. M. Bollwitzer, A. Lee-Chair, K. Barndollar, and R. Trotschel. "The Automated Will: Nonconscious Activation and Pursuit of Behavioral Goals." *Journal of Personality and Social Psychology* 81 (2001): 1014–27.
Bejczy, Istvan, ed. *Virtue Ethics in the Middle Ages: Commentaries on Aristotle's Nicomachean Ethics, 1200–1500*. Boston: Brill, 2008.
Bowersock, G. W. *Martyrdom and Rome*. Cambridge: Cambridge University Press, 1995.
Brown, Peter. *Poverty and Leadership in the Later Roman Empire*. Hanover, NH: Brandeis University Press, 2002.
Cavadini, John. "Simplifying Augustine." *Educating People of Faith: Exploring the History of Jewish and Christian Communities*, edited by John Van Engen, 63–84. Grand Rapids, MI: Eerdmans, 2004.
Chartrand, T. L., and J. A. Bargh. "Automatic Activation of Impression Formation and Memorization Goals: Nonconscious Goal Priming Reproduces Effects of Explicit Task Instructions." *Journal of Personality and Social Psychology* 71 (1996): 464–78.
Clark, Elizabeth A. "Asceticism, Pre-Augustine," in *Augustine Through the Ages*, edited by Allan D. Fitgerald, 71–76. Grand Rapids, MI: Eerdmans, 1999.
Colish, Marcia. "*Habitus* Revisited: A Reply to Cary Nederman." *Traditio* 48 (1993): 80–82.
Condon, P., G. Desbordes, W. Miller, and D. DeSteno. "Meditation Increases Compassionate Responses to Suffering." *Psychological Science* 24, no. 10 (October 2013): 2125–27.
Darley, J. M., and C. D. Batson. "From Jerusalem to Jericho: A Study of Situational and Dispositional Variables in Helping Behavior." *Journal of Personality and Social Psychology* 27 (1973): 100–108.
Devine, P. G., and M. J. Monteith. "Automaticity and Control in Stereotyping." In *Dual-Process Theories in Social Psychology*, edited by S. Chaiken and Y. Trope, 339–60. New York: Guilford, 1999.
Doris, John. *Lack of Character: Personality and Moral Behavior*. Cambridge: Cambridge University Press, 2002.
Ehrman, Bart D., ed. *Letter of Ignatius to the Romans*. New York: Oxford University Press, 1998.
Hadot, Pierre. *Philosophy as a Way of Life*. Translated by Michael Chase. Oxford: Blackwell, 1995.
Hauerwas, Stanley. *Vision and Virtue*. Notre Dame, IN: University of Notre Dame Press, 1986.

Hauerwas, Stanley, and L. Gregory Jones, eds. *Why Narrative? Readings in Narrative Theology*. London: Wipf & Stock, 1997.

Herdt, Jennifer A. *Putting On Virtue: The Legacy of the Splendid Vices*. Chicago: University of Chicago Press, 2008.

Herdt, Jennifer A. "Rain on the Just and the Unjust: The Ethical Implications of Indiscriminate Divine Love." *Studies in Christian Ethics* 22, no. 1 (2009): 34–47.

Herdt, Jennifer A. "The Theater of the Virtues: Augustine's Critique of Pagan Mimesis." In *Augustine's City of God: A Critical Guide*, edited by James Wetzel, 111–29. Cambridge: Cambridge University Press, 2012.

Hume, David. *Enquiry Concerning Human Understanding and Concerning the Principles of Morals*. Edited by L. A. Selby-Bigge, text revised by P. H. Nidditch from the 1777 ed. Oxford: Clarendon, 1975.

Isen, A. M., and P. F. Levin, "Effect of Feeling Good on Helping: Cookies and Kindness." *Journal of Personality and Social Psychology* 21 (1978): 145–54.

Joest, Wilfried. *Gesezt und Freiheit*, 4th ed. Goettingen: Vandenhoeck & Ruprecht, 1951.

Kent, Bonnie. "Augustine's *On the Good of Marriage* and Infused Virtue in the Twelfth Century." *Journal of Religious Ethics* 41, no. 1 (2013): 112–36.

Levering, Matthew, and Reinhard Huetter, eds. *Ressourcement Thomism: Sacred Doctrine, the Sacraments, and the Moral Life*. Washington, DC: Catholic University of America Press, 2010.

Luther, Martin. *D. Martin Luthers Werke*. Weimar: Herman Boehlhaus Nachfolger, 1897.

Luther, Martin. *Luther's Works*. Translated by Helmut T. Lehmann. Philadelphia: Fortress Press, 1966.

MacIntyre, Alasdair. *After Virtue*. Notre Dame, IN: University of Notre Dame Press, 1981.

Mahoney, John. *The Making of Moral Theology*. Oxford: Clarendon, 1987.

Malina, Bruce J., and Jerome H. Neyrey. "Honor and Shame in Luke-Acts: Pivotal Values of the Mediterranean World." In *The Social World of Luke-Acts: Models for Interpretation*, edited by Jerome H. Neyrey, 25–66. Peabody, MA: Hendrickson, 1991.

Merritt, Maria. "Virtue Ethics and Situationist Personality Psychology." *Ethical Theory and Moral Practice* 3 (2000): 374–81.

Mischel, W., and Y. Shoda. "A Cognitive-Affective System Theory of Personality: Reconceptualizing Situations, Dispositions, Dynamics, and Invariance in Personality Structure." *Psychological Review* 102, no. 2 (1995): 246–68.

Monroe, K. R. *The Heart of Altruism: Perceptions of a Common Humanity*. Princeton: Princeton University Press, 1996.

Moss, Candida. *The Other Christs: Imitating Jesus in Ancient Christian Ideologies of Martyrdom*. Oxford: Oxford University Press, 2012.

Murphy, Nancey et al., eds. *Virtues and Practices in the Christian Tradition: Christian Ethics after Macintyre*. Harrisburg: Trinity International, 1997.

Neyrey, Jerome H. *Honor and Shame in the Gospel of Matthew*. Louisville, KY: Westminster John Knox Press, 1998.

Oliner, S. P., and P. M. Oliner. *The Altruistic Personality: Rescuers of Jews in Nazi Germany*. London: Collier Macmillan, 1988.

Outka, Gene. "Following at a Distance: Ethics and the Identity of Jesus." *Scriptural Authority and Narrative Interpretation*, edited by Garrett Green, 144–60. Philadelphia: Fortress Press, 1987.

Pinckaers, Servais. *The Sources of Christian Ethics*. Translated by Mary Thomas Noble. Washington, DC: Catholic University of American Press, 1995.

Rush, Alfred C. "Spiritual Martyrdom in St. Gregory the Great." *Theological Studies* 23, no. 4 (1962): 569–89.

Sabini, John, and Maury Silver. "Lack of Character? Situationism Critiqued." *Ethics* 115 (2005): 535–62.

Shanley, Brian. "Aquinas's Exemplar Ethics." *The Thomist* 72 (2008): 349–50.

Snow, Nancy E. *Virtue as Social Intelligence: An Empirically Grounded Theory*. New York: Routledge, 2010.

Stalnaker, Aaron. *Overcoming Our Evil: Human Nature and Spiritual Exercises in Xunzi and Augustine*. Washington, DC: Georgetown University Press, 2006.

Stalnaker, Aaron. "Spiritual Exercises and the Grace of God: Paradoxes of Personal Formation in Augustine." *Journal of the Society of Christian Ethics* 24, no. 2 (2004): 137–70.

Wawrykow, Joseph. "Jesus in the Moral Theology of Thomas Aquinas." *Journal of Medieval and Early Modern Studies* 42, no. 1 (2012): 13–33.

Williams, Bernard. *Ethics and the Limits of Philosophy*. Cambridge, MA: Harvard University Press, 1986.

CHAPTER 10

cⱱᴐ

The Co-Construction of Virtue

Epigenetics, Development, and Culture

DARCIA NARVAEZ

The human sciences are uncovering what virtue theorists surmised long ago: virtue is co-constructed by those around you.[1] But it goes much deeper than previously explained. The effects of co-construction of the self in early life go all the way down to gene expression and the function of immune and neurotransmitter systems. All these can influence one's morality later because physiological function affects the nature of being and being influences morality. A suboptimal set of body/brain systems necessarily is less capable of performing at humanity's highest level, which entails communal imagination, a combination of deep compassion and wisdom in the moment.

On the one hand, although science can verify certain understandings and general patterns concerning virtue and its development, on the other hand, it is limited in its ability to guide virtue *application*. Science is either about pattern description (biology, anthropology) or about predictive laws (physics) and repeatable, lawful application. Yet, virtue application is neither following a pattern nor applying a law. When virtue is conceptualized as doing the right thing in the right way at the right time, as understood here, situatedness is critical. In this case, science cannot guide implementation because "Situations do not come in duplicates."[2] Applied ethics requires noticing the uniqueness of the situation, interpreting the landscape of implications and possibilities for those circumstances, dramatically rehearsing options, prioritizing the best option for that situation, implementing the option in the appropriate way for those circumstances, and following it through to completion. There is no law of action that one can follow to know which principles to apply and how to apply them in a virtuous way for a particular situation. Though one may hold conscious general principles (e.g., compassion, honesty), they are too general and too narrow to guide specific action.[3] If it's virtuous, the specific action taken in a particular situation will be unique, tailored to the entities and circumstances at hand. Virtue is not about repetition and doggedness but about variation and agility.

Cognitive scientist Wilma Koutstaal provides a brilliant analysis and theory of an "agile mind."[4] The "representational accessibility landscape" in which a person resides includes emotion, perception, and conceptual memory, as well as representations of actions and goals. These different aspects move in and out of awareness, including into and out of focal and peripheral attention. Representational accessibility landscapes are continuously affected, moment by moment and over time, through environments experienced and selected, including physical, symbolic, and social contexts. The individual moves constantly in a spiral of perception-action (perceiving, acting, perceiving effects) or between goals and intentions and the options the world provides. The agile mind can shift among representations, from concreteness to abstraction, from controlled (intentional) to automatic (spontaneous) functioning, as needed. Those with cognitive, emotional, or psychopathological limitations tend not to display an agile mind.

An agile mind is a necessary component of a virtuous moral life, but so is a wide range of capacities. As one moves through shifting moral contexts, one needs a host of flexible application skills, skills that allow one to be socially and practically effective and for which one has built confidence through frequent appropriate deployment.[5] Moreover, orientation or mindset is also involved. It's not just any mindset that leads to humanity's highest moral capacities. One must cultivate the more prosocial orientations—those that allow one to swim in the social landscape with humility and sense of extensive social consequence.

How does one best develop flexible skills and optimal mindsets for life and morality? First, the body/brain has to work well. Much of the guidance for action emerges from the unconscious, implicit mind, which is more powerful in social situations and draws from knowledge and capacities developed and established in early life.[6] Optimizing capacities take a great deal of supportive social experience, and it starts from birth (if not during conception-gestation).

EARLY LIFE EXPERIENCE

To understand virtue development, one must understand humanity's evolutionary and developmental unfolding. Over the course of human evolution encompassing such things as bipedalism, human babies became increasingly helpless and immature at birth, emerging from the womb nine to eighteen months early, compared to other animals. Humans have 75 percent of the brain left to develop over a lengthy period of maturation (over 20 years) but most of it by age 5.[7] As a result, the early caregiving environment has enormous effects on all of a child's systems, including the development of the self, sociality, and capacities for self-regulation.[8]

Although the paradigm shift has started toward acknowledging the primacy of *epigenetics* (the fact that genes must be turned on, or "expressed" by experience), the majority of people are still led to believe that static genes play the largest role in whom a person becomes.[9] On the contrary, genes provide only a blueprint that requires experience, some during critical periods, for gene expression to occur. For example, Michael Meaney and colleagues have documented a critical period for rat pups in the first ten days of life when proper gene expression for controlling anxiety is switched on, but which only occurs when one has a normal nurturant mother; if one lacks a nurturant mother (high licking), the gene may never be properly expressed and new situations will cause anxiety for a lifetime.[10] If a species-typical developmental context is altered, modifications in gene activation, regulation, and selection will occur, creating species-atypical epigenetic outcomes that can get transferred across generations. Moreover, the developmental plasticity in early life means that the set points, parameters, and thresholds for many physiological systems are influenced as they are being established. As a result, the early caregiving environment will have long-term effects on the health and well-being of the offspring.[11]

Although many dichotomize nature and nurture, as if they can be separated, genes and environment form part of a shifting context for the ongoing development and functioning of an active, changing organism, marking "a host of recurrent interactions or coactions situated temporally and physically within complex developmental manifolds or systems."[12] Early life represents the complex beginning of a dynamic system: "Features of available prenatal and early postnatal sensory stimulation (such as amount, intensity, or the timing of presentation of stimulation) can co-act with specific organismic factors (such as the stage of organization of the sensory systems, previous history with the given properties of stimulation, and the current state of arousal of the young organism) to guide and constrain the developmental course of species-typical perceptual preferences, learning, and memory."[13]

What is the developmental manifold or nest for humans? What type of caregiving did human young evolve to need? To match the immaturity of newborns, over the course of mammalian and human evolution, humans developed intense parenting practices.[14] My colleagues and I call these caregiving practices the *evolved developmental niche* (EDN). This EDN, shaped over 30 million years of social and human mammalian development, is a form of support that matches the maturational schedule of the needy infant and young child. It may be critical for optimal physiological and social development.[15] The EDN for young children includes responsiveness to child needs, natural childbirth, two to five years of breastfeeding, frequent and pervasive positive touch, extensive free play, multiple adult caregivers, and positive social climate and support.[16]

Most research involving early life experience thus far has focused on the first in the list, responsive caregiving, particularly within the mother-child relationship. Attentive and supportive early caregiving results in what Fogel and colleagues[17] call a kind of "relational communication system," in which parent and child successfully modulate their behaviors to achieve an optimal level of physiological arousal and coordinated action.[18] Within the EDN, the child exists in a web of relationships (with other adults beyond the mother) that guide and shape systems which underlie perception and attention. As Murdoch[19] wisely pointed out, attention shapes desires and, in psychoperception lingo, *affordances* or action possibilities.[20] Perception and action also depend on mindset—which emotion systems are active (more below). In early life, capacities for cognition and emotion develop together in early implicit rational knowledge that underlies conscious thought.[21] As noted by Colwyn Trevarthen, through experiences of positive intersubjectivity with caregivers, which involve emotional presence and responsiveness, young children build flexible responsiveness-in-the-moment to others.[22] With EDN-consistent care, children experience companionship care that fosters not only emotional attachment but also deep social and cognitive intelligence. Caregiver and child co-construct their own narratives and play patterns that familiarize the child with a world of joyous being-in-the-moment. This sets the child on a trajectory for true (wise) rationality, which integrates well-trained emotions. In fact, without well-trained emotions, reason can be stupid and/or destructive.[23] Anthropologist Colin Turnbull offered a concrete example.[24] He contrasted his own British upbringing with that of the Mbuti, whom he studied. The Mbuti, with EDN-consistent care, reach adolescence with full sensory capacities and energy for adulthood, whereas he arrived with emptiness and almost a self-disownership, lacking emotional depth or sense of being, leaving him vulnerable to manipulation and ideologies of domination and aggression toward others.

Responsive caregiving shapes the regulation of physiological, but also emotion systems and social foundations, during sensitive periods for their establishment. Emotions and cognitive structures develop together in early life, from repeated or intense experiences.[25] Emotion systems (e.g., FEAR, PANIC, CARE) are placed centrally in the brain, interacting with more evolved cognitive structures and with lower-level physiological and motor outputs to guide behavior.[26] Emotion systems represent an inheritance of characteristics that worked for our ancestors for behaving in adaptive ways. With EDN-consistent support during development, physiological and emotional self-regulation increases and moderates action.[27] The mammalian brain actually has evolved to (learn to) delay impulsive actions, allowing for the selection and elaboration of a plan of action. With good developmental support, the action tendencies of more primitive brain systems interact with the planning, memory, and attentional components of higher order systems, both tuning into interindividual communication of affect and meaning. But to coordinate social action well, brains must be nurtured well. For example, young children who are cared for with little warmth and responsivity, even if their physical needs are met, show more depressed affect and fewer social bids than children with a nurturing caregiver.[28] Poor physiological self-regulation is associated with insecure or disorganized attachment to caregivers, a sign of misguided development from an evolutionary perspective.[29]

Self-regulation is a multilayered component underlying all functioning in mammals, including mental and social health.[30] But self-regulation is not the task of the offspring alone; it requires adult support for optimal development and is initially fostered by caregiver interaction in early life.[31] Self-regulation is by definition a social, and primarily dyadic, process that begins at (or even before) birth. The human infant is characterized by significant neurological immaturity, and thus even such basic physiological processes as regulating temperature and the sleep/wake cycle require support from a responsive, caring adult. Specifically, maternal sensitivity has been identified as an important component of an infant's physiological regulation.[32] Hofer's work, examining the deterioration of various systems when infant rats are separated from their mothers, indicates that mammalian self-regulation comprises multiple physiological systems.[33] At this level, self-regulation is mostly outside conscious awareness. So, for example, the stress response system is set up well with responsive parenting (i.e., limiting distress, providing comfort, meeting needs immediately). Systems related to the stress response include the hypothalamic-pituitary-adrenal gland axis and the vagus nerve. Unresponsive parenting is linked to maladaptive functioning in both systems.[34] Repeated experience of stress in early development can become a pattern that establishes a suboptimal foundation for future development.[35]

When things go right in early life, the individual becomes not only well self-regulated but also highly socially skilled, with full empathic and socially flexible skills.[36] Because requisites for affection, autonomy, and other basic needs were met, the individual is able to be attuned to others and take up social experience with vigor. She has less self-preoccupation than a child whose needs were denied. She is able to be emotionally present with others and solve social problems with others in mind, based on her own life experience with caregivers. However, when things go poorly in early life, neurobiology and social development can be deformed. This is evident in insecure attachment. In one type, anxious attachment, cognition is underdeveloped and emotions are out of control.[37] In another type, avoidant attachment, emotions are underdeveloped and cognition becomes detached (a type that is increasing among U.S. college students).[38] The effects of insecure attachment are most apparent in social relations—people have difficulty getting along as flexibly intimate companions and instead they emotionally disassociate or move to domination and control of others.[39]

Well-constructed socio-emotional systems are fundamental to virtue. Indeed, Kochanska's extensive work on mother-child relations and the development of morality indicates that secure attachment style and moral development are greatly influenced by responsive care.[40] A mutually responsive orientation in the mother-child relationship from the beginning has long-term beneficial effects on the development of empathy, conscience, cooperation, and prosocial behavior.

Although we know through decades of research that responsivity has long-term effects on children's well-being, responsive care is only one of the characteristics of the evolved developmental niche. Research into the effects of the other practices characteristic of the evolved developmental niche shows that they matter for physiological health.[41] For example, breast milk provides all the building blocks for the immune system, which is housed primarily in the gut, as well as supports healthy brain development. Touch is important for promoting growth, healthy stress response, and other systems. Rough-and-tumble play develops executive brain functions. Interfering with natural birth processes can negatively impact child health and maternal-child bonding. The EDN fosters healthy, well-functioning neurobiology and self-regulation from the first hours of life (or earlier, such as from conception, though grandparental experience also has effects). Extensive research with animals and humans demonstrates that lifelong deficits can occur when early experience is suboptimal. Like the foundation for a house, later development builds upon early development. Touch also influences stress response in that, as noted above, without plenty of nurturing touch, genes (e.g., those that control anxiety) may not be expressed properly for the rest of life.[42] Such findings should not come as a surprise, as each human is a dynamic system, whose initial conditions matter for later outcomes.[43] For optimal moral development, the vast immaturity and neediness of human infants may require more than responsive relationships with caregivers.

My colleagues and I are examining whether each of the EDN components (e.g., breastfeeding, touch, play, social support, natural childbirth, and responsivity) matters for child moral outcomes in early life. In two studies (in the United States and China) with mothers of 3- to 5-year-old children,[44] Our data show that after controlling for maternal income and education as well as maternal responsivity, children's *empathy* was influenced by type of childbirth (lower with cesarean birth) and by touch in infancy; and at age 3, by play with mom and with other adults. Maternal reports of child *self-regulation* were correlated with no C-section, and with positive touch in infancy; and at age 3, with play with mom and with other adults, multiple caregivers, and family cohesion. Children's *inhibitory control* was associated with breastfeeding length and with positive touch in infancy; and at age 3, with play with mom and with other adults, and with family cohesion. Children's *conscience* was correlated with breastfeeding length, positive touch, play with other adults, and multiple adult caregivers. A third study used a pre-collected longitudinal dataset.[45] We examined children's prosocial behavior (cooperation, social competence), behavior problems (internalizing, externalizing), and cognitive ability (intelligence, auditory comprehension, and verbal expression). We controlled for maternal responsivity to see if responsivity, breastfeeding, touch, and maternal social support would influence child outcomes. Here are a few findings. *Prosocial behavior* (measured at 18 and 30 months) at 18 months was predicted by breastfeeding initiation and at both 18 and 30 months prosocial behavior was predicted by maternal responsivity at 4 months and maternal social support. These results suggest that early life experience influences the development of moral capacities.

Generally speaking, prosocial behavior is an indicator of well-functioning social and emotional systems and proper right hemisphere development in early life. Breastfeeding initiation corresponds to maternal responsivity, which fosters good attachment and the corresponding brain development. Maternal social support encourages a mother to be responsive. Overall, our findings suggest that more than responsivity may be needed for moral development. The EDN may provide the necessary grounding for bottom-up virtue development among humans.[46]

VIRTUE AND MORAL ORIENTATION

Critical features of virtue involve basic capacities that were traditionally formed in an early life evolved developmental niche (though some may be remedied later with extensive, immersive experience).[47] Ongoing experience with caregivers in the EDN includes the practices of emotional presence, reverence (openness to the depth of the Other), synchrony and repair of dysynchrony in communication, intersubjective mutual influence, empathy, and perspective taking.[48] Babies are prepared for all these aspects and rapidly develop reciprocal skills in a supportive environment. Such deep and ongoing experience with caregivers leads to social pleasure and social effectivity—capacities that foster what I call *empathic effectivity roots*. Without these capacities, one is less able to be relationally attuned and display the social fittedness that Aristotle included in his list of virtues, resulting in mismanagement or misjudgments of social relations and a more self-focused personality.[49] See figure 10.1 for an illustration of moral developmental systems theory and life trajectories related to the EDN.

The EDN fosters frontal controls of subcortical emotion systems—networks that are scheduled to develop during early life and that are necessary for controlling self-protective (fight-flight-freeze-faint) emotions in social relations.[50] The self-protective emotions that occur with the stress

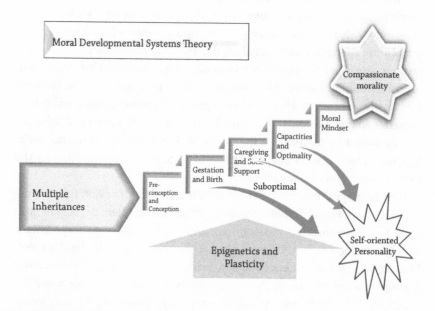

Figure 10.1.
Moral Developmental Systems Theory Showing Evolved Developmental Niche Trajectories.

response (fear, anger) can otherwise take over mind and attention, derailing the more delicate capacities for abstract thinking and reflection. The inter-relations of executive function, emotion, and cognition neurobiology in the development of social functioning matter for moral functioning and are integrated in triune ethics theory.

Triune ethics theory (TET) describes three basic moral propensities with evolutionary roots.[51] MacLean noted three distinctive evolved brain strata that establish different global brain states.[52] TET identifies how making moral decisions and taking moral action from each brain state represents a different ethical orientation. The moral orientations emerge from distinctive cognitive-emotional-perceptual states that shift the processing of life events. For example, emotions change vision;[53] and goals and needs shift affordances (perceived action possibilities).[54]

Triune ethics theory identifies three basic moral orientations (with multiple subtypes): Safety (relational self-protection), Engagement (relational attunement), and Imagination (reflective abstraction). They are fostered by distinctive early experience and general cultural milieu. The ethic of Safety represents a stress-reactive orientation that focuses on the self. Although most theorists consider morality to be necessarily concerned with the welfare of others, from a subjective position egoism is a moral orientation. (More on this later.) The Safety ethic is based primarily in instincts for survival (rooted in the brain stem, lower limbic system), which are systems available at birth, shared with all animals, and useful in moments of physical threat.[55] The Safety mindset is primed by perception of a fearful social climate or situation and focuses on "me and mine." It can be acted on as a general orientation to life, filtering life events at a subliminal level (e.g., rejecting a new idea out of hand, inflexibly applying categorization to new experience). It can also fluctuate between an aggressive or withdrawing stance propelled by social stress reactivity. The stress response activates the sympathetic nervous system, taking over attention and depleting resources for higher order processes.[56] Anger and striving (related to "grasping" or hoarding of some kind for self-protection) indicate that the sympathetic autonomic system is active, driving an aggressive-defensive orientation—self-preservational externalizing behavior. It can become a habitual orientation for those who were abused or traumatized, especially in early life, and can be seen in bullying and scapegoating. A second subtype of Safety ethic occurs when the parasympathetic system kicks in (after an immediate or historic unsuccessful sympathetic system response to flee or fight). It is represented by dissociation, freezing, and paralysis. One becomes passive and/or withdrawn from relationship, a self-preservational internalizing behavior.

The second ethic, Engagement, is rooted in prosocial mammalian emotion systems linked to intimacy (care, play)[57] and the capacities underlying

Darwin's "moral sense" (e.g., social pleasure, social skills, concern for the opinion of others).[58] The ethic of Engagement represents relational presence and attunement with the Other in the present moment ("you and me"). It is fostered by the EDN and primed by supportive, caring relationships and environments. It underlies compassionate response, the force behind "positive" moral behavior, such as the Gentile rescuers of Jews in World War II, who stated they were driven by "pity, compassion, concern, and affection" when faced with another human being in need.[59] The ethic of Engagement is not innate, but its development requires a receptive, emotionally supportive early environment (or during subsequent sensitive periods). It relies on well-functioning systems that are lateralized to the right hemisphere, brain circuitries that develop in the first years of life, that are necessary for successful social intimacy.[60]

Humans, like all mammals, evolved to favor face-to-face relationships and have difficulty imagining those not present. However, with the third brain strata to evolve, humans have a further capacity that is largely theirs alone: an extensive frontal lobe with the added complexities of the prefrontal cortex. The frontal lobe allows humans to think about those not present and make plans for the future based on the past. The ethic of Imagination is rooted here, expanding capacities beyond what is face-to-face, using abstraction, deliberation, and imagination to coordinate instincts, intuitions, and principles; to integrate the goals/needs of the self with the goals/needs of others; and to adjudicate reactions and outcomes of the self and others within a shifting representational landscape. All of this supports reflective abstraction and macro morality (taking into account those not physically present). It provides a narrative grounding for relationships ("it's about more than me and you").

There are multiple types of imagination; for example, one is connected to engaged prosocial emotions (communal imagination), another to deliberate self-protection (vicious imagination), and another is divorced from emotional connection (detached imagination). *Communal* imagination involves an ethic of love, sympathetic action, egalitarian respect. *Vicious* imagination involves a deliberate divorce from engagement (hardening of the heart). The one I consider most dominant in explicit Western culture is *detached* imagination, which represents a focus on predominantly "left hemisphere directed," conscious thought, predominantly emotionally cool or cold. It categorizes and stereotypes, objectifies, dissects and orders, decontextualizes; aims for control and power over objects; seeks a firm, certain answer; calculates the usefulness of other people and things.[61] According to Flynn himself, hypothetical thinking, which is part of detached imagination, is the source of the Flynn effect (the rise in IQ scores in the

United States during the twentieth century).[62] In a detached imagination mindset, the individual is not deeply attuned to relationships, which itself can lead to innovation without a sense of immediate and/or long-term social consequence. Detached imagination is what is usually studied in empirical moral psychology, what Western schooling emphasizes, and what undercare in childhood encourages.

But then, what is an ethic? Both subjective and objective viewpoints are brought together in TET. According to triune ethics theory, when an event occurs (internal or external) and an emotion-cognitive response triggers socially relevant behavior that trumps other values, subjectively it represents an ethic. In any given moment, all animals aim for what they perceive is "the good," and humans are no exception. Thus, when a person acts from the global mindset, in that moment he or she does so with a sense of justice and rightness. In this manner, self-protection, based in the survival systems of the most primitive parts of the brain, operates as an ethical orientation, even though, objectively speaking, taking all possible perspectives into account, it is less "ethical" than a more communal orientation. However, what seems subjectively good may not be objectively good.

The subjective ethic that matches up with the highest form of morality is *mindful morality*. Optimal morality is not so much about *thinking*, although flexible (and postconventional) thinking is vital when needed, as *being* and *behaving*. Mindful morality involves "full beingness with others" in a behavioral manner that promotes flourishing in the broadest sense— inclusive of self, one's family and community, the natural world, and future generations, including those in the natural world. Most indigenous peoples traditionally hold this mindset.[63]

Although each ethic is available to almost everyone because of evolutionary propensities, based on experience individual brain/minds can favor one ethic over others or in particular situations. An individual's perceptions and action capabilities shift by situation and can be handicapped or enhanced by prior experience. How ethical orientations shift from situation to situation, moment to moment, is reflected in a person-by-context manner.[64] However, it is easy and satisfying to downshift to self-protective mindsets.[65] It is also easy to *build* a brain that has a propensity to favor self-protective moralities. Without early life EDN, the resulting human nature can become disordered in multiple ways, depending on the type, duration, intensity, and timing of undercare, plus epigenetic inheritances from ancestors.[66] The Safety ethic, conditioned during sensitive developmental periods or from traumatic experiences, can impair higher order reasoning capacities and compassionate response, keeping a focus on self-preservation. Insecure attachment is a sign of neurobiological miswiring in early life.

Those with insecure attachment are less socially adept and less empathic, necessarily caught in a self-nature that is suboptimal. In work from my laboratory, we find that those who have higher scores on a Safety ethic orientation tend to show greater insecure attachment and less trust, empathy, and integrity.[67]

How do TET mindsets relate to the EDN? In a study of over 400 adults, a 10-item adult self-report measure of EDN history was correlated with ethical orientation.[68] Items were about childhood experience in terms of breastfeeding length, responsivity (combination of happiness, support, responsiveness to needs), touch (affection, corporal punishment), play (adult-organized, free inside, free outside), and social support (family togetherness). Those who reported less play and family togetherness activities were more likely to have a safety ethical orientation (either aggressive or withdrawing). A withdrawing moral orientation was also correlated with less reported affectionate touch. Both engagement ethic and communal imagination ethics were related to longer breastfeeding, heightened responsivity, less corporal punishment, greater inside and outside play, and more family togetherness. Engagement was also related to greater affectionate touch. In an examination of mental health, poor mental health was related to more self-concerned moral orientations. That is, anxiety and depression were positively correlated with Safety ethics and negatively correlated with Engagement and Imagination.

In early life, the EDN provides support for optimal development, including moral learning. Like perception, worldview, and everything else truly integrated into the self, moral learning begins first as bottom-up understanding (i.e., intuitions built from immersed experience).[69] This starts in early life, which in the past was a universally shared experience.

UNIVERSALS IN VIRTUE AND THE IMPORTANCE OF CULTURE

Among all animals, a species-typical developmental system (the nest or niche) creates similar species-typical outcomes.[70] How do we know that humans studied in Western cultures by psychologists today, with their low empathy, high self-protectiveness, notorious cheating, and aggression, are *not* the way humans evolved to be? Because those who receive the full complement of early experience that humans evolved to expect (the EDN) do not behave these ways, even under extreme duress.[71] I refer to nomadic hunter-gatherer societies, which are presumed to represent the social context in which humans evolved and reflect 99 percent of human genus history.[72]

Until recently in human genus history, the EDN was universally experienced by humans, and because of this, may have brought about basic similarities in moral foundations of thought and feeling—a "cultural commons." An early cultural commons forms the grounding for mental and moral agility and for a common humanity. In terms of social and moral development, the EDN fosters basic universals in implicit procedural social knowledge that underlies human thought and emotion—a solid empathic core and a sense of autonomy circumscribed by that empathic core. This is evident among small-band hunter-gatherers, for which a similar type of society emerged independently around the world, as documented by anthropologists.[73] These groups share social and personality characteristics that include generosity and sharing, egalitarianism, and lack of coercion. Although there is high individual autonomy, there is also high commitment to relationships. Instead of agency (personal autonomy) and communion (communal relations) being opposing forces, as presumably found in Western mainstream groups, agency and communion align and guide a common purpose of living in harmony with other people and the natural world.[74] After experiencing the EDN in childhood, the uniqueness of a particular culture is the frosting on a cake of a common human nature.

A similar basic culture is found among our hunter-gatherer cousins, one that supports the EDN for children and others throughout life.[75] Adults raised within the early-life EDN appear to be wise about what children need for optimal development and they create a culture that continues the EDN. Social life is deep and satisfying. No one is coerced, even children, who are allowed autonomy as well. In contrast, adults raised outside the EDN, as in the West, create cultures that do not meet the needs of children. In animal studies, poor parenting spirals downward over generations.[76] Along with an early experience that builds the foundations for full human moral capacities, culture is also vital. Cultures not only press caregivers in certain directions for childraising, they immerse their members in a stew of emotions, interpretations, and narratives. They set the parameters for moral concern and lubricate opportunities toward virtue or vice. Among humans, cultures without an early EDN will perpetuate vice from the bottom up, leaning toward self-protective and self-aggrandizing ethics.

When societies curtail the human heritages of close maternal, familial, and community care, so too are curtailed the extensive empathy and self-regulation that otherwise underlie individual autonomy and self-development. Traditions that emphasize detached parenting in early life undermine the development of the components of both Engagement and communal Imagination. Lack of EDN makes one more stress- and threat-reactive and less able to cope with social stressors, leading to habitual use of self-protection in social and moral relations. Diminished are the holistic imagination and receptive intelligence that those raised in indigenous cultures display. As a result, one can argue that today's "civilized" humans are less intelligent, perceptive, well, and wise than their ancestors or cousins who live within a culture supporting the EDN. In terms of morality, today's humans exhibit various levels of self-centeredness, with a fundamental focus on self-aggrandizement and self-protection. Stripping away the evolutionarily evolved principles of childrearing, as some traditions have done, leaves the child with a minimized internal moral compass in early childhood. This leads to the need for externally imposed social learning and morality—explicit rules must be memorized and coerced with sanctions or constructed incentives. With the variability in early life experience, each social group or subgroup may develop or apply an ideology that clashes with another's. Because of the dearth of implicit social knowledge from an EDN-supportive culture, *beliefs* and *thinking* become all important instead of *being*. Individual agency moves *against* others instead of *with* them and *with the natural world*, as is the case among nomadic hunter-gatherers.[77] This stems at least in part from the fact that the individual does not have the early life grounding that provides a previously universal experiential knowledge to guide her.

Thus, socio-moral imagination is shaped in a deep manner (neurobiology and up) by experience. Most of what we know is implicitly held. Conscious reasoning is the veneer on layers of implicit rationality and physiological function built from the interactions of a developing dynamic system. Implicit rationality includes social procedural knowledge constructed in early life, such as the depth and breadth of empathy and the parameters for one's autonomy.[78] These influence worldview and habits of inclusion/exclusion of others (pro-nature vs. contra-nature or humanistic vs. normative).[79] Explicit knowledge works best when it matches up with implicit knowledge; otherwise, implicit knowledge "wins" in behavior, especially under stress, leading to hypocrisy and self-blindness.[80]

As noted above, what EDN care in early life provides is the grounding for fully developed right-hemisphere capacities (encompassing the implicit mind and capacities for sociality). Right-hemisphere processing has greater flexibility, breadth, and inclusive creativity. Right-hemisphere directed processes allow one to be nonevaluative—to notice, enjoy, and receive. Detached imagination, circumventing emotion, shows a lack of awareness that one is attached to all things, missing the sense of enwebbedness where everything one does reverberates on everything else in a given woven fabric of relationships.

Without the EDN creating a grounding for virtue, one's particular culture will matter more, providing narratives and reasons for morality that must be adopted. These often contrast with the distrustful, self-protective orientation that has been learned implicitly. External values then must be coercively imposed to fill the sense of emptiness, to fill the "hungry ghost" of a person without the grounding of an empathic, connected core. Non-EDN care becomes a cycle of misraised adults perpetuating (and making worse) the environments for childraising, further stripping humanity of its evolved moral foundations, influencing the development of self and its relations to others, to nature, and to embodiment. The undermining of the EDN is perpetuated by beliefs that continue the perversion of the early environment (e.g., "human nature as evil," "body as disgusting," "body as machine," "nature as inferior," and extreme individualism imposed on babies). Missing is a wholistic orientation, which requires full right-brain functioning, that allows one to sense the ultimate unity of all living things, as science has shown them to be at the quantum level.[81] A culture without the EDN becomes competitive, operating from Safety-rooted sociobiologies of dominance/withdrawal (see figure 10.2a). Ultimately, it creates humans who are less than fully human.[82] Agency moves against others and communion feels smothering or risky.

What does the alternative look like? Figure 10.2b is an illustration of a cooperative, companionship culture. We see that well-cared-for children become adults who create a different type of culture that gets passed to the next generation through their sociobiology.

COMPANIONSHIP VIRTUE

Hunter-gatherer cultures have a broader sense of moral hospitality than moderns. Not only do they tend to have smaller personal egos, they usually have a large "common self" in which they feel connected to and concerned for other forms in nature as part of themselves. For example, traditional indigenous societies (a mix of small-band hunter-gatherers, complex hunter-gatherers, band, tribal, and chiefdom societies)[83] are respectful of the lives of animals, take on the mind of an animal (perhaps as part of a clan totem), concern themselves about its well-being, attend to its presence, and ask permission to take its life.[84] They maintain a sense of the cyclical nature of life and the importance of maintaining balance for the well-being of All.

In Western cultures, confusions about baselines, human nature, and basic needs have been fostered by the separation of human culture from nature.[85] The experiences of most people living in the United States today are apart from nature (on average, individuals spend less than 24 hours a

Culture of Competitive Detachment

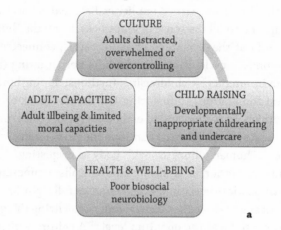

Culture of Cooperative Companionship

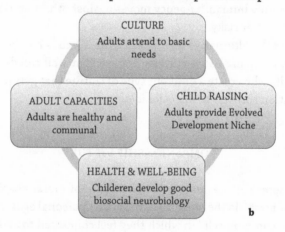

Figure 10.2.
a. Perpetuated Cycles in a Culture of Competitive Detachment and **b.** Cooperative
Companionship.

year outdoors), rendering their understanding of human nature and human
basic needs minimal. Intuitions about children have been shaped by adults'
less than optimal childhoods and by numerous cultural narratives that continue to keep humans unaware of their heritage and promise. In many
places in the West, and perhaps elsewhere, children are forced to "be independent"—from parents, nature, animals, their feelings—and as a result form
large self-protective egos as compensation. From the extensive frustration
of needs for touch, breastmilk, and attunement, they may never feel totally

safe or confident, or, at the other end, take foolish risks that put other lives at stake. After experiencing extensive isolation and despair as infants, they may have nightmares of abandonment and fantasies of dangers lurking in the unfamiliar and the unknown. These may keep them from being able to relax into love and form a sense of commonality with others. Instead, they may brace themselves to survive (fear) or control (anger) events, leading to various clinical and subclinical pathologies. The instincts for a common self are shattered as an excessive ego is born from pain and alienation leading to a "false drive for self-affirmation" and the "having of things" instead of being comfortable with the "unreliable, unsolid, unlasting, unpredictable, dangerous world of relation."[86]

Although an individual may develop—with supportive caregiving and schooling that does not snuff out the spirit—engagement and communal imagination, our heritage of human virtue will be incomplete unless hospitality, care, and commitment are not also extended to the natural world—to all entities (i.e., plants, animals, mountains, streams). Unless a sense of partnership is felt with these other entities, virtue is anthropocentric and does not represent humanity's fullest moral capacities. When humans embrace their mammalian heritage and basic needs, such as intensive parenting and ongoing social support, they are better able to adopt commonself relations with other animals, plants, and forms. A common-self orientation to the natural world is typical of hunter-gatherer societies, where everything can be a relation or at least a responsibility. This may be our most needed moral "learning." A companionship culture not only involves EDN care for children and EDN support for all humans but also includes the natural world as a companion, as agentic, and as equally worthy of care.

THE IMPORTANCE OF AUTOPOEISIS IN VIRTUE DEVELOPMENT

Optimal moral functioning is about virtue—knowing how to act in the right way at the right time, using one's fullest human capacities—a mindful morality encompassing engagement and communal imagination. Virtue is initially bottom-up socio-moral procedural learning, a type of learning that differs from schoolbook learning, in that it does not emphasize thinking and intellect but, rather, feeling, being, and relating with an increasing actionable know-how for everyday life. Socio-moral procedural learning is similar to other forms of actionable learning in that it takes immersion, guidance, and extensive practice to move from novice to greater expertise.

Importantly, organisms that develop actively participate in their own development. In fact, *autopoiesis*—self-development and self-organization—is one of humanity's many inheritances.[87] Although a baby has only minimal autopoietic capacities (hence the importance of EDN-consistent care), with age, development, and education, humans increasingly can take charge of their self-development. With increased maturation, self-monitoring skills facilitate virtue development through the selection of activities and focus. Although they will always need mentors and community support for self-authorship, they can choose the environments in which their implicit mind will learn its intuitions.[88] They can draw their attention to things they prefer as first-order desires.[89] Even individuals who missed the early EDN can learn presence and intersubjective intimacy, building a stronger empathic core. And they can learn to curb their autonomy with a growing sense of communal imagination.

CONCLUSION

Culture shapes contexts for early development. Until recently in human genus history, the evolved developmental niche (EDN) was provided universally in human societies, offering a cultural commons for human personality. The evolved developmental niche provides the essentials for developing humanity's fullest moral capacities. Brain and body systems that underlie moral functioning are influenced by caregivers and social experience. In the last one percent of human genus history (the last 10,000 years or so), and especially recently (last few hundred years), humans outside of small-band hunter-gatherers have often forgotten or ignored their evolutionary history as social mammals (yet which they have not evolved away from) as they have dismantled the EDN. Culture has trumped biology and evolution. Western traditions tend to misshape evolved human nature because of young-child undercare. They undermine the development of the Engagement ethic and instead explicitly emphasize emotionally detached Imagination and implicitly promote the Safety ethic. That is, implicit culture is promoted by the types of care we provide children. As a result, when Engagement is not nurtured with EDN-consistent care, the Safety ethic becomes the default implicit moral mindset, putting at risk health and well-being as well as the natural environment. The Safety ethic, conditioned during sensitive developmental periods, subliminally or through stress reactivity, impairs higher order reasoning capacities and compassionate response, keeping a focus on self-preservation. Thus, a degraded early life (lacking the EDN) leads to a diminishment of humanity.

Adults have choices about the cultures they design and the caregiving they provide. Following the evolved developmental niche will provide its recipients with health and well-being, the foundations for optimal human morality. Although an individual's moral perceptions and action capabilities can be handicapped by prior experience, the individual can author the community and the self toward greater virtue. A companionship culture will further promote mindful morality, the Engagement ethic extended with Imagination into communal imagination.

NOTES

1. Aristotle, *Nicomachean Ethics*, trans. Terence Irwin (Indianapolis: Hackett, 1985).
2. S. Fesmire, *John Dewey and the Moral Imagination: Pragmatism in Ethics* (Bloomington: Indiana University Press, 2003), 59.
3. J. Dewey, *Human Nature and Conduct* (New York: Henry Holt, 1922).
4. W. Koutstaal, *The Agile Mind* (New York: Oxford University Press, 2013).
5. D. Narvaez, "Integrative Ethical Education," in *Handbook of Moral Development*, ed. M. Killen and J. Smetana (Mahwah, NJ: Lawrence Erlbaum, 2006), 703–33; D. Narvaez, "Moral Complexity: The Fatal Attraction of Truthiness and the Importance of Mature Moral Functioning," *Perspectives on Psychological Science* 5, no. 2 (2010): 163–81.
6. A. N. Schore, *The Art and Science of Psychotherapy* (New York: Norton, 2013).
7. W. R. Trevathan, *Human Birth: An Evolutionary Perspective* (New York: Aldine de Gruyter, 2011).
8. Schore, *Psychotherapy*.
9. It should also be noted that very little human genetic material each of us carries is in competition with that of another human being (less than. 01 percent). In fact, 90–99 percent of the genetic material we each carry is not human but all the other organisms keeping us alive. Conservation and cooperation of genetic and extragenetic material is the vast majority of the evolutionary story. See R. Dunn, *The Wild Life of Our Bodies: Predators, Parasites, and Partners that Shape Who We Are Today* (New York: HarperCollins, 2011).
10. M. J. Meaney, "Maternal Care, Gene Expression, and the Transmission of Individual Differences in Stress Reactivity across Generations," *Annual Review of Neuroscience* 24 (2001): 1161–92; M. J. Meaney, "Epigenetics and the Biological Definition of Gene X Environment Interactions," *Child Development* 81, no. 1 (2010): 41–79.
11. D. Narvaez, J. Panksepp, A. Schore, and T. Gleason, eds., *Evolution, Early Experience and Human Development: From Research to Practice and Policy* (New York: Oxford University Press, 2013).
12. R. Lickliter and C. Harshaw, "Canalization and Malleability Reconsidered: The Developmental Basis of Phenotypic Stability and Variability," in *The Handbook of Developmental Science, Behavior,and Genetics*, ed. K. Hood, C. Halpern G. Greenberg, and R. Lerner (Hoboken, NJ: Wiley Blackwell, 2010), 504.
13. Lickliter and Harshaw, "Canalization," 499.
14. M. Konner, *The Evolution of Childhood* (Cambridge, MA: Belknap, 2010).
15. Narvaez, Panksepp, et al., *Evolution*.
16. B. S. Hewlett and M. E. Lamb, *Hunter-gatherer Childhoods: Evolutionary, Developmental and Cultural Perspectives* (New Brunswick, NJ: Aldine, 2005); M. Konner,

"Hunter-gatherer Infancy and Childhood: The !Kung and Others," in *Hunter-gatherer Childhoods: Evolutionary, Developmental and Cultural Perspectives*, ed. B. Hewlett and M. Lamb (New Brunswick, NJ: Aldine, 2005), 19–64.

17. A. Fogel, "Developmental Pathways in Close Relationships," *Child Development* 71, no. 5 (2000): 1150–51; A. Fogel and A. Branco, "Metacommunication as a Source of Indeterminism in Relationship Development," in *Dynamics and Indeterminism in Developmental and Social Processes*, ed. A. Fogel, M. P. Lyra, and J. Valsiner (Hillsdale, NJ: Lawrence Erlbaum, 1997), 65–92.

18. C. A. Evans and C. L. Porter, "The Emergence of Mother-Infant Co-regulation during the First Year: Links to Infants' Developmental Status and Attachment," *Infant Behavior and Development* 32, no. 2 (2009): 147–58.

19. I. Murdoch, *The Sovereignty of Good* (London: Routledge, 1989).

20. J. J. Gibson, *The Ecological Approach to Visual Perception* (Boston: Houghton Mifflin, 1979).

21. S. I. Greenspan and S. I. Shanker, *The First Idea* (Cambridge, MA: Da Capo, 2004).

22. C. Trevarthen, "Stepping Away from the Mirror: Pride and Shame in Adventures of Companionship—Reflections on the Nature and Emotional Needs of Infant Intersubjectivity," in *Attachment and Bonding: A New Synthesis*, ed. C. S. Carter, L. Ahnert, K. E. Grossmann, S. B. Hrdy, M. E. Lamb, S. W. Porges, and N. Sachser, 55–84 (Cambridge, MA: MIT Press, 2005).

23. A. Damasio, *The Feeling of What Happens* (London: Heineman, 1999).

24. C. M. Turnbull, *The Human Cycle* (New York: Simon and Schuster, 1983).

25. A. N. Schore, *Affect Regulation* (Hillsdale, NJ: Lawrence Erlbaum, 1994); Greenspan and Shanker, *The First Idea*.

26. J. Panksepp, *Affective Neuroscience: The Foundations of Human and Animal Emotions* (New York: Oxford University Press, 1998).

27. P. B. Baltes, U. Lindenberger, and U. M. Staudinger, "Life Span Theory in Developmental Psychology," in *Handbook of Child Psychology, Vol. 1: Theoretical Models of Human Development*, 6th ed., ed. W. Damon and R. M. Lerner (New York: Wiley, 2006), 569–664.

28. J. Karrass and T. A. Walden, "Effects of Nurturing and Non-nurturing Caregiving on Child Social Initiatives: An Experimental Investigation of Emotion as a Mediator of Social Behavior," *Social Development* 14, no. 4 (2005): 685–700.

29. G. Spangler and K. E. Grossmann, "Biobehavioral Organization in Securely and Insecurely Attached Infants," *Child Development* 64 (1993): 1439–50.

30. Schore, *Affect Regulation*.

31. A. N. Schore, *Affect Dysregulation & Disorders of the Self* (New York: Norton, 2003); A. Schore, *Affect Regulation and the Repair of the Self* (New York: Norton, 2003); L. A. Sroufe, *Emotional Development: The Organization of Emotional Life in the Early Years* (New York: Cambridge University Press, 1996).

32. G. Spangler, M. Schieche, U. Ilg, and U. Maier, "Maternal Sensitivity as an External Organizer for Biobehavioral Regulation in Infancy," *Developmental Psychobiology* 27, no. 7 (1994): 425–37.

33. M. A. Hofer, "Early Social Relationships as Regulators of Infant Physiology and Behavior," *Child Development* 58, no. 3 (1987): 633–47.

34. S. J. Lupien, B. S. McEwen, M. R. Gunnar, and C. Heim, "Effects of Stress throughout the Lifespan on the Brain, Behaviour and Cognition," *Nature Reviews Neuroscience* 10, no. (6 (2009): 434–45; S. W. Porges, *The Polyvagal Theory: Neurophysiologial Foundations of Emotions, Attachment, Communication, Self-Regulation* (New York: Norton., 2011).

35. Schore, *Psychotherapy*.
36. Greenspan and Shanker, *The First Idea*; Schore, *Psychotherapy*.
37. P. M. Crittenden, "Attachment and Psychopathology," in *Attachment Theory: Social, Developmental, and Clinical Perspectives*, ed. S. Goldberg, R. Muir, and J. Kerr (Hillsdale, NJ: Analytic Press, 1995), 367–406.
38. S. Konrath, W. J. Chopik, C. K. Hsing, and E. O'Brien, "Changes in Adult Attachment Styles in American College Students over Time: A Meta-Analysis, *Personality and Social Psychology Review,* published online, April 12, 2014.
39. D. Narvaez, *Neurobiology and the Development of Human Morality: Evolution, Culture and Wisdom* (New York: Norton, 2014).
40. G. Kochanska, "Mutually Responsive Orientation between Mothers and Their Young Children: A Context for the Early Development of Conscience," *Current Directions in Psychological Science* 11, no. 6 (2002): 191–95.
41. See Narvaez, Panksepp et al., *Evolution*, for details.
42. Meaney, "Maternal Care."
43. P. M. Cole, M. K. Michel, and L. O. Teti, "The Development of Emotion Regulation and Dysregulation: A Clinical Perspective," *Monographs of the Society for Research in Child Development* 59, nos. 2–3 (1994): 73–100; Schore, *Affect Regulation*.
44. D. Narvaez, Y. Cheng, J. Brooks, L. Wang, and T. Gleason. *Does Early Parenting Influence Moral Character Development and Flourishing?* (San Antonio: Association for Moral Education, October 2012); D. Narvaez, L. Wang, T. Gleason, A. Cheng, J. Lefever, and L. Deng. "The Evolved Developmental Niche and Sociomoral Outcomes in Chinese Three-year-olds," *European Journal of Developmental Psychology* 10, no. 2 (2013): 106–27.
45. D. Narvaez, T. Gleason, L. Wang, J. Brooks, J. Lefever, A. Cheng, and Centers for the Prevention of Child Neglect, "The Evolved Development Niche: Longitudinal Effects of Caregiving Practices on Early Childhood Psychosocial Development," *Early Childhood Research Quarterly* 28, no. 4 (2013): 759–73.
46. D. Narvaez, "Development and Socialization within an Evolutionary Context: Growing up to Become 'A Good and Useful Human Being,'" in *War, Peace and Human Nature: The Convergence of Evolutionary and Cultural Views*, ed. D. Fry (New York: Oxford University Press, 2013), 643–72.
47. For suggestions, see Narvaez, *Neurobiology*.
48. Narvaez, *Neurobiology*.
49. M. C. Nussbaum, "Non-relative Virtues: An Aristotelian Approach," in *Midwest Studies in Philosophy, Volume 13: Ethical Theory: Character and Virtue*, ed. P. A. French, T. E. Uehling Jr., and H. K. Wettstein (Notre Dame, IN: University of Notre Dame Press, 1988), 32–53.
50. Schore, *Psychotherapy*.
51. D. Narvaez, "Triune Ethics: The Neurobiological Roots of Our Multiple Moralities," *New Ideas in Psychology* 26 (2008): 95–119; D. Narvaez, "Triune Ethics Theory and Moral Personality," in *Personality, Identity and Character: Explorations in Moral Psychology*, ed. D. Narvaez and D. K. Lapsley (New York: Cambridge University Press, 2009), 136–58.
52. P. D. MacLean, *A Triune Concept of the Brain and Behavior* (Toronto: University of Toronto Press, 1973); P. D. MacLean *The Triune Brain in Evolution: Role in Paleocerebral Functions* (New York: Plenum, 1990).
53. G. Rowe, J. B. Hirsh, and A. K. Anderson, "Positive Affect Increases the Breadth of Attentional Selection," *Proceedings of the National Academy of Sciences* 104, no. 1 (2007): 383–88; T. W. Schmitz, E. De Rosa, and A. K. Anderson, "Opposing Influences

of Affective State Valence on Visual Cortical Encoding," *Journal of Neuroscience* 29 (2009): 7199–207.

54. D. Ariely and G. Loewenstein, "The Heat of the Moment: The Effect of Sexual Arousal on Sexual Decision Making," *Journal of Behavioral Decision Making* 19 (2006): 87–88; L. van Boven and G. Loewenstein, "Projection of Transient Drive States," *Personality and Social Psychology Bulletin* 29 (2003): 1159–68.

55. Panksepp, *Affective Neuroscience*.

56. A. F. T. Arnsten, "Stress Signaling Pathways that Impair Prefrontal Cortex Structure and Function," *Nature Reviews Neuroscience* 10, no. 6 (2009): 410–22.

57. Arnsten, "Stress Signaling."

58. C. Darwin, *The Descent of Man* (Princeton: Princeton University Press, 1871/1981).

59. S. P. Oliner, "Extraordinary Acts of Ordinary People: Faces of Heroism and Altruism," in *Altruistic Love: Science, Philosophy, and Religion in Dialogue*, ed. S. G. Post, L. G. Underwood, J. Schloss, and W. B. Hurlbut (New York: Oxford University Press, 2002), 200.

60. Greenspan and Shanker, *The First Idea*; Panksepp, *Affective Neuroscience*; Schore, *Affect Regulation*.

61. I. McGilchrist, *The Master and His Emissary: The Divided Brain and the Making of the Western World* (New Haven: Yale University Press, 2009).

62. J. R. Flynn, *What Is Intelligence?* (New York: Cambridge University Press, 2007).

63. C. L. Martin, *The Way of the Human Being* (New Haven: Yale University Press, 1999).

64. In other words, individuals show a unique personality signature that changes systematically according to the situation. For example, one person might always be outgoing in family situations but shy with strangers, whereas another person is outgoing only at beach parties.

65. K. Bailey, "Upshifting and Downshifting the Triune Brain: Roles in Individual and Social Pathology," in *The Evolutionary Neuroethology of Paul MacLean: Convergences and Frontiers*, ed. G. A. Cory Jr. and R. Gardner Jr. (Westport, CT: Praeger, 2002), 318–43.

66. P. D. Gluckman and M. A. Hanson, "Living with the Past: Evolution, Development, and Patterns of Disease," *Science* 305, no. 5691: 1733–36.

67. D. Narvaez, S. Hardy, and J. Brooks, *Triune Ethics: A Multidimensional Approach to Moral orientation* (unpublished manuscript).

68. D. Narvaez, A. Lawrence, A. Cheng, and L. Wang, *Evolved Developmental Niche History: The Effects of Early Experience on Adult Health and Morality* (unpublished manuscript).

69. R. M. Hogarth, *Educating Intuition* (Chicago: University of Chicago Press, 2001).

70. G. Gottlieb, "Experiential Canalization of Hehavioral Development Theory," *Developmental Psychology* 27 (1991): 4–13.

71. J. Gowdy, "Gatherer-hunters and the Mythology of the Market," in *The Cambridge Encyclopedia of Hunters and Gatherers*, ed. R. B. Lee and R. Daly (New York: Cambridge University Press, 1999), 391–98; T. Ingold, "On the Social Relations of the Hunter-gatherer Band," in *The Cambridge Encyclopedia of Hunters and Gatherers*, ed. R. B. Lee and R. Daly (New York: Cambridge University Press, 1999), 399–410.

72. D. P. Fry, *The Human Potential for Peace: An Anthropological Challenge to Assumptions about War and Violence* (New York: Oxford University Press, 2006); R. B. Lee and R. Daly, eds., *The Cambridge Encyclopedia of Hunters and Gatherers* (New York: Cambridge University Press, 2005).

73. Ingold, "On the Social Relations."

74. D. Bakan, *The Duality of Human Existence: Isolation and Communion in Western Man* (New York: Beacon, 1966).
75. Narvaez, "Development and Socialization."
76. Meaney, "Epigenetics."
77. Ingold, "On the Social Relations"; T. Ingold, *The Perception of the Environment: Essays on Livelihood, Dwelling and Skill* (New York: Routledge, 2011).
78. Narvaez, *Neurobiology*.
79. S. Tomkins, "Affect and the Psychology of Knowledge," in *Affect, Cognition, and Personality*, ed. S. S. Tomkins and C. E. Izard (New York: Springer, 1965).
80. M. Bazerman and A. Tennbrunsel, *Blindspots: Why We Fail to Do What's Right and What to Do about It* (Princeton: Princeton University Press, 2011).
81. See McGilchrist, *The Master*.
82. Turnbull, *The Human Cycle*.
83. Fry, *The Human Potential*.
84. Martin, *The Way*.
85. C. Merchant, *The Death of Nature: Women, Ecology and the Scientific Revolution* (New York: Harper & Row, 1983).
86. M. Buber, *I and Thou* (New York: Charles Scribner's Sons/ Continuum International, 1937/2004), 136.
87. See Narvaez, *Neurobiology*.
88. Hogarth, *Educating*.
89. H. Frankfurt, *The Importance of What We Care About: Philosophical Essays* (Cambridge: Cambridge University Press, 1988); Murdoch, *The Sovereignty*.

BIBLIOGRAPHY

Ariely, D., and G. Loewenstein. "The Heat of the Moment: The Effect of Sexual Arousal on Sexual Decision Making." *Journal of Behavioral Decision Making* 19 (2006): 87–98.
Aristotle. *Nicomachean Ethics*. Translated by Terence Irwin. Indianapolis: Hackett, 1985.
Arnsten, A. F. T. "Stress Signalling Pathways that Impair Prefrontal Cortex Structure and Function." *Nature Reviews Neuroscience* 10, no. 6 (2009): 410–22.
Bailey, K. "Upshifting and Downshifting the Triune Brain: Roles in Individual and Social Pathology." In *The Evolutionary Neuroethology of Paul MacLean: Convergences and Frontiers*, edited by G. A. Cory Jr., and R. Gardner Jr., 318–43. Westport, CT: Praeger, 2002.
Bakan, D. *The Duality of Human Existence: Isolation and Communion in Western Man*. New York: Beacon, 1966.
Baltes, P. B., U. Lindenberger, and U. M. Staudinger. "Life Span Theory in Developmental Psychology." In *Handbook of Child Psychology. Vol. 1: Theoretical Mmodels of Human Development*, 6th ed., edited by W. Damon and R. M. Lerner, 569–664. New York: Wiley, 2006.
Bazerman, M., and A. Tennbrunsel. *Blindspots: Why We Fail to Do What's Right and What to Do about It*. Princeton: Princeton University Press, 2011.
Buber, M. *I and Thou*. New York: Charles Scribner's Sons/Continuum International, 1937/2004.
Cole, P. M., M. K. Michel, and L. O. Teti. "The Development of Emotion Regulation and Dysregulation: A Clinical Perspective." *Monographs of the Society for Research in Child Development* 59, nos. 2–3 (1994): 73–100.

Crittenden, P. M. "Attachment and Psychopathology." In *Attachment Theory: Social, Developmental, and Clinical Perspectives*, edited by S. Goldberg, R. Muir, and J. Kerr, 367–406. Hillsdale, NJ: Analytic Press, 1995.

Damasio, A. *The Feeling of What Happens*. London: Heineman, 1999.

Darwin, C. *The Descent of Man*. Princeton: Princeton University Press, 1871/1981.

Dewey, J. *Human Nature and Conduct*. New York: Henry Holt, 1922.

Dunn, R. *The Wild Life of Our Bodies: Predators, Parasites, and Partners that Shape Who We Are Today*. New York: HarperCollins, 2011.

Evans, C. A., and C. L. Porter. "The Emergence of Mother-Infant Co-regulation during the First Year: Links to Infants' Developmental Status and Attachment." *Infant Behavior and Development* 32, no. 2 (2009): 147–58.

Fesmire, S. *John Dewey and the Moral Imagination: Pragmatism in Ethics*. Bloomington: Indiana University Press, 2003.

Flynn, J. R. *What Is Intelligence?* New York: Cambridge University Press, 2007.

Fogel, A. "Developmental Pathways in Close Relationships." *Child Development* 7, no. 5 (2000): 1150–51.

Fogel, A., and A. Branco. "Metacommunication as a Source of Indeterminism in Relationship Development." In *Dynamics and Indeterminism in Developmental and Social Processes*, edited by A. Fogel, M. P. Lyra, and J. Valsiner, 65–92. Hillsdale, NJ: Lawrence Erlbaum, 1997.

Frankfurt, H. *The Importance of What We Care About: Philosophical Essays*. Cambridge: Cambridge University Press, 1988.

Fry, D. P. *The Human Potential for Peace: An Anthropological Challenge to Assumptions about War and Violence*. New York: Oxford University Press, 2006.

Gibson, J. J. *The Ecological Approach to Visual Perception*. Boston: Houghton Mifflin, 1979.

Gluckman, P., and M. Hanson. *Fetal Matrix: Evolution, Development and Disease*. New York: Cambridge University Press, 2005.

Gluckman, P. D., and M. A. Hanson. "Living with the Past: Evolution, Development, and Patterns of Disease." *Science* 305, no. 5691 (2004): 1733–36.

Gottlieb, G. "Experiential Canalization of Behavioral Development Theory." *Developmental Psychology* 27 (1991): 4–13.

Gowdy, J. "Gatherer-hunters and the Mythology of the Market." In *The Cambridge Encyclopedia of Hunters and Gatherers*, edited by R. B. Lee and R. Daly, 391–98. New York: Cambridge University Press, 1999.

Greenspan, S. I., and S. I. Shanker. *The First Idea*. Cambridge, MA: Da Capo, 2004.

Hewlett, B. S., and M. E. Lamb. *Hunter-gatherer Childhoods: Evolutionary, Developmental and Cultural Perspectives*. New Brunswick, NJ: Aldine, 2005.

Hofer, M. A. "Early Social Relationships as Regulators of Infant Physiology and Behavior." *Child Development* 58, no. 3 (1987): 633–47.

Hogarth, R. M. *Educating Intuition*. Chicago: University of Chicago Press, 2001.

Ingold, T. "On the Social Relations of the Hunter-gatherer Band." In *The Cambridge Encyclopedia of Hunters and Gatherers*, edited by R. B. Lee and R. Daly, 399–410. New York: Cambridge University Press, 1999.

Ingold, T. *The Perception of the Environment: Essays on Livelihood, Dwelling and Skill*. New York: Routledge, 2011.

Karrass, J., and T. A. Walden. "Effects of Nurturing and Non-nurturing Caregiving on Child Social Initiatives: An Experimental Investigation of Emotion as a Mediator of Social Behavior." *Social Development* 14, no. 4 (2005): 685–700.

Kochanska, G. "Mutually Responsive Orientation between Mothers and Their Young Children: A Context for the Early Development of Conscience." *Current Directions in Psychological Science* 11, no. 6 (2002): 191–95.

Konner, M. *The Evolution of Childhood*. Cambridge, MA: Belknap, 2010.

Konner, M. "Hunter-gatherer Infancy and Childhood: The !Kung and Others." In *Hunter-gatherer Childhoods: Evolutionary,Developmental and Cultural Perspectives*, edited by B. Hewlett and M. Lamb, 19–64. New Brunswich, NJ: Aldine, 2005.

Konrath, S. H., W. J. Chopik, C. K. Hsing, and E. O'Brien. "Changes in Adult Attachment Styles in American College Students over Time: A Meta-Analysis. Personality and Social Psychology Review, online, April 12, 2014. doi: 10.1177/1088868314530516

Koutstaal, W. *The Agile Mind*. New York: Oxford University Press, 2013.

Lee, R. B., and R. Daly, eds. *The Cambridge Encyclopedia of Hunters and Gatherers*. New York: Cambridge University Press, 2005.

Lickliter, R., and C. Harshaw. "Canalization and Malleability Reconsidered: The Developmental Basis of Phenotypic Stability and Variability." In *The Handbook of Developmental Science, Behavior and Genetics*, edited by K. Hood, C. Halpern, G. Greenberg, and R. Lerner, 491–525. Hoboken, NJ: Wiley Blackwell, 2010.

Lupien, S. J., B. S. McEwen, M. R. Gunnar, and C. Heim. "Effects of Stress throughout the Lifespan on the Brain, Behaviour and Cognition." *Nature Reviews Neuroscience* 10, no. 6 (2009): 434–45.

MacLean, P. D. *The Triune Brain in Evolution: Role in Paleocerebral Functions*. New York: Plenum, 1990.

MacLean, P. D. *A Triune Concept of the Brain and Behavior*. Toronto: University of Toronto Press, 1973.

Martin, C. L. *The Way of the Human Being*. New Haven: Yale University Press, 1999.

McGilchrist, I. *The Master and His Emissary: The Divided Brain and the Making of the Western World*. New Haven: Yale University Press, 2009.

Meaney, M. "Epigenetics and the Biological Definition of Gene X Environment Interactions." *Child Development* 81, no. 1 (2010): 41–79.

Meaney, M. "Maternal Care, Gene Expression, and the Transmission of Individual Differences in Stress Reactivity across Generations." *Annual Review of Neuroscience* 24 (2001): 1161–92.

Merchant, C. *The Death of Nature: Women, Ecology and the Scientific Revolution*. New York: Harper & Row, 1983.

Murdoch, I. *The Sovereignty of Good*. London: Routledge, 1970/1989.

Narvaez, D. "Development and Socialization within an Evolutionary Context: Growing up to Become 'A Good and Useful Human Being.'" In *War, Peace and Human Nature: The convergence of Evolutionary and Cultural Views*, edited by D. Fry, 643–72. New York: Oxford University Press, 2013.

Narvaez, D. "Integrative Ethical Education." In *Handbook of Moral Development*, edited by M. Killen and J. Smetana, 703–33. Mahwah, NJ: Lawrence Erlbaum, 2006.

Narvaez, D. "Moral Complexity: The Fatal Attraction of Truthiness and the Importance of Mature Moral Functioning." *Perspectives on Psychological Science* 5, no. 2 (2010): 163–81.

Narvaez, D. "The Neo-Kohlbergian Tradition and Beyond: Schemas, Expertise and Character." In *Nebraska Symposium on Motivation, Vol. 51: Moral Motivation through the Lifespan*, edited by G. Carlo and C. Pope-Edwards, 119–63. Lincoln: University of Nebraska Press, 2005.

Narvaez, D. *Neurobiology and the Development of Human Morality: Evolution, Culture and Wisdom*. New York: Norton, 2014.

Narvaez, D. "Triune Ethics: The Neurobiological Roots of Our Multiple Moralities." *New Ideas in Psychology* 26 (2008): 95–119.

Narvaez, D. "Triune Ethics: Theory and Moral Personality." In *Personality, Identity and Character: Explorations in Moral Psychology*, edited by D. Narvaez and D. K. Lapsley, 136–58. New York: Cambridge University Press, 2009.

Narvaez, D., A. Cheng, J. Brooks, L. Wang, and T. Gleason. *Does Early Parenting Influence Moral Character Development and Flourishing?* San Antonio: Association for Moral Education, October 2012.

Narvaez, D., T. Gleason, L. Wang, J. Brooks, J. Lefever, A. Cheng, and Centers for the Prevention of Child Neglect. "The Evolved Development Niche: Longitudinal Effects of Caregiving Practices on Early Childhood Psychosocial Development." *Early Childhood Research Quarterly* 28, no. 4 (2013): 759–73. doi: 10.1016/j.ecresq.2013.07.003.

Narvaez, D., and S. Hardy, *Moral Mindsets: A Multidimensional Approach.* Unpublished manuscript.

Narvaez, D., A. Lawrence, A. Cheng, and L. Wang. *Evolved Developmental Niche History: The Effects of Early Experience on Adult Health and Morality.* Unpublished manuscript.

Narvaez, D., J. Panksepp, A. Schore, and T. Gleason, eds. *Evolution, Early Experience and Human Development: From Research to Practice and Policy.* New York: Oxford University Press, 2013.

Narvaez, D., L. Wang, T. Gleason, A. Cheng, J. Lefever, and L. Deng. "The Evolved Developmental Niche and Sociomoral Outcomes in Chinese Three-year-olds." *European Journal of Developmental Psychology* 10, no. 2 (2013): 106–27.

Nussbaum, M. C. "Non-relative Virtues: An Aristotelian Approach." In *Midwest Studies in Philosophy, Volume 13: Ethical Theory: Character and Virtue*, edited by P. A. French, T. E. Uehling Jr., and H. K. Wettstein, 32–53. Notre Dame, IN: University of Notre Dame Press, 1988.

Oliner, S. P. "Extraordinary Acts of Ordinary People: Faces of Heroism and Altruism." In *Altruistic Love: Science, Philosophy, and Religion in Dialogue*, edited by S. G. Post, L. G. Underwood, J. Schloss, and W. B. Hurlbut. New York: Oxford University Press, 2002.

Panksepp, J. *Affective Neuroscience: The Foundations of Human and Animal Emotions.* New York: Oxford University Press, 1998.

Porges, S. W. *The Polyvagal Theory: Neurophysiologial Foundations of Emotions, Attachment, Communication, Self-regulation.* New York: Norton, 2011.

Rowe, G., J. B. Hirsh, and A. K. Anderson. "Positive Affect Increases the Breadth of Attentional Selection." *Proceedings of the National Academy of Sciences* 104, no. 1 (2007): 383–88.

Schmitz, T. W., E. De Rosa, and A. K. Anderson. "Opposing Influences of Affective State Valence on Visual Cortical Encoding." *Journal of Neuroscience* 29 (2009): 7199–207.

Schore, A. N. *Affect Dysregulation and Disorders of the Self.* New York: Norton, 2003.

Schore, A. N. *Affect Regulation.* Hillsdale, NJ: Lawrence Erlbaum, 1994.

Schore, A. N. *Affect Regulation and the Repair of the Self.* New York: Norton, 2003.

Schore, A. N. *The Art and Science of Psychotherapy.* New York: Norton, 2013.

Spangler, G., and K. E. Grossmann. "Biobehavioral Organization in Securely and Insecurely Attached Infants." *Child Development* 64 (1993): 1439–50.

Spangler, G., M. Schieche, U. Ilg, and U. Maier. "Maternal Sensitivity as an External Organizer for Biobehavioral Regulation in Infancy." *Developmental Psychobiology* 27, no. 7 (1994): 425–37.

Sroufe, L. A. *Emotional Development: The Organization of Emotional Life in the Early Years.* New York: Cambridge University Press, 1996.

Tomkins, S. "Affect and the Psychology of Knowledge." In *Affect, Cognition, and Personality*, edited by S. S. Tomkins and C. E. Izard, 72–97. New York: Springer, 1965.

Trevathan, W. R. *Human Birth: An Evolutionary Perspective*. New York: Aldine de Gruyter, 2011.

Trevarthen, C. "Stepping Away from the Mirror: Pride and Shame in Adventures of Companionship—Reflections on the Nature and Emotional Needs of Infant Intersubjectivity." In *Attachment and Bonding: A New Synthesis*, edited by C. S. Carter, L. Ahnert, K. E. Grossmann, S. B. Hrdy, M. E. Lamb, S. W. Porges, and N. Sachser, 55–84 (Cambridge, MA: MIT Press, 2005).

Turnbull, C. M. *The Human Cycle*. New York: Simon and Schuster, 1983.

CHAPTER 11

༚

The Development of Virtue

A Perspective from Developmental Psychology

ROSS A. THOMPSON

Virtue ethics, by comparison with other normative theories, emphasizes the character of the actor. It recognizes, as most people intuitively do, that moral evaluations are not just act-based but are also person-centered judgments. How, then, are virtuous character traits cultivated in the person? One approach to this question is to focus, as many ancient and modern theories do, on the refinement of character, such as that which occurs through an individual's self-reflection, the growth of compassion, or other processes discussed in the chapters of this volume.

Another approach is to consider the cultivation of virtue in childhood. The nurturance of character, the capacity for admirable judgment and well-intentioned conduct, is a central childrearing goal of most parents. And ancient and modern theories have also had much to say about the cultivation of virtuous character in children. They have focused, for example, on teaching and nurturing mature judgment, constraining selfish motives through social control, liberating children's natural goodness, fostering the maturation of moral emotions, and other approaches. These views have been based partly on divergent views of human nature: Rousseau's romantic portrayal of the gentle savage, Locke's educable *tabula rasa* and Hobbes's nasty, brutish life of man have very different implications for the cultivation of virtuous character in children.

Further attention to the cultivation of virtue in children has much to offer virtue ethics. Understanding the developmental origins of virtuous character can contribute insight into how and when dispositions toward compassion, benevolence, and equity emerge to guide conduct. It can contribute understanding of how children become morally self-aware and how seeing oneself as a moral actor influences their behavior in different situations. Consideration of the growth of moral character draws attention to the formal and informal moral education that occurs in the context of children's everyday interactions with parents, other family members, and peers. Understanding the cultivation of virtue in children situates the growth of moral character in the context of developmental advances in thinking, emotion, social and moral understanding, the development of self and self-regulation, and the influence of close relationships.

Understanding the growth of moral character in children brings us necessarily to the study of human development. For several decades, developmental scientists have studied the growth of moral understanding and judgment, the origins of differences in moral conduct, and the emergence of moral emotions.[1] Although researchers have rarely focused explicitly on virtue, their studies address the development of empathy and compassion, judgments of fairness and justice, the motivation to help others, conscience, and other relevant issues. One legacy of this work is the widely known theory of Lawrence Kohlberg, which highlighted the development of principled moral judgment in middle childhood and adolescence and its associations with cognitive growth and moral conduct.[2]

Interestingly, however, some of the most vigorous contemporary research related to the development of moral character has focused on young children, whom Kohlberg and others of his time characterized as egocentric and reward-oriented. Newer research, however, offers a much different perspective, which can be summarized in this way. Far from being egocentric, early-developing conceptual and emotional skills provide the basis for a primitive "premoral sensibility" as young children become sensitive to others' feelings and goals, make morally relevant evaluations of others' conduct based on human needs, and become capable of cooperative and prosocial action. This early-emerging premoral sensibility is refined in early childhood as young children engage with adults on everyday issues of responsibility, fairness, and helping. It also contributes to the growth of a "moral self" by which moral appraisals become important to the child. Moral character and virtue are thus constructed from early cognitive-emotional primitives and are advanced by growing understanding of self and others and experience in close relationships. This new, post-Kohlbergian view suggests that the cultivation of virtue begins early in life as young children are developing a sense of who they are in relation to others.[3]

This newer view from current research faces several challenges. What kind of evidence can be adduced to characterize young children as socially and emotionally insightful in this way? Why do young children so often act in a self-centered manner if they are capable of understanding others' needs and feelings? And for present purposes, how is this research relevant to the development of virtue or the growth of moral character?

The purpose of this chapter is to describe recent studies relevant to the development of virtuous character in the early years and its implications for the psychology of moral development and for virtue theory. In the section that follows, I discuss research related to the early development of a "premoral sensibility," an intuitive sense of desirable conduct based on a rudimentary understanding of people's feelings and needs that, while not explicitly moral in nature, provides a psychological foundation for moral growth. Next, I consider research on early conscience that underscores the constructive characteristics of parent-child relationships that contribute to developing cooperation, compliance, concern for others, and other indicators of an internalized moral sense in early childhood. Conscience is also related to a developing "moral self" in young children, which is discussed in the section that follows. Next I consider some of the objections to this portrayal of early-developing aspects of moral character and some of the provisional responses of developmental scientists, before concluding with reflections on the relevance of these studies for the cultivation of virtue.

A comment on method. Studying children's development requires empirical methods with which many readers of this volume may be unacquainted, so I strive to explain relevant research procedures to convey how these conclusions are reached. This is especially important because the conceptual and emotional competencies of very young children can easily be overlooked or misunderstood: toddlers cannot tell us what they know, and often their behavior in everyday situations can lead to multiple intuitive interpretations. This has always been true. Darwin observed his young son, Doddy, and saw an emotionally sensitive, morally perceptive infant, while Piaget saw a budding scientist in his observations of his infant offspring (and Freud gleaned from his adult patients the childhood sexuality at the core of developing personality). The tools of contemporary developmental science do not eliminate observer bias in the interpretation of children's behavior, but scientific method constrains it according to the rules and procedures of empirical inquiry. At times, as readers shall see, these procedures involve carefully designed experiments to try to elucidate young children's understanding when competing influences are controlled; on other occasions, research procedures more closely resemble everyday interactions between children and other people. In most cases, the research described here is representative of a broader range of studies on which these conclusions are based, and I also strive to explain the limits of current understanding as well as what is known.

The most important benefit of these research procedures is that the findings they yield may (and often do) surprise us, and thus question our intuitions, as well as informing us. If the methods described in the discussion that follows seem far afield from the philosophical study of virtue or moral character, it is because we are trying to peer into the mind of a young child to discern the building blocks of mature moral competence. It is a challenging but worthwhile enterprise.

DEVELOPING AN EARLY PREMORAL SENSIBILITY

The challenge of trying to understand what preverbal children think about other people is illustrated by the following experiment.[4] An 18-month-old toddler sits on his mother's lap and faces an experimenter and some unusual objects on the table between them, just out of reach of the child. One at a time, the experimenter manipulates each object in a manner that suggests that he is trying but failing to accomplish what he intends to do. For example, he suspends a string of beads over a cup but fails three times to drop them into the cup, instead causing the beads to fall to the table outside the cup. On another occasion, he holds a small plastic dumbbell before the child and pulls on each end, but his hands slip off one end or the other and he fails to pull apart the dumbbell on each of three trials. After the trials, the object is then placed in front of the toddler. Toddlers immediately picked up each object, but they did not subsequently imitate the behavior of the experimenter. Instead, they performed the act that he was *intending*: pulling apart the dumbbell, or dropping the beads into the cup. Most young children did so easily and without hesitation. Indeed, they performed the intended action at a comparable rate to another group of toddlers who had watched the experimenter successfully demonstrate the target action. But whereas the latter group may have simply imitated what they observed the adult doing, the first group had to infer the adult's intended action.

Are 18-month-olds thus sensitive to the intentions underlying human behavior? A follow-up experiment probed further by repeating the "failed attempt" procedure with the dumbbell, but instead of human fingers slipping off the end of the dumbbell, this action was performed by a mechanical device consisting of metal arms with pincers while the experimenter sat motionless. Toddlers were captivated by the activity of the mechanical device trying, but failing, to pull apart the dumbbell. When the dumbbell was placed before them, however, few performed the intended action. In fact, children were six times more likely to pull apart the dumbbell after watching the human experimenter attempt to do so than after seeing the mechanical arms attempt this.[5] Toddlers appeared to make inferences of intentionality when appraising human, not mechanical, behavior.

Early Understanding of Other People

Other experiments have also demonstrated sensitivity to human goals and intentions in 12- and 18-month-olds,[6] and using different procedures, some researchers have found evidence for infants' rudimentary grasp of human intentions earlier in the first year.[7] When watching people, toddlers interpret their actions in terms of their inferred goals and intentions, and this seems to be an early aspect of social understanding.

Human goals and intentions are not the only psychological processes in others of which very young children become aware. Infants respond appropriately to the emotions they perceive in another's face and voice, responding positively to expressions of happiness and cautiously to angry or sad expressions, and they show concerned attention to the distress of another.[8] By 18 months, toddlers have become adept at using emotional expressions to infer another's desires: they seem to be aware that people are happy when they get what they want and sad when they do not get what they want, or when they get what they do not want. One experiment showed that on this basis, toddlers gave more broccoli to an experimenter who had previously exhibited pleasure when eating broccoli and disgust when eating crackers, even though the children themselves preferred eating the crackers and disliked the broccoli.[9]

Developmental theorists believe that these early achievements in social understanding derive, in part, from children's experience of themselves as agentic, intentional, emotional, desirous beings.[10] In other words, the salient feelings, strong desires, and goal-directed efforts that increasingly characterize their own behavior seem to also afford interpretive lenses for how young children construe the reasons other people act as they do. Watching a parent walk to the refrigerator every day, for example, 1-year-olds infer that the parent is doing so *in order to* open the door and get something inside—and indeed, this inference of goal-directed intentionality is confirmed on most occasions by the adult's subsequent behavior. In experimental situations such as those just described, toddlers demonstrate that they can derive similar inferences even from watching unfamiliar actions of an unacquainted adult.

In making these inferences, infants and toddlers are at a very early stage of constructing a theory-like understanding of how others' minds function. This conceptual task will continue throughout childhood and contribute to their social and emotional competence as children better understand different mental elements (e.g., mistaken thoughts, memories) and mental functions (e.g., biases, expectations, and other mentally constructive processes).[11] These early achievements illustrate the non-egocentric quality of early social understanding because young children exhibit no confusion of their own perspective, understanding, or intention with that of another. In addition, these achievements are important for present purposes in two ways. First, they provide a basis for the development of *shared intentionality* by which young children become capable of spontaneously entering into and sharing the intentions, goals and feelings of another, and behaving accordingly. Second, they provide a basis for young children's responses to people who help or hinder others' needs, desires, or goals.

Shared Intentionality

Consider again the "failed-attempt" study profiled earlier. The conclusion that toddlers could infer the experimenter's intended action was based on young children completing that action successfully. In a sense, these children readily accomplished for the adult the goal that he was trying but failing to achieve for himself. The conclusion that toddlers reveal their understanding of others' goals by helping to accomplish them was studied further in another experiment. In this study, researchers observed 18-month-olds in a variety of simple situations in which the child could provide assistance to an adult.[12] An adult was drawing with a marker and then accidentally dropped it on the floor near the child, for example, or mistakenly dropped a spoon he was using through a hole in a box where the child could reach it. In the experimental conditions, the adult signaled a need for help in several ways, such as by reaching toward the marker that had been accidentally dropped, or reaching for the spoon that had been lost through the hole, while looking perplexed. In the control conditions, the same outcome was reached through the deliberate action of the adult (e.g., intentionally tossing the marker on the floor; deliberately putting the spoon through the hole), and the adult did not try to retrieve the lost object or otherwise signal a need for assistance.

Toddlers were significantly more likely to help the adult in the experimental than in the control conditions—that is, when the adult's intentions were waylaid by accidental misfortune and the adult appeared to need assistance. Toddlers were never thanked or rewarded by the adult for helping, and another experiment showed that providing extrinsic rewards undermined the frequency of their assistance.[13] Toddlers instead seemed to be motivated to spontaneously assist an adult stranger independently of reward when they could discern the adult's goals and were capable of helping the adult achieve them.

These and related behaviors reflect, according to several researchers, a developing capacity for shared intentionality, in which young children participate in activity with another that involves shared psychological states, especially their goals and intentions.[14] Shared intentionality is believed to be a uniquely evolved human characteristic that enables people not only to understand another's intentions (which some primates can do) but also to share them and other psychological states. Why would children do so? One reason is that this enables young children to better understand other people, since participating in their intentionality is one way of comprehending what they are doing, how they are doing it, and why. It also contributes to social communication and understanding. Viewed broadly, shared intentionality provides the basis for language learning, collaborative problem solving, cooperative social games (including shared pretend play), and many forms of cultural learning. It is reflected in the simple helping acts observed in the experiments reported here, as well as how 1-year-olds point and gesture to prompt another person's attention or continue with a shared activity.[15] The development of shared intentionality means that much socially constructive conduct of this kind develops, not through external incentives and rewards, but as a natural accompaniment to children's understanding others' intentions and their spontaneous participation in the intentional orientation of another.[16]

Responding to the Actions of Others

What happens, then, when young children observe someone else helping or hindering another person from accomplishing his goals? If shared intentionality derives from young children understanding the goals of others' behavior, then they might also apply this understanding to their appraisal of the behavior of third parties. They might respond differently, in other words, when an actor assists in the achievement of someone's goals compared to another actor who impedes that achievement. This was explored in an experiment in which 18- to 24-month-olds sat on their mothers' laps while they watched two adults interacting with each other across a table.[17] In the experimental condition, one adult showed the child her necklace and belt, drew a picture, and created a clay sculpture, admiring the object in each case. The second adult watched her, and then took the necklace and belt for herself or destroyed the picture and sculpture. The victim did not respond to these actions and appeared emotionally impassive. In the control condition, the adult displayed the necklace and belt and created the drawing and sculpture as described above, but the second adult instead took a different necklace and belt that were within the child's view and destroyed a blank sheet of paper and a clay ball. Thus, the significant difference between these two conditions was whether one adult's goals (enjoying the objects she owned or made) were undermined by the actions of another adult.

Afterward, the second adult brought three balloons into the room, and gave one to the first adult and gave the remaining two balloons to the child. A minute later, the adult's balloon was "accidentally" released and it rose to the ceiling, out of reach, and the adult looked sad. Children's responses were observed for two minutes before the adult found a chair and retrieved her balloon. Young children who had previously witnessed that adult being victimized by another in the experimental condition were significantly more likely to help that person, such as by giving her a balloon, hugging or patting the adult, or making suggestions for retrieving the balloon, compared to children in the control condition who were much more likely to simply pay attention to the situation without doing anything else. Although there was nothing the toddlers could do to restore the victim's necklace, belt, or artwork, children appeared to respond more positively and helpfully to the victim when they had the opportunity to do so.

Similar results have been found in other studies using comparable procedures. Using a puppet stage, for example, another study found that 19- to 23-month-olds were more likely to provide rewards to a puppet who was previously observed as helpful to another puppet (i.e., retrieving a ball the other puppet had dropped), and to take rewards from a puppet who had previously acted harmfully to another (i.e., taking away the dropped ball).[18] It is noteworthy that in these situations, young children's helping could not directly address the consequences to the victim of what was done. Instead, children provided benefits to the victim, or denied them to the perpetrator.

At somewhat older ages, children respond similarly in more complex circumstances. In one study, 3 1/2-year-olds were told a story, with pictures, of two girls who were baking cookies, but in which one girl quit to play while the other finished the baking alone. When it was time to allocate the cookies, even though most children were initially inclined to distribute them equally, three-fourths of the children made a simple distributive justice judgment and indicated that the child who contributed more should receive more of the cookies.[19] In another study using doll play, children of the same age showed that they believed that a protagonist would prefer to give rewards to another doll who had previously helped her compared to one who had not. They also indicated that a protagonist would prefer to give rewards to a doll who had previously been generous to another doll compared to one who had not.[20]

Yet another study showed that 3-year-olds not only assist the victim of harm that they have witnessed but also protest the harmful act and tattle on the perpetrator.[21] And contrary to the traditional view that young children are consequentialist rather than focused on good or bad intentions, 3-year-olds also respond based on a person's intentions. In a study by Vaish, Carpenter, and Tomasello, 3-year-olds participated in an experimental condition involving an adult showing her necklace and belt, drawing a picture, and creating a clay sculpture as before.[22] In this situation, however, the second adult tried but failed to damage or destroy the objects and, after a moment, returned them to the table. When children were observed in a subsequent helping task, however, they were much less likely to provide assistance to the adult who had intended harm compared to another adult who had been present but uninvolved. Even though the "victim" had not really been harmed at all, 3-year-olds still denied benefits to the adult with apparently bad intentions.

Taken together, these studies suggest that from a very early age, young children are constructing a rudimentary understanding of why people act as they do—more specifically, the internal, mental states that account for people's actions. Along with their understanding that people act on the basis of their perceptions and sensations, they also become aware that intentions, desires, emotions, and goals are also significant motivators of human conduct.[23] This understanding further allows young children to participate in these internal experiences of others—to look where another person is glancing (shared attention), participate in another's happiness or distress (shared emotion or empathy), and help achieve another person's goals.

Shared intentionality has at least two important implications for the development of a premoral sensibility. First, young children are capable of cooperative, prosocial behavior not because of external incentives but, rather, as a spontaneous result of understanding and sharing others' goals, and knowing how to assist in their achievement. The motivation for doing so does not necessarily derive from its moral value as much as from the intrinsic rewards of social participation and understanding, but it can become enlisted into a moral value system, such as when parents explicitly associate helpful acts with consideration for others. Second, young children appraise the behavior of other people in terms of its effects on others' goals, and they reward those who assist, punish those who hinder, and offer beneficence to those who were previously victimized by a hinderer. The motivation for children's responses in these contexts is not necessarily explicitly moral, but there are suggestions in these findings of children's approval of helpers and disapproval of hinderers.

Thus from early in life, young children are developing an intuitive and non-egocentric sense of right or desirable conduct based on its consequences for others' goals and desires, and which may provide the basis for judgments of fairness, equity, and even simple justice.[24] There are many unanswered questions remaining to be studied, however. Some relate to furthering this developmental account, and better understanding whether and how this premoral sensibility becomes associated with later forms of moral understanding and judgment, as well as the development of virtue. Other questions concern the wide individual variability in young children's responses to these experimental tasks and understanding the origins of these differences (in the next section, I discuss some of these influences in the context of conscience development). Other questions require elucidating the reasons for young children's differential responding to helpers, hinderers, and victims in these experimental procedures, and the intuitive judgments they entail. Several research groups are currently at work on these tasks.

Our research group is one of them. In a recent study, we observed 18-month-olds in the kinds of helping situations described above involving dropped markers and spoons. We also observed these children in more demanding kinds of tasks, such as deciding whether to share snack crackers or toys with an adult experimenter who had none, or whether to try to repair the adult's favorite toy that had broken and this made her sad.[25] We found that even at this early age, toddlers were consistent in their responses, with one group providing assistance in each kind of situation and another group responding minimally each time. Furthermore, two characteristics of the child's interaction with the mother, observed independently, were associated with whether children were consistent helpers or not. First, when mothers made frequent references to the thoughts, emotions, and desires of story characters during a book-reading task, their children were more likely to assist the adult, perhaps because these mental state references help the young child understand the feelings and thoughts of others. Second, mothers who were more sensitively responsive to the child's interests and intentions during a free-play observation had children who were more likely to assist the adult. Viewed from the perspective of shared intentionality, it is possible that having experienced the mother entering helpfully into their own intentional states, these children generalized this understanding to their interactions with other people.

Emotion Understanding

Shared intentionality is manifested in joint activities based on shared attention, goals, and intentions. It is also apparent in shared emotions. Indeed, some researchers believe that a very early capacity for resonant or empathic responding to another's distress provides a foundation for more complex forms of shared emotion, such as compassion, and their association with helping and caring at later ages.[26] As earlier noted, young children understand that emotions are linked to the satisfaction or frustration of goals and desires, and thus by reading another's emotional expressions one gains insight into other mental states. Another's distress, sadness, or anger also increases the salience of the causes of these emotions and the actions that might alleviate them. For these reasons, emotion understanding is part of an early premoral sensibility because of how emotions are associated with situations related to helping or hindering another's goals and, more generally, the well-being of other people. The connection of emotion understanding to others' needs and interests and the sharing of that emotion may also contribute, for some children, to the development of virtuous qualities such as compassion and respect for others.

Emotion understanding is part of an early premoral sensibility also because of how parents enlist emotion understanding in early values socialization. Mothers justify their enforcement of moral rules with their 2- and 3-year-old children on the basis of people's needs and welfare, but they justify social conventional rules instead in terms of social order and regulation.[27] Consequently, by age 3 or 4, young children view moral violations as more serious, and moral rules as irrevocable (i.e., valid regardless of social guidelines), justifying their judgments in terms of unfairness and the harm to others entailed in moral violations.[28] The needs of others and the feelings associated with them early distinguish their conceptions of moral values from other kinds of social rules.

Despite their skills in interpreting others' emotions, however, the sight and sound of another person in distress is a conceptually and motivationally complex event for a young child. Understanding the causes of another person's distress, whether those causes have implications for oneself, and whether—and how—that person's upset can be allayed are cognitively challenging considerations for young children. Because in most circumstances they may be incapable of acting in a helpful manner or unaware of how to do so, even if they are motivated sympathetically to help, many young children can be observed in a demeanor of "concerned attention" in response to a distressed person. Acting helpfully in everyday situations requires, therefore, the development of a sympathetic response to another's distress and the behavioral competence to intervene helpfully, and these capacities develop according to different timelines in the early years.

CONSCIENCE DEVELOPMENT

The term *conscience* has a long and complex heritage in philosophy and religious traditions. As the term has recently been appropriated by psychologists, it refers to the developmental processes by which young children construct and act consistently with internal, generalizable standards of conduct.[29] The capacity for internalized moral conduct has traditionally been viewed as an achievement of late childhood or adolescence, but contemporary research on conscience development has focused on early childhood as the period when the foundations of conscience are established. Developmental researchers have focused on the growth of conscience in early childhood and the influences associated with individual differences in conscience development, which may be viewed as foreshadowing the development of moral character. Consistent with the preceding discussion, conscience is based on the premoral sensibility that develops in the early years, and is influenced by the young child's temperamental characteristics and developing capacities for self-regulation. Most important, researchers have found that the quality of parent-child relationships is central to the development of conscience and the growth of individual differences in moral conduct that may be associated with virtuous character.

According to one prominent developmental theory by Grazyna Kochanska, early conscience development is founded on the growth of a mutually responsive orientation between parent and child that sensitizes the young child to the reciprocal obligations of close relationships.[30] Young children are accustomed to others caring for them. But as they become more competent, children are increasingly expected to help with household tasks, cooperate with family members, comply with adult requests, accommodate the needs and desires of others, resist impulses to behave in disapproved ways, and act in a socially appropriate manner. Most young children are capable of doing so—at least some of the time—owing to their sensitivity to others' goals and needs, together with the rewards derived from compliant conduct and the sanctions associated with misbehavior. Kochanska argues that a further incentive is the quality of the parent-child relationship.[31] Parental warmth and sensitive responsiveness elicit complementary responses in young children, who are thus motivated to cooperate and respond constructively to parental requests to maintain this relational harmony. Such a view is consistent with the research findings discussed earlier concerning maternal sensitivity and toddlers' prosocial responding in the context of shared intentionality. These positive relational incentives also motivate children to adopt parental values and seek to behave accordingly. Such a view is consistent with the ideas of contemporary attachment theory, but contrasts with traditional conceptualizations of early moral compliance motivated by fear of punishment or parental love withdrawal.[32]

How is conscience measured in young children? As early as age 2 1/2, children are observed at home or in laboratory playrooms as their mothers seek to elicit their cooperation either when mother is present (e.g., asking the child to put away toys the child had been playing with) or absent (e.g., prohibiting the child from touching attractive toys on a shelf, and then leaving the room).[33] Children's willing cooperation and compliance in maternal absence are viewed as reflecting conscience development at this early age. For older children, conscience assessments include children's rule-compliant behavior when there are opportunities and incentives to cheat, responses to hypothetical stories involving moral dilemmas, emotional responses to apparent mishaps (e.g., believing that the child had broken a toy that was rigged to fall apart), sympathetic concern for another's distress, and children's morally relevant self-perceptions ("moral self").[34] These different assessments are intended to resemble everyday age-appropriate circumstances of cooperation, concern for others, and obedience, and although they are early oriented toward young children's compliance, these assessments increasingly encompass the more complex cognitive, emotional, and self-referential dimensions of moral conduct at older ages.

Children's conscience-related behavior develops significantly with age, as would be expected. Young children better understand behavioral standards and become more cooperative and compliant with increasing age.[35] Individual differences on measures of early conscience tend to remain consistent during this time: toddlers who are more enthusiastically cooperative and compliant become older preschoolers who are less likely to cheat on difficult games, provide socially constructive responses to hypothetical moral dilemmas, and describe themselves as children who try to do the right thing.[36] This consistency over time could result from the growth of characteristics related to moral dispositions or virtuous character, the influence of hereditary temperamental qualities related to conscience, and/or the continuing quality of the parent-child relationship, and there is research evidence that all three processes are influential.[37] There is a strong association, for example, between children's conscience and measures of the positive, mutual responsiveness between child and mother that are derived from independent observations of their shared activity.[38] This association is confirmed longitudinally when positive mutuality is observed when children are toddlers and conscience is assessed as they enter school several years later.[39] Children's temperamental characteristics are also influential, especially as they interact with the quality of the parent-child relationship to influence conscience development. One study showed that children with a hereditary vulnerability to self-regulatory problems were lower on conscience at age 5 1/2 when maternal care was poorly responsive, but children with the same hereditary vulnerability were more advanced in conscience development in the context of responsive maternal care.[40]

Further research has focused on other relational influences on early conscience. What happens, for example, when young children misbehave? In our lab, we recorded the conversations of mothers with their 2 1/2-year-old children during conflict episodes in the lab and at home, and subsequently measured the child's conscience development at age 3.[41] Mothers who more frequently discussed people's feelings and who tried to resolve conflict by explaining and justifying their requests had children who were more advanced on measures of conscience six months later. Even though maternal references to rules and the consequences of breaking them were also coded in these conversations, they were unrelated to conscience development. These findings were substantively replicated in another study that focused on the conversations of mothers with their 4-year-olds about past instances of the child's good or bad behavior.[42] Maternal comments about people's feelings, not to rules and the consequences of breaking them, were associated with conscience development. In another study, 2- to 3-year-old children whose mothers used reasoning and conveyed humanistic concerns when resolving conflict with them were more advanced in measures of moral understanding at kindergarten and first grade.[43] Consistently with young children's developing comprehension of moral standards in terms of human needs and welfare, therefore, mothers who discuss misbehavior in terms of the emotional consequences of morally relevant conduct are more likely to foster conscience development than those who focus on judgments of rule-oriented compliance.[44]

Although the behavioral manifestations of conscience in young children provide only a glance into the development of moral character or virtue, the relational influences highlighted by this work are potentially important. These studies contribute to the view that the positive incentives for moral growth provided in parent-child relationships may be more important than the negative incentives afforded by punishment and the threat of love withdrawal. In a manner also found to be true of older children and adolescents, young children are sensitized to issues of fairness, responsibility, and care through parent-child relationships that exemplify mutual respect and cooperation and through parent-child conversations that highlight the human consequences of the child's conduct.[45]

The importance of parent-child relationships and emotion sensitivity extends also to circumstances of voluntary assistance. In another study from our lab, Thompson and Winer observed 4-year-olds in a series of age-appropriate helping, sharing, and repair/assistance tasks, and also elicited mother-child conversations about past instances in which the child was helpful or not helpful to another person.[46] As in our earlier research, these 4-year-olds showed considerable consistency in their assistance to the experimenter across the different tasks. Mothers whose children were most prosocial more often discussed people's emotions and made more frequent evaluative comments about the child's behavior in conversation. As in the studies of conscience, maternal discussion of rules and rule-based justifications for helping others was never associated with preschoolers' actual helping in the lab. These findings, although preliminary, suggest that sensitivity to people's feelings, especially in the context of supportive parent-child relationships, is important not only to children's compliance with adult requests but also to their motivation to offer voluntary assistance.

The importance of conversational catalysts to the development of moral understanding is not limited to early childhood. Although the early years may be formative, Lapsley and Narvaez have argued that the quality of parent-child discourse may also be important at later ages, particularly as parents incorporate moral evaluations, causal attributions, and behavioral expectations into their conversations with older children about the child's experiences.[47] As a consequence, they argue, some children develop easily primed and readily activated nonconscious moral schemas that cause them to appraise everyday situations in morally relevant ways and that guide their conduct. This gets us closer to the development of moral character and the cultivation of virtue, especially as these moral appraisals extend to volitional moral conduct (such as helping and sharing), in addition to the obligatory moral standards that are more often the focus of early moral socialization. Our research suggests that both aspects of moral conduct begin to develop early and are influenced by the quality of parent-child relationships and conversation.

In sum, research in this area suggests that positive moral dispositions develop in the context of responsive relationships of mutuality in the family, and are enhanced in parent-child conversations that highlight the feelings and needs of others, rather than rule-oriented compliance. Unanswered questions in this field remain important, however. Some concern the nature of "conscience" and its relevance to the development of moral character. Although behaving consistently with internalized values is a developmentally important accomplishment, do young children with strong conscience development become conventional, compliant adolescents and adults, or does conscience provide a foundation for deeper moral judgment, flexibility, and even courage? The relevant longitudinal studies remain to be done. Moreover, little is known of how assessments of conscience are associated with young children's behavior with people outside the family, such as peers and other adults.[48] Extending research in this area to other contexts and partners will enable researchers to better understand the generality and robustness of the characteristics observed primarily with mothers in these studies.

DEVELOPMENT OF THE "MORAL SELF"

Moral identity, as it is studied by psychologists, can be defined as the construction of a sense of self around moral values.[49] Adults for whom moral concerns are central to identity and self-understanding are more likely to feel an obligation to act consistently with moral values, even though many other influences also affect conduct in specific situations.[50] Little is known, however, about the early development of moral identity and how moral values become important to self-understanding and the development of virtuous character.

Developmental researchers have begun to explore the growth of the "moral self" in early childhood. The moral self can be defined as the child's view of himself or herself as a "good" person who tries to do the right thing, as defined by parental expectations and internal moral values.[51] Developmental scientists who study young children's self-understanding must do so using unconventional approaches because preschoolers lack the linguistic skills to convey clearly, in response to direct questions, their sense of themselves according to abstract personality qualities or moral virtues. They can, however, respond competently to simpler kinds of inquiries. One such procedure invites children to interact with a pair of puppets in a theatre who explain that they want to find out about "kids your age" and, to do so, they will describe themselves and the child can then describe himself or herself. The two puppets then proceed to describe themselves in terms of opposite characteristics before asking the child to respond. For example, one puppet says, "I like to be with other people" and the other responds "I like to be by myself," and then the child is asked what he or she is like. Several research groups have found that when young children respond in this way to a carefully designed range of bipolar descriptors designed to assess specific personality characteristics, children provide consistent judgments that seem to reflect an underlying, coherent representation of their internal qualities.[52] Preschoolers' self-descriptions are internally consistent, for example, and are similar to parent and teacher descriptions of the child. These studies show that personality qualities like positive or negative mood, timidity, aggressiveness, and agreeableness emerge as salient aspects of early self-awareness, together with a more generally positive or negative self-concept.

Kochanska and colleagues have adapted this procedure to examine 5-year-olds' moral selves by presenting children with puppets whose self-descriptions anchor opposite ends of a series of moral characteristics (e.g., "When I break something, I try to hide it so no one finds out" and "When I break something, I tell someone about it right away"). The characteristics assessed in this interview include children's self-awareness of behaviors associated with moral conduct (e.g., apology; spontaneously confessing wrongdoing; attempting reparation), moral emotions (e.g., empathy, discomfort after wrongdoing), moral motivation (e.g., internalized conduct), and other characteristics.[53] In a longitudinal study, these researchers found that measures of conscience development when children were age 2 to 4 1/2 were significantly associated with the "moral self" at age 5 1/2 which, in turn, predicted school-age measures of competent conduct.[54] More specifically, preschoolers who were more cooperative and compliant with the parent described themselves at age 5 1/2 as children who try to do the right thing, and these children were rated by parents and teachers as showing more social-emotionally competent behavior at age 6 1/2. The latter included broad assessments of the child's school engagement, peer acceptance, emotional health, and prosocial behavior by teachers and parents. These findings suggest, therefore, the emergence of relatively consistent individual traits that might be associated with the growth of moral character or virtuous qualities.

Developmental researchers who use these puppet interview procedures do not assume that young children comprehend their personality or moral qualities with the conceptual richness of an adult. But these findings suggest that preschoolers have a richer sense of self than has been traditionally assumed. Young children also vary in the extent to which being a "good boy" or "good girl" is important to them, and this is associated with independent measures of conscience development and later behavior. These findings are consistent with other research that underscores how much developing self-awareness is colored by parental responses to behavior of young children. Children begin to exhibit behaviors reflecting self-evaluative emotions like pride, shame, and guilt late in the second year, and these emotions most often appear in achievement or moral contexts in which parents applaud children's desirable behavior and are critical of undesirable conduct.[55]

Parents' evaluative comments (e.g., "that was not a good thing to do," "you were nice to help in that way") occur frequently in discussions of morally relevant behavior, and constitute an important influence on how young children evaluate their own conduct.[56] In light of this, we might expect that young children begin to perceive themselves in ways relevant to their compliance with parental expectations as they are also developing a broader and morally relevant understanding of themselves as persons.

Much less is known, however, about the characteristics of parent-child interaction that contribute to differences in the "moral self" in young children—that is, why some children perceive themselves as striving to be cooperative, make amends, feel badly after misbehavior, while other children do not. Moreover, the longitudinal studies have not yet been conducted that would enable researchers to associate the developing moral self in preschoolers with moral identity at older ages. Thus there remain important questions requiring further study.

CULTIVATING VIRTUE?

Crafting a theoretical argument from research findings is necessarily limited by the available evidence, and readers may feel that they are faced with a glass half empty/glass half full dilemma from the preceding discussion. On one hand, there is much that is *not* known about the development of virtuous character in early childhood, particularly the relevance of early achievements in moral awareness to more mature forms of judgment, identity, and conduct. Whereas research in this area has focused on the developmentally relevant challenges of early childhood—becoming sensitive to the needs of other people, learning how to respond appropriately to those needs, and beginning to develop an internalized compass concerning personal conduct—little is known of how these relate to the later development of moral character or to virtuous qualities of the person. Moreover, the reliance of researchers on carefully designed laboratory procedures highlights the need for further inquiry into young children's conduct in everyday circumstances with peers and adults other than mother. To a developmental scientist, this constitutes an exciting research agenda, but to others it identifies glaring gaps in current knowledge.

On the other hand, what *is* known about the early development of moral awareness is noteworthy. By contrast with traditional portrayals of the egocentric, self-interested young child, it is apparent that early conceptual achievements afford children considerable sensitivity to the internal experiences of others, and this influences children's conduct and their evaluations of the behavior of others. This premoral sensibility is refined in parent-child interaction that affords an integration of the child's developing conception of desirable conduct in relation to others' goals and feelings with parental values and their justification in relation to others' well-being. Parent-child interaction is also a forum for children's developing self-awareness as moral actors. Virtue has developmental origins, therefore, in an intuitive premoral sensibility that emerges from early psychological understanding and its cultivation in the context of a parent-child relationship that builds on it—particularly positive relational experiences that afford mutual responsiveness, respect, and understanding. Any developmental account that overlooks these early influences risks misunderstanding the origins of moral awareness and of formative influences on moral character.

It is important to clarify what this argument does *not* claim. First, this is not an argument that morality is innate, although other developmental scientists have proposed this.[57] Nativist arguments are problematic in psychology because they are easy to formulate and difficult to validate. The view that a premoral sensibility builds on a network of early-developing cognitive-emotional primitives does not require assumptions about evolutionary preparedness or natural instincts relevant to morality. Second, this argument does not claim that all or even the most important constituents of moral character emerge in early childhood. It seems undeniable that significant aspects of moral character and virtue develop with subsequent growth in personality, self-regulation, cognitive complexity, self-awareness, and relational experience. This argument claims, rather, that instead of perceiving early childhood as irrelevant to the development of moral character or affording obstacles (such as egocentric thinking) to virtuous conduct, it should instead be regarded as a developmental foundation to the humanistic, cooperative, relational morality that flourishes at later ages.

A more basic question concerns the whether the kinds of behaviors studied in young children are relevant to morality at all. A prominent psychologist who studies moral character, Augusto Blasi, has raised this question.[58] Blasi has identified criteria of the "common everyday understanding" of moral behavior that require that genuinely moral actions are intentional, that they are informed by moral motives, and that "the agent must want it because it is morally good." These criteria cause him to disregard the kinds of behavior studied in young children as genuinely moral, relegating the advent of truly moral conduct to middle childhood. His analysis raises further questions, of course, about whether moral motives must be explicitly recognized by the actor or can be implicitly influential, and what cognitive prerequisites are required to fulfill the criteria of genuinely moral conduct. In any case, whether the capabilities of young children are defined as moral or premoral in nature, it seems undeniable that a serious developmental analysis requires understanding how complex competencies at any age emerge from earlier skills that are progenitors to those that come later.

A more searching question concerns the inconsistency between young children's behavior and the capabilities revealed in these experimental studies. If toddlers and preschoolers exhibit such sensitivity to the feelings, goals, and desires of other people, for example, why do their actions in everyday circumstances often seem so self-centered and oblivious to the interests of others? A toddler who shows concerned attention to another child in distress, for instance, may subsequently walk away, laugh, or seek comfort for himself rather than assisting the other child. Advances in developmental neuroscience may provide some insight into this incongruity. Research on brain development has shown that neurobiological regions related to self-regulation are among the slowest to mature.[59] The neurobiological development of self-regulatory capacities, such as those governing impulse control, attentional focusing, cognitive flexibility, and emotional self-control, begins early but has an extended maturational course, lasting through adolescence into early adulthood.[60] Because of this, the behavior of young children is often characterized by impulsivity (such as taking an attractive toy from another's grasp), distractibility (such as turning to another activity after watching a peer hurt herself), cognitive inflexibility (such as becoming mentally fixed on a desired activity despite the needs of another), and limited emotional self-regulation—each of which can make young children appear very egocentric.

One reason, therefore, that young children often behave inconsistently with the competencies revealed in experimental studies is that self-regulation mediates between knowing and doing. Young children may be aware of another person's goals and feelings, but acting appropriately on this knowledge requires self-regulatory competencies that are neurobiologically very immature, and need many years for their full development. Carefully designed experimental studies control many of the distractions and competing influences that otherwise might undermine the ability of young children to enact what they know about others' goals, intentions, desires, feelings, and needs. In everyday experience, however, these competing influences often overwhelm their limited self-regulatory skills and undermine performance. Stated simply, what appears to be self-centered conduct may actually be self-regulatory limitations imposed by a slowly maturing brain.[61]

To be sure, the behavior of young children is better characterized as inconsistent than as unregulated. Episodes of generosity and cooperation alternate with periods of impulsivity and self-centeredness in the home as well as the lab. This is one of the reasons why early childhood has typically been disregarded in psychological research on moral development and philosophical reflections on the cultivation of virtue. How can one talk about virtue cultivated when it is so little enacted? But this conundrum may help explain why relational influences are so important to the early growth of conscience and moral awareness. Sensitivity and mutual responsiveness in early parent-child relationships may be important because in these contexts, adults can support young children's limited self-regulatory competencies and enlist them in positive conduct as the child's brain is slowly maturing to support independent self-control. By contrast, a parental emphasis on rule-oriented compliance requires the capacities for independent self-control that young children lack. In the end, virtue may be cultivated even when it is not reliably enacted because its developmental foundations are being established in a premoral sensibility, built on children's understanding of other people, and the responsive relationships that provide support for positive behavior and the development of a moral self.

CONCLUSION

What is the place of early childhood development in moral psychology and virtue ethics? The topics discussed in this review of research on young children—empathy and compassion, emotion understanding of others, moral self-awareness, fairness and equity, helping and benevolence—suggest that it should have an important place in developmental analysis. A conceptual foundation for the growth of moral character emerges in young children's understanding of other people and their relevance to the self, and the quality of early parent-child relationships enlists that understanding into a broader network of values. The problem is that in the past, in both psychology and philosophy, early childhood has been portrayed in extremes—the young child is either the untamed, egocentric beast in need of civilizing, or the morally perceptive altruist in need of liberation. Developmental science suggests that neither depiction is accurate. Rather, virtue is cultivated as children's intuitive premoral sensibility is nurtured in the context of relationships that exemplify, as well as discuss, responsiveness and support.

Unfortunately, in far too many parts of the world, young children are not growing up in such relationally supportive contexts, and their representations of the characteristics of other people and their relevance to the self do not reliably support the growth of virtuous conduct. Thus a concern with early childhood has practical as well as theoretical importance, and is relevant to public policy as well as to moral psychology and philosophical ethics. Early experiences of children growing up in conditions of adversity and stress merit attention for what these experiences mean for the character that they are developing.[62]

NOTES

1. For a review, see Melanie Killen and Judith Smetana, eds., *Handbook of Moral Development*, 2nd. ed. (New York: Taylor & Francis, 2013).
2. Lawrence Kohlberg, "Stage and Sequence: The Cognitive Developmental Approach to Socialization," in *Handbook of Socialization Theory and Research*, ed. D. Goslin (New York: Rand McNally, 1969), 347–480.
3. Ross A. Thompson, "Whither the Preconventional Child? Toward a Life-span Moral Development Theory," *Child Development Perspectives* 6, no. 4 (2013): 423–29.
4. Andrew N. Meltzoff, "Understanding the Intentions of Others: Re-enactment of Intended Acts by 18-month-old Children," *Developmental Psychology* 31, no. 5 (1995): 838–50.
5. Meltzoff, "Understanding the Intentions."
6. Malinda Carpenter, Josep Call, and Michael Tomasello, "Twelve- and 18-month-olds Copy Actions in Terms of Goals," *Developmental Science* 8, no. 1 (2005): F13–F20.
7. Amanda Woodward, "Infants' Grasp of Others' Intentions," *Current Directions in Psychological Science* 18, no. 1 (2009): 53–57.
8. Ross A. Thompson and Kristin Lagattuta, "Feeling and Understanding: Early Emotional Development," in *The Blackwell Handbook of Early Childhood Development*, ed. Kathleen McCartney and Deborah Phillips (Oxford: Blackwell, 2006), 317–37.
9. Betty M. Repacholi and Alison Gopnik, "Reasoning about Desires: Evidence from 14- and 18-month-olds," *Developmental Psychology* 33, no. 1 (1997): 12–21.
10. Meltzoff, "Understanding the Intentions"; Woodward, "Infants."
11. Henry M. Wellman, "Developing a Theory of Mind," in *The Wiley-Blackwell Handbook of Childhood Cognitive Development*, 2nd ed., ed. Usha Goswami (Oxford: Wiley-Blackwell, 2011), 258–84.
12. Felix Warneken, Frances Chen, and Michael Tomasello, "Cooperative Activities in Young Children and Chimpanzees," *Child Development* 77, no. 3 (2006): 640–63.
13. Felix Warneken and Michael Tomasello, "Extrinsic Rewards Undermine Altruistic Tendencies in 20-month-olds," *Developmental Psychology* 44, no. 6 (2008): 1785–88.
14. Michael Tomasello, Malinda Carpenter, Josep Call, Tanya Behne, and Henrike Moll, "Understanding and Sharing Intentions: The Origins of Cultural Cognition," *Behavioral and Brain Sciences* 28, no. 5 (2005): 675–735.
15. Warneken, Chen, and Tomasello, "Cooperative Activities."
16. Ross A. Thompson and Emily K. Newton, "Baby Altruists? Examining the Complexity of Prosocial Motivation in Young Children," *Infancy* 18, no. 1 (2013): 120–33.
17. Amrisha Vaish, Malinda Carpenter, and Michael Tomasello, "Sympathy through Affective Perspective Taking and Its Relation to Prosocial Behavior in Toddlers," *Developmental Psychology* 45, no. 2 (2009): 534–43.

18. J. Kiley Hamlin, Karen Wynn, Paul Bloom, and Neha Mahajan, "How Infants and Toddlers React to Antisocial Others," *Proceedings of the National Academy of Sciences* 108, no. 50 (2011): 11931–36.

19. Nicholas Baumard, Olivier Mascaro, and Coralie Chevallier, "Preschoolers Are Able to Take Merit into Account When Distributing Goods," *Developmental Psychology* 48, no. 2 (2012): 492–98.

20. Kristina R. Olson and Elizabeth S. Spelke, "Foundations of Cooperation in Young Children," *Cognition* 108, no. 1 (2008): 222–31.

21. Amrisha Vaish, Manuela Missana, and Michael Tomasello, "Three-year-old Children Intervene in Third-party Moral Transgressions," *British Journal of Developmental Psychology* 29, no. 2 (2011): 124–30.

22. Amrisha Vaish, Malinda Carpenter, and Michael Tomasello, "Young Children Selectively Avoid Helping People with Harmful Intentions," *Child Development* 81, no. 6 (2010): 1661–69.

23. See Wellman, "Developing."

24. See also Michael Tomasello and Amrisha Vaish, "Origins of Human Morality and Cooperation," *Annual Review of Psychology* 64 (2013): 231–55.

25. Emily K. Newton, Ross A. Thompson, and Miranda Goodman, "Individual Differences in Toddlers' Prosociality: Experiences in Early Relationships Explain Variability in Prosocial Behavior," manuscript submitted for review, University of California, Davis. See also Emily K. Newton, Miranda Goodman, and Ross A. Thompson, "Why Do Some Toddlers Help a Stranger? Origins of Individual Differences in Prosocial Behavior," *Infancy* 19, no. 2 (2014): 214–26.

26. Nancy Eisenberg, Natalie D. Eggum, and Alison Edwards, "Empathy-related Responding and Moral Development," in *Emotions, Aggression, and Morality in Children*, ed. William F. Arsenio and Elizabeth A. Lemerise (Washington, DC: American Psychological Association, 2010), 115–35; Martin L. Hoffman, *Empathy and Moral Development: Implications for Caring and Justice* (Cambridge: Cambridge University Press, 2000).

27. Judith G. Smetana, "Toddlers' Social Interactions in the Context of Moral and Conventional Transgressions in the Home," *Developmental Psychology* 25, no. 4 (1989): 499–508.

28. Larry Nucci and Elsa K. Weber, "Social Interactions in the Home and the Development of Young Children's Conceptions of the Personal," *Child Development* 66, no. 5 (1995): 1438–52; Smetana, "Toddlers."

29. Grazyna Kochanska and Nazan Aksan, "Children's Conscience and Self-regulation," *Journal of Personality* 74, no. 6 (2006): 1587–617; Ross A. Thompson, "Conscience Development in Early Childhood," in *Handbook of Moral Development*, 2nd ed., ed. Melanie Killen and Judith Smetana (New York: Taylor & Francis, 2013).

30. Grazyna Kochanska, "Mutually Responsive Orientation between Mothers and Their Young Children: A Context for the Early Development of Conscience," *Current Directions in Psychological Science* 11, no. 6 (2002): 191–95; Kochanska and Aksan, "Children's Conscience."

31. Kochanska, "Mutually Responsive...A Context."

32. Judith Cassidy and Philip R. Shaver, eds., *Handbook of Attachment*, 2nd ed. (New York: Guilford, 2008).

33. See, e.g., Grazyna Kochanska, "Mutually Responsive Orientation between Mothers and Their Young Children: Implications for Early Socialization," *Child Development* 68, no. 1 (1997): 94–112.

34. E.g., Grazyna Kochanska, David R. Forman, Nazan Aksan, and Stephen B. Dunbar, "Pathways to Conscience: Early Mother-Child Mutually Responsive Orientation and Children's Moral Emotion, Conduct, and Cognition," *Journal of Child Psychology and Psychiatry* 46, no. 1 (2005): 19–34; Grazyna Kochanska, Jamie L. Koenig, Robin A. Barry, Sanghag Kim, and Jeung Eun Yoon, "Children's Conscience during Toddler and Preschool Years, Moral Self, and a Competent, Adaptive Developmental Trajectory," *Developmental Psychology* 46, no. 5 (2010): 1320–32.

35. Grazyna Kochanska, Nazan Aksan, and Amy L. Koenig, "A Longitudinal Study of the Roots of Preschoolers' Conscience: Committee Compliance and Emerging Internalization," *Child Development* 66, no. 6 (1995): 1752–69.

36. Kochanska, Aksan, and Koenig, "A Longitudinal Study"; Kochanska, Koenig et al., "Children's Conscience"; Grazyna Kochanska and Kathleen T. Murray, "Mother-Child Mutually Responsive Orientation and Conscience Development: From Toddler to Early School Age," *Child Development* 71, no. 2 (2000): 417–31.

37. See Thompson, "Conscience," for a review of this research.

38. Kochanska, "Mutually Responsive…A Context"; Deborah J. Laible and Ross A. Thompson, "Mother-Child Discourse, Attachment Security, Shared Positive Affect, and Early Conscience Development," *Child Development* 71, no. 5 (2000): 1424–40.

39. Kochanska, Forman et al., "Pathways"; Kochanska and Murray, "Mother-Child."

40. Grazyna Kochanska, Sanghag Kim, Robin A. Barry, and Robert A. Philibert, "Children's Genotypes Interact with Maternal Responsive Care in Predicting Children's Competence: Diathesis-stress or Differential Susceptibility?," *Development and Psychopathology* 23, no. 3 (2011): 605–16.

41. Deborah J. Laible and Ross A. Thompson, "Mother-Child Conflict in the Toddler Years: Lessons in Emotion, Morality, and Relationships," *Child Development* 73, no. 4 (2002): 1187–203.

42. Laible and Thompson, "Mother-Child Conflict."

43. Judy Dunn, Jane R. Brown, and M. Maguire, "The Development of Children's Moral Sensibility: Individual Differences and Emotion Understanding," *Developmental Psychology* 31, no. 4 (1995): 649–59.

44. Smetana, "Toddlers."

45. Martin L. Hoffman, "Moral Development," in *Carmichael's Manual of Child Psychology*, vol. 2, ed. Paul H. Mussen (New York: Wiley, 1970), 261–360.

46. Ross A. Thompson and Abby C. Winer, "Moral Development, Conversation, and the Development of Internal Working Models," *Talking about Right and Wrong: Parent-Child Conversations as Contexts forMmoral Development*, ed. Celia Wainryb and Holly Recchia (New York: Cambridge University Press, 2014), 299–333.

47. Daniel K Lapsley and Darcia Narvaez, "A Social-Cognitive Approach to the Moral Personality," in *Moral Development, Self, and Identity*, ed. Daniel K. Lapsley and Darcia Narvaez (Mahwah, NJ: Lawrence Erlbaum, 2004), 189–212.

48. But see Kochanska and Murray, "Mother-Child," for an example of research involving peer interaction.

49. Sam A. Hardy and Gustavo Carlo, "Identity as a Source of Moral Motivation," *Human Development* 48, no. 3 (2005): 232–56.

50. Hardy and Carlo, "Identity as a Source."

51. Grazyna Kochanska, "Committed Compliance, Moral Self, and Internalization: A Mediational Model," *Developmental Psychology* 38, no. 2 (2002): 339–51.

52. E.g., Geoffrey L. Brown, Sarah C. Mangelsdorf, Jean M. Agathen, and Moon-Ho Ho, "Young Children's Psychological Selves: Convergence with Maternal Reports of Child Personality," *Social Development* 17, no. 2 (2008): 161–82; Rebecca

Goodvin, Sara Meyer, Ross A. Thompson, and Rachel Hayes, "Self-understanding in Early Childhood: Associations with Child Attachment Security and Maternal Negative Affect," *Attachment & Human Development* 10, no. 4 (2008): 433–50; Herbert W. Marsh, Louise A. Ellis, and Rachel G. Craven, "How Do Preschool Children Feel about Themselves? Unraveling Measurement and Multidimensional Self-concept Structure," *Developmental Psychology* 38, no. 3 (2002): 376–93.

53. Kochanska, "Committed"; Kochanska, Koenig et al., "Children's Conscience."
54. Kochanska, Koenig, et al., "Children's Conscience."
55. Kristin Lagattuta and Ross A. Thompson, "The Development of Self-conscious Emotions: Cognitive Processes and Social Influences," in *Self-conscious Emotions,* 2nd ed., ed. Richard W. Robins and Jess Tracy (New York: Guilford, 2007), 91–113; Deborah Stipek, "The Development of Pride and Shame in Toddlers," in *Self-conscious Emotions,* ed. Judith Tangney and Kurt Fischer (New York: Guilford, 1995), 237–52.
56. Laible and Thompson, "Mother-Child Discourse"; Laible and Thompson, "Mother-Child Conflict"; Thompson and Winer, "Moral Development."
57. Cf. Paul Bloom, "Moral Nativism and Moral Psychology," in *The Social Psychology of Morality: Exploring the Causes of Good and Evil,* ed. Mario Mikulincer and Phillip R. Shaver (Washington, DC: American Psychological Association, 2012), 71–89; Felix Warneken and Michael Tomasello, "The Roots of Human Altruism," *British Journal of Developmental Psychology* 100, no. 3 (2009): 455–71.
58. Augusto Blasi, "Moral Understanding and the Moral Personality: The Process of Moral Integration," in *Moral Development: An Introduction,* ed. William M. Kurtines and Jacob L. Gewirtz (Boston: Allyn & Bacon, 2005), 121.
59. Silvia Bunge, Allison Mackey, and Kirstie J. Whitaker, "Brain Changes Underlying the Development of Cognitive Control and Reasoning," in *The Cognitive Neurosciences,* 4th ed., eds. Michael J. Gazzinaga (Cambridge, MA: MIT Press, 2009): 73–85.
60. Ross A. Thompson and Charles A. Nelson, "Developmental Science and the Media: Early Brain Development," *American Psychologist* 56, no. 1 (2000): 5–15.
61. Ross A. Thompson, "Doing What *Doesn't* Come Naturally: The Development of Self-regulation," *Zero to Three Journal* 30, no. 2 (2009): 33–39.
62. Ross A. Thompson, "Stress and Child Development," *The Future of Children* 24, no. 1 (2014): 41–59.

BIBLIOGRAPHY

Baumard, Nicholas, Olivier Mascaro, and Coralie Chevallier. "Preschoolers Are Able to Take Merit into Account when Distributing Goods." *Developmental Psychology* 48, no. 2 (2012): 492–98.

Blasi, Augusto. "Moral Understanding and the Moral Personality: The Process of Moral Integration." In *Moral Development: An Introduction,* edited by William M. Kurtines and Jacob L. Gewirtz, 229–53. Boston: Allyn & Bacon, 2005.

Bloom, Paul. "Moral Nativism and Moral Psychology." In *The Social Psychology of Morality: Exploring the Causes of Good and Evil,* edited by Mario Mikulincer and Phillip R. Shaver, 71–89. Washington, DC: American Psychological Association, 2012.

Brown, Geoffrey L., Sarah C. Mangelsdorf, Jean M. Agathen, and Moon-Ho Ho. "Young Children's Psychological Selves: Convergence with Maternal Reports of Child Personality." *Social Development* 17, no. 2 (2008): 161–82.

Bunge, Silvia, Allison Mackey, and Kirstie J. Whitaker. "Brain Changes Underlying the Development of Cognitive Control and Teasoning." In *The Cognitive Neurosciences,* 4th ed., edited by Michael J. Gazzinaga, 73–85. Cambridge, MA: MIT Press, 2009.

Carpenter, Malinda, Josep Call, and Michael Tomasello. "Twelve- and 18-month-olds Copy Actions in Terms of Goals." *Developmental Science* 8, no. 1 (2005): F13–F20.

Cassidy, Judith, and Philip R. Shaver, eds. *Handbook of Attachment,* 2nd ed. New York: Guilford, 2008.

Dunn, Judy, Jane R. Brown, and M. Maguire. "The Development of Children's Moral Sensibility: Individual Differences and Emotion Understanding." *Developmental Psychology* 31, no. 4 (1995): 649–59.

Eisenberg, Nancy, Natalie D. Eggum, and Alison Edwards. "Empathy-related Responding and Moral Development." In *Emotions, Aggression, and Morality in Children,* edited by William F. Arsenio and Elizabeth A. Lemerise, 115–35. Washington, DC: American Psychological Association, 2010.

Goodvin, Rebecca, Sara Meyer, Ross A. Thompson, and Rachel Hayes. "Self-understanding in Early Childhood: Associations with Child Attachment Security and Maternal Negative Affect." *Attachment & Human Development* 10, no. 4 (2008): 433–50.

Hamlin, J. Kiley, Karen Wynn, Paul Bloom, and Neha Mahajan. "How Infants and Toddlers React to Antisocial Others." *Proceedings of the National Academy of Sciences* 108, no. 50 (2011): 11931–36.

Hardy, Sam A., and Gustavo Carlo. "Identity as a Source of Moral motivation." *Human Development* 48, no. 3 (2005): 232–56.

Hoffman, Martin L. *Empathy and Moral Development: Implications for Caring and Justice.* Cambridge: Cambridge University Press, 2000.

Hoffman, Martin L. "Moral Development." In *Carmichael's Manual of Child Psychology,* vol. 2, edited by Paul H. Mussen, 261–360. New York: Wiley, 1970.

Killen, Melanie, and Judith Smetana, eds. *Handbook of Moral Development,* 2nd ed. New York: Taylor & Francis, 2013.

Kochanska, Grazyna. "Committed Compliance, Moral Self, and Internalization: A Mediational Model." *Developmental Psychology* 38, no. 2 (2002): 339–51.

Kochanska, Grazyna. "Mutually Responsive Orientation between Mothers and Their Young Children: A Context for the Early Development of Conscience." *Current Directions in Psychological Science* 11, no. 6 (2002): 191–95.

Kochanska, Grazyna. "Mutually Responsive Orientation between Mothers and Their Young Children: Implications for Early Socialization." *Child Development* 68, no. 1 (1997): 94–112.

Kochanska, Grazyna, and Nazan Aksan. "Children's Conscience and Self-regulation." *Journal of Personality* 74, no. 6 (2006): 1587–617.

Kochanska, Grazyna, Nazan Aksan, and Amy L. Koenig. "A Longitudinal Study of the Roots of Preschoolers' Conscience: Committee Compliance and Emerging Internalization." *Child Development* 66, no. 6 (1995): 1752–69.

Kochanska, Grazyna, David R. Forman, Nazan Aksan, and Stephen B. Dunbar. "Pathways to conscience: Early mother-child mutually responsive orientation and children's moral emotion, conduct, and cognition." *Journal of Child Psychology and Psychiatry* 46, no. 1 (2005): 19–34.

Kochanska, Grazyna, Sanghag Kim, Robin A. Barry, and Robert A. Philibert. "Children's Genotypes Interact with Maternal Responsive Care in Predicting Children's Competence: Diathesis-stress or Differential Susceptibility?" *Development and Psychopathology* 23, no. 3 (2011): 605–16.

Kochanska, Grazyna, Jamie L. Koenig, Robin A. Barry, Sanghag Kim, and Jeung Eun Yoon. "Children's Conscience during Toddler and Preschool Years, Moral Self, and a Competent, Adaptive Developmental Trajectory." *Developmental Psychology* 46, no. 5 (2010): 1320–32.

Kochanska, Grazyna, and Kathleen T. Murray. "Mother-Child Mutually Responsive Orientation and Conscience Development: From Toddler to Early School Age." *Child Development* 71, no. 2 (2000): 417–31.

Kohlberg, Lawrence. "Stage and Sequence: The Cognitive Developmental Approach to Socialization." In *Handbook of Socialization Theory and Research*, edited by D. Goslin, 347–480. New York: Rand McNally, 1969.

Lagattuta, Kristin, and Ross A. Thompson. "The Development of Self-conscious Emotions: Cognitive Processes and Social Influences." In *Self-conscious Emotions*, 2nd. ed., edited by Richard W. Robins and Jess Tracy, 91–113. New York: Guilford, 2007.

Laible, Deborah J., and Ross A. Thompson. "Mother-Child Conflict in the Toddler Years: Lessons in Emotion, Morality, and Relationships." *Child Development* 73, no. 4 (2002): 1187–203.

Laible, Deborah J., and Ross A. Thompson. "Mother-Child Discourse, Attachment Security, Shared Positive Affect, and Early Conscience Development." *Child Development* 71, no. 5 (2000): 1424–40.

Lapsley, Daniel K., and Darcia Narvaez. "A Social-Cognitive Approach to the Moral Personality." In *Moral Development, Self, and Identity*, edited by Daniel K. Lapsley and Darcia Narvaez, 189–212. Mahwah, NJ: Lawrence Erlbaum, 2004.

Marsh, Herbert W., Louise A. Ellis, and Rachel G. Craven. "How Do Preschool Children Feel about Themselves? Unraveling Measurement and Multidimensional Self-concept Structure." *Developmental Psychology* 38, no. 3 (2002): 376–93.

Meltzoff, Andrew N. "The 'Like Me' Framework for Recognizing and Becoming an Intentional Agent." *Acta Psychologica* 124, no. 1 (2007): 26–43.

Meltzoff, Andrew N. "Understanding the Intentions of Others: Re-enactment of Intended Acts by 18-month-old Children." *Developmental Psychology* 31, no. 5 (1995): 838–50.

Newton, Emily K., Miranda Goodman, and R. A. Thompson. "Why Do Some Toddlers Help a Stranger? Origins of Individual Differences in Prosocial Behavior." *Infancy* 19, no. 2 (2014): 214–26.

Newton, Emily K., R. A. Thompson, and Miranda Goodman. "Individual Differences in Toddlers' Prosociality: Experiences in Early Relationships Explain Variability in Prosocial Behavior." Manuscript submitted for review, University of California, Davis.

Nucci, Larry, and Elsa K. Weber. "Social Interactions in the Home and the Development of Young Children's Conceptions of the Personal." *Child Development* 66, no. 5 (1995): 1438–52.

Olson, Kristina R., and Elizabeth S. Spelke. "Foundations of Cooperation in Young Children." *Cognition* 108, no. 1 (2008): 222–31.

Repacholi, Betty M., and Alison Gopnik. "Reasoning about Desires: Evidence from 14- and 18-month-olds." *Developmental Psychology* 33, no. 1 (1997): 12–21.

Smetana, Judith G. "Toddlers' Social Interactions in the Context of Moral and Conventional Transgressions in the Home." *Developmental Psychology* 25, no. 4 (1989): 499–508.

Stipek, Deborah. "The Development of Pride and Shame in Toddlers." In *Self-conscious Emotions*, edited by Judith Tangney and Kurt Fischer, 237–52. New York: Guilford, 1995.

Thompson, Ross A. "Conscience Development in Early Childhood." In *Handbook of Moral Development*, 2nd ed., edited by Melanie Killen and Judith Smetana, 73–92. New York: Taylor & Francis, 2013.

Thompson, Ross A. "Doing What *Doesn't* Come Naturally: The Development of Self-regulation." *Zero to Three Journal* 30, no. 2 (2009): 33–39.

Thompson, Ross A. "Stress and Child Development." *The Future of Children* 24, no. 1 (2014): 40–59.

Thompson, Ross A. "Whither the Preconventional Child? Toward a Life-span Moral Development Theory." *Child Development Perspectives* 6, no. 4 (2013): 423–29.

Thompson, Ross A., and Kristin Lagattuta. "Feeling and Understanding: Early Emotional Development." In *The Blackwell Handbook of Early Childhood Development*, edited by Kathleen McCartney and Deborah Phillips, 317–37. Oxford: Blackwell, 2006.

Thompson, Ross A., and Charles A. Nelson. "Developmental Science and the Media: Early Brain Development." *American Psychologist* 56, no. 1 (2000): 5–15.

Thompson, Ross A., and Emily K. Newton. "Baby Altruists? Examining the Complexity of Prosocial Motivation in Young Children." *Infancy* 18, no. 1 (2013): 120–33.

Thompson, Ross A., and Abby C. Winer. "Moral Development, Conversation, and the Development of Internal Working Models." In *Talking about Right and Wrong: Parent-Child Conversations as Contexts for Moral Development*, edited by Celia Wainryb and Holly Recchia, 299–333. New York: Cambridge University Press, 2014.

Tomasello, Michael, Malinda Carpenter, Josep Call, Tanya Behne, and Henrike Moll. "Understanding and Sharing Intentions: The Origins of Cultural Cognition." *Behavioral and Brain Sciences* 28, no. 5 (2005): 675–735.

Tomasello, Michael, and Amrisha Vaish. "Origins of Human Morality and Cooperation." *Annual Review of Psychology* 64 (2013): 231–55.

Vaish, Amrisha, Malina Carpenter, and Michael Tomasello. "Sympathy through Affective Perspective Taking and Its Relation to Prosocial Behavior in Toddlers." *Developmental Psychology* 45, no. 2 (2009): 534–43.

Vaish, Amrisha, Malinda Carpenter, and Michael Tomasello. "Young Children Selectively Avoid Helping People with Harmful Intentions." *Child Development* 81, no. 6 (2010): 1661–69.

Vaish, Amrisha, Manuela Missana, and Michael Tomasello. "Three-year-old Children Intervene in Third-Party Moral Transgressions." *British Journal of Developmental Psychology* 29, no. 2 (2011): 124–30.

Warneken, Felix, Frances Chen, and Michael Tomasello. "Cooperative Activities in Young Children and Chimpanzees." *Child Development* 77, no. 3 (2006): 640–63.

Warneken, Felix, and Michael Tomasello."Altruistic Helping in Human Infants and Young Chimpanzees." *Science* 311, no. 5765 (2006): 1301–303.

Warneken, Felix, and Michael Tomasello. "Extrinsic Rewards Undermine Altruistic Tendencies in 20-month-olds." *Developmental Psychology* 44, no. 6 (2008): 1785–88.

Warneken, Felix, and Michael Tomasello. "The Roots of Human Altruism." *British Journal of Developmental Psychology* 100, no. 3 (2009): 455–71.

Wellman, Henry M. "Developing a Theory of Mind." In *The Wiley-Blackwell Handbook of Childhood Cognitive Development*, 2nd ed., edited by Usha Goswami, 258–84. Oxford: Wiley-Blackwell, 2011.

Woodward, Amanda. "Infants' Grasp of Others' Intentions." *Current Directions in Psychological Science* 18, no. 1 (2009): 53–57.

CHAPTER 12

⚭

Psychological Science and
the *Nicomachean Ethics*

Virtuous Actors, Agents, and Authors

DAN P. McADAMS

U ntil recently, empirical psychologists tended to shy away from the
study of moral virtue. The topic seemed too philosophical, even
theological, for their intellectual tastes, and many may have worried that venturing into the virtue domain might compromise their scientific objectivity. Moreover, throughout much of the twentieth century,
American behavioral scientists questioned the extent to which human lives
displayed enough internal coherence and temporal consistency to justify
the attribution of character traits. In the spirit of Skinner, behaviorists
explained regularities in conduct as the predictable outcomes of environmental stimuli, rather than resulting from inherent qualities of mind.[1]
Dominating American psychology between the 1920s and 1960s, the behaviorist perspective not only ruled out virtues but went much further to
doubt the existence of *any* internal dispositions in human beings, including
basic temperament traits. The one branch of psychological science historically given over to the study of dispositional traits in human beings—
personality psychology[2]—came to question its very legitimacy in the 1970s
and 1980s, as many researchers proclaimed the tenets of *situationism*—the
idea that behavior is driven primarily by environmental (situational) contingencies rather than stable characteristics of the person.[3] People are not
good or bad, the argument went; nor do they even possess good or bad

qualities. Instead, good situations produce good behavior, and bad situations produce bad behavior.

In the 1990s, at least two developments in psychological science cleared a pathway for the study of moral virtues. First, personality psychologists marshaled empirical and rhetorical forces to demonstrate that internal personality traits show considerable consistency over time,[4] are robustly associated with distinctive behavioral trends across different situations,[5] and predict consequential life outcomes, like physical health, psychological well-being, occupational success, marital adjustment, and even mortality.[6] Whereas the situationist critique offered useful corrective points for the field of personality psychology, it ultimately lost the intellectual war. Today, very few psychological scientists of note take seriously the once fashionable claim that dispositional traits—consistent individual differences in feeling, thought, and action as expressed in the people psychologists study—are merely fictions in the minds of the psychologists who study them. Second, the 1990s witnessed the emergence of a broad-based movement in psychological science and clinical work dedicated to the study of psychological health and flourishing, prosocial tendencies in human behavior, and positive character traits.[7] What has come to be known as *positive psychology* seeks to explore the meaning and manifestation of human virtues and character strengths, as well as the nature of happiness and meaning in life. In a landmark volume, Peterson and Seligman laid out a broad agenda for the scientific study of twenty-four character strengths, grouped into the six broad virtue domains of wisdom, courage, humanity, justice, temperance, and transcendence.[8]

In this chapter, I will consider some of the main empirical themes running through contemporary personality psychology and positive psychology as they speak to the *development* of human virtues. I will also draw selectively from the fields of developmental and social psychology, cognitive science, evolutionary biology, and sociology. I will argue that the development of virtues may be usefully construed within an integrative model for the development of human selfhood more generally, a model that traces the development of self from infancy through old age.[9] The model proposes that the psychology of virtue may be understood from three different psychological perspectives, each of which corresponds to a layer of human selfhood developing over time. As such, the self may be construed as (1) a social actor, (2) a motivated agent, and (3) an autobiographical author. From the standpoint of the self as social actor, virtue is expressed through *temperament* traits; from the standpoint of the motivated agent, virtue is instantiated in long-term moral *choices*; from the standpoint of the autobiographical author, virtue is embodied in and narrated through a lifelong moral *vocation*. The development of virtue across the human life course, therefore, follows three separable but interacting trajectories—virtue as temperament, choice, and vocation. Let me suggest, furthermore, that hints of this tripartite conception of virtue may be found in one of the great canonical texts in the philosophical literature on virtue: Aristotle's *Nicomachean Ethics*.

VIRTUE AS TEMPERAMENT: THE SOCIAL ACTOR

As a practical treatise on human happiness and virtue, the *Nicomachean Ethics* poses the question: How do we live a good life? Happiness (*eudaimonia*) is the ultimate aim of human action, Aristotle wrote, the natural consequence of a life well lived. For Aristotle, life is akin to playing the harp (or any musical instrument). Like the best harpist who achieves an exalted level of musical virtuosity, the happiest man or woman attains a kind of excellence (*arête*) in living. But whereas the harpist endeavors to make beautiful music, the man or woman who lives an excellent and happy life strives to express virtue, for human happiness comes through virtue, and virtue only:

> Now, if the function of man is activity of the soul in accordance with, or implying, a rational principle; and if we hold that the function of an individual of the same kind—e.g., of a harpist and of a good harpist and so on generally—is generically the same, the latter's distinctive excellence being attached to the name of the function (because the function of the harpist is to play the harp, but that of the good harpist is to play it well); and if we assume that the function of man is a kind of life, an activity or series of actions of the soul, implying a rational principle; and if the function of a good man is to perform these well and rightly; and if every function is performed well when performed in accordance with its proper excellence; if all this is so, the conclusion is that the good for man is an activity of the soul in accordance with virtue, in accordance with the best and most perfect kind.[10]

In the *Nicomachean Ethics*, Aristotle discussed a number of different virtues, including courage, temperance, generosity ("liberality"), and friendship. Each is conceived as an ideal mode of conduct situated between two extremes. For example, courage sits somewhere between cowardice and foolhardy rashness; temperance, between licentiousness and insensibility. Finding the golden mean or psychological sweet spot for any given virtue within any given situation is a difficult task, calling upon the strongest powers of reason, or what Aristotle called the "rational principle." Human beings aim, or should aim, to experience and express virtue because virtue flows from the fundamental nature of human beings as rational organisms. But there is more to it than cool rationality, for the topic of virtue would likely never enter the rational mind of any human being if human behavior were not so exquisitely *social*. It is because we interact in social groups that such virtues as temperance and friendship are required in the first place. "Man is a social creature, and naturally constituted to live in company," Aristotle wrote.[11] Virtues are guidelines or standards for how rational organisms achieve moral excellence, and thereby happiness, in social contexts.

Rational Human Conduct in Social Groups

To the extent Aristotle identified rationality and sociality as cardinal characteristics of human nature, his perspective anticipated contemporary scientific understandings of what it means to be a human being. Compared to every other species on earth, what most clearly distinguishes the bipedal organisms who, over the past 6 million years, evolved on the African savannah to become *Homo sapiens* are our capacious cerebral cortex and the exquisitely social nature of our existence. We are brainy creatures who evolved to live in complex social groups.[12] For all species, individuals must adapt to environmental challenges in order to survive and reproduce, or else the species fails. For human beings, survival and reproductive efficacy have always been tied to success in social life, which typically translates into the abilities to *get along* with others (social acceptance) and to *get ahead* in the face of limited resources (social status).[13] This is why social exclusion and loss of status are among the most painful experiences human beings can know today, for being excluded from the group, or downgraded in status, has throughout evolutionary history often led to death, or at best a significant decline in reproductive fitness. No matter how smart a human being may be, he or she cannot typically go it alone.

Whereas getting along and getting ahead in the group may sometimes be enhanced through brute force and other forms of overt coercion, more often than not human beings sort themselves out in more subtle and complex ways, relying heavily on the currency of *social reputation*. Whether we are considering the bands and tribes to which our evolutionary ancestors belonged or the complex social ecology of contemporary modern life, developing a positive social reputation has always gone a long way in determining the extent to which a person will thrive in social life, which means life writ large, for human life is always social life. Social reputation implies personality, which ultimately implies character and virtue. In its most basic sense, an individual person's social reputation consists largely of those *dispositional traits* that other group members attribute to him or her. How friendly is this person? How honest, kind, caring, conscientious, courageous, or socially dominant? Can I count on this person when I need help? Can I trust this person? Should I collaborate with this person on a joint venture? Would he or she make a good ally? Would he or she make a good mate? Individual differences in personality traits, therefore, owe their very existence to the attributions that human beings make about each other (and themselves)—the social reputations they invoke and cultivate—as they interact with each other over time and across different situations.[14] Among the most important attributions that ever get made are those that pertain to the moral goodness of a person, to virtue.

In all human societies, attributions of moral goodness and virtue signify a positive relationship between the individual and the group. Aristotle's virtues of justice and generosity promote the well-being of the person him- or herself, because they enhance his or her social reputation in the group. But they also promote the well-being of other group members, most of whom, in principle, should benefit from societal norms that encourage people to be fair, generous, and caring. Whether we are considering the tribes and bands of hominids who roamed the African savannah a million years ago or contemporary nation-states, the very integrity of human groups—their ability to survive and flourish as groups from one generation to the next—depends, to some degree, on the virtuous conduct of group members, or at least their tendency (willed or coerced) to behave in ways that benefit the group. The prosocial nature of virtue is especially apparent in the moral traditions espoused by the world's great religions, which celebrate such virtues as love, hope, charity, humility, mercy, gratitude, loyalty, filial piety, *ahimsa* (nonviolence: Hinduism), *mudita* (altruistic joy: Buddhism), and the like. For the cognitively gifted and exquisitely social creatures we call human beings, individual survival and individual well-being hinge on group survival and group well-being. Put simply, virtue is (usually) good for the individual *because* it is (nearly always) good for the group.

Recognizing that viable human groups depend on the virtuous conduct of individual group members, Aristotle devoted considerable attention to the problem of inculcating virtue in the young. The problem is especially salient for parents, of course, but it is also a matter for the state. In the *Nicomachean Ethics*, Aristotle instructed parents, teachers, and legislators to provide opportunities wherein young people may practice the arts of virtue. Socialization and education for virtue require extensive practice, as would be the case for playing a musical instrument or learning a craft. We learn by doing, Aristotle contended. Young children, therefore, must be taught how to behave in ways that are consistent with the virtues of temperance, justice, friendship, and so on, even before they are able to comprehend the meanings of these abstract terms:

> But the virtues we do acquire by first exercising them, just as happens in the arts. Anything that we have to learn to do we learn by the actual doing of it: people become builders by building and instrumentalists by playing instruments. Similarly, we become just by performing just acts, temperate by performing temperate ones, brave by performing brave ones. This view is supported by what happens in city-states. Legislators make their citizens good by habituation.... In a word, then, like activities produce like dispositions. Hence, we must give our activities a certain quality, because it is their characteristics that determine the resulting dispositions. So it is a matter of no small importance what sort of habits we form from the earliest age—it makes a vast difference, or rather all the difference in the world.[15]

In Aristotle's implicit theory of psychological development, *social action precedes motivated intention*. Children first learn *habits* of proper conduct, and these eventually pave the way for the development of *character* (in Greek: *ethos*). Her parents and teachers tell four-year-old Helen that she should share her toys with other children in the playgroup. While she is reluctant to do so at first, she eventually complies, and over time her sharing behavior may generalize to other interpersonal situations. As she practices sharing, she gets better at it—she shares more consistently, even when authorities are not looking, and she begins to express other acts of kindness and consideration that suggest a growing sense of fairness and of empathy for others. In Aristotle's view, little Helen is well on her way to internalizing the broad virtue of justice, but she is not quite there yet. She is learning how to display habits of justice; eventually, justice may become a full-fledged virtue within her character structure. The full expression of any virtue, Aristotle maintained, requires *moral intentionality*. Put differently, through instruction and practice, Helen is learning how to be a virtuous *social actor*, even if she has not quite yet achieved the higher level of virtue indicative of a *motivated agent*.

The distinction between the self as social actor and the self as motivated agent helps to inform the growing empirical literature on the psychological development of prosocial personality traits, and other human characteristics that might fall under the wide rubric of virtue.[16] Like Aristotle, contemporary researchers in developmental psychology construe moral development in children as involving instruction from parents, teachers, and other socializing agents and institutions.[17] Of special significance in this regard is the development of caregiver-infant attachment bonds. A large body of research suggests that when children enjoy secure bonds of attachment with their caregivers, they tend to exhibit higher levels of instrumental and interpersonal competence, giving them a slight edge in the development of virtue compared to their less securely attached peers.[18] As Aristotle knew, children must be taught good habits, and it turns out to be easier to teach them such habits when children are securely attached to their parents. However, the quality of attachment is but one factor to consider in sorting out the developmental antecedents of virtuous conduct. Just as important, if not more so, are inherent individual differences between children, presumed to be strongly shaped, though not completely shaped, by genetic differences between people. From the very beginning, different kinds of children appear predisposed to encounter the social demands of virtue in different kinds of ways.

Temperament Differences: Three Lines of Development

Children are not born good or bad, of course. But they are born different. Individual differences in basic *temperament* dimensions are readily observed in the first year or two of human life.[19] Temperament refers to broad differences in behavioral and emotional style, and in the regulation of behavior and emotion, as expressed early in the human life course.[20] Although these dimensions are assumed to be a product of genetic differences between social actors, they are also amenable to the influence of environments, including especially the influence of parents, peers, and teachers. Over the human life course, then, temperament dimensions develop through a long and complex series of gene × environment interactions. Eventually, such dimensions become fully articulated as broad dispositional traits of adult personality. Temperament and personality are about more than virtue, for sure. But because these broad dimensions of individual differences encode the most important ways in which human beings differ from each other as social actors, they cannot help but capture aspects of virtuous behavior, as expressed in habitual tendencies to engage in actions that benefit the self and benefit others.

Research in personality psychology points to three developmental lines that track the gradual transformation from infant temperament traits to dispositions of adult personality.[21] Each has implications for comprehending the virtuous conduct of social actors.

The first line begins with the broad temperament dimension of *positive emotionality*. Within the first few months of life, human infants demonstrate remarkable differences in characteristic mood and emotional responses to social events. Whereas some three-month olds will smile in response to a wide range of stimuli, others appear more withdrawn and emotionally subdued. High levels of positive emotionality indicate an active behavioral approach system, which governs the social actor's tendency to seek out rewards in the environment and to feel high levels of positive emotion when rewards are achieved. Over time and in response to a wide range of environmental inputs, differences in positive emotionality gradually morph into the personality trait of *extraversion*. Social actors high in extraversion are described by themselves and by others as especially gregarious, assertive, enthusiastic and upbeat, fun loving, and socially dominant; individuals low in extraversion (introverts) develop the opposite kinds of social reputations—as relatively withdrawn, quiet, and socially inhibited actors. In that personality dispositions typically assume a normal (bell-shaped) distribution in any population, most people show a mix of extraverted and introverted tendencies, falling somewhere toward the middle of the bell-shaped curve.[22]

Behavioral manifestations of extraversion are widely observed in everyday social life. But what is their relation to virtue? A growing body of research shows that when people feel positive emotion they are more likely to help others and engage in a range of prosocial behaviors. In the words of Barbara Fredrickson, high levels of positive emotion tend to "broaden and build" a strong and resilient personality, sustaining the social actor's hope and optimism in everyday life and providing the energy and confidence he or she needs to meet interpersonal and instrumental challenges.[23] It is easy to see, then, how high levels of hope and joy might promote virtuous conduct in many different social situations. At the same time, studies also suggest that when people feel high levels of positive emotion, they may also tend to *cheat* more, perhaps because they feel especially confident about getting away with it.[24]

A second developmental line tracks how early temperament differences in *negative emotionality* eventually grow into the broad personality trait of *neuroticism*. Highly irritable, fearful, and emotionally volatile infants are more likely than their easy-going counterparts (those low in negative emotionality) to demonstrate characteristics of neuroticism as adults. Social actors high in neuroticism see themselves (and are seen by others) as especially fearful, anxious, vulnerable, emotionally conflicted, and tending toward depression.[25] Social actors low in neuroticism are calm and emotionally stable. In that high levels of neuroticism are associated with myriad social problems and negative social outcomes, it would follow that neuroticism should prove a general psychological impediment to the development of many virtuous habits. Because social actors high in neuroticism experience chronic levels of fear, moreover, one might expect that they would find it extraordinarily difficult to demonstrate the Aristotelian virtue of courage. Other things being equal, it follows that individuals who enjoy persistently *low* levels of neuroticism should be predisposed to display virtues like courage and tranquillity; moreover, being relatively free of debilitating negative emotions, like anxiety and sadness, may facilitate the development of many other virtues, as well.

The third developmental line may exert the broadest influence for virtue. Beginning in the second year of life, children demonstrate marked individual differences in their abilities to focus on tasks, delay immediate gratification, and inhibit impulsive responses in order to attain important social and instrumental ends. This broad temperament disposition goes by the name of *effortful control*.[26] Effortful control enables children to inhibit impulses so that they can focus their attention on tasks. The ability to do so on a consistent basis has profound implications for social adaptation. When social actors can set aside immediate desires (I want this), emotions (I feel this), and potentially distracting perceptions (I notice this), they clear a path in consciousness so that they can focus attention on the complex exigencies of a given social situation, including the desires, feelings, and perceptions *of others*. Effective effortful control, therefore, helps to support *empathy* and raises a child's awareness regarding the appropriate standards of social conduct, which when violated lead to the salutary experience of *guilt*.[27] Empathy and guilt are key ingredients in the development of children's *conscience*[28] and, over developmental time, may form the emotional cores, respectively, for the adult personality traits of *agreeableness* and *conscientiousness*.[29]

Social actors high in agreeableness are empathic, friendly, caring, modest, and altruistic. Those low in agreeableness carry the social reputation of being disagreeable, antagonistic, callous, mean-spirited, selfish, and even cruel. In the realm of virtuous habits, research consistently shows that people who score high on measures of agreeableness are more sensitive to the suffering of others, more positively disposed toward fairness and reciprocity, and more loyal to others with whom they feel close bonds, compared to those lower in agreeableness.[30] Social actors high in conscientiousness are industrious, reliable, persevering, rule abiding, and achievement oriented. They are more prone to guilt, compared to less conscientious individuals, and guilt proves to be a strong motivator for self-regulation and prosocial behavior. In Aristotle's terms, therefore, they often appear to be paragons of temperance. Research shows that adults who score high on the trait of conscientiousness tend to invest more heavily in family and work roles, tend to be more religiously observant, and tend to be more involved in prosocial volunteer activities, compared to individuals low in conscientiousness.[31]

Table 12.1. THREE LINES OF DEVELOPMENT, TRACING HOW INFANT TEMPERAMENT DIMENSIONS EVENTUALLY DEVELOP INTO ADULT PERSONALITY TRAITS, EACH OF WHICH PROVIDES SOCIAL ACTORS WITH PSYCHOLOGICAL RESOURCES FOR THE PERFORMANCE OF VIRTUOUS CONDUCT

Temperament Origins	Related Emotions	Adult Personality Trait	Habits of Virtuous Conduct
1. Positive emotionality	joy, excitement	extraversion	The ability to approach social situations with hope and confidence; energy, vitality, sociability. Qualities of personality that promote virtues related to ambition, industry, and wit.
2. Negative emotionality	fear, anxiety sadness	neuroticism	Being *low* in neuroticism suggests emotional stability and equanimity, which promotes virtues related to courage, humility, and serenity.
3. Effortful control	empathy	agreeableness	The ability to care for others and express kindness and interpersonal regard; altruism, friendliness, sincerity, gentleness, warmth. Qualities of personality that promote virtues related to love, charity, generosity, justice, loyalty, peace, and honesty.
	guilt	conscientiousness	The ability to focus attention on long-term goals and socially important tasks; self-control and discipline; perseverance, determination, duty, following rules. Qualities of personality that promote virtues related to temperance, prudence, order, resolution, respect for authority, chastity, and faithfulness.

Especially low levels of conscientiousness, by contrast, predict a wide range of outcomes that implicate deficiencies in virtue—from substance abuse to dishonesty in the workplace.[32]

Table 12.1 summarizes the three lines of psychological development I have described for the self as social actor. The three basic temperament dimensions repeatedly identified in research on infants—positive emotionality, negative emotionality, and effortful control—provide the socio-emotional raw materials out of which adult personality traits may develop. Each of the four corresponding basic traits of personality provides psychological resources for habits of virtuous conduct that social actors display in human groups. Positive emotionality in infancy helps pave the way for the development of extraversion, which promotes virtues that draw upon vitality, sociability, and hope. Negative emotionality in infancy is a precursor to adult neuroticism; individuals who score *low* on the trait of neuroticism are rarely plagued by fear and anxiety and instead develop social reputations as calm and emotionally stable actors—qualities that may promote virtues like courage and serenity. Finally, effortful control in infancy and early childhood paves the way for the development of two personality traits that are crucial for mature behavior in social groups—agreeableness and conscientiousness. Agreeableness may promote those qualities of love, care, and friendship that underlie a wide range of virtues, from generosity to justice, whereas conscientiousness may promote conduct indicative of temperance, prudence, and other virtues that require strong self-control.

VIRTUE AS CHOICE: THE MOTIVATED AGENT

When we observe a social actor perform a behavior that we deem to be praiseworthy or virtuous, we may nonetheless be uncertain as to *why* the social actor did what he or she did. A person may smile and offer a helping hand in a given situation, but the gracious gesture may be motivated by a desire to curry favor with the person helped, or by a need to impress other actors attending the scene, or by the behavioral demands necessitated by the social role that the actor finds himself or herself playing in the particular situation (e.g., the role of mother, the role of supervisor). The behavior, then, is one thing—what the social actor does. The underlying motive, goal, or intention may be something very different—the reason why the motivated agent makes the choice that he or she makes.

In a similar sense, the temperament dispositions or personality traits that comprise the lion's share of a social actor's reputation do not typically speak directly to the reasons behind the conduct that he or she repeatedly displays. Knowing that a person is highly extraverted or conscientious tells us little, if anything, about what that person wants in life, what goals he or she is likely to pursue, what values he or she is likely to espouse. A highly agreeable actor may be friendly and caring in many different situations. It is probably fair to say that the friendly and caring person *intends* to be friendly and caring much of the time, in that the actor could certainly quit being friendly and caring if the situation warranted, or if he or she no longer felt the urge to be so nice. Habitual behavior is not usually completely mindless; there is typically some modicum of volition and will. But how much deliberation and choice are involved? Did the person high in agreeableness wake up this morning and explicitly decide to help other people? A year or two ago, did he or she carefully consider a range of life choices and then develop an altruistic life plan or project to promote the well-being of others and make a positive contribution to society? Probably not—but maybe. The point here is that the social actor's recurrent behavioral and emotional displays do not typically reveal what he or she, as a motivated agent, wants or strives to achieve in life. In the lexicon of personality psychology, traits are one thing, but motives may be quite another.[33]

The distinction between trait and motive roughly parallels Aristotle's distinction between habit and character. To be virtuous, a person must practice virtuous acts, must learn and repeatedly perform the habits of virtuous social conduct. But more is required, Aristotle maintained. The full expression of virtue entails deliberation and choice. In the *Nicomachean Ethics*, Aristotle wrote: "Acts that are incidentally virtuous [should be] distinguished from those that are done knowingly, of choice, and by a virtuous disposition."[34] Aristotle used the example of courage to illustrate the distinction: "The quasi-courage that is due to spirit seems to be the most natural, and if it includes deliberate choice and purpose it is considered to be courage."[35] Translating Aristotle's insight into modern psychological parlance, positive emotionality may spur the social actor to behave boldly and with great confidence, even fearlessness, which may function as a kind of behavioral and emotional precursor to courage; courage in the fullest sense, however, is manifest only when the motivated agent rationally considers various contingencies and then purposefully makes a choice. Reality—dictated by nature and society—presents us with the contingencies. Within these constraints, we must deliberate and ultimately exercise our human agency:

> Choice involves deliberation.... What we deliberate about is practical measures that lie within our power; this is the class of things that actually remains for the accepted types of cause are nature, necessity, and chance, and also mind and human agency of all kinds.... The effects about which we deliberate are those which are produced by our agency.[36]

Virtue, then, involves "a *purposive* disposition, lying in a mean that is relative to us and determined by a rational principle, and by that which a prudent man would use to determine it."[37] Like the modern concept of temperament, the (quasi-) virtuous habits that children show are pre-rational, pre-deliberate. They do not directly suggest purpose. They do not fully exploit the powers of human agency. Accordingly, many modern theories of psychological development suggest that children do not engage in the kind of rational deliberation that Aristotle described until the early grade-school years. Sameroff and Haith have identified an *age 5–7 shift* in human development, roughly marking the transition from spontaneous acting to mindful agency.[38] In Piaget's terms, the general move is from the preschooler's *preoperational thought* (spontaneous, intuitive, bound by present concerns) to the third-grader's *concrete operations* (systematic, rational, goal-oriented mental activity).[39] Young children exhibit a *heteronomous* structure of morality, Piaget also asserted.[40] Their moral choices and rationalizations are dictated by external contingencies of reward and punishment and by momentary feeling states. Older children, by contrast, show *autonomous* morality, wherein moral decisions are guided by internalized rules and norms. The same developmental move is captured in Kohlberg's transition from *preconventional* (egocentric) to *conventional* (socio-centric) moral reasoning.[41]

In most societies, children begin systematic schooling between the ages of five and seven years. Parents, teachers, and other socializing agents provide systematic instruction in matters of mind and body, from science to soccer, and they begin to expect children to exhibit rational thought and goal-directed behavior.[42] Children learn to plan their daily activities, strive toward important academic and personal goals, and sublimate their impulses in the service of a long-term motivational agenda. In Erikson's theory of psychosocial development, the motivated agency of the elementary school years plays out within a dynamic of *industry versus inferiority*.[43] Industrious, goal-oriented schoolchildren strive to master the *roles* and the *tools* that society provides for them, and when their agentic efforts fall short of society's standards, they may feel a sense of inferiority. In Erikson's psychodynamic view, schoolchildren are ready to take on the challenges of industry versus inferiority because, by the age of five or six, they have likely worked through the unconscious conflicts of the Oedipus complex. Parental authority has now been internalized, such that the seven-year-old can readily submit his or her behavior to the dictates of the superego, and other authority figures as well. Whether or not one buys into the idea of an Oedipus complex, psychological theory tends to suggest that children must, in some sense, come to terms with authority before they can subordinate their personal needs to societal norms, develop long-term goals that are consistent with societal expectations, and realize the potential of virtuous character. Aristotle seems to make a similar point in his discussion of licentiousness:

Licentious people are like spoilt children.... The metaphor seems not to be a bad one, because restraint is necessary for anything that has low appetites and a marked capacity for growth; and these qualities are possessed in the highest degree by desires and also by children. For children too live as their desires impel them, and it is in them that the appetite for pleasant things is strongest; so unless this is rendered docile and submissive to authority it will pass all bounds. For in an irrational being the appetite for what gives it pleasure is insatiable and indiscriminate, and the exercise of the desire increases its latent tendency; and if these appetites are strong and violent, they actually drive out reason. So they must be moderate and few, and in no way opposed to the dictates of principles— this is what we mean by "docile" and "restrained"—and just as the child ought to live in accordance with the directions of his tutor, so the desiderative elements in us ought to be controlled by the rational principle.[44]

Psychologically speaking, then, human beings are social actors from the beginning of life, but eventually they are more, too. In the middle-childhood years, a second layer of selfhood begins to form. Recurrent personal *goals* (things I want to achieve today, tomorrow, in my life) begin to layer over dispositional traits in the elementary-school years, as the child begins to understand him- or herself from the standpoint of a motivated agent. In a rudimentary sense, even infants behave in a goal-directed manner, but it is not until middle childhood that consistent individual differences in children may be seen with respect to the particular goals, plans, programs, and projects they expressly lay out for themselves—desired ends to which they orient their will.[45] At this developmental juncture, the language of rational agency—will, choice, deliberation, decision—becomes a legitimate part of discourse on the self, and on virtue.

Nine-year-old Kristin is a highly outgoing and impulsive girl (social actor: trait) who has *decided* that she wants Jesus to come into her heart, *plans* to make Erika her best friend, and *hopes* that her estranged mother and father will reconcile (motivated agent: goal). Unlike traits (the social actor), goals (the motivated agent) orient the person toward the future; they are expressly teleological constructs, and therefore carry the connotations of planning, choice, and prospection. Some personal goals suggest virtue—either in terms of their content (my New Year's resolution to become a more loving spouse) or by the complicated or conflicted calculus (Aristotle's rational deliberation) that the agent plays out in his or her mind in an effort to come to a morally defensible decision, or to figure out the means whereby a moral end may be achieved. The rational calculus may require considerable cognitive effort, for, as Aristotle contended, virtue aims to express a valued end "at the right times on the right grounds toward the right people for the right motive and in the right way."[46] As a motivated agent, then, a person expresses virtue when he or she commits the self to achieve an end that society deems to be good and praiseworthy, deliberates about the means and social complexities that are relevant to the end, develops a plan to achieve the end, and then strives to make good on the plan.

Spurred by the recent rise of positive psychology, psychological researchers have developed and validated measures of individual differences in the extent to which people express such virtues as gratitude[47] and forgiveness,[48] among others. These research programs implicitly assume that motivated agents engage in rational deliberation, through which they take into consideration the thoughts, feelings, and desires of other people, and even the multiple perspectives presented by conflicting groups. Other research programs examine virtues as expressed in the content and structure of people's goals. For example, studies have shown that personal goals focused on caring for others and making positive contributions to society are associated with psychological well-being and reports of higher life meaning.[49] Still other programs subsume the concept of virtue within the related domains of *values* and *personal ideology*.[50] These research programs aim to map the psychological geography of those envisioned end states that moral agents deem praiseworthy. Through self-report surveys, they determine the relative importance that moral agents ascribe to such personal values as honesty and hard work, and such societal values as security, equality, freedom, and world peace.

VIRTUE AS VOCATION: THE AUTOBIOGRAPHICAL AUTHOR

In the *Nicomachean Ethics*, Aristotle argued that human happiness is inextricably tied to virtue. In that human beings are rational creatures who always live in social groups, the happiest men and women are those who engage in rational social conduct, consistently exhibiting moral excellence in their interpersonal affairs. As children, they learn virtuous habits; with development, their rational powers grow to the point that they are able to deliberate about means and ends in social behavior, enabling them to express virtue in a purposive, goal-directed manner, through choice and planning. There are many different kinds of virtues that human beings may display, from courage to temperance. But the highest or most exalted virtues, Aristotle suggested, are those that are most fully infused with the rational activity of the mind. As such, Aristotle reserved a special place in his conception of virtue for wisdom and contemplation:

We have already said that it [happiness] is a contemplative activity. This may be regarded as consonant both with our earlier arguments and with the truth. For contemplation is both the highest form of activity (since the intellect is the highest thing in us, and the objects that it apprehends are the highest things that can be known), and also it is the most continuous, because we are more capable of continuous contemplation than we are of practical activity . . . the wise man can practice contemplation by himself, and the wiser he is, the more he can do it.[51]

If, then, politics and warfare, although pre-eminent in nobility and grandeur among practical activities in accord with goodness, are incompatible with leisure and, not being desirable in themselves, are directed towards some other end, whereas the activity of the intellect is considered to excel in seriousness, taking as it does the form of contemplation, and to aim at no other end beyond itself and to possess a pleasure peculiar to itself, which intensifies its activity; and if it is evident that self-sufficiency and leisuredness and such freedom from fatigue as is humanly possible, together with all other attributes assigned to the supremely happy man, are those that accord with this activity; then this activity will be the perfect happiness for man—provided that it is allowed a full span of life.[52]

Wisdom, Contemplation, and the Psychology of Adulthood

As Aristotle saw it, the wisest men (and women) enjoy the highest form of happiness as they exercise their rational minds through contemplation. In contemplation, they survey facts and situations, synthesize existing knowledge, and arrive at broad truths and integrative insights regarding human nature, interpersonal relationships, and the state of society. Contemplation is a self-sufficient activity; it is done for its own sake, rather than for other ends, and it can be done anywhere and anytime. Yet contemplation does require leisure. In order to contemplate, a person must enjoy some degree of freedom from the practical demands of everyday life, and from "fatigue," and other physical or material ailments that might undermine the powers of rationality. Moreover, contemplation may require the perspective of "a full span of life," Aristotle suggested. Children may daydream, and adolescents may fantasize, but contemplation would appear to be a quality of human consciousness that is more common among adults, perhaps even older adults. Children may be smart, but only adults can be wise, for adults have lived long enough to gain the knowledge and perspective that contemplation requires.

Aristotle's conception of the highest human expressions of happiness and virtue, reserved as they are for the mature adult, anticipate two notable strands of research and theory in life-span developmental psychology today. First, one highly influential line of work conceives of *wisdom* as expertise in the pragmatics of life.[53] According to this conception, adults demonstrate wisdom when they draw upon a rich base of factual and procedural knowledge that they have accumulated over the course of life in order to address difficult, even intractable, personal and interpersonal problems. To measure wisdom, researchers ask adults to describe what kind of advice they might give to a person who is facing a particularly difficult life problem, such as whether or not to have an abortion or what kind of action to take in the face of relentless suffering. The wisest responses are those that take into careful consideration the life-span context at play (e.g., the person's age and stage in life, unique personal circumstances, class and gender constraints, demographic factors, and so on), that weigh competing moral principles and values, and that bring many relevant sources of knowledge to bear while remaining cognizant of the limitations of human expertise and the ultimate ambiguity of human life. As with Aristotle, the contemporary conception views wisdom as a synthetic rational activity that requires a broad base of knowledge and experience. But the research focuses on the application of this knowledge to solving life problems, rather than on the contemplative activity itself, through which wisdom may be gained over time.

A second line of research and theory examines *reminiscence* and *life review*.[54] As people age, they are more likely to look back on their lives and take stock, a contemplative activity that often brings benefits for mental health. Through reminiscing about the past and reviewing important or memorable autobiographical events, adults may gain a broader and more meaningful perspective on their lives. Indeed, a retrospective understanding of life in full may be a feature of wisdom itself. In order to work through the most vexing challenges in life pragmatics, the wise man or woman needs to be able to see a life—one's own or another's—in its full temporal complexity, as an ongoing *narrative* situated in society and culture and articulated through a series of social actions and motivated projects stretched across lived time.

For Aristotle, the wise man's (or woman's) contemplative activity seems to share with the modern concept of reminiscence a "looking back upon" quality. In contemplation, an adult surveys the knowledge he or she has attained in the past and, likewise, surveys the past itself. With the leisure and perspective that comes with age, then, the adult should be able to adopt a broad, retrospective perspective on life and on the world. Indeed, should the person reach an advanced age whereby he or she is no longer active in social life or in productive work, contemplation may become the dominant mode of rational existence—so much so that the person's activity comes to resemble what the gods mainly do. Aristotle wrote:

> But if a living being is deprived of action, and still further of production, what is left but contemplation? It follows, then, that the activity of the gods, which is supremely happy, must be a form of contemplation; and therefore among human activities that which is most akin to the gods' will be the happiest.[55]

As (assumedly) practiced by the gods and by wise men and women, Aristotelian contemplation is less like navel-gazing and more like an active synthetic process. In the conceptions of contemporary psychological science, this kind of cognitive activity involves *constructing* truths and *reconstructing* the past. With respect to reminiscence and life review, therefore, the individual does more than merely survey what has happened in the past, as if the past were but a video recording for passive viewing. Instead, he or she selectively appropriates and makes meaning of the past. In his psychobiography of Martin Luther, Erikson contended that this kind of autobiographical activity—constructing one's own life as a story, in retrospect and prospect—is a form of contemplation that marks the status of adulthood.[56] In other words, adopting a reconstructive, retrospective understanding for determining who one is—past, present, and anticipated future—is something that children and younger adolescents simply cannot do, but adults do it:

> To be adult means among other things to see one's own life in continuous perspective, both in retrospect and prospect. By accepting some definition as to who he is, usually on the basis of a function in an economy, a place in the sequence of generations, and a status in the structure of society, the adult is able to selectively reconstruct his past in such a way that, step for step, it seems to have planned him, or better, he seems to have planned it. In this sense, psychologically we *do* choose our parents, our family history, and the history of our kings, heroes, and gods. By making them our own, we maneuver ourselves into the inner position of proprietors, of creators.[57]

In this evocative passage, Erikson implies that becoming an adult means assuming the role of an *autobiographical author*, a storyteller of the self. In contemporary psychological science, this idea is captured in the concept of *narrative identity*.[58] Narrative identity is an internalized and evolving story of the self that a person constructs to provide his or life with a sense of unity and temporal continuity. As a selective reconstruction of the past and an imagined vision for the future, a person's narrative identity tells a story, for the self and for others, regarding how the person believes he or she came to be the person that he or she is becoming. It is my story about how the "me" of my past became the "me" of my present, and will become the anticipated "me" of the future.

A growing literature in personality, developmental, and cognitive psychology has identified some of the cognitive skills[59] and social processes[60] that are instrumental in the development of a narrative identity in adulthood. Chief among these psychological factors is *autobiographical reasoning*, which refers to a range of socio-cognitive practices whereby autobiographical authors draw personal meanings from past events. Through autobiographical reasoning, for example, authors may identify an organizing theme in their life stories or chart a causal sequence to explain a transformation in their identity over time. Through autobiographical reasoning, authors may derive life lessons or personal truths from past events. In Aristotelian terms, autobiographical reasoning is human rationality given over to making sense of a life in time. It is contemplation in the service of self-authorship.

How Exemplars of Virtue Author Their Lives

Beyond the social actor and the motivated agent, then, human selfhood is manifest in the stories people live by—the self as autobiographical author. Adults construct multilayered selves, wherein stories layer over goals and values, which layer over traits.[61] The construction of a life story is both a psychological and a moral project, for authors always position themselves within an assumptive world regarding what they (explicitly and implicitly) believe to be good and true.[62] Nonetheless, the content and the structure of individual life stories vary wildly, as a function of different experiences that people have, different inclinations regarding how to make meaning out of those experiences, and different cultural conventions about what constitutes a good life and a coherent life story.[63] The expression of virtue may be a minor, even nonexistent, motif in many life stories, but for some it may serve as the central organizing theme.

In a handful of exemplary life stories, authors express virtue as a life's *vocation*. The protagonists in these stories may feel a sense of calling[64] or personal destiny[65] with respect to the role of virtue in their lives. More than social actors who regularly display habits of virtuous conduct, more than motivated agents who deliberately make virtuous choices and pursue virtuous goals, some people may construe their lives writ large as grand narratives of virtue. Whereas some examples of doing so may indicate pathological narcissism, others may reveal the stories produced by what

Ann Colby and William Damon call *moral exemplars*—people who exemplify moral commitment and passion, and who are recognized, by themselves and by others, as exemplifying a life of deep and abiding virtue.[66]

Psychological research on moral exemplars has begun to reveal common patterns in the stories they author to make meaning in their lives. For example, Lawrence Walker and Jeremy Frimer interviewed twenty-five men and women who had been recognized by the Canadian government for exemplary lives of caring and community service ("caring exemplars"), twenty-five who were similarly recognized for bravery or heroism ("brave exemplars"), and a matched sample of fifty more or less well-functioning adults who received no such commendation.[67] Their analyses revealed that the caring and brave exemplars were significantly more likely than the matched control group to construct stories that repeatedly (1) illustrated the use of personal power to accomplish prosocial ends, and (2) featured the transformation from emotionally negative events to positive outcomes.

The latter finding captures what I have called a *redemption sequence* in life narratives.[68] In a redemption sequence, the author describes how an especially painful or emotionally difficult situation in his or her life (e.g., loss, failure, illness, deprivation) eventually led to a positive turn of events, or resulted in a positive development in life (e.g., an insight, a lesson, a positive personal transformation). The protagonist is ultimately delivered from suffering to an enhanced status or state. In other words, the hero of the story first experiences a strongly negative state of affairs, but this state eventually gives way (either as remembered in the event itself or as a matter of retrospective interpretation) to a positive result. The negative past is salvaged, saved, or redeemed by what follows. A number of studies suggest that narrating one's life in redemptive terms is associated with independent measures of psychological well-being and mental health.[69]

Redemption sequences appear often in the life stories constructed by American adults who also display high levels of *generativity*.[70] Derived from Erikson's theory of psychosocial development, generativity is an adult's concern for and commitment to promoting the well-being of future generations, through parenting, teaching, mentoring, and engaging in a wide range of activities aimed at leaving a positive legacy for the future.[71] Erikson conceived of generativity itself as something akin to a virtue, and a large body of research shows that adults who score high on self-report measures of generativity do indeed exhibit caring and prosocial behavior in a wide range of contexts, from parenting to community service.[72] With respect to life stories, generative adults are much more likely than their less generative counterparts to construct narratives that feature an early awareness of a moral or spiritual calling in life, sensitivity to suffering and injustice in the world, moral steadfastness, redemption sequences, and the tendency to anticipate a future of growth and fruition.[73] McAdams has argued that constructing this kind of redemptive story for one's life serves as a psychological resource for highly generative adults.[74] If one's story affirms the power of human redemption and proclaims that one has been called to do good work in the world, even in the face of suffering and injustice, then one may be better prepared, psychologically speaking, for the disappointments and frustrations that invariably accompany a life dedicated to generativity. Living out one's vocation of virtue is hard work; it helps to have a good story.

At the same time, individual life narratives reflect the values and conventions that a society holds dear.[75] Going back to the founding myths regarding the Puritan migration to the New World, Americans have always cherished narratives of personal redemption. In my book, *The Redemptive Self*, I have explored the historical, cultural, and literary sources of redemptive stories in American society, focusing on narratives of religious atonement, upward social mobility (the "American Dream"), personal liberation, and recovery.[76] Highly generative American adults tend to draw upon these master narratives to make sense of their own lives, blending cultural sources and personal experience to comprehend a virtuous life in time. In that autobiographical authors cannot help but borrow images and metaphors from the culture wherein they live and they narrate, individual stories of virtuous lives invariably reflect the dominant categories that particular social groups and societies writ large employ in order to understand themselves as social collectives and to comprehend their place in the world.

CONCLUSION

From the standpoint of contemporary psychological science, theory and research on human virtue follow the three broad characterizations of self-development that I have outlined in this essay: the self as social actor, motivated agent, and autobiographical author. As social actors, human beings develop dispositional traits—habitual patterns of feeling and behavior—that come to comprise their social reputations. As motivated agents, human beings articulate goals, plans, and values as they aim to achieve desired ends and avoid undesired ends. As autobiographical authors, human beings construct life stories that integrate the reconstructed past and imagined future in order to provide life with some semblance of unity and temporal continuity. Hints of this tripartite conception may be discerned in Aristotle's *Nicomachean Ethics*, a canonical text in Western thinking on virtue. For Aristotle, virtue begins with learning habits of good conduct (akin to the social actor's traits), which ideally paves the way for the consolidation of purposive tendencies (the motivated agent's goals and values) that capture the deliberative and future-oriented nature of virtue. Finally, a virtuous life culminates in the wisdom and contemplation ideally associated with mature adulthood, Aristotle argued, a developmental move that roughly parallels the psychological emergence of the autobiographical author and the construction of a self-defining life story.

As potentially rational creatures who evolved to live in complex social groups, human beings begin life as social actors, performing emotion and behavior in the presence of others. Early social performance is shaped by the temperament dispositions that appear in the first two years of life—positive emotionality, negative emotionality, and effortful control. Through complex gene × environment interactions, these dispositions eventually become full-fledged personality traits. In its most basic developmental sense, virtue is expressed through the habitual patterns of feeling and behavior that temperament dispositions and the broader traits of personality are able to afford. Most notably, the developmental line that tracks how effortful control gradually morphs into the traits of agreeableness and conscientiousness has widespread implications for a psychology of virtue. By recruiting the socializing power of empathy and guilt, this particular line of development clears a pathway for the many different forms of virtuous conduct that require some considerable degree of self-control.

Whereas certain dispositional traits may promote virtuous behavior, traits do not directly speak to the motivation behind behavior. As children move into elementary school, they gradually become motivated agents, as well as social actors. This developmental move paves the way for the articulation of long-term goals and values, which themselves layer over the (still developing) dispositional traits of the social actor. In Aristotle's terms, motivated agents are capable of rational deliberation; they can systematically sort through the contingencies of a given situation in order to derive plans and articulate purpose. They can make virtuous choices. In contemporary psychological science, many different theories mark the emergence of motivated agency in middle-childhood, and with it enhanced expectations regarding moral development and the articulation of virtue. Moreover, research in this area has shown that articulating personal goals that emphasize the virtues of benevolence and friendship tend to be associated with higher levels of psychological well-being and mental health.

In the adult years, the self thickens to encompass the life stories that people construct in order to make meaning of their lives in time. Life stories eventually layer over goals and values, which layer over dispositional traits. Adults employ the powers of autobiographical reasoning to craft narratives that explain how they came to be the person they are now becoming, and how they will continue to develop in the future. As imaginative reconstructions of the past and anticipations of the future, life stories also draw upon the themes, metaphors, and models for living that prevail in a given culture. From the perspective of life narrative, some people are able to affirm a vocation in virtue—a life in full dedicated, as the narrator sees it, to the fulfillment of a personal destiny or calling toward virtue. As shown in studies of moral exemplars and highly generative American adults, these stories often celebrate the power of human redemption, tracking how suffering can ultimately lead to personal and social enhancement.

For some people, then, habits of virtuous conduct, as captured in dispositional traits, may promote goals and values aimed at virtuous ends, as social actors become motivated agents, too. And virtuous goals may become so salient in a person's life that they result in a vocation of virtue, which may express itself as a redemptive life story wherein the protagonist feels called to live a life of higher purpose. But such an idealization is certainly the exception, rather than the rule. As social actors, we may behave in ways that promote or obstruct the wellbeing of others and ourselves. As motivated agents, we sometimes make choices that suggest a purposive engagement of virtue, and sometimes we choose an alternative path. As autobiographical authors, we may recall and cherish key scenes or plot lines in our lives that exemplify the expression of virtue, and we remember with regret many others through which we failed to achieve anything close to moral excellence. There are so many different ways to succeed in the expression of human virtue. And so many ways to fall short.

AUTHOR NOTE

Work on this chapter was supported, in part, by a grant from the University of Chicago and the Templeton Foundation under the aegis of "A New Science of Virtues." Address correspondence to: Dan P. McAdams, Department of Psychology, Northwestern University, 2120 N. Campus Drive, Evanston, IL 60208. dmca@northwestern.edu.

NOTES

1. B. F. Skinner, *Behavior of Organisms* (New York: Appleton-Century-Crofts, 1938).
2. G. W. Allport, *Personality: A Psychological Interpretation* (New York: Holt, Rinehart & Winston, 1937).

3. W. Mischel, *Personality and Assessment* (New York: Wiley, 1968).
4. B. W. Roberts and W. F. DelVecchio, "The Rank-order Consistency of Personality Traits from Childhood to Old Age," *Psychological Bulletin* 126 (2000): 3–25.
5. S. Epstein, "The Stability of Behavior across Time and Situations," in *Personality and the Prediction of Behavior,* ed. R. A. Zucker, J. Aronoff, and A. I. Rabin (New York: Academic Press, 1984): 209–68.
6. B. W. Roberts, N. R. Kuncel, R. Shiner, A. Caspi, and L. R. Goldberg, "The Power of Personality: The Comparative Validity of Personality Traits, Socioeconomic Status, and Cognitive Ability for Predicting Important Life Outcomes," *Perspectives on Psychological Science* 2 (2007): 313–45.
7. M. E. P. Seligman, and M. Csikszentmihalyi, "Positive Psychology: An Introduction," *American Psychologist* 55 (2000): 5–14.
8. C. Peterson and M. E. P. Seligman, *Character Strengths and Virtues: A Handbook and Classification* (New York: Oxford University Press, 2004).
9. D. P. McAdams, "The Psychological Self as Actor, Agent, and Author," *Perspectives on Psychological Science* 8 (2013): 272–95.
10. Aristotle, *The Nicomachean Ethics*, trans. J. A. K. Thomson, ed. H. Tredennick (London: Penguin, 2004), 16.
11. Aristotle, *Nicomachean Ethics,* 246.
12. E. O. Wilson, *The Social Conquest of Earth* (New York: Liveright, 2012).
13. R. Hogan, "A Socioanalytic Theory of Personality," *Nebraska Symposium on Motivation,* vol. 29, ed. M. Page (Lincoln: University of Nebraska Press, 1982), 55–89.
14. D. P. McAdams and J. L. Pals, "A New Big Five: Fundamental Principles for an Integrative Science of Personality," *American Psychologist* 61 (2006): 204–17.
15. Aristotle, *Nicomachean Ethics,* 32.
16. D. P. McAdams, "The Moral Personality," in *Personality, Identity and Character: Explorations in Moral Psychology,* ed. D. Narvaez and D. K. Lapsley (New York: Cambridge University Press, 2009), 11–29; McAdams, "The Psychological Self"; D. P. McAdams and B. Olson, "Personality Development: Continuity and Change over the Life Course," In *Annual Review of Psychology,* vol. 61, ed. S. Fiske, D. Schacter, and R. Sternberg (Palo Alto, CA: Annual Reviews, 2010), 517–43.
17. D. Narvaez and D. K. Lapsley, eds., *Personality, Identity, and Character: Explorations in Moral Psychology* (New York: Cambridge University Press, 2009).
18. E.g., M. L. Diener, S. C. Mangelsdorf, J. L. McHale, and C. A. Frosch, "Infants' Behavioral Strategies of Emotion Regulation with Fathers and Mothers: Associations with Emotional Expressions and Attachment Quality," *Infancy* 3 (2002): 153–74.
19. M. Zentner and R. L. Shiner, eds., *Handbook of Temperament* (New York: Guilford, 2012).
20. M. K. Rothbart, "Temperament, Development, and Personality," *Current Directions in Psychological Science* 16 (2007): 207–12.
21. R. L. Shiner and C. G. De Young, "The Structure of Temperament and Personality Traits: A Developmental Perspective," In *Handbook of Developmental Psychology,* ed. P. D. Zelazo (New York: Oxford University Press, 2013), 113–41.
22. R. R. McCrae and P. T. Costa Jr., "The Five-Factor Theory of Personality," in *Handbook of Personality: Theory and Research,* 3rd. ed., ed. O. P. John, R. W. Robins, and L. A. Pervin (New York: Guilford, 2008): 159–80.
23. B. L. Fredrickson, "The Role of Positive Emotions in Positive Psychology: The Broaden-and-Build Theory of Positive Emotions," *American Psychologist* 56 (2001): 218–26.
24. L. C. Vincent, K. J. Emich, and J. A. Goncalo, "Strengthening the Moral Gray Zone: Positive Affect, Moral Disengagement, and Dishonesty," *Psychological Science* 24 (2013): 595–99.

25. McCrae and Costa, "The Five-Factor Theory."
26. Rothbart, "Temperament."
27. M. R. Rueda, "Effortful Control," in *Handbook of Temperament*, ed. M. Zentner and R. L. Shiner (New York: Guilford, 2012), 145–67.
28. G. Kochanska and N. Aksan, "Children's Conscience and Self-regulation," *Journal of Personality* 74 (2006): 1587–617.
29. J. V. Fayard, B. W. Roberts, R. W. Robins, and D. Watson, "Uncovering the Affective Core of Conscientiousness: The Role of Self-conscious Emotions," *Journal of Personality* 80 (2012): 1–32.
30. M. K. Matsuba, and L. J. Walker, "Extraordinary Moral Commitment: Young Adults Working for Social Organizations," *Journal of Personality* 72 (2004): 413–36.
31. J. Lodi-Smith, and B. W. Roberts, "Social Investment and Personality: A Meta-analysis of the Relationship between Personality Traits and Investment in Work, Family, Religion, and Volunteerism," *Personality and Social Psychology Review* 11 (2007): 68–86.
32. T. Bogg and B. W. Roberts, "Conscientiousness and Health-related Behavior: A Meta-analysis of the Leading Behavioral Contributors to Mortality," *Psychological Bulletin* 130 (2004): 887–919; B. W. Roberts and R. Hogan, eds., *Personality Psychology in the Workplace* (Washington, DC: American Psychological Association Press, 2001).
33. Allport, *Personality*.
34. Aristotle, *Nicomachean Ethics*, 37.
35. Aristotle, *Nicomachean Ethics*, 72.
36. Aristotle, *Nicomachean Ethics*, 57.
37. Aristotle, *Nicomachean Ethics*, 42, italics added.
38. A. J. Sameroff and M. M. Haith, eds., *The Five to Seven Year Shift* (Chicago: University of Chicago Press, 1996).
39. J. Piaget, "Piaget's Theory," in *Carmichael's Manual of Child Psychology*, vol. 1, 2nd ed., ed. P. H. Mussen (New York: Wiley, 1970), 703–32.
40. J. Piaget, *The Moral Judgment of the Child* (New York: Free Press, 1965).
41. L. Kohlberg, "Stage and Sequence: The Cognitive Developmental Approach to Socialization," in *Handbook of Socialization Theory and Research*, ed. D. A. Goslin (Skokie, IL: Rand McNally, 1969), 347–480.
42. Sameroff and Haith, *The Five*.
43. E. H. Erikson, *Childhood and Society*, 2nd ed. (New York: Norton, 1963).
44. Aristotle, *Nicomachean Ethics*, 80–81.
45. McAdams, "The Psychological Self"; T. A. Walls and S. H. Kollat, "Agency to Agentic Personalities," in *Handbook of Personality Development*, ed. D. Mroczek and T. Little (Mahwah, NJ: Lawrence Erlbuam, 2006), 231–44.
46. Aristotle, *Nicomachean Ethics*, 41.
47. M. E. McCullough, R. A. Emmons, and J. A. Tsang, "The Grateful Disposition: A Conceptual and Empirical Topography," *Journal of Personality and Social Psychology* 82 (2002): 112–27.
48. J. W. Berry, E. L. Worthington, L. Parrott, L. E. O'Connor, and N. G. Wade, "Dispositional Forgiveness: Development and Construct Validity of the Transgression Narrative Test of Forgiveness (TNTF)," *Personality and Social Psychology Bulletin* 27 (2001): 1277–90.
49. J. J. Bauer and D. P. McAdams, "Growth Goals, Maturity, and Well-being," *Developmental Psychology* 40 (2004): 114–27; T. Kasser and R. M. Ryan, "Further Examining the American Dream: Well-being Correlates of Intrinsic and Extrinsic Goals," *Personality and Social Psychology Bulletin* 22 (1996): 281–88.

50. E. g., E. de St. Aubin, "Personal Ideology Polarity: Its Emotional Foundation and its Manifestation in Individual Value Systems, Religiosity, Political Orientation, and Assumptions Concerning Human Nature," *Journal of Personality and Social Psychology* 71 (1996): 152–65; S. H. Schwartz and W. Bilsky, "Toward a Theory of the Universal Content and Structure of Human Values: Extensions and Cross-cultural Replications," *Journal of Personality and Social Psychology* 58 (1990): 878–91.
51. Aristotle, *Nicomachean Ethics*, 270.
52. Aristotle, *Nicomachean Ethics*, 271–72.
53. P. B. Baltes and U. M. Staudinger, "Wisdom: A Metaheuristic (Pragmatic) to Orchestrate Mind and Body Towards Excellence," *American Psychologist* 55 (2000): 122–36.
54. R. N. Butler, "The Life Review: An Interpretation of Reminiscence in Old Age," *Psychiatry* 26 (1963): 65–76; J. P. Serrano, J. M. Latorre, M. Gatz, and J. Montanes, "Life Review Therapy Using Autobiographical Retrieval Practice for Older Adults with Depressive Symptomatology," *Psychology and Aging* 19 (2004): 358–62.
55. Aristotle, *Nicomachean Ethics*, 275.
56. E. H. Erikson, *Young Man Luther* (New York: Norton, 1958).
57. Erikson, *Young Man Luther*, 111–12.
58. D. P. McAdams, *Power, Intimacy, and the Life Story: Personological Inquiries into Identity* (Homewood, IL: Dorsey, 1985; D. P. McAdams and K. C. McLean, "Narrative Identity," *Current Directions in Psychological Science* 22 (2013): 233–38.
59. T. Habermas and S. Bluck. "Getting a Life: The Emergence of the Life Story in Adolescence," *Psychological Bulletin* 126 (2000): 748–69.
60. K. C. McLean, M. Pasupathi, and J. L. Pals, "Selves Becoming Stories Becoming Selves: A Process Model of Self-development," *Personality and Social Psychology Review* 11 (2007): 265–78.
61. McAdams, "The Psychological Self."
62. A. MacIntyre, *After Virtue* (Notre Dame, IN: University of Notre Dame Press, 1981); C. Taylor, *Sources of the Self: The Making of the Modern Identity* (Cambridge, MA: Harvard University Press, 1989).
63. D. P. McAdams, *The Redemptive Self: Stories Americans Live by*, rev. ed. (New York: Oxford University Press, 2013).
64. M. Weber, *The Protestant Ethic and the Spirit of Capitalism* (New York: Charles Scribner's Sons, 1958).
65. McAdams, *The Redemptive Self*.
66. A. Colby and W. Damon, *Some Do Care: Contemporary Lives of Moral Commitment* (New York: Free Press, 1992).
67. L. J. Walker and J. A. Frimer, "Moral Personality of Brave and Caring Exemplars," *Journal of Personality and Social Psychology* 93 (2007): 845–60; J. A. Frimer, L. J. Walker, W. L. Dunlop, B. H. Lee, and A. Riches, "The Integration of Agency and Communion in Moral Personality: Evidence of Enlightened Self-interest," *Journal of Personality and Social Psychology* 101 (2011): 149–63.
68. McAdams, *The Redemptive Self*.
69. McAdams, *The Redemptive Self*; D. P. McAdams, J. Reynolds, M. Lewis, A. Patten, and P. J. Bowman, "When Bad Things Turn Good and Good Things Turn Bad: Sequences of Redemption and Contamination in Life Narrative, and Their Relation to Psychosocial Adaptation in Midlife Adults and in Students," *Personality and Social Psychology Bulletin* 27 (2001): 472–83.
70. McAdams, *The Redemptive Self*; D. P. McAdams, A. Diamond, E. de St. Aubin, and E. D. Mansfield, "Stories of Commitment: The Psychosocial Construction of Generative Lives," *Journal of Personality and Social Psychology* 72 (1997): 678–94.

71. Erikson, *Childhood*.
72. B. K. Jones and D. P. McAdams, "Becoming Generative: Socializing Influences in the Life Stories of Euro-American and African-American Adults in Late Midlife," *Journal of Adult Development* 20 (2013): 158–72; McAdams, *The Redemptive Self*.
73. McAdams, *The Redemptive Self*; D. P. McAdams et al., "Stories of Commitment."
74. McAdams, *The Redemptive Self*.
75. A. Giddens, *Modernity and Self-identity: Self and Society in the Late Modern Age* (Stanford, CA: Stanford University Press, 1991); P. L. Hammack, "Narrative and the Cultural Psychology of Identity," *Personality and Social Psychology Review* 12 (2008): 222–47; MacIntyre, *After Virtue*.
76. McAdams, *The Redemptive Self*.

BIBLIOGRAPHY

Allport, G. W. *Personality: A Psychological Interpretation*. New York: Holt, Rinehart & Winston, 1937.

Aristotle. *The Nicomachean Ethics*. Translated by J. A. K. Thomson, revised with notes and appendices by H. Tredennick. London: Penguin, 2004.

Baltes, P. B., and U. M. Staudinger. "Wisdom: A Metaheuristic (Pragmatic) to Orchestrate Mind and body Towards Excellence." *American Psychologist* 55 (2000): 122–36.

Bauer, J. J., and D. P. McAdams. "Growth Goals, Maturity, and Well-being." *Developmental Psychology* 40 (2004): 114–27.

Berry, J. W., E. L. Worthington, L. Parrott, L. E. O'Connor, and N. G. Wade. "Dispositional Forgiveness: Development and Construct Validity of the Transgression Narrative Test of Forgiveness (TNTF)." *Personality and Social Psychology Bulletin* 27 (2001): 1277–90.

Bogg, T., and B. W. Roberts. "Conscientiousness and Health-related Behavior: A Meta-analysis of the Leading Behavioral Contributors to Mortality." *Psychological Bulletin* 130 (2004): 887–919.

Butler, R. N. "The Life Review: An Interpretation of Reminiscence in Old Age." *Psychiatry* 26 (1963): 65–76.

Colby, A., and W. Damon. *Some Do Care: Contemporary Lives of Moral Commitment*. New York: Free Press, 1992.

de St. Aubin, E. "Personal Ideology Polarity: Its Emotional Foundation and Its Manifestation in Individual Value Systems, Religiosity, Political Orientation, and Assumptions Concerning Human Nature." *Journal of Personality and Social Psychology* 71 (1996): 152–65.

Diener, M. L., S. C. Mangelsdorf, J. L. McHale, and C. A. Frosch. "Infants' Behavioral Strategies of Emotion Regulation with Fathers and Mothers: Associations with Emotional Expressions and Attachment Quality." *Infancy* 3 (2002): 153–74.

Epstein, S. "The Stability of Behavior across Time and Situations." In *Personality and the Prediction of Behavior*, edited by R. A. Zucker, J. Aronoff, and A. I. Rabin, 209–68. New York: Academic Press, 1984.

Erikson, E. H. *Young Man Luther*. New York: Norton, 1958.

Erikson, E. H. *Childhood and Society*, 2nd ed. New York: Norton, 1963.

Fayard, J. V., B. W. Roberts, R. W. Robins, and D. Watson. "Uncovering the Affective Core of Conscientiousness: The Role of Self-conscious Emotions." *Journal of Personality* 80 (2012): 1–32.

Fredrickson, B. L. "The Role of Positive Emotions in Positive Psychology: The Broaden-and-Build Theory of Positive Emotions." *American Psychologist* 56 (2001): 218–26.

Frimer, J. A., L. J. Walker, W. L. Dunlop, B. H. Lee, and A. Riches. "The Integration of Agency and Communion in Moral Personality: Evidence of Enlightened Self-interest." *Journal of Personality and Social Psychology* 101 (2011): 149–63.

Giddens, A. *Modernity and Self-identity: Self and Society in the Late Modern Age.* Stanford, CA: Stanford University Press, 1991.

Habermas, T., and S. Bluck. "Getting a Life: The Emergence of the Life Story in Adolescence." *Psychological Bulletin* 126 (2000): 748–69.

Hammack, P. L. "Narrative and the Cultural Psychology of Identity." *Personality and Social Psychology Review* 12 (2008): 222–47.

Hogan, R. "A Socioanalytic Theory of Personality." In *Nebraska Symposium on Motivation,* vol. 29, edited by M. Page, 55–89. Lincoln: University of Nebraska Press, 1982.

Jones, B. K., and D. P. McAdams. "Becoming Generative: Socializing Influences in the Life Stories of Euro-American and African-American Adults in Late Midlife." *Journal of Adult Development* 20 (2013): 15872.

Kasser, T., and R. M. Ryan. "Further Examining the American Dream: Well-being Correlates of Intrinsic and Extrinsic Goals." *Personality and Social Psychology Bulletin* 22 (1996): 281–88.

Kochanska, G., and N. Aksan. "Children's Conscience and Self-regulation." *Journal of Personality* 74 (2006): 1587–617.

Kohlberg, L. "Stage and Sequence: The Cognitive Developmental Approach to Socialization." In *Handbook of Socialization Theory and Research,* edited by D. A. Goslin, 347–480. Skokie, IL: Rand McNally, 1969.

Lodi-Smith, J., and B. W. Roberts. "Social Investment and Personality: A Meta-analysis of the Relationship between Personality Traits and Investment in Work, Family, Religion, and Volunteerism." *Personality and Social Psychology Review* 11 (2007): 68–86.

MacIntyre, A. *After Virtue.* Notre Dame, IN: University of Notre Dame Press, 1981.

Matsuba, M. K., and L. J. Walker. "Extraordinary Moral Commitment: Young Adults Working for Social Organizations." *Journal of Personality* 72 (2004): 413–36.

McAdams, D. P. "The Moral Personality." In *Personality, Identity, and Character: Explorations in Moral Psychology,* edited by D. Narvaez and D. K. Lapsley, 11–29. New York: Cambridge University Press, 2009.

McAdams, D. P. *Power, Intimacy, and the Life Story: Personological Inquiries into Identity.* Homewood, IL: Dorsey, 1985.

McAdams, D. P. "The Psychological Self as Actor, Agent, and Author." *Perspectives on Psychological Science* 8 (2013): 272–95.

McAdams, D. P. *The Redemptive Self: Stories Americans Live By,* rev. ed. New York: Oxford University Press, 2013.

McAdams, D. P., A. Diamond, E. de St. Aubin, and E. D. Mansfield. "Stories of Commitment: The Psychosocial Construction of Generative Lives." *Journal of Personality and Social Psychology* 72 (1997): 678–94.

McAdams, D. P., and K. C. McLean. "Narrative Identity." *Current Directions in Psychological Science,* 22 (2013): 233–38.

McAdams, D. P., and B. Olson. "Personality Development: Continuity and Change over the Life Course." In *Annual Review of Psychology,* vol. 61, edited by S. Fiske, D. Schacter, and R. Sternberg, 517–43. Palo Alto, CA: Annual Reviews, 2010.

McAdams, D. P., and J. L. Pals. "A New Big Five: Fundamental Principles for an Integrative Science of Personality." *American Psychologist* 61 (2006): 204–17.

McAdams, D. P., J. Reynolds, M. Lewis, A. Patten, and P. J. Bowman. "When Bad Things Turn Good and Good Things Turn Bad: Sequences of Redemption and Contamination in Life Narrative, and Their Relation to Psychosocial Adaptation in Midlife Adults and in Students." *Personality and Social Psychology Bulletin* 27 (2001): 472–83.

McCrae, R. R., and P. T. Costa Jr. "The Five-Factor Theory of Personality." In *Handbook of Personality: Theory and Research,* 3rd ed., edited by O. P. John, R. W. Robins, and L. A. Pervin, 159–80. New York: Guilford, 2008.

McCullough, M. E., R. A. Emmons, and J. A. Tsang, J. A. "The Grateful Disposition: A Conceptual and Empirical Topography." *Journal of Personality and Social Psychology* 82 (2002): 112–27.

McLean, K. C., M. Pasupathi, and J. L. Pals. "Selves Becoming Stories Becoming Selves: A Process Model of Self-development." *Personality and Social Psychology Review* 11 (2007): 265–78.

Mischel, W. *Personality and Assessment.* New York: Wiley, 1968.

Narvaez, D., and D. K. Lapsley, eds. *Personality, Identity, and Character: Explorations in Moral Psychology.* New York: Cambridge University Press, 2009.

Peterson, C., and M. E. P. Seligman. *Character Strengths and Virtues: A Handbook and Classification.* New York: Oxford University Press, 2004.

Piaget, J. *The Moral Judgment of the Child.* New York: Free Press, 1965.

Piaget, J. "Piaget's Theory." In *Carmichael's Manual of Child Psychology,* vol. 1, 2nd. ed., edited by P. H. Mussen, 703–32. New York: Wiley, 1970.

Roberts, B. W., and W. F. DelVecchio. "The Rank-order Consistency of Personality Traits from Childhood to Old Age." *Psychological Bulletin* 126 (2000): 3–25.

Roberts, B. W., and R. Hogan, eds. *Personality Psychology in the Workplace.* Washington, DC: American Psychological Association Press, 2001.

Roberts, B. W., N. R. Kuncel, R. Shiner, A. Caspi, and L. R. Goldberg. "The Power of Personality: The Comparative Validity of Personality Traits, Socioeconomic Status, and Cognitive Ability for Predicting Important Life Outcomes." *Perspectives on Psychological Science* 2 (2007): 313–45.

Rothbart, M. K. "Temperament, Development, and Personality." *Current Directions in Psychological Science* 16 (2007): 207–12.

Rueda, M. R. "Effortful Control." In *Handbook of Temperament,* edited by M. Zentner and R. L. Shiner, 145–67. New York: Guilford, 2012.

Sameroff, A. J., and M. M. Haith, eds. *The Five to Seven Year Shift.* Chicago: University of Chicago Press, 1996.

Schwartz, S. H., and W. Bilsky. "Toward a Theory of the Universal Content and Structure of Human Values: Extensions and Cross-cultural Replications." *Journal of Personality and Social Psychology* 58 (1990): 878–91.

Seligman, M. E. P., and M. Csikszentmihalyi. "Positive Psychology: An Introduction." *American Psychologist* 55 (2000): 5–14.

Serrano, J. P., J. M. Latorre, M. Gatz, and J. Montanes. "Life Review Therapy Using Autobiographical Retrieval Practice for Older Adults with Depressive Symptomatology." *Psychology and Aging* 19 (2004): 358–62.

Shiner, R. L., and C. G. De Young. "The Structure of Temperament and Personality Traits: A Developmental Perspective." In *Handbook of Developmental Psychology,* edited by P. D. Zelazo, 113–41. New York: Oxford University Press, 2013.

Skinner, B. F. *Behavior of Organisms.* New York: Appleton-Century-Crofts, 1938.

Taylor, C. *Sources of the Self: The Making of the Modern Identity.* Cambridge, MA: Harvard University Press, 1989.

Vincent, L. C., K. J. Emich, and J. A. Goncalo. "Strengthening the Moral Gray Zone: Positive Affect, Moral Disengagement, and Dishonesty." *Psychological Science* 24 (2013): 595–99.

Walker, L. J., and J. A. Frimer. "Moral Personality of Brave and Caring Exemplars." *Journal of Personality and Social Psychology* 93 (2007): 845–60.

Walls, T. A., and S. H. Kollat. "Agency to Agentic Personalities." In *Handbook of Personality Development,* edited by D. Mroczek and T. Little, 231–44. Mahwah, NJ: Lawrence Erlbaum, 2006.

Weber, M. *The Protestant Ethic and the Spirit of Capitalism.* New York: Charles Scribner's Sons, 1958.

Wilson, E. O. *The Social Conquest of Earth.* New York: Liveright, 2012.

Zentner, M., and R. L. Shiner, eds. *Handbook of Temperament.* New York: Guilford, 2012.

INDEX

Acceptance, social, 310
Aesthetics, Mill and moral
    sentimentalism on, 55
  rationalism and judgments on, 57
  virtue and, 56–57
Agape, 123–124
Aggregation effect, situationism and,
    138–139
Agile mind, 252
Agreeableness, 315, 316t
Altruism
  in empathy, 72
  gratitude in, 72
  pathological, 124–125
Anger
  from childhood lack of love and abuse,
    68, 69, 70, 73, 78
  generalization of, 73
Angle, Stephen, 123–124
Annas, Julia, 111, 215
Applied ethics, 251–252
Aquinas, Thomas, 235, 236
Aristotle
  on licentiousness, 319–320
  on pleasure and pain, early shaping
    of, 25
  rational principle of, 310, 320
  on wisdom and contemplation,
    321–323
Aristotle, on virtue
  as cultivated, 17–18
  definition of, 20–21
  as excellence, 20–22, 309
  as getting better, 18
  happiness in, 309, 321–322
  as *hexis* (attribute), 21, 24, 26, 30
  mean of, 122–123
  as mundane, 20–23

nature of, 17
  in *Nicomachean Ethics*, 23, 234,
    307–329 (*See also Nicomachean
    Ethics*)
  path-dependent approach of,
    19–20, 30
  vs. practical intelligence, 22
  right instruments for, 128
Aristotle, on virtue acquisition
  central contention of, 30
  as mundane, 23–27
  ethos in, 23–25
  political power in, 32
  psychology of skill and moral
    development in, 32–36
  research program of, 30–32
  as skills acquisition, 18, 20, 22, 23, 26,
    31, 311–312
  Kahneman on, 37
  messiness of, 40–41
  mundane, 24, 27–29
  regularity of learning environment
    and feedback in, 37–39
Art of life, Mill's, 55–61
  aesthetics in, 55
    rationalism and judgments on, 57
    virtue and, 56–57
  calm passions in, 59
  duty in, sense of
    vs. sin, 59–60
    vs. supererogation, 55
  sympathies and enlightened
    self-interest in, 56
  happiness of all sentient beings in, 59
  imaginative engagement in, 58
  impartial spectator standard in, 59
  inner life focus in, 61
  literary fiction in, 60

Art of life *(continued)*
  morality in, 55
  perspective-taking in, 56–59
  prudence in, 55
  sympathies in
    enlarged, 58
    happiness and, 61
    variability of, 58
Asceticism
  in Christianity, 229–230, 231,
    233–234
  Ibn Misawayh's rejection of, 206
  modern views on, 239
Associative empathy, 69
  mediated, 71–72
Attribution error, fundamental, 153–154
Attributions
  of moral goodness, 311
  of virtue, 240
Augustine
  on humility as dependency on God,
    233
  on love of God in virtue, 235
  on sexuality as flawed, 204
Augustinians, modern, rejection of
    virtue by, 236–238
Authority, in moral sentimentalism, 53
Autobiographical author, 308–309,
    321–329
  authoring of life by exemplars of
    virtue in, 325–327
  wisdom and contemplation in,
    321–323
  wisdom and contemplation in, and
    psychology of adulthood,
    322–325
Autobiographical reasoning, 325
Automaticity, in skill development, 36
Autopoieisis, in virtue development, 267

Baptism, in Christianity, 230
Behaviorist perspective, 307
Being-in-the-world, in Buddhism, 173
Benevolence, as instinct, 78
Blasi, Augusto, 297–298
Bodily practices, Islam on, 201–204
  veiling and, 210–211
Brave exemplars, 326
Breastfeeding, 256–257
Brin, David, 128

Buddhism, 171–188
  compassion and loving-kindness in,
    173, 178, 186
  conceptual *vs.* non-conceptual truths
    in, 172, 182
  core of, 174–176
  education of youth in, 187–188
  as form of life, 172–174
  Four Noble Truths in, 174, 179
  getting *vs.* conveying, 188
  individual and communal work in,
    183–187
  meditation and mindfulness in,
    180–182, 186
  naturalization of, 185
  Noble Eightfold Path in, 175–176
  normative ethics and, 173
  path and Four Immeasurables in,
    177–178
  philosophical wisdom in, 178–180
  self-cultivation in, 178
  skillful means in, 184
  stories of exemplars *(Jakatas)* in,
    183–184
  on virtue as goodness, 173
Buddhist ethics
  alleviating suffering and bringing
    happiness in, 172
  as empiricist, 179
Bystander effect
  Christianity on, 239, 240, 242
  meditation on, 239

Calm passions, 59
"Cardinal" Christian virtues, love and
    humility as, 232–234, 236
Care ethics, 72, 80–81
Caring, 80–81
Caring exemplars, 326
Character cultivation. *See also specific
    traditions*
  in Christianity, 238–242
  in Confucianism, 150
  in Islam, 205–208
Charismatic virtue, 151
Chase, William, 33–34
Chess skill
  Chase and Simon on, 33–34
  regularity and feedback in learning of,
    39–40

Choice, virtue as, 308, 317–321, 328
  Aristotle on, 21, 36
  in children, 319–320
  habit *vs.* character in, 318
  Kant on, 89–91
  motivation in, 317
  personal goals in, 320
  purposive disposition in, 318–319
  research on, 321
  temperament dispositions and,
    317–318
Christ
  conformity to, 228–229
  as exemplar of virtues, 228–229, 236
  perfection of, 237, 240
Christianity, 227–243
  asceticism in, 229–230, 231, 233–234
  classical virtue ethics in, development
    of, 234–236
  conclusions on, 242–243
  cultivating virtue in, 238–242
  divine exemplarity and conformity to
    Christ in, 228–229
  emulating character of God in, 228
  ethical formation in, 227
  faith *vs.* virtuous activity in, 229
  heart in, 203
  on how to live, 227
  love and humility in, 230–231, 236
    as "cardinal" virtues, 232–234
  pagan reflection on virtues in, 227
  practices of, 242
    Christian formation, 229–232
    meditation, 231–232, 233, 237,
      242–243
    self-control, 231–232
  practice *vs.* theory in, 228, 243
  repudiation of virtue and its recovery
    in, 236–238
Co-construction of virtue, 251–269
  agile mind in, 252
  applied ethics in, 251–252
  autopoieisis in, 267
  companionship virtue in, 265–267, 269
  early life experience in, 253–257
  evolved developmental niche in,
    254–257, 268–269
    (*See also* Evolved developmental
    niche (EDN))
  moral orientation in, 258–262, 258f

  universals in virtue and culture in,
    262–265, 266f
Cognitive control models, 136
Cohen, Jonathan, 156
Colby, Ann, 326
Communal work, in Buddhism,
  183–187
Community involvement, in character
    cultivation in Islam, 205–208
Companionship, cooperative, 265, 266f
Companionship virtue, 265–267, 269
Compassion, 173, 178, 186
Compassion-extension
  in *The Mencius*, 146–149
  Snow on, 146
Competitive detachment, 265, 266f
Conceptual truths, 172
Conduct
  good and bad, 55
  in social groups
    rational human, 310–313
    virtuous, 311
  virtuous, habits of, 329
Confucianism
  on cultivation of moral traits,
    145–146
  rationality and willpower in, 155
  self-cultivation as manipulation of
    situation in, 150–154
  virtue ethics of
    situationist critique and, 135–158
    (*See also* Situationist critique, and
    early Confucian virtue ethics)
    as time-delayed cognitive control, 156
  virtue terms in, 143
Conscience
  definition of, 290
  development of
    early, 281, 290–294
    positive incentives on, 292–293
  measurement of, in young children, 291
Conscientiousness, 315–316, 316t
Contemplation
  adulthood and, psychology of,
    322–325
  happiness as, 321–322
  virtue from, Aristotle on, 321–323
Cooperative companionship, 265, 266f
Corporate virtue, of Ibn Miskawayh,
  206, 208, 213

Correlation coefficient
  0.3, 139–140, 144
  0.227 and cheating, 141–142
  debate about, 140
Cross-cultural diversity, 216–218
Cultivating virtue. *See also specific topics*
  in adolescent moral education, Kant
    on, 99–100
  in developmental psychology,
    279–280, 296–299 (*See also*
    Developmental psychology)
Cultural commons, 263
Culture
  diversity of virtue across, 216–218
  in virtue development, 262–265, 266f

Damon, William, 326
Definitions, of virtue
  by Aquinas, 235
  by Aristotle, 20–21
  by Ibn Miskawayh, 200
Deliberation, in choice, 318
Dependent being, 175
Dependent origination, 175
Detachment, competitive, 265, 266f
Developmental psychology, 279–300.
    See also specific topics
  conscience development in, 281,
    290–294
  cultivating virtue in, 279–280, 296–299
  growth of moral character in, 280
  moral self in, 280, 281, 291, 294–296
  premoral sensibility in, early, 281,
    282–288, 297
  research on younger children in,
    280–282
  virtue ethics in, 279
Dhammapada, 171, 177, 180, 184–185
Discipline
  of children, Kant on, 97–99
  inductive, 66
Disconnect objection, 114–115
Dispositional "extension," in Confucian
    moral training, 145–150
Dispositional traits
  habits of virtuous conduct in, 329
  for social reputation, 311
Divine exemplarity, 228–229
Doctrine of Virtue. *See* Kant, on virtue
  and the virtues

Donnellan, Brent, 141–142
Doris, John, 136, 142–143. *See also*
    Situationism, strong
Dreier, James, 118
Duty
  feelings of, 51
  Kant on, 93, 95
    to perfect oneself morally, 126–127
    perfect *vs.* imperfect, 101–102, 103
  sense of
    vs. sin, 59–60
    vs. supererogation, 55
    sympathies and enlightened
      self-interest in, 56

Early life experience, 253–257
Ecological theory for skill, 34–35
Education, moral
  Kant on
    in adolescents, 99–100
    in children, 97–99
  parent–child interactions in, early,
    66–67
Effortful control, 315, 316t
Emotion understanding, in early
    childhood, 289–290
Empathic affectivity roots, 258
Empathy, 263, 315, 316t
  associative (receptive), 69
  definition of, 71
  identification with other in, 71
  lack of, in sociopaths and psychopaths,
    67, 69–70
  literary fiction on, 60
  mediated associative, 71–72
  projective, 69
  vs. sympathy, 71
Empathy, roots of, 65–82
  altruistic motivation in, 72
  caring in, 80–81
  child's need for love in, 68–70, 79–80
  child's taking in love in, 76–77
  ethics of care in, 72
  gratitude in (*See also* Gratitude)
    in adults, 73–74
    as empathically absorbed sympathy
      for another, 74–79
    toward loving parents, 68, 70–73
  induction in, 66
  parental behavior on, 67–68

parent–child interactions in, early, 66–67
psychopathy and sociopathy *vs.*, 67,
68–70
sympathy toward us in, 74–76
Empirical inquiry, 135–136
Emptiness, 176, 182
Engagement ethic, 259–260, 263,
268–269
Enlightened self-interest, in sense of
duty, 56
Epigenetics, 253
Equanimity, 178
Erikson, Eric, 319, 324
Ethical formation, in Christianity, 227
Ethics, applied, 251–252
Ethos, 23–25
Eudaimonia, 111, 309
Christianity on, 234
in disconnect objection, 114
in narcissism objection, 112–113
Evolution, human, 253
Evolved developmental niche (EDN),
254–257, 268–269
breastfeeding and touch in, 256–257
in hunter-gatherer societies, nomadic,
262–264, 265
moral developmental systems theory
in, 258, 258f
prosocial behavior and, 257
responsive caregiving in, 254–255, 256
self-regulation in, 255–256, 257
social skills in, 256
triune ethics theory in, 259–262
Excellence, Aristotle on virtue as,
20–22, 309
Exemplars of virtue
authoring of life by, 325–327
in Buddhism, 183–184
Christ as, 236
redemption sequence in, 326–327
Expertise effects research, 34–35
Experts *vs.* novices, 32–33
Extent, of self-improvement, 123–124
Extraversion, 314, 316t

Faith *vs.* virtuous activity, in
Christianity, 229
Feedback, in skills acquisition, 37–39
Feelings
of duty, 51

social, sympathy in, 54
in virtue, Kant on, 91–92
Fiction, literary, on empathy, 60
Five Factor Model of Personality, 125
Flanagan, Owen, 135
Fogel, A., 254
Foucault, Michel, 201
Four Immeasurables, 177–178
Four Noble Truths, 174, 179
Fragmentation, in Christianity.
See Christianity
Frailty, in Christianity, 240, 242.
See also Christianity
Freedom, Kant on virtue as, 95–96
Frimer, Jeremy, 326
Fulfillment of moral nature, Kant on
virtue as, 95–97
Fundamental attribution error, 153–154
Funder, David, 141–142

Gendered, Islam on virtue as, 214–216
Generativity, 326–327
Generosity, 311
Good
in itself, virtue as, 49
Mill on, 49, 50
partial, eudaimonia and virtue as,
116–117
pleasure as, 50
Good conduct, 55
Goodness
Buddhism on virtue as, 173
Ibn Miskawayh on, 116–117, 203–204
moral, attributions of, 311
Good will, Kant on, 88–90
Grace, Divine, in Christianity, 229,
233, 236
Gratitude
in adults, 73–74
in altruism, 72
as empathically absorbed sympathy
for another, 74–79
in empathy, 70–73
from love, 232
in moral education, 68
spread of, 75
sympathy toward us in, 74–76
toward loving parents, 68, 70–73
Growth, of moral character, 280
Guilt, 315, 316t

Habit
 ethos as, 24
 hexis as, 21, 24, 26
 in infused virtues, 235–236
 in virtue, 318
 of virtuous conduct, 329
Habituation
 Aristotle on, 25
 of sexual appetites in Islam, 204–205
 veiling and, 211–212
Hadot, Pierre, 201, 231, 233
Haith, M. M., 319
Happiness. *See also* Eudaimonia
 of all sentient beings, 59
 as contemplative activity, 321–322
 as excellence, 309
 sympathy and, 61
 through virtue, to Aristotle, 309,
  321–322
 from virtue, 49
Harman, Gilbert, 136
Harshorne, Hugh, 141–142
Health, Kant on virtue as, 97
Heart, in Christianity, 203
Hedonism, Mill on, 50
Heteronomy, 135
Hexis (hexeis)
 virtues as, 21, 24, 26, 30
 virtue *vs.* skill in, 27–29
"High bar" argument
 definition of, 144
 early Confucian virtue ethics and,
  144–154
  Confucian self-cultivation as
   manipulation of situation in,
   150–154
  moral training and dispositional
   "extension" in, 145–150
 inapplicability of, to Confucianism, 145
Hill, Patrick, 157
Hoffman, Martin, 66
Horney, Karen, 125–126
Hume, David, 54, 56, 135, 239
Humility
 in Christianity, 231, 232–234, 236,
  237, 239, 242
 from prostration in prayer, in Islam, 202
Hunter-gatherer societies, nomadic,
  262–264, 265
Hutton, Eric, 154

Ibn Miskawayh, 199–200
 on character, 200
 ethics of, 200–201
 on virtue, 200
Ibn Miskawayh's synthesis. *See* Islam
Ibn Miskawayh's theory of virtue,
  199–208, 214–216
 bodily practices in, 201–204
  veiling and, 210–211
 cross-cultural diversity of virtue in,
  216–218
 ethics in, 200–201
 Greek thought and, 199–201
 self- and character formation in, 206
 sexual appetites in, habituating,
  204–205
  veiling and, 211–212
 on vanity, 205
 virtue as gendered in, 214–216
 virtue as social in, 205–208
  veiling in public and, 212–213
 virtues defined in, 200
Imagination ethic, 259, 260–261,
  263, 269
Imaginative engagement, 58
Impartial spectator standard, 59
Impermanence, 175, 179
Individual work, in Buddhism, 183–187
Inductive discipline (induction), 66
Inference of intentionality, in toddlers,
  282–283
Infused virtues, 235–236
Innate, morality as, 297
Instruments of self-improvement,
  128–129
Intentionality, in early childhood
 inference of, 282–283
 shared, 284–285, 288, 289, 291
Islam, 197–218
 cross-cultural diversity of virtue in,
  216–218
 etiquette *(adab)* in, 198–199
 heart in, 203
 Ibn Miskawayh's theory of virtue in,
  199–208 (*See also* Ibn
   Miskawayh's theory of virtue)
 legal *(fiqh)* thought and virtue ethics
  in, 198
 revelation and moral conduct in, 198
 virtue as gendered in, 214–216

virtue of the veil in, 208–214
  (*See also* Veil(ing), virtue of)
Ivanhoe, P. J., 149, 150–151

Johnson, Mark, 135
Johnson, Robert, 112, 118–120
Joy
  feeling another's, 67, 74 (*See also*
    Empathy)
  sympathetic, 178
Justice, 311

Kahneman, Daniel, on skills acquisition, 37
Kant, on virtue and the virtues, 87–104
  choice in, 89–91 (*See also* Choice,
    virtue as)
  duties in, 93, 95, 101–102, 103
    duty to perfect oneself morally,
      126–127
    perfect *vs.* imperfect, 101–102, 103
  feelings in, 91–92
  instruments for development of, 129
  moral education of children and
    adolescents in, 97–100
  moral luck and accomplishments in,
    91–93
  moral perfection in, 95
  moral self-improvement in, 100–102
  moral virtue as good, strong will to do
    what is right in, 87–91
  objections and replies to, 102–104
  self-improvement in, 127–128
  success/results and, 92–93
  unity of the virtues in, 93–95
  variety of virtues of, 93–94
  virtue as fulfillment of moral nature
    in, 95–97
Knowledge, Aristotle on, 22
Kochanska, Grazyna, 290, 295
Kohlberg, Lawrence, 280
  on moral development, 19–20, 319
  moralized psychology of, 19
Koustaal, Wilma, 252

Lapsley, Daniel, 157
  on experts *vs.* novices, 32–33
  on path-dependent approach, 20
  psychologized morality of, 19, 20
Learning as conceptual priming, in
  Confucianism, 152

Legal thought in Islam, moral conduct
  and, 198
Licentiousness, Aristotle on, 319–320
Life experience, early, in virtue
  development, 253–257
Life review, 323–324
Li (ritual), 150–151
Literary fiction, on empathy, 60
Local traits *vs.* global traits, 138–144.
  See also Situationism, strong
  anti-globalist critique of, 140–141
  Doris mechanic argument on, 142–143
  Hartshorne and May study on,
    141–142
  as spectrum *vs.* analytic dichotomy, 141
Love
  in Christianity, 230–231
    as "cardinal" virtue, 232–234
    Divine, Jesus as, 228
  on empathy
    child's need for, 68–70, 79–80
    child's taking in of, 68–70
Loving-kindness, 173, 178, 186
Lucas, Richard, 141–142
Luther, Martin, 237

Manipulation of situation, in Confucianism
  character training as, 150
  self-cultivation as, 150–154
Manner of self-improvement, 128
Martyrdom, in Christianity, 229–230
May, Mark, 141–142
McAdams, D. P., 327
Mean of virtue, Aristotle on, 122–123
Mediated associative empathy, 71–72
Meditation
  in Buddhism, 180–182, 186
  in Christianity, 231–232, 233, 237,
    242–243
Mencius, The, 146–149
Merrit, Maria, 236
Meta-ethics, 173
Metcalf, Barbara, 215
Mill, John Stuart
  on good, 49, 50
  on hedonism, 50
  on moral sentimentalism and virtue
    cultivation, 49–61
    art of life in, 55–61 (*See also* Art of
      life, Mill's)

Mill, John Stuart (*continued*)
   moral sentimentalists in, 51–55
     (*See also* Sentimentalism, moral,
     Mill and)
   virtue as good in itself in, 49
   virtue for utilitarians and, 50–51
   on virtue, 54
Mindful morality, 261
Mindfulness, 180–182
Mischel, Walter, 137–138, 139, 155
Mistreatment, parental, in psychopathy, 67
Modesty, in Islam. *See* Ibn Miskawayh's
   theory of virtue; Veil(ing), virtue of
Monastic spiritual practices, Christian, 231
Moral character, growth of, 280
Moral development
   as path-independent *vs.* path-dependent,
   19–20
   psychology of skill and, Aristotle on,
   32–36
Moral education, virtue from, 53
   Kant on
     in adolescents, 99–100
     in children, 97–99
     parent–child interactions in, early,
     66–67
Moral exemplars, 326. *See also*
   Exemplars of virtue
Moral identity, 294
Moral intentionality, 312
Morality. *See also specific topics*
   Mill on, 55
Morality, psychologized, 19
   of Aristotle, 30
   of Lapsley and Narvaez, 19, 20
Moralized psychology, 19
Moral life
   in Buddhism, 172–174 (*See also*
   Buddhism)
   systematicitiy and, 174
Moral luck, Kant on accomplishments
   and, 91–93
Moral orientation, virtue and, 258–262, 258f
Moral perfection, of Kant, 95
Moral self
   definition of, 294
   development of, 280, 281, 291,
   294–296
Moral self-improvement, Kant on,
   100–102

Moral sentimentalism, in utilitarian
   virtue cultivation, 49–61
   art of life in, 55–61 (*See also* Art of
   life, Mill's)
   moral sentimentalists in, 51–55 (*See also*
   Sentimentalism, moral, Mill and)
   virtue as good in itself in, 49
   virtue for utilitarians and, 50–51
Moral sentimentalists, 51–55
Moral training, Confucian, dispositional
   "extension" in, 145–150
Moral virtue as good, strong will to do
   what is right, 87–91
Motivated agent, 308–309, 317–321,
   328. *See also* Choice, virtue as
   vs. social actor, 312–313
Motivated intention, social action for, 312
Motive, for self-improvement, 124–126
Mundane, Aristotle on
   virtue acquisition as, 23–27
   virtue as, 20–23
Mundane skills acquisition, Aristotle on
   virtue acquisition as, 27–29
Murdoch, Iris, 58, 60, 254
Myles-Worsley, Marina, 34

Narcissism objection, 112–113
Narrative identity, 324–325
Narvaez, Darcia
   on experts *vs.* novices, 32–33
   on path-dependent approach, 20
   psychologized morality of, 19, 20
Nativist arguments, for morality, 297
Negative emotionality, 314–315, 316t
Neuroticism, 314–315, 316t
Nicomachean Ethics, 23, 234, 307–329.
     See also Aristotle; *specific concepts*
   habits of virtuous conduct in, 329
   virtue as choice (motivated agent) in,
   308, 317–321, 328
   virtue as temperament (social actor)
   in, 309–317, 328
   virtue as vocation (autobiographical
   author) in, 308–309, 321–329
   virtue for Aristotle in, 327–328
Nietzsche, Friedrich, on pathological
   altruism, 124–125
Noble Eightfold Path, 175–176
Noddings, Nel, 66, 80–81
Non-conceptual truths, 172, 182

No-self, 175–176, 182, 186
Nussbaum, Martha, 122

Pagan reflection, on virtues, in origins of
    Christianity, 227
Pain
    Aristotle on early shaping of, 25
    feeling another's, 67
    Plato on early shaping of, 25
Parent–child interactions (relationship),
        early
    on conscience development, 290–294
    on inductive disciplines, 66
    on moral education, 66–67
    on morality development, 67, 296, 313
    in psychopathy and sociopathy, 67–68
    sensitivity and mutual responsiveness
        in, 299
Path-dependent approach
    of Aristotle, 19–20, 30
    definition of, 19
    messiness of, 40–41
    Narvaez and Lapsley on, 20
Path-independent approach, 19–20
Pathological altruism, 124–125
People, in self-improvement, 127–128
Perfect duty, Kant on, 101–102, 103
Personality coefficient, 139–140
    0.3, 139–140, 144
Personality psychology, development of
        human virtues in, 308. *See also*
        Nicomachean Ethics
Personality traits. *See also* Temperament
    isomorphism between skill and, 35
    psychological science on, 308
    temperament differences in, 316t, 317
Personality traits, in situationism,
        137–144
    critique of, 308
    origins of person *vs.* situation debate
        in, 137–138
    strong situationism as anti-globalist
        argument in, 138–144
        conceptual issues in, 140–144
        empirical issues in, 138–140
Personal virtue motivation, rebuttal of
        virtue ethics as, 115–116
Perspective-taking, moral
        sentimentalism and
        emotional responses from, 58

motivation and, 57–58
training in, 56–59
Philosophical wisdom, in Buddhism,
    178–180
Piaget, Jean, on psychosocial develop-
    ment, 319
Plato
    on early conditioning, 25
    on pleasure and pain, early shaping of, 25
Pleasure
    Aristotle on early shaping of, 25
    higher *vs.* lower, 50
    as intrinsic good, 50
    Plato on early shaping of, 25
    virtue and, 52
Positive emotionality, 313–314, 316t
Positive psychology, 308
    development of human virtues in, 308
        (*See also Nicomachean Ethics*)
Practical intelligence, *vs.* skill,
        Aristotle on, 28
Premoral sensibility, developing early,
        280, 281, 282–288
    Blasi on, 297–298
    emotion understanding in, 289–290
    inference of intentionality in,
        282–283
    nativists on, 297
    parent–child interaction on, 297
    responding to actions of others in,
        285–288
    shared intentionality in, 284–285,
        288, 289, 291
    understanding of other people in,
        283–284
    virtue in, 297, 299
Projective empathy, 69
Prosocial behavior, 257
Prudence, Mill on, 55
Psychological science. *See also specific
        topics*
    moral virtues in, study of, 307–308
    recent history of, 307–308
    self as autobiographical author in, 308
    self as motivated agent in, 308–309,
        317–321, 328
    self as social actor in, 308,
        309–317, 328
        vs. motivated agent, 312–313
    theory and research on virtue in, 327

Psychologized morality, 19
  of Aristotle, 30
  of Lapsley and Narvaez, 19, 20
Psychopathy
  lack of emotional responsiveness in,
      69–70
  origins of, 79
  parental neglect or abuse in, 67, 79
  parent–child interactions in, early, 67
  rage in, 79
  sadistic, 69
Psychosocial development
  Erikson on, 319
  Piaget on, 319
  Sameroff and Haith on, 319

Radiologist skills, 34
Rage
  from childhood lack of love and abuse,
      68, 69, 70, 73, 78
  generalization of, 73
  in psychopaths, 79
Rationalism, aesthetic judgments and, 57
Rationality, in Confucianism, 155
Rational principle, of Aristotle, 310, 320
Reasoning, autobiographical, 325
Receptive empathy, 69
Redemption sequence, 326–327
Regularity, in skills acquisition, 37–39
Relational communication system, 254
Religious traditions, 197
Reminiscence, 323–324
Representational accessibility
      landscape, 252
Reputation, social, 310–311
Research on younger children, 280–281
  methods in, 281–282
Responding to actions of others, in early
      childhood, 285–288
Responsive caregiving, 254–255, 256
Revelation, moral conduct and, in
      Islam, 198
Rich, Kant on virtue as making us, 97
Right, meanings of, 122
Right action
  in Buddhism, 176, 177
  Ibn Miskawayh on, 201–204
"Right but not virtuous" objection,
      120–122
Right Concentration, 176

Right Effort, 176
Right Livelihood, 176, 177
Right Mindfulness, 176
Right Speech, 176, 177
Ritual, in Confucian virtue ethics, 150–151
Rosenthal, Robert, 140
Rubin, Donald, 140
Russell, Daniel, 121

Sadists, 69
Safety ethic, 259, 261–262, 268
Samadhi, 181–182
Sameroff, A. J., 319
Self-centeredness objection, 111–115
  disconnect objection in, 114–115
  narcissism objection in, 112–113
  rebutting "deeper level" of
      first attempt in, 115–117
      second attempt in, 117–120
  self-effacing objection in, 113
Self-control, as virtuous
  Aristotle on, 24–25
  Christianity on, 231–232, 233
  Kant on, 96, 99
  neurobiological development of, early,
      298, 299
Self-cultivation
  in Buddhism, 173, 178, 184, 189
  in Confucianism, 145, 157
    as manipulation of situation,
      150–154
  in Islam, 206
Self-development
  in autopoiesis, 267–268
  in evolved developmental niche, 263
  in Nicomachean Ethics, 308–329
    (See also Nicomachean Ethics)
Self-effacing objection, 113
Self-improvement as virtue, 112,
      122–129
  extent in, 123–124
  instruments in, 128–129
  Kant on, 100–102, 127–128
  manner in, 128
  motive in, 124–126
  people in, 127–128
  time in, 126–127
Self-interest
  enlightened, in sense of duty, 56
  in moral sentimentalism, 53

Self-organization, in autopoiesis,
    267–268
Self-regulation
    in conscience developmental, 290
    in cultivation of virtue, 280, 297
    early caregiving on capacity for, 253
    evolved developmental niche on,
        255–256, 257, 263
    guilt in, 315
    Hume on, 54, 56
    neurobiological development of, 298
    sentimentalists on, 56
    on social stereotypes, 146
Sentimentalism, moral
    fundamentals of, 51
    on moral education (*See* Empathy,
        roots of)
    in utilitarian virtue cultivation, 49–61
        (*See also* Sentimentalism, moral,
        Mill and)
Sentimentalism, moral, Mill and, 51–55
    authority in, 53
    feelings of duty in, 51
    good and bad conduct and virtue
        in, 55
    vs. Hume, 54
    moral education and virtue in, 53
    pleasure and virtue in, 52
    self-interest in, 53
    sympathetic engagement with others
        in, 53–54
    sympathy in, natural, 52
    utilitarians and, 52
    whole person in, 54–55
Sexual appetites
    Apostles and Christianity on, 204
    Islam on, 204–205
        veiling and, 211–212
Shared intentionality, in early childhood,
    284–285, 288, 289, 291
Simon, Herbert, 33–34
Situationism
    principles of, 307–308
    strong, as anti-globalist argument,
        138–144
        empirical issues in, 138–140
    subtle, unnoticed situations and
        environments on behavior in, 157
Situationist critique, and early Confucian
    virtue ethics, 135–158

concluding argument on, 155–158
    "high bar" argument in, 144–154
        (*See also* 'High bar' argument)
    Hume and empirical inquiry in,
        135–136
    key issues in, 136–137
    personality traits in, 137–144
        (*See also* Personality traits, in
        situationism)
Skill
    Aristotle on
        vs. practical intelligence, 28
        vs. virtue, 27–29
    personality attributes and,
        isomorphism between, 35
    psychology of, in moral development,
        32–36
        vs. Aristotle's approach, 36
        automaticity in, 36
        central hypothesis of, 33–36
        chess skill in, 33–34, 39–40
        ecological theory in, 34–35
        expertise effects research in, 34–35
        experts *vs.* novices in, 32–33
        messiness of, 40–41
        radiologist skills in, 34
        research on, ongoing, 35
Skillful means, 184
Skills acquisition
    Aristotle on virtue acquisition as, 18,
        22, 23, 26, 31
    Kahneman on, 37
    regularity and feedback in, 37–39
Snow, Nancy, 146, 156–157
Social, Ibn Miskawayh on virtue as,
    205–208
    veiling in public and, 212–213
Social acceptance, 310
Social action, for motivated
    intention, 312
Social actor, 308, 309–317, 328
    Aristotle on, 309–310
    vs. motivated agent, 312–313
    rational human conduct in social
        groups in, 310–313
    temperament differences in, 313–317,
        316t (*See also* Temperament
        differences, in social actor)
Social dependency, in Christianity.
    See Christianity

Social feeling, sympathy in, 54
Social groups, rational human conduct in, 310–313
Social reputation, 310–311
Social status, 310
Sociopathy
    lack of emotional responsiveness in, 69–70
    parent–child interactions in, early, 67
    projective empathy in, 69
Solomon, David, 114–115
Status, social, 310
Stereotype modification, 146, 156–157
Stereotype priming, 151–152
Success, Kant on virtue and, 92–93
Suffering, in Buddhism
    alleviation of, for all sentient beings, 172, 173
    in Four Noble Truths, 175
    meditation for release from, 182
Sympathetic engagement, in moral sentimentalism, 53–54
Sympathetic joy, 178
Sympathetic motivation, rebuttal of virtue ethics as, 115
Sympathetic response, variability of, 58
Sympathy(ies)
    vs. empathy, 71
    enlarged, 58
    happiness and, 61
    in moral sentimentalism, natural, 52
    in sense of duty, 56
    toward another
        empathically absorbed, gratitude as, 74–78
        as instinct, 78
    toward us, in empathy, 74–76
    variability of, 58

Tahdhib al-akhlaq, 199–200. *See also* Ibn Miskawayh's theory of virtue
Targets, of virtue, 118–120, 121
Temperament, 313. *See also* Personality traits
Temperament, virtue as, 308, 309–317, 328
    Aristotle on, 309–310
    rational human conduct in social groups in, 310–313
    temperament differences in, 313–317,

316t (*See also* Temperament differences, in social actor)
Temperament differences, in social actor, 313–317, 316t
    agreeableness in, 315, 316t
    conscientiousness in, 315–316, 316t
    effortful control in, 315, 316t
    negative emotionality in, 314–315, 316t
    personality traits and, 316t, 317
    positive emotionality in, 313–314, 316t
Temperament traits, 308
Thick concept of virtue, 123
Thin concept of virtue, 122–123
Time, in self-improvement, 126–127
Toddlers, research on, 280–281
    methods in, 281–282
Toner, Christopher, 117
Touch, 256–257
Trevarthen, Colwyn, 254
Triune ethics theory, 259–262
Turnbull, Colin, 254

Understanding of other people, in early childhood, 283–284
Unity of virtues, Kant on, 93–95
Universals, in virtue, 262–265, 266f
Utilitarians
    moral sentimentalism in virtue cultivation by, 49–61
        art of life in, 55–61 (*See also* Art of life, Mill's)
        moral sentimentalists in, 51–55 (*See also* Sentimentalism, moral, Mill and)
        virtue as good in itself in, 49
    virtue for utilitarians and, 50–51
    sentimalism of, 52
    virtue for, 50–51

Vanity, Ibn Miskawayh on, 205
Variety of virtues, Kant on, 93–94
Veil(ing), virtue of, 208–214
    bodily practices and, 210–211
    habituating sexual appetites on, 211–212
    Ibn Miskawayh's virtue theory on, 209–210
    Islam scriptures on, 208–209

as symbol, 209, 214
virtue as social in, 212–213
Vice, Kant on, 94
Vicente, Kim, 34–35
Virtue ethics, 111–129, 279
in Christianity, 234–236
classical, development of, 234–236
Confucian, situationist critique and,
135–158 (*See also* Situationist
critique, and early Confucian
virtue ethics)
definition of, 1, 198
vs. deontology and utilitarianism, 136
fundamentals of, 111–112
key issues in, 136
"right but not virtuous" objection in,
120–122
self-centeredness objection in,
111–115
disconnect objection in, 114–115
narcissism objection in, 112–113
self-effacing objection in, 113
self-centeredness objection in,
rebutting "deeper level" of
first attempt in, 115–117
second attempt in, 117–120
self-improvement as virtue in, 112,
122–129
extent in, 123–124
instruments in, 128–129
Kant on, 100–102, 127–128
manner in, 128
motive in, 124–126
people in, 127–128
time in, 126–127

thin *vs.* thick account of virtue in,
122–123

Virtue terms
Confucian, 143
loose use of, 143–144
Vocation, virtue as, 308–309, 321–329
authoring of life by exemplars of
virtue in, 325–327
wisdom and contemplation in,
321–323
wisdom and contemplation in, and
psychology of adulthood, 322–325

Walker, Lawrence, 326
Wang, JoAnne, 34–35
Whole person, in moral sentimalism,
54–55
Will, Kant on
good will in, 88–90
weakness or strength of, 90–91
Williams, Bernard, 113
Willpower, in Confucianism, 155
Will to do what is right, Kant on moral
virtue as, 87–91
Wisdom
in Buddhism, 178–180
as expertise in pragmatics of life, 323
psychology of adulthood and,
322–325
reminiscence and life review in,
323–324
virtue from, Aristotle on, 321–323

xin, 143